Otitis Media
in Young Children

Otitis Media in Young Children

Medical, Developmental, and Educational Considerations

edited by

Joanne E. Roberts, Ph.D.
Frank Porter Graham Child Development Center
University of North Carolina
Chapel Hill

Ina F. Wallace, Ph.D.
Research Triangle Institute
Research Triangle Park, North Carolina

and

Frederick W. Henderson, M.D.
Frank Porter Graham Child Development Center
University of North Carolina School of Medicine
Chapel Hill

·P A U L·H·
BROOKES
PUBLISHING CO.

Baltimore • London • Toronto • Sydney

Paul H. Brookes Publishing Co.
Post Office Box 10624
Baltimore, Maryland 21285-0624

Typeset by PRO-Image Corporation, York, Pennsylvania.
Manufactured in the United States of America by
Thomson-Shore, Inc., Dexter, Michigan.

Library of Congress Cataloging-in-Publication Data

Otitis media in young children : medical, developmental, and
    educational considerations / edited by Joanne E. Roberts, Ina F.
    Wallace, and Frederick W. Henderson.
      p.   cm.
    Includes bibliographical references and index.
    ISBN 1-55766-278-9
    1. Otitis media in children. 2. Children—Language. 3. Otitis
media in children—Complications. I. Roberts, Joanne Erwick,
1950–   . II. Wallace, Ina F., 1950–   . III. Henderson,
Frederick W.
RF225.O756 1997
618.92′09784—dc20   96-42315
                                                    CIP

British Library Cataloguing in Publication data are available from
the British Library.

Contents

About the Authors

The Editors

Joanne E. Roberts, Ph.D., Investigator, Frank Porter Graham Child Development Center; Research Professor, Division of Speech and Hearing Sciences, University of North Carolina at Chapel Hill School of Medicine, Campus Box 8180, 105 Smith Level Road, Chapel Hill, North Carolina 27599-8180.

Dr. Roberts is a speech-language pathologist who is widely known for her research on the communication sequelae of otitis media. She has published extensively in speech-language, pediatric, early childhood, and audiology journals and has made many presentations on how otitis media affects children's communication and the implications for health care professionals, teachers, and families. She served on a multidisciplinary panel from the Agency for Health Care Policy and Research that developed guidelines for management of otitis media.

Ina F. Wallace, Ph.D., Senior Research Psychologist, Research Triangle Institute; Post Office Box 12194, Research Triangle Park, North Carolina 27709-2194; Visiting Associate Professor, Department of Otolaryngology, Albert Einstein College of Medicine; and Research Associate Professor, Department of Pediatrics, University of North Carolina at Chapel Hill School of Medicine.

Dr. Wallace is a psychologist whose principal research interests have been in the area of communication and cognitive skills in children at high risk for developmental disorders, including children born prematurely and children with recurrent otitis media. Her research publications have examined the communicative and academic consequences of otitis media as well as the impact of caregivers' communication styles on language outcomes of children with otitis media. She also has been evaluating the effects of preventive interventions for infants and young children.

Frederick W. Henderson, M.D., Professor, Department of Pediatrics; Investigator, Frank Porter Graham Child Development Center, University of North Carolina at Chapel Hill School of Medicine, Campus Box 7220, Chapel Hill, North Carolina 27599-7220.

Dr. Henderson is a pediatrician who is known for his research on the epidemiology and pathogenesis of viral and bacterial respiratory infections in young children, including otitis media. His recent research is on the transmission of antibiotic resistant *Streptococcus pneumoniae* in the child care setting, as well as other respiratory diseases in this environment. He has published articles in pediatric and infectious disease journals.

The Contributors

Anthea Counsell, M.Sc., Clinical Research Fellow, Department of Otolaryngology and Head and Neck Surgery, St. Michael's Hospital, University of Bristol, Bristol, BS2 8EG, United Kingdom.

Ms. Counsell was involved in the Avon Longitudinal Study of Pregnancy and Childhood (ALSPAC) in Bristol and more recently was Clinical Research Fellow in the Department of Otolaryngology, University of Bristol.

Kathleen A. Daly, Ph.D., M.P.H., Assistant Professor, Department of Otolaryngology, Investigator, Otitis Media Research Center, University of Minnesota Medical School, Box 396 UMHC, Harvard Street at East River Parkway, Minneapolis, Minnesota 55455.

Dr. Daly is widely known for her research on the epidemiology of otitis media. She has published in pediatric, audiology, otolaryngology, public heath, and epidemiology journals. She served as a panel member for the NIH Consensus Development Conference on Cochlear Impants in Adults and Children.

Amelia F. Drake, M.D., F.A.C.S., Associate Professor, Divisions of Otolaryngology/Head and Neck Surgery and Pediatrics, University of North Carolina at Chapel Hill School of Medicine, Campus Box 7070, Chapel Hill, North Carolina 27599-7070.

Dr. Drake is an otolaryngologist with expertise in the management of all conditions encountered in pediatric otolaryngology. She has published in leading otolaryngology and pediatric journals and in texts on otitis media and airway compromise. She has just completed a phase I clinical trial in the topical treatment of otitis media and is pursuing additional research in this area.

Judith S. Gravel, Ph.D., Associate Professor, Departments of Otolaryngology and Pediatrics, Director of Audiology, Albert Einstein College of Medicine/Montefiore Medical Center, Rose F. Kennedy Center, Room 842, 1300 Morris Park Avenue, Bronx, New York 10461.

Dr. Gravel is an audiologist whose clinical activities, research, and teaching have been in the area of pediatric audiology. She is widely recognized as an expert in the behavioral assessment of infants and children, neonatal screening for hearing loss, and the audiological consequences of otitis media. She has published extensively in audiological, speech-language, and pediatric journals.

John H. Grose, Ph.D., Assistant Professor, Division of Otolaryngology/ Head and Neck Surgery, University of North Carolina at Chapel Hill School of Medicine, Campus Box 7070, Chapel Hill, North Carolina 27599- 7070.

Dr. Grose is a psychoacoustician whose research interests include the effects of hearing impairment on the perception of complex sounds and the extraction of signals from background noises. His research reports have made important contributions to the understanding of how auditory function is affected by both short-term and long-term changes in hearing status, such as those associated with chronic otitis media and its resolution.

Joseph W. Hall, III, Ph.D., Professor, Division of Otolaryngology/Head and Neck Surgery, University of North Carolina at Chapel Hill School of Medicine, Campus Box 7070, Chapel Hill, North Carolina 27599-7070.

Dr. Hall is an audiologist and psychophysicist who is widely recognized as an expert in the area of central auditory system processing. His principal research interest is in the auditory analysis of signals in complex noise backgrounds. He has published extensively in audiologic and medical journals.

Stephen R. Hooper, Ph.D., Psychology Section Head and Director of Child and Adolescent Neuropsychology, Clinical Center for the Study of Development and Learning, Child Development Institute, Associate Professor, Department of Psychiatry, University of North Carolina at Chapel Hill School of Medicine, Campus Box 7255, BSRC UNC, Chapel Hill, North Carolina 27599-7255.

Dr. Hooper is a neuropsychologist who has been widely published in the areas of child neuropsychology and child psychopathology. His expertise is in the diagnosis and management of learning disorders. He is a member of many leading editorial boards, and he reviews regularly for other major journals in the fields of school psychology, clinical psychology, and neuropsychology.

Richard Maw, M.S., F.R.C.S., Consultant Otolaryngologist and Senior Clinical Lecturer, Department of Otolaryngology, University of Bristol, Bristol, BS2 8EG, United Kingdom.

Dr. Maw is recognized for his research on the surgical management and sequelae of otitis media with effusion and has published widely on this subject. He is undertaking a study to demonstrate the effects of early or late intervention for otitis media with effusion, with speech, language, cognition, and behavior as the outcome measures.

Maria Mody, Ph.D., Visiting Research Scientist, Ecole Nationale Superiure des Telecommunications Department Signal, Paris, France.

Dr. Mody is a speech-language pathologist who has worked on several longitudinal projects examining speech and language development in young children with otitis media. Her other research interests have included speech perception in children who are poor readers and the emergence of gestural units in speech production.

Robert J. Nozza, Ph.D., Professor and Acting Department Head, Department of Communication Sciences and Disorders, University of Georgia, 576 Aderhold Hall, Athens, Georgia 30602.

Dr. Nozza, an audiologist, is widely known for his research in auditory development, the measurement of hearing in infants, and screening and diagnosis of middle ear effusion using acoustic immittance. He has chaired or served as a member on committees related to the development of guidelines for identification of middle ear effusion for the American Speech-Language-Hearing Association and for the American Academy of Audiology.

Jack L. Paradise, M.D., Professor, Departments of Pediatrics, Family Medicine and Clinical Epidemiology, and Otolaryngology, University of Pittsburgh School of Medicine, 3075 Fifth Avenue, Pittsburgh, Pennsylvania 15213-2583.

Dr. Paradise is a pediatrician who has devoted his research efforts to the understanding and management of diseases and disorders of the upper respiratory tract and related structures in children. He has studied the indications for tonsillectomy and adenoidectomy; the medical management of infants with cleft plate; and the diagnosis, treatment, and possible developmental consequences of otitis media. He received the 1994 Ambulatory Pediatric Association Research Award.

Kakia Petinou, Ph.D., Research Assistant, Speech-Language Laboratory, Rose F. Kennedy Center, Albert Einstein College of Medicine, Bronx, New York 10461.

Dr. Petinou's research focuses on speech perception and speech production in children with otitis media. She has investigated acoustic characteristics of children's productions of stressed and unstressed syllables.

Jackson Roush, Ph.D., Associate Professor and Director, Division of Speech and Hearing Sciences, University of North Carolina at Chapel Hill School of Medicine, Campus Box 7190, Chapel Hill, North Carolina, 27599-7190.

Dr. Roush is an audiologist whose principal clinical and research interests are in the identification and management of children with otitis media. He chaired the American Academy of Audiology's Task Force on Screening for Hearing Loss and Middle Ear Disorders.

Richard G. Schwartz, Ph.D., Director, Speech-Language Laboratory, Rose F. Kennedy Center, Visiting Professor, Department of Otolaryngology, Albert Einstein College of Medicine and Professor, Department of Speech and Hearing Sciences, City University of New York, 33 West 42nd Street, New York, New York 10036.

Dr. Schwartz's research has focused on early phonological and lexical acquisition in typically and atypically developing children, including those with recurrent otitis media. He serves as editor and advisor on the editorial boards of leading journals and served as a member of the panel that developed the National Institutes of Health Consensus Report on Cochlear Implantation.

Sylvan E. Stool, M.D., Senior Clinical Instructor, Department of Pediatric Otolaryngology—Head and Neck Surgery, University of Colorado Health Sciences Center and The Children's Hospital of Denver.

Dr. Stool is a widely known pediatric otolaryngologist who has published extensively on pediatric issues in otolaryngology. He served as the co-chairman for the recently published guidelines on otitis media by the Agency for Health Care Policy and Research.

Douglas H. Todd, M.D., Clinical Assistant Professor of Otolaryngology/ Head and Neck Surgery, University of Texas Health Science Center at San Antonio; Major, United States Army Medical Corps, Attending Surgeon, Otolaryngology/Head and Neck Surgery, Brooke Army Medical Center, Fort Sam Houston, Houston, Texas 78234.

Dr. Todd is an otolaryngologist who has presented and published papers regarding carcinoma of the head and neck, otitis media, and head and neck manifestations of lightning strike injuries. He and Dr. Stool have taught many pneumatic otoscopy courses to otolaryngology, pediatric, and family practice residents.

Pamela J. Winton, Ph.D., Research Fellow and Investigator, Frank Porter Graham Child Development Center, Clinical Associate Professor, School of Education, University of North Carolina at Chapel Hill, Campus Box 8185, 521 South Greensboro Street, Chapel Hill, North Carolina 27599-8185.

Dr. Winton is recognized for her research, training, and curricula development in the areas of family–professional and interprofessional collaboration within the context of early intervention. She has published extensively on this topic in addition to providing training at the state, national, and international levels.

Susan A. Zeisel, Ed.D., RNC, PNP, Project Coordinator, Frank Porter Graham Child Development Center, Adjunct Assistant Professor, Department of Nursing, University of North Carolina at Chapel Hill School of Medicine, Campus Box 8180, 105 Smith Level Road, Chapel Hill, North Carolina 27599-8180.

Dr. Zeisel is both a pediatric nurse practitioner and a health educator. She has published several articles in leading pediatric and early childhood journals on the incidence of otitis media in young children and implications of otitis media for families and early childhood educators.

Foreword

Otitis media (OM) is an illness that affects nearly all young children, accounting for $3.5 billion annually in direct and indirect costs (Gates, 1996; Stool et al., 1994). It has become so widespread that the Agency for Health Care Policy and Research developed guidelines for management of OM in children birth to 3 years of age. Although there has been a 30-year history of research on the nature and sequelae of OM, there has not been a consensus about the long-term effects on children. Nevertheless, there has been concern that OM is often associated with language and learning difficulties in young children.

The communication deficits linked with OM are believed to be due to changes in auditory acuity, both detection and discrimination, at a time when the central nervous system is developing the capacity for perceiving speech and mapping other aspects of communication. Although the incidence of OM tends to decline with age, the effect on communication skills may be more long lasting. One explanation for this is that older children have a diminished ability to acquire skills for speech perception and other basic auditory–linguistic processes even when their hearing acuity returns to normal. One possibility is that OM-linked auditory degradations may result in neurolinguistic structures and functions that do not allow for the optimal development of communication. Impairments of this sort could have long-term implications for anyone in a society such as ours, which requires a high level of communicative competence.

The effects of OM are variable and appear to depend, in part, on the age and the type of functions assessed, the amount of hearing loss, and other sequelae of OM, as well as the environment of the child. There are data that indicate that some children are at greater risk from the communication deficits caused by OM than others. Moreover, there is some evidence that there are differential incidence rates of OM as a function of ethnicity, socioeconomic background, and child-rearing practice, factors that also can affect outcomes.

In recent years, OM research has incorporated more sophisticated methods and has thereby been able to address some of the complex issues in this area. Therefore, there is the need for a timely, thorough, and scholarly compilation of the information concerning the disease and its effects on development. The scope of this book is broad, covering the areas of epidemiology, diagnosis, management, and sequelae of OM. This book should be of interest to educational and health care professionals as well as to families.

Section I of this book includes chapters that cover the definition, diagnosis, and epidemiology of OM. It is clear that there is a critical need for consistent terminology and accurate diagnostic criteria both for describing the disease and for researching its effects in children. Daly's chapter gives an outstanding synthesis of the current knowledge of the prevalence of and the risk factors for OM. The chapter by Henderson and Roush provides a comprehensive discussion of otoscopic and tympanometric procedures for diagnosing otitis media and implications for screening.

The chapters of Section II describe the auditory, language, cognitive, and behavioral sequelae of OM and management strategies. Because of the controversy surrounding the sequelae of OM, this comprehensive review of this literature is welcome. Gravel and Nozza thoroughly discuss the nature of hearing loss associated with OM, carefully describe common procedures for screening and diagnosing hearing loss, and provide useful techniques for the audiologic management of OM-related hearing loss. In Hall, Grose, and Drake's scholarly treatment of auditory sequelae, they describe the psychophysiologic consequences of auditory deprivation, current techniques (e.g., auditory brain stem response, masking level difference) for assessing central auditory abilities, and implications for classroom learning. Models of speech processing, how otitis media affects the development of speech, and implications for management of children with chronic OM are discussed in the well-conceptualized theoretical and empirical chapter by Schwartz, Mody, and Petinou. Roberts and Wallace present a well-reasoned model of the OM–language relationship, critically review the large body of language outcomes research, and offer a variety of intervention and management strategies for clinicians, caregivers, and teachers. After a comprehensive review of the literature on the effects of OM on cognition, academic skills, and behavior, Wallace and Hooper propose several mechanisms for how OM can cause learning and behavioral difficulties and suggest intervention strategies for classroom teachers. Finally, Winton, Roberts, and Zeisel give a thoughtful treatment of the issues families face when their children have chronic or recurrent OM and offer practical suggestions for professional–family collaborations.

The chapters in Section III cover the latest techniques for medical and surgical management of OM. There continues to be a need for an empirically based discussion of surgical and medical options for treating children who have persistent or frequent episodes of OM. Henderson provides a detailed and scholarly discussion of pathogenic characteristics of OM and how various antibiotics can be used to treat the different OM agents. While acknowledging the controversies surrounding surgical issues in the management of OM, Todd and Stool clearly and carefully identify the various surgical procedures for young children with OM.

Finally, the chapters in Section IV present an international perspective on OM and a discussion of future directions in research on the effects of OM and development. Maw and Counsell thoroughly trace the differences in OM prevalence and medical and surgical management across such diverse countries as the United States, Great Britain, the Netherlands, Denmark, and New Zealand. Paradise offers a useful perspective for the future directions in OM research and clinical practice. Specific suggestions are made for the design of research to answer the many questions that continue to exist on the sequelae of OM.

An understanding of the current state of research in OM, as detailed in this book, should be welcomed by all professionals working with young children. This book makes an important contribution to the synthesis of and description of deficiencies in the current body of literature that could lead to better-designed research protocols. This book opens the way for a better understanding of procedures for identifying susceptible children, mechanisms by which OM can affect children's development, and management strategies that will prevent OM sequelae. It is hoped that such information will be used to improve the communication and learning functions of children that are so necessary for our society's success as well as for our children's.

Robert J. Ruben, M.D., F.A.C.S., F.A.A.P.
Professor and Chairman
Department of Otolaryngology
Professor of Pediatrics
Albert Einstein College of Medicine
Bronx, New York

REFERENCES

Gates, G.A. (1996). Cost-effectiveness considerations in otitis media treatment. *Otolaryngology—Head and Neck Surgery, 114*(4), 525–530.

Stool, S.E., Berg, A.O., Berman, S., Carney, C.J., Cooley, J.R., Culpepper, L., Eavey, R.D., Feagans, L.V., Finitzo, T., Friedman, E.M., Goertz, J.A., Goldstein, A.J., Grundfast, K.M., Long, D.G., Macconi, L.L., Melton, L., Roberts, J.E., Sherrod, J.L., & Sisk, J.E. (1994). *Otitis media with effusion in young children: Clinical practice guideline no. 12* (AHCPR Publication No. 94-0622). Rockville, MD: Agency for Health Care Policy and Research.

Preface

In recent years, otitis media has emerged as one of the major health problems in young children. Whereas researchers have used more sophisticated techniques for the documentation of otitis media and clinicians have broadened their approaches to management, the rates of otitis media are increasing and bacterial resistance to some antibiotics is on the rise. Moreover, there is no consensus regarding the long-term consequences of otitis media. This has resulted in uncertainty among those individuals with responsibility for the physical and educational well-being of children with otitis media.

This book was conceived as a forum for the discussion of clinical and management issues of otitis media by many of the leading researchers in the field. We selected topics that we believed were important to health care professionals and educators as well as clinicians who work with young children. The topics covered are broad, including the epidemiology, diagnosis, and medical management of middle ear disorders, the auditory and communicative sequelae of otitis media, and the impact of otitis media on families. We have also included an international perspective on the epidemiology and management of otitis media. Within each chapter is a review of the literature, discussion of the clinical implications for practitioners, and directions for future research. We welcome the opportunity this book has provided us to bring these different areas together and to review the current research in otitis media and its sequelae on aspects of child development.

The publication of this book is based on our collective experience conducting research in the area of otitis media and working clinically with young children. We were particularly influenced by the ongoing studies of illness and child development at the Frank Porter Graham Child Development Center of the University of North Carolina at Chapel Hill and at the Rose F. Kennedy Center of the Albert Einstein College of Medicine, where we had observed high rates of otitis media in children followed from infancy.

This book is our attempt to synthesize what is currently known about otitis media and its sequelae. The authors realize that there is yet much

more to learn about these topics and that there is important ongoing research in progress. We hope that this book helps to clarify some of the
controversial issues surrounding otitis media. If it provides useful information to other researchers and clinicians, we will feel that we have made
a contribution to the children who inspired our work.

Acknowledgments

There are many people whose support and encouragement helped us complete this book. First, we want to thank the contributing authors, who added their own perspective to the understanding of otitis media in young children. Second, we would like to express our appreciation to our colleagues at the Frank Porter Graham Child Development Center and our many colleagues working at other institutions in otitis media research. Third, we greatly appreciate the support of the Maternal and Child Health Bureau (MCJ-370599 and 370649; Title V, Social Security Act), Health Resources and Services Administration, Department of Health and Human Services, in completing this book. Fourth, we acknowledge Sarah Henderson for her dedication, assistance, and excellent organizational skills in handling the many details of this book. Fifth, we are grateful to the many children and their families who have participated in our research projects and were part of our clinical populations. On a personal side, we are very grateful to our spouses, Barry S. Roberts and Pamela F. Henderson, for their constant support and willingness to allow us to work on yet another project. Finally, we want to acknowledge our children—Justin Roberts, Matthew Roberts, Ellen Pieper, Heather Henderson, and Fred Henderson—who used real everyday experiences to teach us about otitis media and child development.

To our children—
Justin, Matthew, Ellen, Heather, and Fred

I

DEFINITION, PREVALENCE, AND DIAGNOSIS

1

Definition and Epidemiology of Otitis Media

Kathleen A. Daly

Otitis media (OM) was the most commonly diagnosed disease among children in the United States in 1990 (Schappert, 1992). Between 1975 and 1990, the annual visit rate for children younger than 2 years with a principal diagnosis of OM increased from 31.5 to 102.1 per 100 children (Schappert, 1992). In addition, among children younger than 5 years, parent-reported acute ear infections rose from 43 to 67 per 100 between 1982 and 1990 (Adams & Benson, 1991; National Center for Health Statistics, 1985). Direct and indirect costs for OM in 1991 were estimated at $1.1 billion for 2-year-olds (Stool et al., 1994). An earlier estimate was $3.5 billion annually for all children (Stool & Field, 1989).

Otitis media is the general term for a continuum of related diseases, including asymptomatic middle ear effusion, recurrent acute OM, and middle ear effusion that persists for months. Recurrent OM and chronic otitis media with effusion (OME) are associated with temporary conductive hearing loss (Fria, Cantekin, & Eichler, 1985; McDermott, Giebink, Le, Harford, & Paparella, 1983), which may result in speech and language difficulties (Chalmers, Stewart, Silva, & Mulvena, 1989; Gravel & Wallace, 1992; Teele et al., 1990). Children with OM also

This chapter was supported in part by National Institutes of Health Grant No. P01-DC00133 from the National Institute on Deafness and Other Communication Disorders.

3

have an increased likelihood of developing middle ear pathologies (Maw, 1991; Maw & Bawden, 1994b; Paparella & Schachern, 1984; Schilder, Zielhuis, & van den Broek, 1993; Tos, Stangerup, Holm-Jensen, & Sorensen, 1984) that may result in long-term hearing loss (Wright & Meyerhoff, 1994).

This chapter describes the terminology used to define OM and OME, reports the worldwide incidence and prevalence of OME, discusses the host and environmental factors that increase (or decrease) the risk of OME, and points out the strengths, limitations, and unresolved issues of extant OME research. In addition, the chapter explores the application of epidemiologic knowledge to the prevention and management of OME.

TERMINOLOGY

The Fourth Research Conference on Recent Advances in Otitis Media (Klein et al., 1989) was the last of several such conferences to address OM terminology (Paparella et al., 1985; Senturia et al., 1980). The Panel on Definition and Classification used clinical criteria to define the following terms (Klein et al., 1989):

- Otitis media: An inflammation of the middle ear. This general term encompasses all the diseases of the OM continuum.
- Acute suppurative otitis media (AOM): Clinically identifiable infection of the middle ear of sudden onset and short duration. Synonyms include acute otitis media and acute purulent otitis media.
- Secretory otitis media: Presence of middle ear effusion behind an intact tympanic membrane without acute signs or symptoms. This category includes the clinically noninfectious forms of otitis media. Common synonyms are chronic otitis media with effusion, otitis media with effusion, nonsuppurative otitis media, serous otitis media, mucoid otitis media, catarrh, serotympanum, and mucotympanum.
- Chronic suppurative otitis media, or chronic otitis media: Chronic otorrhea through a tympanic membrane perforation.

These terms were essentially unchanged from the previous conference (Paparella et al., 1985) except for the elimination of red tympanic membrane as a criterion for AOM. The research panels recommended that authors define their terms to facilitate communication about related OM conditions (Klein et al., 1989; Paparella et al., 1985).

Although experts have recommended using standard terms with standard definitions when communicating about OM, in practice, researchers have used a variety of definitions to describe conditions in the OM continuum. For example, *OME* is the recommended term to describe asymptomatic middle ear effusion detected by pneumatic otoscopy, tympanometry, or acoustic reflectometry. However, many authors used OM or OME as synonyms for middle ear effusion, independent of the presence or assessment of symptoms (Birch & Elbrønd, 1986a, 1986b; Casselbrant, Mandel, Rockette, & Bluestone, 1993; Fiellau-Nikolajsen, 1980; Karma, Penttilä, Sipilä, & Kataja, 1989; Marchant et al., 1984; Møller & Tos, 1990; Owen et al., 1993; Roland et al., 1989; Tos, Poulsen, & Borch, 1978; Zielhuis, Straatman, Rach, & van den Broek, 1990).

Otitis media modifiers such as *acute, chronic, persistent,* and *recurrent* also have not been used in a standard fashion (Bluestone, 1984). North American researchers tend to use the terms *acute* and *chronic* to define both duration and clinical state, whereas Europeans use them to describe clinical characteristics (Paparella et al., 1985). *Persistent OME* has been used to describe effusion that is present after treatment for AOM (Schwartz, Rodriguez, & Grundfast, 1984) and OME that persists for 2 or more months (Kraemer et al., 1983). Definitions of recurrent OM vary with the number of episodes in a specific time period and the criteria used to demarcate episodes. Recurrent OM has been defined as three episodes before age 1, 3, or 7 (Teele, Klein, Rosner, & the Greater Boston Otitis Media Study Group, 1989); six or more episodes before age 6 (otitis-prone) (Howie, Ploussard, & Sloyer, 1975); or six or more episodes during a 12-month period (Harsten, Prellner, Heldrup, Kalm, & Kornfält, 1989). Because of variation in OM definitions, disease criteria, and accuracy of diagnostic methods, comparison of study results presents a challenge for the reader.

INCIDENCE AND PREVALENCE STUDIES

Incidence and prevalence rates are measures of disease frequency in a population. The incidence rate is determined in a study using prospective surveillance for disease and assumes the population is disease-free at the beginning of the study. The OME *incidence rate* is calculated by dividing the number of *new* cases of OME (individuals with disease or episodes of disease) during a specified time period by the population at risk during that time period. When individuals with OME are used in the numerator, the incidence rate conveys the probability that an individual will develop OME during the specified time period. When episodes of OME constitute the numerator, the incidence rate communicates the burden of disease in the population for that time period. If some subjects do not participate for the entire follow-up period, the denominator should be the sum of each individual's follow-up time. For example, 100 children followed for 1 year plus 100 children followed for 6 months equals 150 child-years of follow-up. Incidence rates of OME specific for demographic characteristics are also reported. Age-specific OME incidence for children from birth to 5 years is the number of new cases of OME among children 5 years old or younger during a given time period divided by the number of birth- to 5-year-olds in the population.

The OME *prevalence rate* is the number of cases of OME at one point in time divided by the population at that point in time. This is the definition for *point prevalence,* which does not require a prospective study for determination. *Period prevalence,* in contrast, combines both prevalence and incidence. Period prevalence of OME includes all cases of OME at one point in time (prevalence) plus new cases of OME that develop during a specified follow-up period (incidence). Prevalence depends on both incidence and duration of disease. For a disease that is common but generally of short duration (e.g., AOM), incidence exceeds prevalence because a prevalence rate captures only those with AOM at the time of the survey, whereas an incidence study includes all those who develop AOM over a specified follow-up period.

The incidence and prevalence studies summarized in Tables 1 and 2 were conducted among different populations around the world, and the reported rates vary widely. Whether study results can be generalized to children as a whole depends on the method of subject selection. Population-based studies (i.e., all children born during a specific period in a locale) represent all children from the community. Clinic-based studies reflect the experience of children who are actively involved in the health care system. Studies conducted in child care centers, schools, or reservations describe more narrowly defined groups of children. The wide variability in rates reported in these studies may represent true disparities in susceptibility (e.g., differences in age, race, or ethnicity; child care attendance; other risk factors), or it may be the result of artifactual influences on OM rates (e.g., access to or utilization of health care, dissimilarities in study diagnostic methods and criteria, frequency or season of examination, length of follow-up, ear rather than child as the unit of analysis).

Although researchers may agree in general about the signs and symptoms required to diagnose OME, there is no precise "gold standard" for OME. The presence of middle ear effusion is often used as a gold standard for OME, but effusion cannot be ascertained unequivocally with common diagnostic methods. The middle ear is not observed directly during examination. Rather, it is inspected with an otoscope through the tympanic membrane and tested by observing tympanic membrane mobility in response to positive and negative pressure and by measuring response to sound (tympanometry). All these tests provide

Table 1. Otitis media incidence studies in childhood, 1970–1994

Study (year)	N	Population	Surveillance	Diagnostic criteria[a]	Follow-up/ exam schedule	Age (yr)	Incidence[b] AOM	Incidence[b] OME	OM[c]
UNITED STATES									
Reed & Dunn (1970)[d]	641	Community based	Passive	NS	1 yr/monthly	0–10 0–1			43% 83/100 75%
Howie et al. (1975)	488	Clinic based	Passive	↓ TM mobility	6 yr/N/A	0–1 0–2 0–6			49% 61% 67%
Biles et al. (1980)	1,018 174 136	Community based	Passive	M.D. diagnosis	1 yr/N/A	0–8 0–1 1–2			35% 97/100 81/100
Goodwin et al.(1980)[e]	1,710 1,206	Community based	Passive	Red, bulging TM or TM perforation with drainage	1 yr/N/A	0–1 1–2	60% 43%		
Henderson et al. (1982)	110	Research child care	Active	↓ TM mobility; MEE seen	Variable when ill	0–0.5 0.5–1 1–2 2–3 3–6		178/100 381/100 232/100 106/100 20/100	
Marchant et al. (1984)	70	Clinic based	Active	↓ TM mobility, or air–fluid level	1 yr/every 1–3 mo	0–1			77%
Teele et al. (1989)	877 698 498	Clinic based	Passive and active	Otorrhea, or ↓ TM mobility, or air–fluid level + ≥1 symptom	6 mo/ 1 yr/ 3 yr/ 7 yr/ All clinic visits for 3 yr; every 4 mo yrs 4–7	0.5 0–1 0–3 0–7	35% 62% 83% 93%		

(continued)

7

Table 1. (continued)

Study (year)	N	Population	Surveillance	Diagnostic criteria[a]	Follow-up/ exam schedule	Age (yr)	Incidence[b]		OM[c]
							AOM	OME	
Stewart (1989)[d]	344	Community based	Passive	M.D. diagnosis	1 yr/N/A	0–0.5 0–1			55% 78%
Roland et al. (1989)	483	Clinic based	Active	Algorithm: flat tympanogram or air–fluid level, or MEE by otoscopy	1 yr/6–8 wk	0.5–1.5		74%	
Casselbrant et al. (1985)	103	Child care center	Active	Cantekin (1983) algorithm	2 yr/monthly	2–6		57%	
Casselbrant et al. (1993)	218 110	Clinic	Active and passive	MEE + 1 sign and 1 symptom	1 yr/monthly	0–1 0–2	34% 59%		78%[f] 92%[f]
Duncan et al. (1993)	1,013	Clinic (HMO)	Passive	M.D. diagnosis	1 yr/N/A	0–1	64%		
Owen et al. (1993)	435	Community based	Active	Otorrhea, or acoustic reflex ≥5, or type B tympanogram	2 yr/2–4 wk	0–0.5 0–1 0–2		85% 97% 99%	
Clements et al. (1993)	147	Research child care	Active	Evidence of MEE, red or bulging TM	2 yr/monthly	0–0.5 0.5–1 1–1.5 1.5–2	120/100 420/100 280/100 160/100		
DENMARK									
Lous & Fiellau-Nikolajsen (1981)	387	Community based	Active	B tympanogram	1 yr/monthly	7–8		25/100	
Birch & Elbrønd (1984)	373	Child care center	Active	B tympanogram	3 mo/every 2 wk	0.75–7		53% 192/100	
Birch & Elbrønd (1986b)	210	Community based	Active	B tympanogram	3 mo/every 2 wk	1–7		74% 324/100	

Study	N	Setting	Surveillance	Diagnostic criteria	Duration/frequency	Age (yr)	Incidence
Stangerup & Tos (1986)	729	Community based	Active	TM perforation, or effusion at paracentesis, or red, bulging TM + pain or fever	3 yr/every 3 mo	0–1 0–2 0–3	22% 37% 49%
Møller & Tos (1990)	51	School based	Active	B tympanogram	1 mo/daily	3–6	6–24%[g]
FINLAND							
Pukander et al. (1984)	NA	Community based	Passive	Symptoms + otoscopic signs or otorrhea	1 yr/ 18 mo./ N/A	0–1 0–1.5	28% 37%
Kero & Piekkala (1987)	4,868	Community based	Active and passive	Parent report	1 yr/3, 6, & 12 mo	0–1	35%
Sipila et al. (1987)	1,642	Community based	Active and passive	Symptoms + otoscopic signs, or MEE at myringotomy	1 yr/N/A 18 mos/NA	0–1 0–1.5	45% 100/100 57% 170/100
Alho et al. (1991)	2,512	Community based	Passive	M.D. diagnosis	1 yr/ 2 yr/ N/A	0–1 0–2	42% 71% 93/100
SWEDEN							
Ingvarsson et al. (1984)	2,404	Community based	Passive	Red, bulging TM	5 yr/N/A	0–1 0–5	18% 58%
Ingvarsson, Lundgren, & Olofsson (1988)	2,978	Community based	Passive	Red, bulging TM	1 yr/N/A	1–2 0–7	38–44/100[h] 65–70%[h]
Harsten et al. (1989)	113	Clinic based	Active and passive	Earache + red, bulging TM; + URI symptoms	3 yr/N/A	0–3	62%
Rasmussen (1994)	1,306	Community based	Passive	Red TM + fever or earache	7 yr/N/A	0–1 0–3 0–7	14% 38% 61%

(continued)

Table 1. (continued)

Study (year)	N	Population	Surveillance	Diagnostic criteria[a]	Follow-up/ exam schedule	Age (yr)	Incidence[b] AOM	Incidence[b] OME	Incidence[b] OM[c]
NETHERLANDS									
Zielhuis et al. (1989)	1,439	Community based	Active	B tympanogram	15 mo/3 mo	2 3		20%[i] 18%[i]	
Zielhuis et al. (1990)	609	Community based	Active	B tympanogram	2 yr/3 mo	2–4		65%	
JAPAN									
Kaneko et al. (1984)	347	School based	Active	B or C tympanogram + MEE at myringotomy	3 yr/2 per yr	6–9		0.5–4%	
UNITED KINGDOM									
Ross, Croft, & Collins (1988)	278	Clinic based	Active	Red TM	1 yr/N/A	0–3	19% 22/100		

Adapted from Daly, K. (1991). Epidemiology of otitis media. *Otolaryngologic Clinics of North America, 24,* 776–777.
[a] I, Decreased; MEE, middle ear effusion; N/A, not available; NS, not specified; TM, tympanic membrane; URI, upper respiratory infection.
[b] Incidence is expressed as percentage of children with 1 or more episodes during the follow-up, or as episodes/100 children/years of follow-up.
[c] Type of OM as designated by author.
[d] Eskimo.
[e] Native American.
[f] Middle ear effusion.
[g] Varied by diagnostic instrument; impedance tympanoscope greater than impedance audiometer.
[h] Varied by gender; male greater than female.
[i] Average incidence over three 3-month periods.

Table 2. Otitis media prevalence studies in childhood, 1974–1993

Study (year)	N	Population	Diagnostic criteria[a]	Age (yr)	Season	OME prevalence
UNITED STATES						
Kessner et al. (1974)	2,780	Community based	TM amber, blue, or yellow, or air–fluid level, or retraction pocket, or tube present	0.5–11	Winter	6%
	497			0.5–3		10%
	412			4–5		7%
	451			6–7		4%
	797			8–11		3%
Griffith (1979)	274	School based	B or C_2 tympanogram	3–11	Winter	12%
Casselbrant et al. (1985)	103	Child care center	Cantekin (1983) algorithm	2–6	All year	5–25%[b,c]
DENMARK						
Poulsen & Tos (1980)	240	Community based	B tympanogram	2	Winter–spring	11–15%[c,d]
Tos et al. (1982)	288	Community based	B tympanogram	4	All year	10–19%[c,d]
Tos et al. (1978)	278	Community based	B tympanogram	1–2	Winter	11%
Tos, Poulsen, & Hancke (1979)	150	Community based	B tympanogram	1	All year	13%[d]
Lous & Fiellau-Nikolajsen (1981)	387	Community based	B tympanogram	7	All year	2–9%[b,c]
Fiellau-Nikolajsen (1980)	938	Community based	B tympanogram	3–4	Summer Winter	8–10%[c,d]
Birch & Elbrønd (1986)	210	Community based	B tympanogram	1–7	Fall	20%[d,e]
Møller & Tos (1990)	51	School based	B tympanogram	3–5	Fall	16–22%[f]
FINLAND						
Virolainen et al. (1980)	1,207	School based	MEE at tympanocentesis	7–8	Spring	3%
NETHERLANDS						
Schilder et al. (1993)	946	Community based	B tympanogram	7–8	Fall–winter	10%

(continued)

11

Table 2. (continued)

Study (year)	N	Population	Diagnostic criteria[a]	Age (yr)	Season	OME prevalence
BELGIUM						
Van Cauwenberge & Kluyskens (1984)	2,069	Child care center	B tympanogram + absent reflex + otoscopic Dx of OME	2–6	Summer–fall	12%
	97		B tympanogram		School year	9–27%[c,d]
UNITED KINGDOM						
Hallet (1982)	553	School based	B tympanogram	5	Spring/fall	20–30%[c,d]
SPAIN						
Suarez Nieto et al. (1984)	5,950	School based	NS	4–9	Winter	8%
GREENLAND						
Pedersen & Zachau-Christiansen (1986)	56	Community based	B tympanogram	3–4 5–8	Spring	18%[d] 5%[d]
NEW ZEALAND						
Chalmers et al. (1989)	881 847 770 790	Community based	B tympanogram	5 7 9 11	All year	14%[d] 9%[d] 4%[d] 3%[d]
AUSTRALIA						
Dugdale et al. (1978)	52	Community based	Abnormal TM color and thickness, ↓ TM mobility	<6	Winter	44%[d]
MICRONESIA						
Dever et al. (1985)	56 334	Clinic and school based	Otorrhea, or ↓ TM mobility, severe retraction pocket	0–2 5–16	NS	46%[d] 15%[d]
SOUTH AFRICA						
Halama et al. (1986)	267	Community based	Cantekin (1983) algorithm	<15	Winter	4%[b]

	N	Setting	Diagnostic criteria	Age	Season	Prevalence
NIGERIA						
Miller et al. (1983)	334	Community based	Cantekin (1983) algorithm	<15	Cooler season	19%[b]
Okeowo (1985)	764	Community based	B tympanogram	3–11	NS	6%
Ogisi (1988)	407	School based	B tympanogram Dull, retracted TM, air–fluid level	5–6	NS	1%[d] 8%[d]
KUWAIT						
Holmquist, Al Fadala, & Qattan (1987)	893	School based	B or C tympanogram	7–9	Winter	31%[d]
JAPAN						
Motohashi et al. (1993)	1,252 1,422 1,528	School based	B tympanogram	6–7 8–9 10–11	Spring	15% 7% 4%

Adapted from Daly, K. (1991). Epidemiology of otitis media. *Otolaryngologic Clinics of North America, 24,* 776–777.

[a]↓, Decreased, Dx, diagnosis; MEE, middle ear effusion; NS, not specified; TM, tympanic membrane.
[b]Based on worse ear.
[c]Monthly or seasonal variation.
[d]Based on ears, not children.
[e]Mean for six exams.
[f]Varied by instrument.

indirect evidence of OME. A fluid level or bubbles can sometimes be seen behind the tympanic membrane, which provides strong evidence of OME. Myringotomy provides access to the middle ear and allows the examiner to directly ascertain the presence of middle ear fluid. This diagnostic method is commonly used in European countries but is not used routinely in North America to diagnose OME. Although myrin-gotomy provides direct evidence of middle ear fluid, absence of fluid does not equate to absence of OM. A proportion of children who have myringotomy and tympanostomy tube placement for chronic OME have dry but not disease-free ears (Le, Daly, Margolis, Lindgren, & Giebink, 1992). None of these methods is 100% accurate in diagnosing OME. For example, tympanometry is considered to be a more objective test than otoscopy. However, it may be less reliable in young infants because of differences in ear canal compliance (Keefe & Bulen, 1993), or the results may be affected by crying or restless subjects.

Many studies reporting incidence are record reviews or do not use active surveillance in which the child is examined at frequent, regularly scheduled intervals determined by the investigator. Because OME is a labile disease, the ideal study design would combine frequent active surveillance (visits 1–2 months apart) with passive surveillance (data on middle ear status that are routinely recorded in the medical record as part of health supervision). Another important component in a prospec-tive study is subject retention. If a large proportion of study subjects withdraw early in the study, results may be biased or inaccurate. In many studies, OME status was ascertained at well-child and illness visits. With this type of surveillance, children were examined when their parents elect to schedule a clinic visit rather than on a schedule determined by the investigator.

Literature Review
Several U.S. researchers have reported OM incidence rates during the first year of life among nonnative populations ranging from 49% to 97% (Table 1) (Casselbrant et al., 1993; Duncan et al., 1993; Howie et al., 1975; Marchant et al., 1984; Owen et al., 1993; Teele et al., 1989). In contrast, estimates of OM incidence for Scandinavian infants were much lower: 14%–18% in Sweden (Ingvarsson, Lundgren, & Olofsson, 1984; Rasmussen, 1994); 22% in Denmark (Stangerup & Tos, 1986); and 28%–42% in Finland (Alho, Koivu, Sorri, & Rantakallio, 1991; Kero & Piekkala, 1987; Pukander, Sipila, & Karma, 1984; Sipila, Pukander, & Karma, 1987). The broader criteria used by U.S. researchers is a partial explanation for the differences in OM incidence between the United States and Scandinavia. The major criterion for OM in most of the U.S. studies was the presence of middle ear effusion, with the ad-

dition of one or more otitis-related signs or symptom in two studies (Casselbrant et al., 1993; Teele et al., 1989). Another study used physician diagnosis as the criterion for OM (Duncan et al., 1993). In contrast, the Scandinavian studies typically estimated the incidence of symptomatic AOM, requiring the presence of acute signs (red tympanic membrane, otorrhea, middle ear effusion at myringotomy). However, one study used parental report (Kero & Piekkala, 1987), one used physician diagnosis (Alho et al., 1991), and another required tympanic membrane signs without symptoms for a diagnosis of OM (Ingvarsson et al., 1984).

Although experience with OM during childhood appears to be almost universal (Owen et al., 1993; Roberts, Burchinal, Davis, Collier, & Henderson, 1991; Teele et al., 1989), middle ear effusion tends to resolve rapidly. Prospective studies of OM incidence and randomized studies of antibiotic treatment for AOM reveal that, for 60%–70% of children, OME resolved within 30 days after diagnosis, irrespective of treatment with standard antibiotics, extended-spectrum antibiotics, or placebo (Rosenfeld et al., 1994; Teele, Klein, & Rosner, 1980; Schwartz et al., 1984). Among children with OME, 40%–56% resolve it in 2 weeks (Birch & Elbrønd, 1984; Marchant et al., 1984), 71%–86% resolve it in 8 weeks, and 60%–94% resolve it in 12 weeks (Bartolozzi, Sacchetti, Scarane, & Becherucci, 1992; Birch & Elbrønd, 1986b; Casselbrant et al., 1984; Marchant et al., 1984; Teele et al., 1980; Zielhuis et al., 1990). The estimate of 60% resolution in 12 weeks may be an underestimate (Zielhuis et al., 1990). It was derived from a study with 3-month examination intervals in which OME resolution followed by recurrence between examinations would be misclassified as continuous OME. These studies all included children younger than 7 years, but each group consisted of a different age subset (e.g., birth to 1 year, 2–4 years). In general, children younger than age 1 year tended to have slower OME resolution. Children younger than 3 years are developing speech and language and are more vulnerable to the effects of OME-related hearing impairment. Roland et al. (1989) reported that, between the ages of 6 and 18 months, 27% of children have no OME, 17% have OME for 1–30 days, 16% have OME for 31–60 days, 15% have OME for 61–90 days, and 25% have OME for more than 90 days. Others have reported similar proportions of children with OME for more than 90 days (Roberts, Burchinal, & Henderson, 1993; Teele et al., 1989). Fourteen percent of children in the first year of life (Marchant et al., 1984), and 28% in the first 2 years of life experienced chronic OME (Bartolozzi et al., 1992). Other researchers have reported median OME durations of 17–44 days during the first year and 23–52 days during the second year of life, 40%–72% of this time was spent with bilateral

OME (Roberts et al., 1993; Teele et al., 1989). In these two studies, the duration of OME among children 3–5 years declined significantly to 14 days or less. Sixty-five percent of children followed in a child care center from 6 to 24 months of age had bilateral OME for 4 or more continuous months (Zeisel et al., 1995). The natural history of bilateral OME is an important research focus because a young child with OME in both ears is at greater risk of experiencing hearing impairment and treatment with tympanostomy tubes than a child with unilateral OME. Bilateral OME has been shown to predict chronic OME (Daly et al., 1988).

Recurrent OM (defined as three or more episodes in a year) is experienced by 3%–17% of children (Biles, Buffler, & O'Donell, 1980; Casselbrant et al., 1984; Rasmussen, 1994; Teele et al., 1989). However, 20%–40% of children experience two or more episodes in the first year of life, and 19%–30% experience two or more OM episodes between 1 and 2 years of age (Goodwin, Shaw, & Feldman, 1980; Kero & Piekkala, 1987; Teele et al., 1989).

Tympanic membrane and middle ear sequelae of recurrent OM and chronic OME were reported in population-based samples of 7- to 8-year-old children (Schilder et al., 1993; Tos et al., 1984) and summarized among children followed after tympanostomy tube treatment (Giebink, 1988). Among the population-based samples, less than 1% had tympanic membrane perforation or retraction pocket, 10%–18% had atrophy, 7%–23% had tympanosclerosis, and 22%–30% had attic retraction. However, among children followed after tympanostomy tube insertion, the weighted annual incidence of sequelae (new occurrences per year) was as follows: perforations, 1%; atrophy, 8%; tympanosclerosis, 10%; and attic retractions, 15% (Daly, 1994).

RISK FACTORS FOR OTITIS MEDIA

Age
Children are more likely to develop AOM and OME in infancy and early childhood than in later childhood (Biles et al., 1980; Birch & Elbrønd, 1986a, 1986b; Casselbrant et al., 1985; Chalmers et al., 1989; Clements, Henderson, & Neebe, 1993; Dever, Stewart, & David, 1985; Dugdale, Canty, Lewis, & Lovell, 1978; Fiellau-Nikolajsen, 1983; Goodwin et al., 1980; Halama, Voogt, Musgrave, 1986; Henderson et al., 1982; Kessner, Snow, & Singer, 1974; Miller, Omene, Bluestone, & Torkelson, 1983; Okeowo, 1985; Pedersen & Zachau-Christiansen, 1986; Teele et al., 1989; Van Cauwenberge & Kluyskens, 1984). Researchers reported the following age-specific OME prevalence rates (Table 2): age 1 year, 13% (Tos, Poulsen, & Hancke, 1979); age 2 years, 11%–15% (Poulsen & Tos, 1980); ages 3–5 years, 5%–30% (Birch &

Elbrønd, 1984; Chalmers et al., 1989; Fiellau-Nikolajsen, 1980; Hallet, 1982; Ogisi, 1988; Pedersen & Zachau-Christiansen, 1986; Tos, Holm-Jensen, Sørenson, & Mogensen, 1982); ages 6–8 years, 3%–15% (Chalmers et al., 1989; Kessner et al., 1974; Lous & Fiellau-Nikolajsen, 1981; Motohashi et al., 1993; Schilder et al., 1993; Virolainen et al., 1980); and ages 9–11 years, 3%–6% (Chalmers et al., 1989; Kessner et al., 1974; Motohashi et al., 1993). Most of the estimates of prevalence among preschool children were based on ears rather than children, and probably underestimate prevalence.

OM incidence peaks between 6 and 18 months of age (Alho et al., 1991; Clements et al., 1993; Teele et al., 1989). The number of AOM episodes per 100 children per year during the first year of life have been estimated to be 97–100 (Biles et al., 1980; Sipila et al., 1987). Higher estimates of 120 and 178 (birth to 6 months) and 381 and 420 (6–12 months, respectively), were obtained among children in a research child care center (Clements et al., 1993; Henderson et al., 1982). The proportion of children experiencing at least one episode of OME during the first year of life ranged from 14% in Sweden (Rasmussen, 1994) to 97% in the United States (Owen et al., 1993).

Among cohorts of U.S. children, 35%–85% had their first episode of middle ear effusion by age 6 months (Casselbrant et al., 1993; Marchant et al., 1984; Owen et al., 1993; Stewart, 1989; Teele et al., 1989) and 36%–56% of episodes during the first year of life were asymptomatic (Casselbrant et al., 1993; Marchant et al., 1984). These rates are much higher than the 13% prevalence reported by Tos, Poulsen, and Hancke (1979) because they represent an entire 6-month period rather than the single point in time in which the prevalence survey was conducted.

Children who experience their first OM episode at an early age are at two to eight times greater risk of chronic OME (Kraemer et al., 1983; Marchant et al., 1984) and recurrent OM (Biles et al., 1980; Harsten et al., 1989; Howie et al., 1975; Lundgren, Ingvarsson, & Olofsson, 1984; Teele et al., 1989) than children who have a later first episode. Early OM may be attributed in part to an infant's immature immune system, which increases his or her susceptibility to respiratory pathogens. Children under age 2 years have demonstrated poor antibody response to 23-valent pneumococcal vaccine containing the serotypes commonly implicated in OM (Giebink, 1994). In addition, anatomical and physiological differences in the infant eustachian tube play a role in early OM onset by impeding drainage of effusion formed in the middle ear during the inflammatory process (Proctor, 1967; Sadler-Kimes, Siegel, & Todhunter, 1989). The combination of innate predisposition (e.g., decreased ability to produce antibodies against common OM pathogens,

differences in eustachian tube anatomy and function) and early exposures to risk factors (e.g., child care attendance) probably results in
earlier OM onset. Identified risk factors for earlier onset of OM are male
gender, cessation of breast feeding before 6 months, feeding in a supine
position, and group child care attendance (Aniansson et al., 1994; Owen
et al., 1993).

Gender

Many studies reported that boys are at higher risk of AOM and OME
than girls (Adams & Benson, 1991; Alho, Kikku, Oja, Koivu, & Sorri,
1993; Casselbrant et al., 1984; Chalmers et al., 1989; Kero & Piekkala,
1987; Teele et al., 1989), but others reported no difference in OM incidence or prevalence by gender (Goodwin et al., 1980; Hallet, 1982;
J.L. Stewart, 1989; Tos et al., 1978). Based on available data, the male:
female ratio in OM incidence and prevalence is probably less than 2:1.
Chronic OME and recurrent OM were also reported to be more common
(Duncan et al., 1993; Fiellau-Mikolajsen, 1983; Hardy & Fowler, 1993;
Onion & Taylor, 1977; Stewart, Kirkland, Simpson, Silva, & Williams,
1984; Teele et al., 1989) or more severe (Le et al., 1992) among boys
than girls, but others have concluded there is no gender disparity in
these two conditions (Gates, Wachtendorf, & Holt, 1986; Harsten et al.,
1989; Shurin, Pelton, Donner, & Klein, 1979). One study demonstrated
that girls had a longer duration of OME than boys during the second
year of life (Owen et al., 1993), whereas another reported a longer
duration for boys during the first 3 years of life (Teele et al., 1989).

Race

Several studies conducted in Native American (Nelson & Berry, 1984;
Todd & Bowman, 1985; Zonis, 1968) and Eskimo (Pedersen & Zachau-
Christiansen, 1986) communities reported a lower prevalence of OME
and a higher prevalence of chronic OM compared to rates reported for
Caucasian populations. Among school-age children, 4%–8% of Native
Americans had chronic tympanic membrane perforations, compared
with 0.5% of a U.S. population–based sample (National Center for
Health Statistics, 1972; Nelson & Berry, 1984; Zonis, 1968). However,
the few prospective studies of infants and young children in native populations reported age-specific OM incidence rates similar to those for
Caucasian and African American children (Casselbrant et al., 1993;
Goodwin et al., 1980; Reed & Dunn, 1970; Stewart, 1989; Teele et al.,
1989). In population-based studies, OME prevalence (Kessner et al.,
1974; National Center for Health Statistics, 1972) and the annual OM
visit rate were greater in Caucasians than in African Americans (Schappert, 1992). A small clinical study in which Caucasian and African
American children were examined monthly from birth to age 2 reported

no differences in the incidence of AOM or OME in these children (Casselbrant, Mandel, Kurs-Lasky, Rockette, & Bluestone, 1995). Although African American parents were less likely to be employed than Caucasian parents, OM rates did not differ by race within employment strata.

Parent-reported OM and recurrent OM were significantly higher for Caucasian, non-Hispanic children than for African American or Hispanic children (Adams & Benson 1991; Hardy, 1991). However, in a community-based study in Texas, the observed OM incidence rates did not differ among Caucasians, African Americans, and Hispanics (Biles et al., 1980). Chronic OME was not related to race in two studies (Kraemer et al., 1983; Marchant et al., 1984), although, compared with African American children, Caucasian children were more likely to have persistent OME (Shurin et al., 1979). Investigators using the same algorithm (Cantekin, 1983) to diagnose OME among 2- to 5-year-olds reported similar OME prevalence rates among black children in Nigeria and Caucasian children in Pittsburgh (28% and 22%–33%, respectively) (Casselbrant et al., 1985; Miller et al., 1983). These rates were considerably higher than the 4% rate reported for black children in South Africa (Halama et al., 1986). Differences in OM rates by Native American tribe also have been reported (Shaw, Todd, Goodwin, & Feldman, 1981). Direct comparisons of race-specific incidence and prevalence rates from separate studies may be inappropriate because of differences in study methodology and subject selection. However, race-specific rates would be comparable if a study applied the same subject selection, diagnostic methods, disease definitions, data collection techniques, and active surveillance to a multiracial subject group. Nevertheless, disparities in utilization of health care may be responsible, in part, for differences in race-specific rates reported from a single study.

Socioeconomic Status
The effect of socioeconomic status on OM is ambiguous. Although socioeconomic status did not influence prevalence of OME or the risk of recurrent OM in some studies (Chalmers et al., 1989; Kessner et al., 1974; Taino et al., 1988; Teele et al., 1989), others reported that AOM and recurrent OM are more common (Kero & Piekkala, 1987; Ståhlberg, Ruuskanen, & Virolainen, 1986) or less common (Tos et al., 1978) in lower socioeconomic classes. In a population-based U.S. study, children from families with higher income, health insurance, or a regular source of health care had higher rates of recurrent OM than children without these benefits. Shaw and colleagues (1981) explored the influence of living conditions on AOM in the first year of life among four groups of Native American children. For all four groups, children who lived within

5 miles of the health facility had a higher AOM incidence than those who lived farther away. Regular access to health care may lead to more frequent examinations and a greater likelihood that OM will be ascertained, suggesting that OM may be underdiagnosed in populations with less access to health care.

Birth Weight and Neonatal Factors

Most researchers have concluded that there is no relationship between birth weight or gestational age and AOM, OME, chronic OME, and OME duration (Alho, Koivu, Hartikainen-Sorri, et al., 1990; Black, 1985; Chalmers et al., 1989; Gravel, McCarton, & Ruben, 1988; Kraemer et al., 1983; Teele et al., 1989; Zielhuis, Heuvelmans-Heinen, Rach, & van den Broek, 1989). Similarly, head circumference and use of neonatal ventilation were not related to risk of AOM (Alho, Koivu, Hartikainen-Sorri, et al., 1990). Lower birth weight and prematurity increased AOM or OME risk in two studies, however (Kero & Piekkala, 1987; Van Cauwenberge & Kluyskens, 1984).

Immune Status

The principal etiologic agents in AOM are *Streptococcus pneumoniae* (the most common pathogen), nontypable *Haemophilus influenzae, Moraxella catarrhalis,* respiratory syncytial virus, adenovirus, influenza A and B, and parainfluenza (Bluestone, Stephenson, & Martin, 1992; Henderson et al., 1982). Compared with older children and adults, infants and children younger than 2 years do not produce protective levels of antibody to pneumococcal capsular polysaccharide vaccine antigens and are at greater risk of AOM and recurrent OM (Giebink, 1994; Klein, 1981). This is due to the immature immune response of infants and young children and the T-cell–independent characteristics of the pneumococcal polysaccharide antibody response, which is a response without immunologic memory. Because *S. pneumoniae* is the most common OM pathogen in children, inability to mount an adequate immune response to this organism leaves a young child susceptible to AOM. In addition, researchers have shown that some children who are susceptible to AOM have subtle immune defects. Prellner and colleagues demonstrated that children with recurrent OM in the first year of life had a significantly lower antibody response to rubella vaccine (Prellner, Harsten, Löfgren, Christenson, & Heldrup, 1990) and lower levels of specific immunoglobulin G (IgG) antibodies to *S. pneumoniae* Types 6A and 19F than healthy children (Prellner, Kalm, Harsten, Heldrup, & Oxelius, 1989). Otitis-prone children had significantly lower levels of IgG2 at 12 and 32 months than age-matched controls and were more likely to have *H. influenzae* cultured from their nasopharynx during episodes of AOM if their IgG2 level was below the mean (Freijd, Oxelius, & Rynnel-

Dagöö, 1985). Because most pneumococcal antibodies are of the IgG2 subclass, this study also suggests an inability of otitis-prone children to mount a specific antibody response to pneumococcal polysaccharides.

Other Diseases and Conditions

Respiratory diseases are closely associated with the development of OME. These include recent or concurrent upper-respiratory infection (Casselbrant et al., 1984; Daly et al., in press; Ruuskanen & Heikkinen, 1994; Suarez Nieto, Malluguiza Calvo, & Barthe Garcia, 1984; Van Cauwenberge & Kluyskens, 1984), nasal congestion, nasal obstruction, and tonsillitis (Chalmers et al., 1989; Van Cauwenberge & Kluyskens, 1984). Children who had bacterial and viral pathogens cultured from the nasopharynx and upper respiratory tract were at greater risk of developing AOM and OME than children lacking these pathogens (Aniansson et al., 1994; Faden, Stanievich, Brodsky, Bernstein, & Ogra, 1990; Faden et al., 1991; Henderson et al., 1982; Tos, Poulsen, & Borch, 1979). Adenoid or tonsillar hypertrophy and sinusitis were also associated with chronic OME (Ishidoya, Takasaka, & Shimizu, 1988).

The role of allergy in OM has not been clearly established. Children with atopic manifestations or asthma were reported to be at higher risk of acute and recurrent OM in the first 2 years of life than children without these symptoms (Alho et al., 1993; Hardy & Fowler, 1993; Taino et al., 1988). Serum immunoglobulin E levels at 9 and 12 months of age were similar in children with recurrent OM in the first year of life and in children with no OM (Taino et al., 1988). Immunoglobulin E levels were significantly lower in a third group who experienced recurrent OM later. Prior history of allergy and frequent atopic symptoms, including nasal congestion, were more common in children being treated with tympanostomy tubes for chronic OME than in controls (Kraemer et al., 1983). Others reported no relation between personal or family history of allergy and chronic OME (Black, 1985) or recurrent OM (Teele et al., 1989).

Children with craniofacial abnormalities such as Down syndrome and cleft palate have a high incidence of recurrent OM, OME, and chronic OME (Paradise, Bluestone, & Felder, 1969; Downs, 1980; Schwartz & Schwartz, 1978). A group of children with cleft palate all had OM by 3 years of age, but their type 6A and 19F pneumococcal antibody levels did not differ significantly from those of normal, age-matched controls (Rynnel-Dagöö, Lindberg, Bagger-Sjöbäck, Larson, 1992). Cleft uvula, which is an atypical variation of cleft palate, was not predictive of the number of AOM episodes in a cohort of Native American children (Fischler, Todd, & Feldman, 1987). Cystic fibrosis is characterized by abnormal mucus secretions and lower respiratory tract infections, which could predispose a child to OME. However, studies suggest that children with cystic fibrosis are actually at lower risk of OME than the general pediatric population, perhaps because of the long-term use of antibiotics in children with this condition (Haddad, Gonzalez, Kurland, Orenstein, & Casselbrant, 1994).

Familial Clustering

The risk of AOM, recurrent OM, OME, and chronic OME is greater in children with a family history of these conditions (Black, 1985; Harsten et al., 1989; Kraemer et al., 1983; Rasmussen, 1993; Sipila, Karma, Pukander, Timonen, & Kataja, 1988; Teele et al., 1989; Zielhuis et al., 1989). Children with an affected sibling have a 1.6- to 4.2-fold increase in OM risk. The development of OM in siblings may be due to inherited biologic susceptibility, common environmental exposures, or both. Evidence of OM history across two or more generations is probably the result of genetic factors because parent and child are in different environments at the period of highest risk. Risk factors for OM may cluster in families and across generations as a result of cultural practices, however, so environmental factors cannot be ruled out as a cause of OM in families with more than one affected generation.

Studies that have investigated sibling and parental history separately have reported increased AOM or OME risk if a child has an affected sibling, but not if a parent is affected (Teele et al., 1989; Zielhuis et al., 1989). Parent history of OM significantly predicted OME duration (Teele et al., 1989), and parents of children undergoing surgical treatment for chronic OME were five times more likely to have tympanic membrane abnormalities consistent with an OM history than control parents (Rockley & Rhys Evans, 1986). In studies that classified the OM status of first-degree relative pairs, the observed number of normal–normal or abnormal–abnormal pairs was significantly greater than expected by chance (Todd, 1987; Todd & Settle, 1988).

Human leukocyte antigens (HLA), which are genetically determined, are associated with immune response. Associations between specific HLA antigens and a variety of diseases and conditions have been demonstrated (De Vries, 1992). The HLA antigen A2 was found to be significantly more frequent and A3 significantly less frequent in children with recurrent OM than in healthy adults or children without OM. Children with chronic OME had HLA profiles similar to those of the control groups (Kalm, Johnson, & Prellner, 1994; Kalm, Johnson, Prellner, & Ninn, 1991). In a study designed to separate the effects of genes and environment, OM rates of Apache children adopted into non-Apache families were similar to those of Apache children living in the reservation, and higher than those of their non-Apache siblings (Spivey & Hirschhorn, 1977).

Season

Prevalence of OME is highest in the winter and lowest in the summer (Bartolozzi et al., 1992; Casselbrant et al., 1985; Chalmers et al., 1989; Griffith, 1979; Hallet, 1982; Lous & Fiellau-Nikolajsen, 1981; Tos, Holm-Jensen, & Sorensen, 1981; Van Cauwenberge & Kluyskens, 1984; Zielhuis et al., 1989). OME is associated with upper respiratory infection (Birch & Elbrønd, 1984; Casselbrant et al., 1985; Tos, Poulsen, & Borch, 1979), and the seasonal distributions of AOM and respiratory viral illness closely coincide (Henderson et al., 1982). Although OME is more common in the winter months, no relationship has been demonstrated between OME and weather patterns (temperature, wind speed, precipitation, and humidity) (Hilditch, 1985; Reed & Dunn, 1970; Suarez Nieto et al., 1984).

A child born at the beginning of the respiratory illness season could be at greater risk for viral respiratory illnesses commonly associated with AOM. A community-based study in Texas reported that recurrent OM was more common among children born during the last half of the calendar year (Biles et al., 1980), but a large clinic-based study found that the risk of recurrent OM and the duration of OME did not differ by season of birth (Teele et al., 1989).

Infant Feeding Practices

Many studies reported that breast feeding significantly reduced the risk of OME, AOM, and recurrent OM and decreased the duration of OME (Alho, Koivu, Sorri, & Rantakallio, 1990; Aniansson et al., 1994; Chalmers et al., 1989; Cunningham, 1977; Duncan et al., 1993; Kero & Piekkala, 1987; Owen et al., 1993; Paradise, Elster, & Tan, 1994; Saarinen, 1982; Sassen, Brand, & Grote, 1994; Schaefer, 1971; Shaaban & Hamadnalla, 1993; Teele et al., 1989). Estimates of the protective effect of breast feeding suggest that the risk of AOM is reduced by 30% and the risk of recurrent OM is reduced by 30%–50% in the first 2 years of life (Alho, Koivu, Sorri, et al., 1990; Duncan et al., 1993; Sipila et al., 1988; Teele et al., 1989). A few studies have shown that its protective effect may persist 1 to several months after cessation of breast feeding (Alho, Koivu, Sorri, et al., 1990; Aniansson et al., 1994; Duncan et al., 1993; Kero & Piekkala, 1987; Sassen et al., 1994), and Teele and colleagues in Boston (1989) established that a short duration of breast feeding was as protective as a long duration of breast feeding during the first 12 months of life. Most studies have considered the effect of breast feeding without regard to supplementation or concurrent formula feeding; only a few studies have evaluated the effects of exclusive breast feeding (Aniansson et al., 1994; Duncan et al., 1993). Aniansson et al.

(1994) found that children who were exclusively breast fed had a greater reduction in OM than those who were mixed fed or weaned. In addition, the age at first OM episode was inversely related to duration of exclusive breast feeding. Duncan and colleagues in Arizona (1993) determined that exclusive breast feeding for at least 6 months conferred the greatest protection against OM, and breast feeding for at least 4 months with or without supplementation conferred lower levels of protection compared with a group that was not breast fed. This study used multivariate analysis to control for gender, child care, maternal smoking, parental hay fever, and number of siblings.

Not all studies have reported that breast feeding decreased OM (Harsten et al., 1989; Kraemer et al., 1983; Ståhlberg et al., 1986; Taino et al., 1988). The decreased risk of OM in breast-fed infants may be due to other factors that are not controlled or adjusted for in many of the studies.

Infants fed in a supine position have an increased risk of OME and AOM (Owen et al., 1993; Teele et al., 1989). This method of feeding may cause milk or formula to reflux up the eustachian tube into the middle ear (Duncan, 1960). Formula and cow's milk may contain constituents that contribute to the development of OM. In vitro studies have shown that the addition of infant formulas to human breast milk significantly reduced the milk's lysozyme activity, suggesting that formula may adversely affect the protective properties of breast milk when formula and breast milk are used together (Quan et al., 1994).

A unique study evaluated the effect of breast milk in infants with cleft palate (Paradise et al., 1994). Those who were fed breast milk via a compressible feeder were significantly more likely than infants fed formula or cow's milk to have OME-free study visits. This finding suggests that breast milk provided protection from OME. Constituents of human breast milk that have antimicrobial, anti-inflammatory, or immunomodulating properties include secretory immunoglobulin A, leukocytes, lactoferrin, lysozyme, lipids, prostaglandins, and cytokines. These components may protect against OM during breast feeding and even after breast feeding has ceased (Goldman, 1993). Casein in human milk plays an important role in preventing *S. pneumoniae* and *H. influenzae* from adhering to pharyngeal epithelial cells (Aniansson, Andersson, Lindstedt, & Svanborg, 1990). However, the method of feeding does not appear to affect the colonization of the infant nasopharynx with OM pathogens (Harabuchi et al., 1994; Kaleida et al., 1993).

Child Care and Siblings

Exposure to siblings or to children in a child care setting has been reported to increase the risk of AOM and OME. The majority of researchers report a 1.5- to 5-fold increase in risk of OME, chronic OME, AOM, and recurrent OM among child care attendees (Alho et al., 1993; Aniansson et al., 1994; Birch & Elbrønd, 1986a; Black, 1985; Daly, Giebink, et al., 1988; Duncan et al., 1993; Fiellau-Nikolajsen, 1979; Fleming, Cochi, Hightower, & Broome, 1987; Hardy & Fowler, 1993; Kero & Piekkala, 1987; Rasmussen, 1993; Ståhlberg et al., 1986; Strangert, 1977; Taino et al., 1988; Teele, Klein, Rosner, & the Greater Boston Otitis Media Study Group, 1993; Zielhuis et al., 1989). An increased duration of OME was also reported among children in child care settings (Owen et al., 1993). Children in large child care centers are at greater risk of AOM and OME (Alho et al., 1993; Rasmussen, 1993; Sipila et al., 1988; Strangert, 1977; Tos et al., 1978) than those in family child care settings. Researchers have demonstrated that duration of OME and risk of AOM increased as the number of children (Friel-Patti, Finitzo, Chinn, & Lindgren, 1993; Hardy & Fowler, 1993) or hours in the child care setting (Owen et al., 1993) increased. Child care center environments facilitate the transmission of bacterial and viral agents that cause respiratory disease and in turn increase the risk of AOM and OME (Birch & Elbrønd, 1984; Casselbrant et al., 1985; Henderson & Giebink, 1986; Tos, Poulsen, & Borch, 1979).

Risk of AOM and OME also rises as the number of siblings increases, presumably by increasing the exposure to infectious agents that cause acute respiratory infection (Alho et al., 1993; Duncan et al., 1993; Kero & Piekkala, 1987; Zielhuis et al., 1989). Chronic OME, which results from persistent middle ear inflammation rather than acute infection, has not been associated with daily exposure to small children or to number of siblings (Black, 1985; Kraemer et al., 1983).

Passive Smoking
Studies have shown that exposure to parental smoking increases the risk of recurrent OM (Alho et al., 1993; Ey et al., 1995; Sipila et al., 1988; Ståhlberg et al., 1986), OME (Etzel, Pattishall, Haley, Fletcher, & Henderson, 1992; Hinton, 1989; Iversen, Birch, & Lundqvist, 1985; Strachan, Jarvis, & Feyerabend, 1989), chronic OME (Black, 1985; Kraemer et al., 1983), and OME recurrence after surgical treatment for chronic OME (Maw & Bawden, 1994a; Maw, Parker, Lance, & Dilkes, 1992). Exposure to passive smoke also lengthens the duration of OME (Etzel et al., 1992; Owen et al., 1993). These studies reported a 1.1- to 2.0-fold increase in risk associated with exposure to passive smoke. Others have reported no relationship between exposure to passive smoke and OME (Chalmers et al., 1989; Van Cauwenberge & Kluyskens, 1984; Zielhuis et al., 1989), chronic OME (Rasmussen, 1993; Rowe-Jones & Brockbank, 1992), or recurrent OM (Harsten et al., 1989; Teele et al.,

1989). Exposure in these studies was usually assessed by parental report of their smoking status and may underestimate the true exposure if infants were exposed to smokers in other settings or if smoking parents described themselves as nonsmokers or underestimated the amount they smoked. Studies that quantified cotinine, a nicotine metabolite, in the child's serum or saliva reported a significant relationship between cotinine level and OME (Etzel et al., 1992; Strachan et al., 1989).

There are several possible mechanisms by which exposure to passive smoke could increase the risk of OM among infants and children. Passive smoke may inflame the mucosa of the nasopharynx, eustachian tube, and middle ear, increasing susceptibility to viral and bacterial invasion. Constituents of tobacco smoke are involved in goblet cell hyperplasia, facilitating the production of mucoid middle ear effusion. Once formed, middle ear effusion may not be readily cleared because of smoke-induced eustachian tube obstruction and decreased mucociliary clearance. Passive smoke may also act indirectly by inflaming the small airways of the respiratory tract, leaving a child more susceptible to respiratory infections and subsequent AOM and chronic OME (Hinton, 1989; U.S. Department of Health and Human Services, 1986). Alternatively, smoking parents are at increased risk of upper respiratory infection, which can be spread to their children (Hinton, 1989; Strachan et al., 1989).

Multivariate Analysis
Most of the reported analytic studies used univariate analysis to explore the relationship between individual risk factors and OM. Others used stratification to examine the effect of one risk factor while controlling for another (Etzel et al., 1992; Paradise et al., 1994; Zielhuis et al., 1989). Still others used multivariate analysis to control for confounding variables (Alho et al., 1993; Daly, Giebink, et al., 1988; Duncan et al., 1993; Etzel et al., 1992; Hardy & Fowler, 1993; Kero & Piekkala, 1987; Maw & Bawden, 1994a; Owen et al., 1993; Rasmussen, 1993; Strachan et al., 1989; Taino et al., 1988). A confounding variable is one that is related to the outcome (OM) and one or more risk factors under study. For example, children with OM are more likely to have parents who smoke, and parents who smoke are more likely to be of lower socioeconomic status. Once smoking is taken into account, OM rates may not vary by socioeconomic status. Similarly, women who elect to breast feed their infants are more likely to be Caucasian, not employed outside the home (and their children not in child care), nonsmokers, more educated and with higher incomes than women who do not breast feed (Ryan, Rush, Kreiger, & Lewandowski, 1991); all these factors could impact OME incidence and should be controlled in analysis. Even the

studies employing multivariate analysis used different combinations of variables, and not all confounders were controlled in every analysis. Studies that fail to control for confounding should be interpreted cautiously.

UNRESOLVED ISSUES

There is little dispute about the fact the OM clusters in families, but the relative contributions of genetics and environment have not been clarified. Specific genes or chromosomes have not yet been implicated in the transmission of OM susceptibility. Although an HLA antigen has been associated with recurrent OM, the clustering of specific genotypes in affected family members has not been explored. The most likely model for genetic influence in OME is multifactorial, in which genes and environmental exposures play a role in predisposing a child to OME, recurrent OM, and chronic OME. Studies currently underway compare OM rates in monozygotic and dizygotic twins to estimate the degree of heritability (Casselbrant, Golden, Doyle, Rockette, & Steele, 1988; Kvaerner & Tambs, in press) and to examine the hypothesis that aggregation of OM in families fits a specific mode of inheritance while controlling for environmental covariates (Rich et al., in press).

The effect of socioeconomic status on the risk of OM should be more clearly defined. On the one hand, the prevalence of OM risk factors is inversely related to socioeconomic status (Alho, Koivu, Sorri, et al., 1990; Owen et al., 1993). On the other hand, there is evidence that the risk of OM (or the likelihood of having OM diagnosed) is greater in children with greater access to health care, which is associated with higher family income. Risk of recurrent OM was greater for children of lower socioeconomic status in a Finnish study, but the association disappeared after controlling for the confounding factors of parental smoking and duration of breast feeding (Alho, Koivu, Sorri, et al., 1990). Of the two studies reporting a higher incidence of OM among children with lower socioeconomic status, one did not control for confounders (Ståhlberg et al., 1986), whereas the other controlled for breast feeding, child care, gender, and number of siblings but not for parental smoking (Kero & Piekkala, 1987). Correlates of social class that are important in OM risk require further illumination. Studies controlling for risk factors for OM and access to and utilization of health care are necessary to more clearly define the role of socioeconomic status in the development of OM.

Allergy, as a potential risk factor for AOM and OME, has been studied with equivocal results. Some studies suggest that children with respiratory allergies are at increased risk of OM; however, it is possible that they also have increased surveillance for OM. More studies are needed to illuminate the potential relationship between allergy and OM.

Early-onset OM is often a predictor of recurrent and chronic disease. Research to explore the relative contributions of innate characteristics, biologic susceptibility, and early exposure to the development of OM in the first few months of life would be beneficial. For example, although infants with cleft palate experience almost continuous OME, those fed breast milk with a compressible feeder had a greater proportion of effusion-free health care visits than those fed cow's milk or formula (Paradise et al., 1994). This suggests that the high incidence and long duration of OME in children with cleft palate may be the result of a number of factors and not solely caused by anatomic predisposition. The interrelationship of risk factors for OME in early infancy may produce groups of children at very high risk. Children of smokers are breast fed for a shorter duration, and they enter group child care earlier than children of nonsmokers (Owen et al., 1993; Alho, Koivu, Hartikainen-Sorri, et al., 1990). In addition, women who smoke also may have lower levels of IgG, which are transferred to the infant across the placenta (Ferson, Edwards, Lind, Milton, & Hersey, 1979). Although all young infants lack immunocompetence, subgroups with the lowest levels of antibody would be at higher risk than infants with higher antibody levels (Salazar et al., in review).

At the other end of the spectrum, little is known about risk factors for OM sequelae (tympanic membrane and middle ear pathology). Some of these conditions, although relatively uncommon, can lead to cholesteatoma with intracranial complications and permanent hearing loss (Wright & Meyerhoff, 1994). Identification of risk factors could lead to development of strategies to prevent sequelae, with increased surveillance and more aggressive treatment for high-risk children.

Prevention of OME, particularly recurrent and chronic OME, is a worthwhile goal. Several preventive approaches should be studied. Risk factor reduction could presumably be effective in primary prevention. However, little is known about parents' knowledge of modifiable risk factors for OME and about barriers to change. In three studies, interventions did not significantly reduce infant exposure to passive smoke as measured by infant urine cotinine, but interventions did not include information about the increased risk of OM for infants exposed to passive smoke, nor was OM measured as an outcome (Chilmonczyk, Palomaki, & Knight, 1992; Greenberg et al., 1994; Woodward, Owen, Grgurinovich, Griffith, & Linke, 1987). One study reported that, compared with the control group, infants in the intervention group were exposed to fewer cigarettes and had a lower prevalence of persistent lower respiratory disease symptoms in the first 12 months of life (Greenberg et al., 1994). No other risk factor reduction trials (i.e., promotion of breast feeding, use of small child care settings) to decrease OME incidence have been attempted. Carefully planned randomized interventions should be designed to measure risk factor reduction as an intermediate measure of success and decreased OME incidence as the outcome.

Newly developed pneumococcal vaccines are being evaluated to determine their effectiveness in reducing OM in the first 2 years of life. Even if these vaccines are effective in reducing OM caused by the vaccine-specific pneumococcal serotypes, OM caused by different pneumococcal serotypes and other organisms could increase, yielding a net effect of no reduction in OM incidence. Vaccines against respiratory virus and nontypable *H. influenzae* are in the early stages of development (Giebink, 1994; Klein, 1994).

Although studies of the epidemiology of OM have become more sophisticated, there is still a need for studies with rigorous design, careful conduct, and multivariate analysis. Some of the methodological issues to be addressed in designing new studies are use of representative samples and appropriate sample size; valid exposure and diagnosis measures; standard, detailed definitions of disease; strategies to reduce loss to follow-up; and design or analytic techniques to control for confounding variables.

IMPLICATIONS FOR MANAGEMENT

With the rise of antibiotic-resistant OM pathogens (Bluestone et al., 1992; Centers for Disease Control and Prevention, 1994) and the continuing debate about appropriate management of AOM, recurrent OM, OME, and chronic OME, developing strategies to prevent these diseases should become a priority. Risk factor modification and development of effective vaccines could be useful strategies in preventing OM. Although research is lacking about the effectiveness of risk factor modification in reducing OM incidence, parental education, physician advice, and changes in public policy could have an impact on OM risk factors, potentially decreasing the incidence of OM. For example, parents could be educated to decrease their child's exposure to tobacco smoke and to choose small child care settings rather than child care centers if possible.

The development of safe and effective vaccines to prevent OM among infants and young children could considerably reduce the morbidity associated with OM diseases. Newly developed pneumococcal vaccines are currently being tested, and vaccines against nontypable *H. influenzae* and respiratory viruses are in the early stages of research. Investigators must address the issue of immunogenicity when several vaccines are administered concurrently.

Not all risk factors can be modified, but they can be used to identify groups of high-risk children for secondary prevention. These children can be targeted for increased observation and earlier intervention to prevent recurrent and chronic OME and their associated sequelae.

CONCLUSIONS

Otitis media is currently the most common childhood disease, with peak incidence in the first 2 years of life. Although OM during childhood is nearly universal, about 5%–20% of children have recurrent OM and chronic OME. Besides age, several host characteristics have been identified as risk factors for OM, including male gender, Caucasian and Native American race, and family history of OM. Environmental risk factors, some of which could be modified to reduce OM incidence, have also been recognized. These include winter season; upper respiratory infection; exposure to other children, especially in child care; and exposure to passive smoke. Breast feeding appears to exert a protective effect, probably because of the protective factors present in human breast milk. Although evidence of an association between these risk factors and OM is relatively strong, other potential risk factors need further study. These include anatomy, allergy, immune status, and socioeconomic status. Development of preventive strategies and studies of their effect on OM should be a priority.

REFERENCES

Adams, P.F., & Benson, V. (1991). Current estimates from the National Health Interview Survey: National Center for Health Statistics. *Vital and Health Statistics. Series 10,* No. 181.

Alho, O.-P., Kilkku, O., Oja, H., Koivu, M., & Sorri, M. (1993). Control of the temporal aspect when considering risk factors for acute otitis media. *Archives of Otolaryngology—Head and Neck Surgery, 119,* 444–449.

Alho, O.-P., Koivu, M., Hartikainen-Sorri, M., Sorri, A.-M., Kilkku, O., & Rantakallio, P. (1990). Is a child's history of acute otitis media and respiratory infection already determined in the antenatal and perinatal period? *International Journal of Pediatric Otorhinolaryngology, 19,* 129–137.

Alho, O.-P., Koivu, M., Sorri, M., & Rantakallio, P.C. (1990). Risk factors for recurrent acute otitis media and respiratory infection in infancy. *International Journal of Pediatric Otorhinolaryngology, 19,* 151–161.

Alho, O.-P., Koivu, M., Sorri, M., & Rantakallio, P. (1991). The occurrence of acute otitis media in infants: A life-table analysis. *International Journal of Pediatric Otorhinolaryngology, 21,* 7–14.

Aniansson, G., Alm, B., Andersson, B., Håkansson, A., Larsson, P., Nylén, O., Peterson, H., Rignèr, P., Svanborg, M., Sabharwal, H., & Svanborg, C. (1994). A prospective cohort study on breast-feeding and otitis media in Swedish infants. *Pediatric Infectious Disease Journal, 13,* 183–188.

Aniansson, G., Andersson, B., Lindstedt, R., & Svanborg, C. (1990). Anti-adhesive activity of human casein against *Streptococcus pneumoniae* and *Haemophilus influenzae*. *Microbial Pathogens, 8,* 315–323.

Bartolozzi, G., Sacchetti, A., Scarane, P., & Becherucci, P. (1992). Natural history of otitis media with effusion in children under six years of age. *Advances in Otorhinolaryngology, 47,* 281–283.

Biles, R.W., Buffler, P.A., & O'Donell, A.A. (1980). Epidemiology of otitis media: A community study. *American Journal of Public Health, 70,* 593–598.

Birch, L., & Elbrønd, O. (1984). Prospective epidemiological investigation of secretory otitis media in children attending day-care centers. *ORL; Journal of Oto-Rhino-Laryngology and Its Related Specialties, 46,* 229–234.

Birch, L., & Elbrønd, O. (1986a). Prospective epidemiological study of secretory otitis media in children not attending kindergarten: A prevalence study. *International Journal of Pediatric Otorhinolaryngology, 11,* 191–197.

Birch, L., & Elbrønd, O. (1986b). Prospective epidemiological study of secretory otitis media in children not attending kindergarten: An incidence study. *International Journal of Pediatric Otorhinolaryngology, 11,* 183–190.

Black, N. (1985). The aetiology of glue-ear—a case-control study. *International Journal of Pediatric Otorhinolaryngology, 9,* 121–133.

Bluestone, C.D. (1984). State of the art: Definitions and classifications. In D.J. Lim, C.D. Bluestone, J.O. Klein, & J.D. Nelson (Eds.), *Recent advances in otitis media with effusion* (pp. 1–4). Philadelphia: B.C. Decker.

Bluestone, C.D., Stephenson, J.S., & Martin, L.M. (1992). Ten-year review of otitis media pathogens. *Pediatric Infectious Disease Journal, 11,* S7–S11.

Cantekin, E.I. (1983). Algorithm for diagnosis of otitis media with effusion. *Annals of Otology, Rhinology, and Laryngology. Supplement, 107,* 6.

Casselbrant, M.L., Brostoff, L.M., Cantekin, E.I., Flaherty, M.R., Doyle, W.J., Bluestone, C.D., & Fria, T.J. (1985). Otitis media with effusion in preschool children. *Laryngoscope, 95,* 428–436.

Casselbrant, M.L., Golden, W.L., Doyle, W.J., Rockette, H.E., & Steele, M.W. (1988). Prospective twin study of otitis media. *Annals of Otology, Rhinology, and Laryngology. Supplement, 133,* 12.

Casselbrant, M.L., Mandel, E.M., Kurs-Lasky, M., Rockette, H.E., & Bluestone, C.D. (1995). Otitis media in a population of black American and white American infants, 0–2 years of age. *International Journal of Pediatric Otorhinolaryngology, 33,* 1–16.

Casselbrant, M.L., Mandel, E.M., Rockette, H.E., & Bluestone, C.D. (1993). Incidence of otitis media and bacteriology of acute otitis media during the first two years of life. In D.J. Lim, C.D. Bluestone, J.O. Klein, J.D. Nelson, & P.L. Ogra (Eds.), *Recent advances in otitis media* (pp. 1–3). Toronto, Ontario, Canada: Decker Periodicals.

Casselbrant, M.L., Okeowo, P.A., Flaherty, M.R., Feldman, R.M., Doyle, W.J., Bluestone, C.D., Rogers, K.D., & Hanley, T. (1984). Prevalence and incidence of otitis media in a group of preschool children in the United States. In D.J. Lim, C.D. Bluestone, J.O. Klein, & J.D. Nelson (Eds.), *Recent advances in otitis media with effusion* (pp. 16–19). Philadelphia: B.C. Decker.

Centers for Disease Control and Prevention. (1994). Drug-resistant *Streptococcus pneumoniae*—Kentucky and Tennessee, 1993. *Morbidity and Mortality Weekly Reports, 43,* 23–25.

Chalmers, D., Stewart, I., Silva, P., & Mulvena, A. (1989). Otitis media with effusion in children—the Dunedin Study. *Clinics in Developmental Medicine, 108,* 1–167.

Chilmonczyk, B.A., Palomaki, G.E., & Knight, G.J. (1992). An unsuccessful cotinine-assisted intervention strategy to reduce environmental tobacco smoke exposure during infancy. *American Journal of Diseases of Children, 146,* 357–360.

Clements, D.A., Henderson, F.W., & Neebe, E.C. (1993). Relationship of viral isolation to otitis media in a research day-care center 1978–1988. In D.J. Lim, C.D. Bluestone, J.O. Klein, J.D. Nelson, & P. L. Ogra (Eds.), *Recent advances in otitis media* (pp. 27–29). Toronto, Ontario, Canada: Decker Periodicals.

Cunningham, A.S. (1977). Morbidity in breast-fed and artifically fed infants. *Journal of Pediatrics, 90,* 726–729.

Daly, K.A. (1994). Risk factors for otitis media sequelae and chronicity. *Annals of Otology, Rhinology, and Laryngology. Supplement, 163,* 39–42.

Daly, K.A., Giebink, G.S., Le, C.T., Lindgren, B., Batalden, P.B., Anderson, R.S., & Russ, J.N. (1988). Determining risk for chronic otitis media with effusion. *Pediatric Infectious Disease Journal, 7,* 471–475.

Daly, K.A., Meland, M., Brown, J., Lindgren, B., Westover, D., & Giebink, G.S. (in press). Epidemiology of early otitis media. In *Proceedings of the 6th International Symposium on Recent Advances in Otitis Media,* Ft. Lauderdale, FL.

Dever, G.J., Stewart, J.L., & David, A. (1985). Prevalence of otitis media in selected populations on Pohnpei: A preliminary study. *International Journal of Pediatric Otorhinoloaryngology, 10,* 143–152.

De Vries, R.R.P. (1992). HLA and disease: From epidemiology to immunotherapy. *European Journal of Clinical Investigation, 22,* 1–8.

Downs, M. (1980). Identification of children at risk for middle ear effusion problems. *Annals of Otology, Rhinology, and Laryngology, Supplement, 68,* 168–191.

Dugdale, A.E., Canty, A., Lewis, A.N., & Lovell, S. (1978). The natural history of chronic middle ear disease in Australian aboriginals: A cross-sectional study. *Medical Journal of Australia Special Supplement,* 6–9.

Duncan, R.B. (1960). Positional otitis media. *Archives of Otolaryngology, 72,* 454–463.

Duncan, R.B., Ey, J., Holberg, C.J., Wright, A.L., Martinez, F.D., & Taussig, L.M. (1993). Exclusive breast-feeding for at least four months protects against otitis media. *Pediatrics, 91,* 867–872.

Etzel, R.A., Pattishall, E.N., Haley, N.J., Fletcher, R.H., & Henderson, F.W. (1992). Passive smoking and middle ear effusion among children in day care. *Pediatrics, 90,* 228–232.

Ey, J.L., Holberg, C.J., Aldous, M.B., Wright, A.L., Martinez, F.D., & Taussig, L.M. (1995). Passive smoke exposure and otitis media in the first year of life: Group Health Medical Associates. *Pediatrics, 95,* 670–677.

Faden, H., Stanievich, J., Brodsky, L., Bernstein, J., & Ogra, P.L. (1990). Changes in nasopharyngeal flora during otitis media of childhood. *Pediatric Infectious Disease Journal, 9,* 623–626.

Faden, H., Waz, M.J., Bernstein, J.M., Brodsky, L., Stanievich, J., & Ogra, P.L. (1991). Nasopharyngeal flora in the first three years of life in normal and otitis-prone children. *Annals of Otology, Rhinology, and Laryngology, 100,* 612–615.

Ferson, M., Edwards, A., Lind, A., Milton, G.W., & Hersey, P. (1979). Low natural killer-cell activity and immunoglobulin levels associated with smoking in human subjects. *International Journal of Cancer, 23,* 603–609.

Fiellau-Nikolajsen, M. (1979). Tympanometry in 3-year-old children: Type of care as an epidemiologic factor in secretory otitis media and tubal dysfunction in unselected populations of 3-year-old children. *ORL; Journal of Oto-Rhino-Laryngology and Its Related Specialties, 41,* 193–205.

Fiellau-Nikolajsen, M. (1980). Tympanometry in three-year-old children: Prevalence and spontaneous course of MEE. *Annals of Otology, Rhinology, and Laryngology. Supplement, 68,* 223–227.

Fiellau-Nikolajsen, M. (1983). Tympanometry and secretory otitis media: Observations on the diagnosis, epidemiology, treatment, and prevention in prospective cohort studies of three-year-old children [Monograph]. *Acta Oto-Laryngologica. Supplement, 394,* 7–73.

Fischler, R.S., Todd, N.W., & Feldman, C.M. (1987). Lack of association of cleft uvula with otitis media in Apache Indian children. *American Journal of Diseases of Children, 141,* 866–867.

Fleming, D.W., Cochi, S.L., Hightower, A.W., & Broome, C.V. (1987). Childhood upper respiratory tract infections: To what degree is incidence affected by daycare attendance? *Pediatrics, 79,* 55–60.

Freijd, A., Oxelius, V.-A., & Rynnel-Dagöö, B. (1985). A prospective study demonstrating an association between plasma IgG2 concentrations and susceptibility to otitis media in children. *Scandinavian Journal of Infectious Diseases, 17,* 115–120.

Fria, T.J., Cantekin, E.I., & Eichler, J.A. (1985). Hearing acuity of children with otitis media with effusion. *Archives of Otolaryngology—Head and Neck Surgery, 111,* 10–16.

Friel-Patti, S., Finitzo, T., Chinn, K.M., & Lindgren, B. (1993). Effects of daycare setting on incidence of OME and language development in a cohort of children followed prospectively. In D.J. Lim, C.D. Bluestone, J.O. Klein, J.D. Nelson, & P. L. Ogra (Eds.), *Recent advances in otitis media* (pp. 569–573). Toronto, Ontario, Canada: Decker Periodicals.

Gates, G.A., Wachtendorf, C., & Holt, G.R. (1986). Medical treatment of chronic otitis media with effusion (secretory otitis media). *Otolaryngology—Head and Neck Surgery, 94,* 350–354.

Giebink, G.S. (1988). Epidemiology of otitis media with effusion. In F.H. Bess (Ed.), *Hearing impairment in children* (pp. 75–90). Parkton, MD: York Press.

Giebink, G.S. (1994). Preventing otitis media. *Annals of Otology, Rhinology, and Laryngology. Supplement, 163,* 20–23.

Goldman, A.S. (1993). The immune system of human milk: Antimicrobial, antiinflammatory and immunomodulating properties. *Pediatric Infectious Disease Journal, 12,* 664–671.

Goodwin, M.H. Jr., Shaw, J.R., & Feldman, C.M. (1980). Distribution of otitis media among four Indian populations in Arizona. *Public Health Reports, 95,* 589–594.

Gravel, J.S., McCarton, C.M., & Ruben, R.J. (1988). A prospective study of otitis media in infants born at very-low birthweight. *Acta Oto-Laryngolocia, 105,* 516–521.

Gravel, J.S., & Wallace, I.F. (1992). Listening and language at 4 years of age: Effects of early otitis media. *Journal of Speech and Hearing Research, 35,* 588–595.

Greenberg, R.A., Strecher, V.J., Bauman, K.E., Boat, B.W., Fowler, M.G., Keyes, L.L., Denny, F.W., Chapman, R.S., Stedman, H.C., LaVange, L.M., Glover, L.H., Haley, N.J., & Loda, F.A. (1994). Evaluation of a home-based intervention program to reduce infant passive smoking and lower respiratory illness. *Journal of Behavioral Medicine, 17,* 273–290.

Griffith, T.E. (1979). Epidemiology of otitis media—an interracial study. *Laryngoscope, 89,* 22–29.

Haddad, J., Jr., Gonzalez, C., Kurland, G., Orenstein, D.M., & Casselbrant, M.L. (1994). Ear disease in children with cystic fibrosis. *Archives of Otolaryngology—Head and Neck Surgery, 120,* 491–493.

Halama, A.R., Voogt, G.R., & Musgrave, G.M. (1986). Prevalence of otitis media in children in a black rural community in Venda (South Africa). *International Journal of Pediatric Otorhinolaryngology, 11,* 73–77.

Hallet, C.P. (1982). The screening and epidemiology of middle-ear disease in a population of primary school entrants. *Journal of Laryngology and Otology, 96,* 899–914.

Harabuchi, Y., Faden, H., Yamanaka, N., Duffy, L., Wolf, J., Krystofik, D., & Tonawanda/Williamsville Pediatrics. (1994). Nasopharyngeal colonization with nontypable *Haemophilius influenzae* and recurrent otitis media. *Journal of Infectious Diseases, 170,* 862–866.

Hardy, A.M. (1991). Incidence and impact of selected infectious diseases in childhood: Center for Health Statistics. *Vital Health Statistics, 10,* 1–22.

Hardy, A.M., & Fowler, M.G. (1993). Child care arrangements and repeated ear infections in young children. *American Journal of Public Health, 83,* 1321–1325.

Harsten, G., Prellner, K., Heldrup, J., Kalm, O., & Kornfält, R. (1989). Recurrent otitis media. A prospective study of children during the first three years of life. *Acta Otolaryngologica, 107,* 111–119.

Henderson, F.W., Collier, A.M., Sanyal, M.A., Watkins, J.M., Fairclough, D.L., Clyde, W.A., & Denny, F.W. (1982). A longitudinal study of respiratory viruses and bacteria in the etiology of acute otitis media with effusion. *New England Journal of Medicine, 306,* 1377–1383.

Henderson, F.W., & Giebink, G.S. (1986). Otitis media among children in day care: Epidemiology and pathogenesis. *Review of Infectious Diseases, 8,* 533–538.

Hilditch, J.R. (1985). Otitis media: Seasonality and absence of association with weather. *Journal of Otolaryngology, 14,* 365–368.

Hinton, A.E. (1989). Surgery for otitis media with effusion in children and its relationship to parental smoking. *Journal of Laryngology and Otology, 103,* 559–561.

Holmquist, J., Al Fadala, S., & Qattan, Y. (1987). Prevalence of secretory otitis media among school children in Kuwait. *Journal of Laryngology and Otology, 101,* 116–119.

Howie, V.M., Ploussard, J.H., & Sloyer, J. (1975). The "otitis-prone" condition. *American Journal of Diseases of Children, 129,* 676–678.

Ingvarsson, L., Lundgren, K., & Olofsson, B. (1984). Epidemiology of acute otitis media in children—a cohort study in an urban population. In D.J. Lim, C.D. Bluestone, J.O. Klein, & J.D. Nelson (Eds.), *Recent advances in otitis media with effusion* (pp. 19–22). Philadelphia: B.C. Decker.

Ingvarsson, L., Lundgren, K., & Olofsson, B. (1988). Incidence and risk factors of acute otitis media in children: Longitudinal cohort studies in an urban population. In D.J. Lim, C.D. Bluestone, J.O. Klein, & J.D. Nelson (Eds.), *Recent advances in otitis media with effusion* (pp. 6–8). Philadelphia: B.C. Decker.

Ishidoya, M., Takasaka, T., & Shimizu, H. (1988). Risk factors for otitis media with effusion. In D.J. Lim, C.D. Bluestone, J.O. Klein, & J.D. Nelson (Eds.), *Recent advances in otitis media with effusion* (pp. 1–3). Philadelphia: B.C. Decker.

Iversen, M., Birch, L., & Lundqvist, G.R. (1985). Middle ear effusion in children and the indoor environment: An epidemiological study. *Archives of Environmental Health, 40,* 74–79.

Kaleida, P.H., Nativio, D.G., Chao, H., Cowden, S.N., Boltey, K.A., & Clista, B.T. (1993). Bacterial respiratory pathogens in the nasopharynx of breast-fed versus formula-fed infants. In D.J. Lim, C.D. Bluestone, J.O. Klein, J.D. Nelson, & P.L. Ogra (Eds.), *Recent advances in otitis media* (pp. 15–17). Toronto, Ontario, Canada: Decker Periodicals.

Kalm, O., Johnson, U., & Prellner, K. (1994). HLA frequency in patients with chronic secretory otitis media. *International Journal of Pediatric Otorhinolaryngology, 30,* 151–157.

Kalm, O., Johnson, U., Prellner, K., & Ninn, K. (1991). HLA frequency in patients with recurrent acute otitis media. *Archives of Otolaryngology—Head and Neck Surgery, 117,* 1296–1299.

Kaneko, Y., Okitsu, T., Sakuma, M., Shibahara, Y., Yuasa, R., Takasaka, T., & Kawamoto, K. (1984). Incidence of secretory otitis media after acute inflammation of the middle ear cleft and the upper respiratory tract. In D.J. Lim, C.D. Bluestone, J.O. Klein, & J.D. Nelson (Eds.), *Recent advances in otitis media with effusion* (pp. 34–36). Philadelphia: B.C. Decker.

Karma, P.H., Penttilä, M.A., Sipilä, M.M., & Kataja, M.J. (1989). Otoscopic diagnosis of middle ear effusion in acute and non-acute otitis media: I. The value of different otoscopic findings. *International Journal of Pediatric Otorhinolaryngology, 17,* 37–49.

Keefe, D.H., & Bulen, J.C. (1993). Ear-canal impedance and reflection coefficient in human infants and adults. *Journal of the Acoustical Society of America, 94,* 2617–2638.

Kero, P., & Piekkala, P. (1987). Factors affecting the occurrence of acute otitis media during the first year of life. *Acta Paediatrica Scandinavica, 76,* 618–623.

Kessner, D.M., Snow, C.K., & Singer, J. (1974). *Assessment of medical care of children: Contrasts in health status* (Vol. 3). Washington, DC: National Academy of Sciences.

Klein, J.O. (1981). The epidemiology of pneumococcal disease in infants and children. *Reviews of Infectious Diseases, 3,* 246–253.

Klein, J.O. (1994). Otitis media. *Clinical Infectious Diseases, 19,* 823–833.

Klein, J.O., Naunton, R.F., Tos, M., Ohyama, M., Hussl, B., & van Cauwenberge, P.B. (1989). Definition and classification: Panel reports. *Annals of Otology, Rhinology, and Laryngology. Supplement. 139,* 10.

Kraemer, M.J., Richardson, M.A., Weiss, N.S., Furukuwa, C.T., Shapiro, G.G., Pierson, W.E., & Bierman, W. (1983). Risk factors for persistent middle-ear effusions: Otitis media, catarrh, cigarette smoke exposure and atopy. *Journal of the American Medical Association, 249,* 1022–1025.

Kvaerner, C.J., & Tambs, K. (in press). Inheritance of recurrent ear infections in children: A population-based study of genetic and environmental effects. *Annals of Otology, Rhinology, and Laryngology.*

Le, C.T., Daly, K.A., Margolis, R.H., Lindgren, B.R., & Giebink, G.S. (1992). A clinical profile of otitis media. *Archives of Otolaryngology—Head and Neck Surgery, 118,* 1225–1228.

Lous, J., & Fiellau-Nikolajsen, M. (1981). Epidemiology of middle ear effusion and tubal dysfunction: A one-year prospective study comprising monthly tympanometry in 387 non-selected seven-year-old children. *International Journal of Pediatric Otorhinolaryngology, 3,* 303–317.

Lundgren, K., Ingvarsson, L., & Olofsson, B. (1984). Epidemiologic aspects in children with recurrent acute otitis media. In D.J. Lim, C.D. Bluestone, J.O. Klein, & J.D. Nelson (Eds.), *Recent advances in otitis media with effusion* (pp. 22–25). Philadelphia: B.C. Decker,

Marchant, C.D., Shurin, P.A., Turczyk, V.A., Wasikowski, D.E., Tutihasi, M.A., & Kinney, S.E. (1984). Course and outcome of otitis media in early infancy: A prospective study. *Journal of Pediatrics, 104,* 826–831.

Maw, A.R. (1991). Development of tympanosclerosis in children with otitis media with effusion and ventilating tubes. *Journal of Laryngology and Otology, 105,* 614–617.

Maw, A.R., & Bawden, R. (1994a). Factors affecting resolution of otitis media with effusion in children. *Clinical Otolaryngology, 19,* 125–130.

Maw, A.R., & Bawden, R. (1994b). Tympanic membrane atrophy, scarring, atelectasis and attic retraction in persistent, untreated otitis media with effusion and following ventilation tube insertion. *International Journal of Pediatric Otorhinolaryngology, 30,* 189–204.

Maw, A.R., Parker, A.J., Lance, G.N., & Dilkes, M.G. (1992). The effect of parental smoking on outcome after treatment for glue ear in children. *Clinical Otolaryngology, 17,* 411–414.

McDermott, J.C., Giebink, G.S., Le, C.T., Harford, E.R., & Paparella, M.M. (1983). Children with persistent otitis media: Audiometric and tympanometric findings. *Archives of Otolaryngology, 109,* 360–363.

Miller, S.A., Omene, J.A., Bluestone, C.D., & Torkelson, D.W. (1983). A point prevalence of otitis media in a Nigerian village. *International Journal of Pediatric Otorhinolaryngology, 5,* 19–29.

Møller, H., & Tos, M. (1990). Point and period prevalence of otitis media with effusion evaluated by daily tympanometry. *Journal of Laryngology and Otology, 104,* 937–941.

Motohashi, H., Kobayashi, T., Toshima, M., Ohdaira, H., Ishidoya, M., Takasaka, T., Kaneko, Y. (1993). A seven-year school screening for secretory otitis media. In D.J. Lim, C.D. Bluestone, J.O. Klein, J.D. Nelson, & P.L. Ogra (Eds.), *Recent advances in otitis media* (pp. 54–57). Toronto, Ontario, Canada: Decker Periodicals.

National Center for Health Statistics. (1972). Hearing sensitivity and related medical findings among children. *Vital and Health Statistics. Series 11,* No. 114.

National Center for Health Statistics. (1985). Current estimates from the National Health Interview Survey: United States, 1982. *Vital and Health Statistics. Series 10,* No. 150.

Nelson, S.M., & Berry, R.I. (1984). Ear disease and hearing loss among Navajo children—a mass survey. *Laryngoscope, 94,* 316–323.

Ogisi, F.O. (1988). Impedance screening for otitis media with effusion in Nigerian children. *Journal of Laryngology and Otology, 102,* 986–988.

Okeowo, P.A. (1985). Observations on the incidence of secretory otitis media in Nigerian children. *Journal of Tropical Pediatrics, 31,* 295–298.

Onion, D.K., & Taylor, C. (1977). The epidemiology of recurrent otitis media. *American Journal of Public Health, 67,* 472–474.

Owen, M.J., Baldwin, C.D., Swank, P.R., Pannu, A.K., Johnson, D.L., & Howie, V.M. (1993). Relation of infant feeding practices, cigarette smoke exposure, and group child care to the onset and duration of otitis media with effusion in the first two years of life. *Journal of Pediatrics, 123,* 702–711.

Paparella, M.M., Bluestone, C.D., Arnold, W., Bradley, W.H., Hussi, B., Münker, G., Naunton, R.F., Sadé, J., Tos, M., & Van Cauwenberge, P. (1985). Definition and classification. *Annals of Otology, Rhinology, and Laryngology. Supplement, 116,* 8–9.

Paparella, M.M., & Schachern, P.A. (1984). Complications and sequelae of otitis media: State of the art. In D.J. Lim, C.D. Bluestone, J.O. Klein, & J.D. Nelson (Eds.), *Recent advances in otitis media with effusion* (pp. 316–319). Philadelphia: B.C. Decker.

Paradise, J.L., Bluestone, C.D., & Felder, H. (1969). The universality of otitis media in fifty infants with cleft palate. *Pediatrics, 44,* 35–42.

Paradise, J.L., Elster, B.A., & Tan, L. (1994). Evidence in infants with cleft palate that breast milk protects against otitis media. *Pediatrics, 94,* 853–860.

Pedersen, C.B., & Zachau-Christiansen, B. (1986). Otitis media in Greenland children: Acute chronic and secretory otitis media in three- to eight-year-olds. *Journal of Otolaryngology, 15,* 332–335.

Poulsen, G., & Tos, M. (1980). Repetitive tympanometric screenings of two-year-old children. *Scandinavian Audiology, 9,* 21–28.

Prellner, K., Harsten, G., Löfgren, G., Christenson, B., & Heldrup, J. (1990). Responses to rubella, tetanus, and diphtheria vaccines in otitis-prone and non-otitis-prone children. *Annals of Otology, Rhinology, and Laryngology, 99,* 628–632.

Prellner, K., Kalm, O., Harsten, G., Heldrup, J., & Oxelius, V.-A. (1989). Pneumococcal serum antibody concentrations during the first three years of life: A study of otitis-prone and non-otitis-prone children. *International Journal of Pediatric Otorhinoloaryngology, 17,* 267–279.

Proctor, B. (1967). Embryology and anatomy of the eustachian tube. *Archives of Otolaryngology, 86,* 503–514.

Pukander, J., Sipila, M., & Karma, P. (1984). Occurrence and risk factors in acute otitis media. In D.J. Lim, C.D. Bluestone, J.O. Klein, & J.D. Nelson (Eds.), *Recent advances in otitis media with effusion* (pp. 9–13). Philadelphia: B.C. Decker.

Quan, R., Yang, C., Rubinstein, S., Lewiston, N.J., Stevenson, D.K., & Kerner, J.A. (1994). The effect of nutritional additives on anti-infective factors in human milk. *Clinical Pediatrics, 33,* 325–328.

Rasmussen, F. (1993). Protracted secretory otitis media: The impact of familial factors and day-care center attendance. *International Journal of Pediatric Otorhinolaryngology, 26,* 29–37.

Rasmussen, F. (1994). Recurrence of acute otitis media at preschool age in Sweden. *Journal of Epidemiology and Community Health, 48,* 33–35.

Reed, D., & Dunn, W. (1970). Epidemiologic studies of otitis media among Eskimo children. *Public Health Reports, 85,* 699–706.

Rich, S.S., Daly, K.A., Levine, S.C., Savona, K., Lindgren, B.R., & Giebink, G.S. (in press). Familial aggregation of risk factors for chronic/recurrent otitis media. In *Proceedings of the 6th International Symposium on Recent Advances in Otitis Media,* Ft. Lauderdale, FL.

Roberts, J.E., Burchinal, M.R., Davis, B.P., Collier, A.M., & Henderson, F.W. (1991). Otitis media in early childhood and later language. *Journal of Speech and Hearing Research, 34,* 1158–1168.

Roberts, J.E., Burchinal, M.R., & Henderson, F.W. (1993). Otitis media and school age outcomes. In D.J. Lim, C.D. Bluestone, J.O. Klein, J.D. Nelson, & P.L. Ogra (Eds.), *Recent advances in otitis media* (pp. 561–565). Toronto, Ontario, Canada: Decker Periodicals.

Rockley, T.J., & Rhys Evans, P.H. (1986). Secretory otitis media—evidence for an inherited aetiology. *Journal of Laryngology and Otology, 100,* 389–393.

Roland, P.S., Finitzo, T., Friel-Patti, S., Brown, K.C., Stephens, K.T., Brown, O., & Coleman, M. (1989). Otitis media: Incidence, duration and hearing status. *Archives of Otolaryngology—Head and Neck Surgery, 115,* 1049–1053.

Rosenfeld, R.M., Vertrees, J.E., Carr, J., Cipolle, R.J., Uden, D.J., Giebink, G.S., & Canafax, D.M. (1994). Clinical efficacy of antimicrobial drugs for acute otitis media: Metaanalysis of 5400 children from thirty-three randomized trials. *Journal of Pediatrics, 124,* 355–367.

Ross, A.K., Croft, P.R., & Collins, M. (1988). Incidence of acute otitis media in infants in a general practice. *Journal of the Royal College of General Practitioners, 38,* 70–72.

Rowe-Jones, J.M., & Brockbank, M.J. (1992). Parental smoking and persistent otitis media with effusion in children. *International Journal of Pediatric Otorhinoloaryngology, 24,* 19–24.

Ruuskanen, O., & Heikkinen, T. (1994). Viral-bacterial interaction in acute otitis media. *Pediatric Infectious Disease Journal, 13,* 1046–1049.

Ryan, A.S., Rush, D., Kreiger, F.W., & Lewandowski, G. (1991). Recent declines in breast feeding in the United States, 1984 through 1989. *Pediatrics, 88,* 719–727.

Rynnel-Dagöö, B., Lindberg, K., Bagger-Sjöbäck, D., & Larson, O. (1992). Middle ear disease in cleft palate children at three years of age. *International Journal of Pediatric Otorhinolaryngology, 23,* 201–209.

Saarinen, U.M. (1982). Prolonged breast feeding as a prophylaxis for recurrent otitis media. *Acta Paediatrica Scandinavica, 71,* 567–571.

Sadler-Kimes, D., Siegel, M.I., & Todhunter, J.S. (1989). Age-related morphologic differences in the components of the eustachian tube/middle ear system. *Annals of Otology, Rhinology, and Laryngology, 98,* 854–858.

Salazar, J.C., Daly, K.A., Giebink, G.S., Lindgren, B., Liebeler, C., Meland, M., & Le, C.T. (in review). Low cord blood pneumococcal IgG antibodies predict early onset acute otitis media in infancy. *American Journal of Epidemiology.*

Sassen, M.L., & Brand, R., & Grote, J.J. (1994). Breast-feeding and acute otitis media. *American Journal of Otolaryngology, 15,* 351–357.

Schaefer, O. (1971). Otitis media and bottle feeding: An epidemiologic study of infant feeding habits and incidence of recurrent and chronic middle ear disease in Canadian Eskimos. *Canadian Journal of Public Health, 62,* 478–489.

Schappert, S.M. (1992). *Office visits for otitis media: United States 1975–90.* (Vital and Health Statistics, No. 214, pp. 1–20). Hyattsville, MD: National Center for Health Statistics.

Schilder, A.G.M., Zielhuis, G.A., & van den Broek, P. (1993). The otological profile of a cohort of Dutch 7.5–8-years-olds. *Clinical Otolaryngology, 18,* 48–54.

Schwartz, D.M., & Schwartz, R.H. (1978). Acoustic impedance and otoscopic findings in young children with Down's syndrome. *Archives of Otolaryngology, 104,* 652–656.

Schwartz, R.H., Rodriguez, W.J., & Grundfast, K.M. (1984). Duration of middle ear effusion after acute otitis media. *Pediatric Infectious Disease, 3,* 204–207.

Senturia, B.H., Paparella, M.M., Lowery, H.W., Klein, J.O., Arnold, W.J., Lim, D.J., Axelsson, G.-A., Paradise, J., Bluestone, C.D., Sadé, J., Howie, V.M., Woods, R., Hussl, B., Wullstein, H.L., Ingelstedt, S., & Wullstein, S.R. (1980). Definition and classification. *Annals of Otology, Rhinology, and Laryngology. Supplement. 69*, 4–8.

Shaaban, K.M.A., & Hamadnalla, I. (1993). The effect of duration of breast feeding on the occurrence of acute otitis media in children under three years. *East African Medical Journal, 70*, 632–634.

Shaw, J.R., Todd, N.W., Goodwin, M.H., & Feldman, G.M. (1981). Observations on the relation of environmental and behavioral factors to the occurrence of otitis media among Indian children. *Public Health Reports, 96*, 342–349.

Shurin, P.A., Pelton, S.I., Donner, A., & Klein, J.O. (1979). Persistence of middle ear effusion after acute otitis media in children. *New England Journal of Medicine, 330*, 1121–1123.

Sipila, M., Karma, P., Pukander, J., Timonen, M., & Kataja, M. (1988). The Bayesian approach to the evaluation of risk factors in acute and recurrent acute otitis media. *Acta Otolaryngologica, 106*, 94–101.

Sipila, M., Pukander, J., & Karma, P. (1987). Incidence of acute otitis media up to the age of 1½ years in urban infants. *Acta Otolaryngologica, 104*, 138–145.

Spivey, G.H., & Hirschhorn, N. (1977). A migrant study of adopted Apache children. *John Hopkins Medical Journal, 140*, 43–46.

Ståhlberg, M.-R., Ruuskanen, O., & Virolainen, E. (1986). Risk factors for recurrent otitis media. *Pediatric Infectious Disease, 5*, 30–32.

Stangerup, S.-E., & Tos, M. (1986). Epidemiology of acute suppurative otitis media. *American Journal of Otolaryngology, 7*, 47–54.

Stewart, I., Kirkland, C., Simpson, A., Silva, P., & Williams, S. (1984). Some factors of possible etiologic significance related to otitis media with effusion. In D.J. Lim, C.D. Bluestone, J.O. Klein, & J.D. Nelson (Eds.), *Recent advances in otitis media with effusion* (pp. 25–27). Philadelphia: B.C. Decker.

Stewart, J.L. (1989). Otitis media in the first year of life in two Eskimo communities. *Annals of Otology, Rhinology,and Laryngology, 98*, 200–202.

Stool, S.E., Berg, A.O., Berman, S., Carney, C.J., Cooley, J.R., Culpepper, L., Eavey, R.D., Feagans, L.V., Finitzo, T., Friedman, E.M., Goertz, J.A., Goldstein, A.J., Grundfast, K.M., Long, D.G., Macconi, L.L., Melton, L., Roberts, J.E., Sherrod, J.L., & Sisk, J.E. (1994). *Otitis media with effusion in young children: Clinical practice guideline, No. 12* (AHCPR Publication No. 94-0622). Rockville, MD: Agency for Health Care Policy and Research.

Stool, S.E., & Field, M.J. (1989). The impact of otitis media. *Pediatric Infectious Disease Journal, 8*(1, Suppl.), S11–S14.

Strachan, D.P., Jarvis, M.J., & Feyerabend, C. (1989). Passive smoking, salivary cotinine concentrations and middle ear effusion in 7 year old children. *British Medical Journal, 298*, 1549–1552.

Strangert, K. (1977). Otitis media in young children in different types of daycare. *Scandinavian Journal of Infectious Diseases, 9*, 119–123.

Suarez Nieto, C., Malluguiza Calvo, J.R., & Barthe Garcia, P. (1984). Climatic and racial factors related to the aetiology of secretory otitis media. *Otorhinolaryngology, 46*, 318–326.

Taino, V.-M., Savilahti, E., Salmenperä, L., Arjomaa, P., Siimes, M.A., & Perheentupa, J. (1988). Risk factors for infantile recurrent otitis media: Atopy, but not type of feeding. *Pediatric Research, 23*, 509–512.

Teele, D.W., Klein, J.O., Chase, C., Menyuk, P., Rosner, B.A., & the Greater Boston Otitis Media Study Group. (1990). Otitis media in infancy and intellectual ability, school achievement, speech, and language at age 7 years. *Journal of Infectious Diseases, 162,* 685–694.

Teele, D.W., Klein, J.O., & Rosner, B.A. (1980). Epidemiology of otitis media in children. *Annals of Otology, Rhinology, and Laryngology. Supplement, 68,* 5–6.

Teele, D.W., Klein, J.O., Rosner, B., & the Greater Boston Otitis Media Study Group. (1989). Epidemiology of otitis media during the first seven years of life in children in greater Boston: A prospective cohort study. *Journal of Infectious Diseases, 160,* 83–94.

Teele, D.W., Klein, J.O., Rosner, B.A., & the Greater Boston Otitis Media Study Group. (1993). Day-care and risk for recurrent, acute otitis media (AOM) in infancy. In D.J. Lim, C.D. Bluestone, J.O. Klein, J.D. Nelson, & P.L. Ogra (Eds.), *Recent advances in otitis media* (pp. 5–6). Toronto, Ontario, Canada: Decker Periodicals.

Todd, N.W. (1987). Familial predisposition for otitis media in Apache Indians at Canyon Day, Arizona. *Genetic Epidemiology, 4,* 25–31.

Todd, N.W., & Bowman, C.A. (1985). Otitis media at Canyon Day, Arizona. *Archives of Otolaryngology, 111,* 606–608.

Todd, N.W., & Settle, L.L. (1988). Familial predisposition for otitis media in parochial school children. In D.J. Lim, C.D. Bluestone, J.O. Klein, & J.D. Nelson (Eds.), *Recent advances in otitis media with effusion* (pp. 27–29). Philadelphia: B.C. Decker.

Tos, M., Holm-Jensen, S., & Sorensen, C.H. (1981). Changes in prevalence of secretory otitis from summer to winter in four-year-old children. *American Journal of Otology, 2,* 324–327.

Tos, M., Holm-Jensen, S., Sørenson, C.H., & Mogensen, C. (1982). Spontaneous course and frequency of secretory otitis in four-year-old children. *Archives of Otolaryngology, 108,* 4–10.

Tos, M., Poulsen, G., & Borch, J. (1978). Tympanometry in two-year-old children. *ORL; Journal of Oto-Rhino-Laryngology and Its Related Specialties, 40,* 77–85.

Tos, M., Poulsen, G., & Borch, J. (1979). Etiologic factors in secretory otitis. *Archives of Otolaryngology, 105,* 582–588.

Tos, M., Poulsen, G., & Hancke, A.B. (1979). Screening tympanometry during the first year of life. *Acta Otolaryngology, 88,* 388–394.

Tos, M., Stangerup, S.-E., Holm-Jensen, S., & Sorensen, C.H. (1984). Spontaneous course of secretory otitis media and changes of the eardrum. *Archives of Otolaryngology, 110,* 281–289.

U.S. Department of Health and Human Services. (1986). *The health consequences of involuntary smoking: A report of the Surgeon General* (DHHS Publication ND(CDC) 87-8378). Rockville, MD: Office on Smoking and Health.

Van Cauwenberge, P.B., & Kluyskens, P.M. (1984). Some predisposing factors in otitis media with effusion. In D.J. Lim, C.D. Bluestone, J.O. Klein, & J.D. Nelson (Eds.), *Recent advances in otitis media with effusion* (pp. 28–32). Philadelphia: B.C. Decker.

Virolainen, E., Puhakka, H., Aantaa, E., Tuohimaa, P., Ruuskanen, O., & Meurman, O.H. (1980). Prevalence of secretory otitis media in seven- to eight-year-old school children. *Annals of Otology, Rhinology, and Laryngology. Supplement, 68,* 7–10.

Woodward, A., Owen, N., Grgurinovich, N., Griffith, F., & Linke, H. (1987). Trial of an intervention to reduce passive smoking in infancy. *Pediatric Pulmonology, 3,* 173–178.

Wright, C.G., & Meyerhoff, W.L. (1994). Pathology of otitis media. *Annals of Otology, Rhinology, and Laryngology. Supplement, 163,* 24–26.

Zeisel, S.A., Roberts, J.A., Gunn, E.B., Riggins, R. Jr., Evans, G.A., Roush, J., & Henderson, F.W. (1995). Prospective surveillance for otitis media with effusion among African-American infants in group child care. *Journal of Pediatrics, 127,* 875–880.

Zielhuis, G.A., Heuvelmans-Heinen, E.W., Rach, G.H., & van den Broek, P. (1989). Environmental risk factors for otitis media with effusion in preschool children. *Scandinavian Journal of Primary Health Care, 7,* 33–38.

Zielhuis, G.A., Straatman, H., Rach, G.H., & van den Broek, P. (1990). Analysis and presentation of data on the natural time course of otitis media with effusion in children. *International Journal of Epidemiology, 19,* 1037–1044.

Zonis, R.D. (1968). Chronic otitis media in the southwest American Indian. II. Immunologic factors. *Archives of Otolaryngology, 88,* 365–369.

2

Diagnosis of Otitis Media

Frederick W. Henderson
and Jackson Roush

Assessment of middle ear status is a necessary component of both routine and acute illness-related child health evaluations for preschool children. The middle ear space in healthy children is air filled, permitting normal mobility of the intact tympanic membrane and efficient transmission of sound energy from the tympanic membrane to the inner ear. In both otitis media with effusion (OME) and acute otitis media (AOM), the middle ear space is either partially or completely filled with fluid, which impedes tympanic membrane mobility and reduces sound energy transmission from the tympanic membrane to the cochlea. Middle ear fluid ranges from serous or mucoid in OME to suppurative or purulent (i.e., pus-like), in AOM. Immobility of the intact tympanic membrane is the diagnostic hallmark of middle ear effusion. The presence or absence of tympanic membrane mobility can be determined by pneumatic otoscopy and tympanometry. In addition to permitting assessment of tympanic membrane mobility, otoscopy usually allows the clinician to characterize middle ear fluid, when present. Accurate assessment of hearing acuity in the child with long-standing middle ear fluid is required to make appropriate patient management decisions.

In this chapter, we distinguish the physical findings of AOM and OME, identify clinical symptoms suggestive of AOM among children with acute respiratory illness, and identify the otoscopic findings predictive of positive bacterial cultures of middle ear fluid. In addition, we review the techniques of tympanometry and audiometry in middle ear assessment.

43

OTOSCOPIC DIAGNOSIS

Otitis media with effusion is observed frequently both in children who have no overt signs or symptoms of illness and in children being evaluated because of signs and symptoms of acute respiratory infection. Although AOM usually is diagnosed in children being evaluated for acute illness, it also can be observed in asymptomatic children at the time of well-child assessments (Marchant et al., 1984). Thus, symptoms and signs of acute illness are frequently not predictive of the presence or absence of middle ear effusion or of the character of effusion, if present. The extent to which specific clinical signs and symptoms increase or decrease the likelihood of acute suppurative otitis media in children with respiratory illness is addressed in the next section.

Pneumatic otoscopy (i.e., use of an otoscope with a sealed optical system that permits application of positive and negative air pressure in the external auditory canal) is the principal diagnostic technique used to evaluate the middle ear system and its function and to establish an otologic diagnosis. The examining clinician should describe otoscopic findings systematically, including information concerning tympanic membrane position, color, and mobility in response to both positive and negative pressure; tympanic membrane landmarks; the light reflex; and the presence or absence of air–fluid levels behind the tympanic membrane. The presence of middle ear fluid is highly probable when mobility of the intact tympanic membrane is absent in response to both positive and negative pressure or when air–fluid levels are observed in the middle ear space. The character of middle ear fluid usually can be described because the tympanic membrane is typically translucent. In OME, middle ear fluid is characteristically clear and colorless or clear and light to medium straw-yellow in color. In AOM, the fluid is cloudy gray to creamy white or yellow-white in appearance. In OME, the tympanic membrane position is usually neutral to slightly full. In AOM, the tympanic membrane position may be neutral but is frequently full or overtly bulging. To monitor otoscopic accuracy, particularly skill in assessing tympanic membrane mobility, the clinician may compare otoscopic findings with data on middle ear function obtained by tympanometry. Ultimately, relating otoscopic findings to observations at tympanocentesis (aspiration of middle ear contents by needle puncture of the tympanic membrane) provides definitive substantiation of diagnostic accuracy (Kaleida & Stool, 1992).

Diagnosis of Acute Otitis Media

Given the high incidence of AOM and the high proportion of all acute illnesses that are diagnosed as AOM in preschool children, it is surprising how little objective evidence is available regarding clinical and otoscopic clues to an accurate clinical and bacteriological diagnosis (Hayden, 1981). Among children with AOM, over 85% have a history of concurrent or antecedent upper respiratory illness (Pukander, 1983), and laboratory documentation of viral respiratory infection can be obtained in approximately 50% of otitis cases (Chonmaitree et al., 1992; Ruuskanen & Heikkinen, 1994). It has been established using prospective active surveillance that preschool children experience an average of approximately 7–10 acute respiratory illnesses annually (almost all of viral etiology) during the first 3–5 years of life (Dingle, Badger, & Jordan, 1964). Studies in pediatric clinics and practices indicate that parents seek medical advice for approximately three respiratory illnesses per year during this age interval (Teele, Klein, Rosner, & the Greater Boston Otitis Media Study Group, 1989). To obtain a comprehensive understanding of the relationship between respiratory signs and symptoms and the occurrence of AOM would require investigation not only of the illnesses deemed sufficiently worrisome to warrant a physician assessment, but also characterization of less severe respiratory illnesses. To date, most information concerning symptoms and signs of AOM has been derived from studies of children being evaluated in physician offices or clinics; therefore, our clinical knowledge base is incomplete. The bacteriologic database is even less comprehensive because tympanocentesis (i.e., needle aspiration of middle ear space) is required to document active bacterial infection, and performance of this invasive procedure usually is restricted to children deemed by their parents to be ill enough to warrant the investigation. Even when tympanocentesis has been performed, the relationship between specific otoscopic findings and bacteriological results has not been described routinely (Hayden, 1981). It is with the acknowledgment of these limitations that the information that follows is presented.

Heikkinen and Ruuskanen (1995) reported signs and symptoms experienced by children with acute respiratory illnesses and their relationship to AOM. Preschool children attending child care centers ($n = 302$), most of whom were between 1 and 3 years of age, were evaluated during acute respiratory illnesses; one illness was studied per child. Children were examined at a mean of Day 4 of respiratory symptoms; 40% of illnesses were diagnosed as AOM, which was defined as bulging or opacification of the tympanic membrane. Fever was present in 74% of illnesses, but AOM was diagnosed slightly more frequently when fever was absent (47%) than when fever was present (38%), a difference that was not statistically significant. To reiterate, the presence of fever did not increase the likelihood that AOM would be observed. Parents were asked about ear ache and restless sleeping. Both of these symptoms occurred more frequently in children with AOM than in children with respiratory illnesses without AOM, but only the symptom of ear ache contributed significantly to predicting the clinical diagnosis. Overall, ear ache was reported by 30% of children with acute respiratory illness, 60% of those with AOM, and 8% of those without AOM. Thus, although the positive predictive value of ear ache was good (83% of children with ear ache had AOM), the sensitivity of ear ache in detecting children with AOM was only 60%. In other words, children without ear ache accounted for 40% of all AOM episodes. The symptom "restless sleeping" was not clinically useful. Acute otitis media was observed in 46% of children with restless sleeping and in 32% of children without restless sleeping. Among children who were not diagnosed with AOM at the first visit, 85 children were reexamined within 14 days. Among 47 with ongoing respiratory symptoms at a mean of 9 days, AOM was diagnosed in 43% (approximately 50% had ear ache). Among the 38 children who had become asymptomatic, nonpurulent middle ear effusion was observed in 5%.

Otoscopic Findings and
Bacteriologic Results at Tympanocentesis

Bacteria uniformly regarded as otitis pathogens can be recovered from approximately 65%–80% of middle ear fluid samples obtained from symptomatic children with otoscopic findings of AOM. The otoscopic findings most predictive of the presence of purulent fluid in the middle ear space and a positive bacterial culture at the time of tympanocentesis were described by Halstead, Lepow, Balassanian, Emmerich, and Wolinsky (1968). Among children with intact tympanic membranes, they observed the highest rate of positive bacterial cultures when both the pars flaccida and pars tensa of the tympanic membrane were bulging, the landmarks and light reflex were absent, and the tympanic membrane was red or yellow in appearance. In these instances, a "yellow liquid pus" or a "gray cloudy fluid" was obtained by tympanocentesis, and bacteria were isolated from 61 of 67 samples (91%). When the tympanic membrane was slightly red or gray and there was no or minimal bulging, cultures were positive in only 3 of 14 specimens yielding middle ear fluid. When diffuse tympanic membrane erythema was the only finding, fluid was usually absent and no cultures were positive.

Schwartz, Stool, Rodriguez, and Grundfast (1981) confirmed the associations of bulging and the presence of a yellow-opaque appearance to the tympanic membrane as predictive of positive bacterial cultures at the time of tympanocentesis. Among children with *Streptococcus pneumoniae* isolated at tympanocentesis, complete bulging was observed in 15 of 16 ears, and color was described as yellow in 13 ears and red in 3.

Among children in whom *Haemophilus influenzae* was isolated, bulging was observed in 11 of 11 and yellow color was described in 9 of 11. This study is limited by the absence of culture data for children with less convincing otoscopic evidence for middle ear suppuration. In fact, typical otitis pathogens are isolated from approximately 15% of middle ear fluid samples from children with an otoscopic diagnosis of nonpurulent middle ear effusion (Giebink et al., 1979).

In summary, when pneumatic otoscopy reveals an immobile tympanic membrane in a bulging position with a creamy yellow-white, opaque, or cloudy gray fluid behind the tympanic membrane, the probability of a positive culture from the middle ear fluid is highest. Approximately 20% of tympanic membranes that demonstrate these findings will also be diffusely red; however, marked redness is not observed in many cases when the middle ear is filled with purulent liquid. When less stringent otoscopic criteria than these are applied, the probability of a positive culture is decreased. Specifically, when diffuse erythema alone is the criterion for diagnosis, purulent fluid and positive cultures are frequently not obtained at tympanocentesis.

TYMPANOMETRY

Middle ear status can also be determined using tympanometry. A tympanometer is an electromechanical instrument that measures the flow of acoustic energy into the middle ear as air pressure is varied in the sealed external auditory canal. A normally mobile tympanic membrane absorbs acoustic energy, whereas an immobile tympanic membrane reflects acoustic energy. Acoustic admittance measures comprise a battery of tests designed to evaluate various aspects of middle ear function. A routine admittance battery includes measures of tympanometric peak pressure, tympanometric shape (gradient or width), static admittance, and estimates of ear canal volume. Figure 1 describes the various tympanometric measures available, and Figure 2 illustrates a normal tympanogram (type A) and three tympanograms associated with various abnormalities of middle ear function. The tracings in Figure 2 are "single-component" (Y) tympanograms obtained using a low-frequency probe tone (226 Hz). Applied in this manner, tympanometry can be used to corroborate the physical examination or as a sole means of evaluating middle ear function when physical examination is difficult or unavailable.

Static Admittance

Static admittance measures provide an estimate of tympanic membrane mobility. Static admittance, measured in acoustic millimhos (mmho), is calculated by measuring the height of the tympanometric peak relative

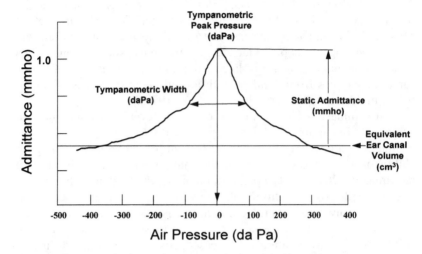

Figure 1. Characteristics and units of measurement for the standard (226-Hz) tympanogram.

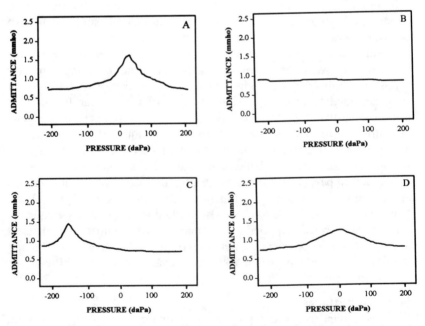

Figure 2. Tympanometric patterns commonly associated with A) normal middle ear function (type A); B) middle ear effusion (type B); C) negative typanometric peak pressure (type C); and D) an abnormally "wide" configuration that may or may not be associated with middle ear effusion.

to its tail value. For children 3–5 years of age with no history of chronic or recurrent OME, mean values are typically 0.6 mmho with a 90% range of 0.2–1.4 mmho (Margolis & Heller, 1987). Infants and toddlers, especially those with significant OME history, are likely to exhibit lower peak static admittance, even when middle ear effusion is not present (Nozza, Bluestone, Kardatzke, & Bachman, 1994; Roush, Bryant, Mundy, Zeisel, & Roberts, 1995). Because effusion reduces the mobility of the middle ear mechanism, a tympanogram associated with OME is characterized typically by low static admittance (0–0.2 mmho). The "flat" tympanogram in Figure 2B, typical of that seen in OME, has no discernible pressure peak. According to the classification scheme recommended by Jerger (1970), this tympanogram would be classified as Type B.

Tympanometric Peak Pressure
The location of the tympanometric pressure peak (pressure in the external canal when static admittance is highest), measured in dekaPascals (daPa) provides an estimate of middle ear pressure. When middle ear pressure is normal, the pressure peak typically ranges from +50 to −150 daPa. The Type C tympanogram (Jerger, 1970) shown in Figure 2C has a pressure peak at approximately −175 daPa. This means that middle ear admittance was maximum when the tympanometer created negative pressure (−175 daPa) in the ear canal. By inference, it is assumed that the middle ear is characterized by negative pressure, presumably as a result of insufficient aeration of the middle ear space. Although it is widely believed that negative-pressure tympanograms are an indication of poor eustachian tube function, Margolis and Hunter (1991) pointed out that changes in middle ear pressure are caused by a complex interaction of many factors ranging from resorption of middle ear gases to sniffing. Thus, it is not surprising that tympanometric peak pressure has proven to be of limited value in the detection of middle ear effusion (e.g., Fiellau-Nikolajsen, 1983).

Tympanometric Width
Tympanometric shape can be altered by middle ear effusion even when a pressure peak is identifiable. For most screening instruments, tympanometric width is reported as the pressure interval (in dekaPascals) observed at a 50% reduction in static admittance (see Figure 1). Several investigators have reported broadly peaked, abnormally wide tympanograms (e.g., Paradise, Smith, & Bluestone, 1976). The tympanogram in Figure 2D is abnormally wide. Such a tympanogram might occur when middle ear effusion occupies a portion of the middle ear space while still allowing some aeration of the middle ear to occur. Abnormally wide tympanograms are also seen in ears with a recent history of OME. Nor-

mative data for tympanometric width appears to vary considerably as a function of age and various population variables (Nozza et al., 1994; Roush et al., 1995). For children 3–5 years of age with no history of chronic or recurrent OME, mean values are typically 100 daPa with a 90% range of approximately 60–150 daPa (Margolis & Heller, 1987). Infants and toddlers, especially those with significant OME history, are likely to exhibit wider tympanograms (up to 200 daPa), even when middle ear effusion is not present (Nozza et al., 1994; Roush et al., 1995).

Ear Canal Volume
Estimates of ear canal volume are useful in identifying a perforation of the tympanic membrane or in checking the patency of a tympanostomy tube. In either case, the volume of the middle ear space is added to the ear canal volume, resulting in an abnormally large equivalent volume (i.e., ≥2.5 cm³). Estimates of equivalent ear canal volume are particularly useful in the interpretation of "flat" tympanograms. Flat tympanograms may be due to perforation of the tympanic membrane, which would result in abnormally large ear canal volume estimates; to OME, which would result in normal ear canal volume estimates; or to occlusion of the probe tip, which would show abnormally small canal volume estimates.

Acoustic Reflex
Measurement of the acoustically evoked contraction of the stapedius muscle may be included in the acoustic admittance test battery (see Wilson & Margolis, 1991). Instruments designed for middle ear screening typically deliver an ipsilateral 1,000-Hz pure-tone stimulus via the admittance probe assembly at a level of approximately 105 dB sound pressure level (SPL). The ipsilateral acoustic reflex is generally absent in an ear with middle ear dysfunction because the conductive hearing loss reduces the sensation level of the acoustic stimulus, the stiffness imposed by middle ear dysfunction obscures its measurement, or both. Inclusion of the acoustic reflex has been shown by some studies to increase the sensitivity of the admittance battery, but usually at the expense of lower specificity (see Wiley & Smith, 1995).

Multifrequency Tympanometry
Some acoustic admittance instruments permit the use of multiple probe tone frequencies ranging from 226 to 2,000 Hz, thus providing a more complete description of how middle ear pathology affects the mechanics of the middle ear. Margolis, Hunter, and Giebink (1994) examined multifrequency tympanograms in children with histories of OME who had previously undergone tympanostomy tube placement but who, at the

time of testing, had normal hearing and no active ear disease. Although two thirds of the 98 ears studied had normal multifrequency tympanograms, one third had unusual patterns that suggested abnormalities of mechanical resonance. The clinical importance of these findings, if any, is still under investigation.

PURE-TONE AND SPEECH AUDIOMETRY

The normal middle ear provides a remarkably effective transfer of energy from the highly compressible medium of air to the fluid-filled inner ear. Impairment of middle ear function as a result of OM causes a reduction in sound transmission resulting in a *conductive* hearing loss. Pure-tone audiometry in conjunction with measures of middle ear function enables the clinician to determine the nature and degree of hearing loss. Speech audiometry provides verification of pure-tone responses as well as an estimate of the extent to which speech reception is affected by conductive hearing loss. These measures, in addition to assisting in the diagnosis of OM, quantify changes in hearing and middle ear function that occur as a result of medical treatment.

The audiogram in Figure 3 was obtained from a child with bilateral OME. Reduction of hearing sensitivity for pure-tone, air-conducted

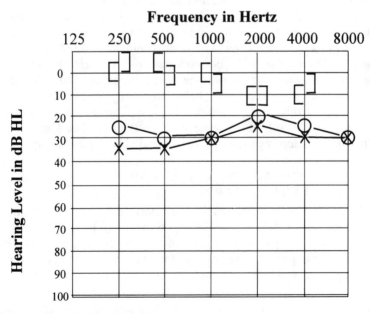

Figure 3.   A typical audiogram for a child with bilateral OME.

stimuli (via earphones) is evident across the frequency range; as expected, bone conduction responses are within normal limits.[1] Measures of pure-tone audiometry are often accompanied by speech audiometry. *Speech reception thresholds* (SRTs) are obtained via air conduction by having the child point to body parts or repeat familiar words. The SRT serves as a cross-check on the accuracy of pure-tone responses while quantifying the loss of hearing sensitivity to speech. When pure-tone audiometry is unsuccessful, the SRT may be obtained by bone conduction as well as air conduction to estimate the degree of conductive impairment. Speech audiometry also includes measures of *word recognition,* obtained by presenting monosyllabic words at one or more levels above threshold. The conductive hearing loss associated with OME generally results in little or no reduction in word recognition ability as long as the speech stimuli are presented at a level high enough to overcome the conductive impairment. However, speech presented at typical conversational levels (e.g., 50 dB hearing level [HL]) may be significantly reduced. Thus, word recognition scores may be useful in documenting the effects of OME on receptive communication.

Clinical Practice Guidelines for the medical management of OME were recently developed by the Agency for Health Care Policy and Research (Stool et al., 1994). These guidelines recommend inclusion of both pure-tone and speech audiometry. Specifically, they recommend that a child with bilateral middle ear fluid for more than 3 months undergo an evaluation of hearing. According to the guidelines, this would optimally include air and bone conduction thresholds at 500, 1,000, 2,000, and 4,000 Hz, corroborated by SRTs. Hearing evaluation in conjunction with medical management is recommended in the guidelines because of the expressed belief that surgery (myringotomy and tympanostomy tubes) is not indicated unless OME is causing a hearing impairment of 20 dB HL or more in the better ear. (See Chapter 3 for further information regarding pure-tone and speech audiometry.)

SCREENING FOR MIDDLE EAR EFFUSION AND CONDUCTIVE HEARING LOSS

Unlike AOM, which is frequently characterized by overt symptoms including ear pain, OME is typically asymptomatic. The mild hearing loss that usually accompanies OME, despite its potentially harmful developmental consequences, may escape the detection of parents and caregivers (Watkin, Baldwin, & Laoide, 1990).

---

[1]Bone conduction responses are affected to a small degree by conductive hearing loss. This is due to the participation of the middle ear in the normal bone conduction response. The effect is minimal, however, and occurs primarily at or around 2,000 Hz.

Tympanometry

When indicated, screening for OME generally is accomplished using one or more of the acoustic admittance measures described previously. At this time there is no consensus on a specific tympanometric screening protocol. Even so, it is widely agreed that the design of a screening protocol will be influenced by the target population, specific procedures employed, and available personnel. Indeed, the lack of consensus surrounding existing protocols is due, in part, to the problems inherent in attempting to apply a single protocol to a wide variety of settings and populations. The protocol will also vary depending on the specific goals of the screening program. For example, a protocol designed to identify children with middle ear effusion would be different from one intended to identify children with *any* abnormality of middle ear function (Nozza, 1995).

Comparison of screening data is complicated by a variety of technical variables, including pump speed, direction of pressure sweep, and other differences in measurement and recording. This has complicated the selection of specific tympanometric measures and the assignment of pass–fail criteria. Still, a general comparison is possible, especially if studies share a common standard for validity. Wiley and Smith (1995) reviewed tympanometric studies based on direct verification of middle ear status from myringotomy, the surgical incision of a tympanic membrane performed by an otologic surgeon prior to placement of a tympanostomy tube. Although direct verification of this nature is not feasible in field-based studies, myringotomy is considered the "gold standard" in assessing the validity of tympanometry. Consequently, several important conclusions can be drawn from Wiley and Smith's review. First, there appears to be substantial evidence supporting the value of peak compensated static admittance. That is, abnormally low static admittance is a relatively good, although imperfect, predictor of middle ear effusion (e.g., Finitzo, Friel-Patti, Chin, & Brown, 1992). Second, abnormalities of tympanometric shape (i.e., "wide" tympanograms) are often associated with middle ear effusion, but there appears to be significant overlap with measures of static admittance (Paradise et al., 1976; Nozza, Bluestone, & Kardatzke, 1992; Nozza, Bluestone, Kardatzke, & Bachman, 1992; Nozza et al., 1994). Third, as a method of identifying perforation of the tympanic membrane, equivalent ear canal volume measures are sensitive to "dry" perforations (e.g., Shanks, Stelmachowicz, Beauchaine, & Schulte, 1992); ears with perforation of the tympanic membrane would not be identified if the middle ear is inflamed or occupied by effusion. Finally, inclusion of the acoustic reflex may improve the performance of a screening battery, although studies have produced mixed findings (Cantekin, Bluestone, et al., 1980; Cantekin, Doyle, Phillips, & Bluestone, 1980; Nozza, Bluestone, Kardatzke, et al., 1992; Roush, Drake, & Sexton, 1992; Silman, Silverman, & Arick, 1992; Utech-Smith, Wiley, & Pyle, 1993; Wachtendorf, Lopez, Cooper, Hearn, & Gates, 1984). Specifically, when acoustic reflexes are elicited at levels typically employed by conventional screening instruments, investigators have reported low specificity. Further research is needed to determine the relative contribution of the acoustic reflex, its effect on specificity as well as sensitivity, and the optimal presentation levels for elicitation (see Silman & Emmer, 1995).

In general, middle ear screening is conducted not with a single measure but with a battery of tests, the success of which will depend on the assignment of pass–fail criteria. In general, improvement in *sensitivity* (correct classification of diseased ears) occurs at the expense of lower *specificity* (correct classification of nondiseased ears). For example, in the study by Nozza, Bluestone, and Kardatzke (1992), sensitivity of static admittance improved from 56% to 82% by increasing the failure criterion from 0.2 mmho or less to 0.3 mmho or less. However, the corresponding specificity decreased from 93% to 63%. Additional research is needed to determine the optimal cutoff values for various combinations of middle ear measures; however, it is important for each program to determine the success of its middle ear screening protocol.

Pure-Tone Screening

Pure-tone screening is commonly used as a method of identifying unsuspected hearing loss in young children. Silman et al. (1992) noted that pure-tone screening at 20 dB HL can be useful as a method of screening for middle ear effusion if the frequency 500 Hz is included in the protocol. Unfortunately, the ambient noise levels present in most screening environments preclude the use of 500 Hz. Moreover, pure-tone screening in isolation would miss OME when hearing levels are better than 20 dB HL. Consequently, if the goal is to identify hearing loss *and* OME, it is recommended that pure-tone screening be done *in conjunction with* tympanometric measures. Manual pure-tone screening at a level of 20 dB HL for the frequencies 1,000, 2,000, and 4,000 Hz can be readily accomplished in most children over the age of 3 years. Behavioral hearing screening of children under 3 years of age should generally be performed by an audiologist using play techniques, visual reinforcement audiometry, or some combination of behavioral and electrophysiologic techniques.

Otoacoustic Emissions

Otoacoustic emissions (OAEs) are sounds generated within the normal inner ear, either spontaneously or in response to acoustic stimulation

(Norton & Stover, 1994). OAEs are present in most normally functioning ears and absent or reduced in ears with mild hearing loss, middle
ear pathology or both. Because of the high sensitivity of OAEs to both
hearing loss and middle ear pathology, OAEs may prove useful as a
first-level screening procedure for *both* conditions (Decreten, Hanssens,
& DeSloovere, 1991; Nozza & Sabo, 1992). Further research using controlled clinical trials is needed to determine the usefulness of OAEs in
the context of routine hearing and middle ear screening of preschool
and school-age children. In the future, it is likely that OAEs will play
an increasingly important role in the identification of auditory dysfunction in children.

Target Populations for Screening
In general, mass screening of children for middle ear dysfunction using
tympanometry is not advocated at this time. Groups that might be targeted include those increased risk for OME as well as those more likely
to be detrimentally affected by the conductive hearing loss that often
accompanies OME. These groups would include children with developmental delays, including learning disabilities; children with delays in
speech-language development; children with known sensorineural hearing loss; children who fail pure-tone screening; children with craniofacial anomalies, including cleft lip/palate and Down syndrome; children
of Native American heritage; children with known histories of chronic
or recurrent OME (American Academy of Audiology, in press). It is
important to note, however, that universal agreement on screening protocols and target populations has never been achieved. This is in part
because most data on middle ear screening have been obtained from
children over 2 years of age, even though OME has its highest prevalence from 6 to 24 months. Infants and young children in this age group
are often difficult to evaluate with tympanometry because of movement
or vocalization artifacts or both. Moreover, the limited data available for
children under 3 years of age are often from selected cohorts with a
high prevalence of middle ear disease. In the absence of complete data
regarding the sensitivity, specificity, and predictive value of acoustic
admittance measures in various populations of infants and toddlers, clinicians must evaluate the performance of their screening protocols based
on available resources and the outcome of medical referrals. Given the
transient nature of OME and the typical delay between identification
and referral, screening programs must be well coordinated with local
health care providers to whom children will be referred to avoid over-
identification. In general, children suspected of having OME should be
referred initially to a primary care clinician (e.g., pediatrician, family
practice physician) rather than to a specialist (e.g., otolaryngologist).

Summary

Tympanometry is the procedure of choice in screening for middle ear dysfunction. Selection and implementation of a screening protocol should be guided by the specific goals of the screening program. When designing a screening protocol, it is important to apply "norms" obtained from study samples having age and population characteristics relevant to the population of interest, because the best screening test or combination of tests will differ based on the target population (e.g., children from an unselected cohort versus those at high risk). Static admittance is generally the single best tympanometric measure for identification of middle ear effusion; measures of tympanometric width and inclusion of the acoustic reflex are likely to improve the sensitivity of a screening battery, but at the expense of lower specificity. Those responsible for the design and implementation of a screening program are advised to consult with local health care providers and others to whom referrals will be made in order to determine the most appropriate and cost-effective screening and referral criteria. In general, a combination of static admittance and tympanometric width is likely to offer a reasonable balance between sensitivity and specificity. Ears with static admittance of 0.2 mmho or less, tympanometric width greater than 150 daPa, or both on two or more occasions over a 3- to 5-week period should be referred to a physician for determination of need for medical management.

CONCLUSIONS

Acute otitis media and OME occur commonly throughout the preschool and elementary school years; infants and toddlers are at highest risk for both conditions. Skill in pneumatic otoscopy must be developed by all clinicians caring for young children to ensure a high level of diagnostic accuracy for middle ear disease. Tympanometry is an effective electromechanical method of identifying middle ear effusion, but most of our knowledge of the performance characteristics of tympanometry is based on observations in children 2–12 years of age. Further research is needed to determine the accuracy of tympanometry in identifying the presence or absence of middle ear effusion in children 6–24 months of age. Surgical intervention to relieve middle ear effusion may be recommended for children with long-standing effusion associated with conductive hearing loss. Thus, accurate detection of middle ear fluid and measurement of the degree of hearing impairment associated with effusion are critical for appropriate medical and audiological management decisions in young children.

REFERENCES

American Academy of Audiology. (in press). *Position statement on identification of hearing loss and middle ear dysfunction in children.*

Cantekin, E.I., Bluestone, C.D., Fria, T.J., Stool, S.E., Beery, Q.C., & Sabo, D.L. (1980). Identification of otitis media with effusion in children. *Annals of Otology, Rhinology, and Laryngology. Supplement, 68,* 190–195.

Cantekin, E.I., Doyle, W.J., Phillips, D.C., & Bluestone, C.D. (1980). Gas absorption in the middle ear. *Annals of Otology, Rhinology, and Laryngology. Supplement, 68,* 71–75.

Chonmaitree, T., Owen, M.J., Patel, J.A., Hedgpath, D., Horlick, D., & Howie, V.M. (1992). Effect of viral respiratory tract infection on outcome of acute otitis media. *Journal of Pediatrics, 120,* 856–862.

Decreten, S.J.R.C., Hanssens, K., & DeSloovere, M. (1991). Evoked otoaccoustic emissions in infant hearing screening. *International Journal of Pediatric Otorhinolaryngology, 21,* 235–247.

Dingle, J.W., Badger, G.F., & Jordan, W.S., Jr. (1964). *Illness in the home: A study of 25,000 illnesses in a group of Cleveland families.* Cleveland, OH: The Press of Case Western Reserve University.

Fiellau-Nikolajsen, M. (1983). Tympanometry and secretory otitis media. *Acta Oto-Laryngologica, 394*(Suppl.), 1–73.

Finitzo, T., Friel-Patti, S., Chin, K., & Brown, O. (1992). Tympanometry and otoscopy prior to myringotomy: Issues in diagnosis of otitis media. *International Journal of Pediatric Otorhinolaryngology, 24,* 101–110.

Giebink, G.S., Mills, E.L., Huff, J.S., Edelman, C.K., Weber, M.L., Juhn, S.K., & Quie, P.G. (1979). The microbiology of serous and mucoid otitis media. *Pediatrics, 63,* 915–919.

Halstead, C., Lepow, M.L., Balassanian, N., Emmerich, J., & Wolinsky, E. (1968). Otitis media: Clinical observations, microbiology, and evaluation of therapy. *American Journal of Diseases of Children, 115,* 542–551.

Hayden, G.F. (1981). Acute suppurative otitis media in children: Diversity of clinical diagnostic criteria. *Clinical Pediatrics, 20,* 99–104.

Heikkinen, T., & Ruuskanen, O. (1995). Signs and symptoms predicting acute otitis media. *Archives of Pediatric and Adolescent Medicine, 149,* 26–29.

Jerger, J. (1970). Clinical experience with impedance audiometry. *Archives of Otolaryngology, 92,* 311.

Kaleida, P.H., & Stool, S.E. (1992). Assessment of otoscopists' accuracy regarding middle-ear effusion. *American Journal of Diseases of Children, 146,* 433–435.

Marchant, C.D., Shurin, P.A., Turczyk, V.A., Wasikowski, D.E., Tutihasi, M.A., & Kinney, S.E. (1984). Course and outcome of otitis media in early infancy: A prospective study. *Journal of Pediatrics, 104,* 826–831.

Margolis, R.H., & Heller, J.W. (1987). Screening tympanometry criteria for medical referral. *Audiology, 26,* 197–208.

Margolis, R., & Hunter, L. (1991). Audiologic evaluation of the otitis media patient. *Otolaryngologic Clinics of North America, 24,* 877–899.

Margolis, R., Hunter, L., & Giebink, G.S. (1994). Tympanometric evaluation of middle ear function in children with otitis media. *Annals of Otology, Rhinology, and Laryngology, 103,* 34–38.

Norton, S., & Stover, L. (1994). Otoacoustic emissions: An emerging clinical tool. In *Handbook of clinical audiology* (4th ed., pp. 448–462). Baltimore: Williams & Wilkins.

Nozza, R.J. (1995). Critical issues in acoustic-immittance screening for middle-ear effusion. *Seminars in Hearing, 16*(1), 86–98.

Nozza, R.J., Bluestone, C.D., & Kardatzke, D. (1992). Sensitivity, specificity, and predictive values of immittance measures in the identification of middle-ear effusion. In F.H. Bess & J.W. Hall (Eds.), *Screening children for auditory function* (pp. 315–329). Nashville, TN: Bill Wilkerson Press.

Nozza, R.J., Bluestone, C.D., Kardatzke, D., & Bachman, R. (1992). Towards the validation of aural acoustic immittance measures for diagnosis of middle ear effusion in children. *Ear and Hearing, 13,* 442–453.

Nozza, R.J., Bluestone, C.D., Kardatzke, D., & Bachman, R. (1994). Identification of middle ear effusion by aural acoustic admittance and otoscopy. *Ear and Hearing, 15,* 310–323.

Nozza, R.J., & Sabo, D.L. (1992). Transiently evoked OAE for screening school-age children. *The Hearing Journal, 45*(11), 29–31.

Paradise, J.L., Smith, C.G., & Bluestone, C.D. (1976). Tympanometric detection of middle ear effusion in infants and young children. *Pediatrics, 58,* 198–210.

Pukander, J. (1983). Clinical features of acute otitis media among children. *Acta Otolaryngologica, 95,* 117–122.

Roush, J., Drake, A., & Sexton, J.E. (1992). Identification of middle ear dysfunction in young children: A comparison of tympanometric screening procedures. *Ear and Hearing, 13,* 63–69.

Roush, J., Bryant, K., Mundy, M., Zeisel, S., & Roberts, J. (1995). Developmental changes in static admittance and tympanometric gradient in infants and toddlers. *Journal of the American Academy of Audiology, 6,* 334–338.

Ruuskanen, O., & Heikkinen, T. (1994). Otitis media: Etiology and diagnosis. *Pediatric Infectious Disease Journal, 13,* S23–S26.

Schwartz, R.H., Stool, S.E., Rodriguez, W.J., & Grundfast, K.M. (1981). Acute otitis media: Toward a more precise definition. *Clinical Pediatrics, 20,* 549–554.

Shanks, J.E., Stelmachowicz, P.G., Beauchaine, K.L., & Schulte, L. (1992). Equivalent ear canal volumes in children pre- and post-tympanostomy tube insertion. *Journal of Speech and Hearing Research, 35,* 936–941.

Silman, S., & Emmer, M.B. (1995). Ipsilateral acoustic reflex in middle-ear effusion. *Seminars in Hearing, 16*(1), 80–85.

Silman, S., Silverman, C.A., & Arick, D.S. (1992). Acoustic-immittance screening for detection of middle-ear effusion in children. *Journal of the American Academy of Audiology, 3,* 262–268.

Stool, S.E., Berg, A.O., Berman, S., Carney, C.J., Cooley, J.R., Culpepper, L., Eavey, R.D., Feagans, L.V., Finitzo, T., Friedman, E.M., Goertz, J.A., Goldstein, A.J., Grundfast, K.M., Long, D.G., Macconi, L.L., Melton, L., Roberts, J.E., Sherrod, J.L., & Sisk, J.E. (1994). *Otitis media with effusion in young children: Clinical practice guideline No. 12* (AHCPR Publication No. 94-0622). Rockville, MD: Agency for Health Care Policy and Research.

Teele, D.W., Klein, J.O., Rosner, B., & the Greater Boston Otitis Media Study Group. (1989). Epidemiology of otitis media during the first seven years of life in children in greater Boston: A prospective cohort study. *Journal of Infectious Diseases, 160,* 83–93.

Utech-Smith, P., Wiley, T., & Pyle, M. (1993). Efficacy of ASHA guidelines for screening middle-ear function. *Asha, 35*(10), 114.

Wachtendorf, C.A., Lopez, L.L., Cooper, J.C., Hearn, E.M., & Gates, G.A. (1984). The efficacy of school screening for otitis media. In D.J. Lim, C.D.

Bluestone, J.O. Klein, & J.D. Nelson (Eds.), *Recent advances in otitis media with effusion* (pp. 242–246). Philadelphia: B.C. Decker.

Watkin, P., Baldwin, M., & Laoide, S. (1990). Parental suspicion and identification of hearing impairment. *Archives of Disease in Childhood, 65,* 846–850.

Wiley, T.L., & Smith, P.S. (1995). Acoustic-immittance measures and middle-ear screening. *Seminars in Hearing, 16*(1), 60–80.

Wilson, R., & Margolis, R. (1991). Acoustic reflex measurements. In W. Rintelmann (Ed.), *Hearing Assessment* (2nd ed., pp. 247–320). Austin, TX: PRO-ED.

II

AUDITORY, LANGUAGE, AND LEARNING SEQUELAE

3

Hearing Loss Among Children with Otitis Media with Effusion

Judith S. Gravel and Robert J. Nozza

Both a crucial research question and a clinical management issue is whether the developmental sequelae that are sometimes attributed to chronic episodes of otitis media with effusion (OME) in childhood are mediated by the hearing loss that often accompanies the condition. Moreover, if the existence of persistent or fluctuant mild hearing loss does negatively influence speech and language development and later academic performance, then our challenge is to detect any hearing impairment associated with OME soon after it develops, to assess the loss accurately and completely, and to monitor for persistence or recurrence of the condition in the short and long term. Furthermore, when auditory-based communication, behavior, or learning deficiencies are identified, comprehensive evaluation must then be initiated and management plans devised to optimize the child's opportunities to achieve in the learning environment.

This chapter examines the effect of OME on peripheral hearing in the context of our current definition of hearing loss in children. The application of various audiologic test methodologies useful in the identification and assessment of infants and children with middle ear pathology is then reviewed. Next, the influence of the hearing loss

This chapter was supported in part by research grant (5 P50 DC 00223-12) from the National Institute on Deafness and Other Communication Disorders, National Institutes of Health.

associated with OME on speech perception and auditory processing is addressed, first by examining background theory and then by reviewing several current investigations that support a relationship between early conductive hearing impairment and higher-order auditory deficits. Finally, the chapter concludes with suggested approaches to the management of children with conductive hearing loss at home and in the classroom.

For purposes of this discussion, we adopt the premise that persistent mild hearing loss in early life can result in adverse developmental consequences in childhood. It is acknowledged that any sequelae of OME and hearing loss are influenced not only by the degree and duration of the condition but also by the child's stage of development at onset and by the unique demands and constraints of the listening environment under which he or she must function at any point in time. Indeed, the effects of hearing loss associated with OME may be manifested differently over the course of childhood. For example, hearing loss during the first and second years of life can initially result in a delay in emerging receptive or expressive language development or both (e.g., Friel-Patti & Finitzo, 1990; Wallace et al., 1988). Although communication skills may "normalize" before entry into school, other auditory-based deficits may emerge in the classroom situation (Gravel & Wallace, 1995). These may present as problems with listening in competition, in academic achievement, or with attention and behavior (Feagans, Sanyal, Henderson, Collier, & Applebaum, 1987; Gravel & Wallace, 1992, 1995; Roberts et al., 1989).

Although a straightforward formula approach, involving the child's degree of hearing loss and the frequency of episodes experienced, would be useful to clinicians attempting to identify children for whom aggressive management is warranted, such a concept may be too simplistic. Indeed, it is more likely that any deleterious outcomes associated with hearing loss and OME will vary from individual to individual, with audiologic and otologic factors interacting in combination with numerous other variables that are unique to each child and his or her circumstances. Furthermore, two patterns of hearing loss associated with OME may actually exist. The first occurs among children who experienced middle ear effusion and hearing loss persistently in the early years (age 3 and younger) of life, whose condition, except for occasional episodes, resolves by the time they enter public school. The second pattern occurs among children whose OME persists into kindergarten and elementary school, resulting in hearing impairment experienced for various amounts of time within a formal educational setting.

HEARING LOSS IN CHILDREN: DEVELOPING THE DEFINITION

Definitions of what constitutes hearing loss in childhood vary and are, to say the least, somewhat arbitrary (Nozza, 1994). The current lack of an agreed-upon definition of hearing loss in adults compounds the issue. Regardless, even a complete appreciation of the functional consequences of all degrees and configurations of hearing loss in the mature individual would not adequately answer the question for children. Adults who have acquired their communication competencies through an unimpaired auditory system often experience little difficulty from mild, late-onset hearing loss. Children learning language for the first time, however, are confronted with very different auditory requirements when hearing impairment occurs at, or soon after, birth.

In this context, we must consider the implications of the terms *impairment* and *disability*. Fostered by the recommendations of the World Health Organization (1980), a recent report of the American Speech-Language-Hearing Association (ASHA, 1995) described the term *impairment* as a loss or abnormality of a physiologic, anatomic, or psychological structure or function. By comparison, the word *disability* defined a restriction in, or lack of, a person's ability to perform an activity in a manner considered usual for other individuals. Therefore, a "hearing impairment" affects a structure(s), function, or both of the auditory mechanism, whereas a "hearing disability" adversely influences the ability of the individual to function in auditory domains similarly to persons considered to have normal hearing proficiency. We suggest that both of these concepts must be considered in any definition of hearing loss in childhood, because the terms *impairment* and *disability*, particularly in children, are highly interrelated. Indeed, it is the increased risk for developing a disability as a consequence of a hearing impairment that motivates our early identification, assessment, and intervention efforts.

Some suggest that hearing thresholds equal to or better than 15 dB hearing level (HL) bilaterally across the speech range should be considered the upper limit of normal in children (Northern & Downs, 1991). For adults, hearing at 500, 1,000, 2,000 and 4,000 Hz no worse than 25 dB HL is often considered to be normal (Nozza, 1994), and a 20-dB-HL criterion for normal versus impaired hearing in older children and adults has also been suggested (ASHA, 1990). Current attention in the adult hearing literature has focused not only on hearing thresholds, but on any resultant disability the individual experiences as a consequence of the impairment. In adults, a "disabling" hearing loss can now be identified using self-report or self-assessment scales, sometimes termed *handicap inventories*. Using the measure they devised, Ventry and Weinstein (1983) found that the majority of people who are elderly perceived themselves as "handicapped" by their loss when their hearing levels exceeded an average of 40 dB. For more effective intervention planning, screening programs might include both an audiometric screen and a measure to identify those individuals who were concomitantly experiencing disability.

Although newer behavioral and electrophysiologic methods have allowed us to accurately quantify the degree and configuration of any hearing impairment in infants and young children, procedures to examine childhood auditory-based disabilities have not been applied systematically across the pediatric age range. However, it may be that our definition of hearing loss in childhood should consider the functional consequences of the impairment. Delineating this relationship is the key to fully understanding the possible sequelae of the hearing loss that frequently accompanies OME. Therefore, studies designed to examine the effects of OME on child development must assess hearing directly and subsequently relate audiometric data to outcome measures.

CONDUCTIVE HEARING LOSS
ASSOCIATED WITH OTITIS MEDIA WITH EFFUSION

Hearing impairments can result from a pathologic state in the middle ear that causes varying amounts of attentuation of auditory signals arriving at the cochlea. Tympanic membrane, tympanum (middle ear space), and ossicular functions may be differentially affected by the presence of effusion (fluid) within the middle ear space. However, anatomic changes to the tympanic membrane (plaque or scar tissue) or ossicles (adhesions) may also result in some degree of conductive hearing loss. In some cases, chronic perforation of the tympanic membrane (a result of repeated rupturing of the membrane or lack of closure of the eardrum after ventilation tube insertion) can also result in conductive hearing loss. In all cases of purely conductive involvement, cochlear/auditory nerve function is normal.

Because most acute episodes of otitis media in young children resolve fairly rapidly (over half clear spontaneously within 2 weeks and nearly 80% resolve within 4 weeks), only a small number of children (approximately 10%) persist with middle ear effusion (MEE) for prolonged (>8 weeks) periods after initial onset (Pukander & Karma, 1988). Approximately one third of children who experience middle ear disease in the first 3 years of life have recurrent involvement (Teele, Klein, & Rosner, 1980). In the first year, 50%–90% of babies experience at least one episode of otitis media (Gravel, McCarton, & Ruben, 1988; Marchant et al., 1984; Owen, Baldwin, Luttman, & Howie, 1993; Teele et al., 1980). Studies also have suggested that many otitis media episodes are "silent"—that is, manifesting no overt symptomatology (Marchant et al., 1984).

According to the audiogram, the hearing loss associated with otitis media is typically considered to be "slight" to "mild" in degree. The audiogram of children with otitis media is usually depicted as having an average hearing loss of 20–30 dB HL (Bess, 1986; Fria, Cantekin, & Eichler, 1985). A close examination of the average hearing loss associated with otitis media, however, suggests that the impairment may range from less than 10 to greater than 50 dB HL (Bess, 1986). Fria and colleagues (1985) studied over 750 children with otitis media and found that half had average hearing levels poorer than 23 dB and 20% had hearing losses worse than 35 dB HL. It appears that hearing sensitivity is impaired to approximately the same degree in infants experiencing otitis media (Eilers, Widen, Urbano, Hudson, & Gonzales, 1991; Gravel, 1989; Hunter, 1995).

Although the configuration of the hearing loss associated with MEE is often considered to be flat or attenuating equally across the speech range (Bess, 1986), the actual configuration of the impairment may vary, differentially affecting low- and high-frequency areas to a greater degree than mid-frequency regions. These differences in hearing loss configuration may reflect the amount or viscosity of the fluid within the middle ear space, or both, as well as the existence of additional tympanic membrane or ossicular conditions. The characteristics of the hearing loss associated with OME are distinctly different from permanent conductive or sensorineural hearing impairments. The hearing loss resulting from otitis media with effusion is 1) temporary, 2) variable in degree, 3) frequently recurrent, and 4) often asymmetric (Gravel & Ellis, 1995). The inherent variability of hearing loss associated with otitis media may have significant implications for the development of normal speech perception and binaural auditory processing.

METHODS TO QUANTIFY HEARING LOSS
AND MIDDLE EAR INVOLVEMENT IN INFANTS
AND CHILDREN WITH OTITIS MEDIA WITH EFFUSION

Pure-Tone Audiometry

The conventional pure-tone audiogram is the traditional means of quantifying hearing sensitivity across the audiometric range critical for speech recognition. It is the measure most appropriate for the routine documentation of the degree and configuration of any hearing loss associated with OME in children. Ideally, frequency-specific (pure-tone, FM tone, or narrow-band noise) thresholds should be obtained at octave frequencies from 250 through 8,000 Hz in each ear. Often, in infants and very young children, audiometric thresholds cannot be obtained at all of these test frequencies. In these cases, at a minimum, thresholds should be established in low-, mid-, and high-frequency regions (e.g., 500, 1,000, and 4,000 Hz). Ear-specific threshold assessment provides the only means of examining the symmetry of the auditory impairment. In the majority of cases, ear-specific data can be obtained even in infants and young children. Conventional supraaural earphones (attached to a cushioned pediatric headband) or insert receivers (eliminating the need for the bulky transducer/headset assembly) are appropriate for pediatric audiologic assessment. Whereas a sound field audiogram is useful in determining the hearing in the better ear, bilateral sensitivity can be examined only when some means of estimating individual ear responses is used.

Bone conduction thresholds provide important information in audiometric assessment and should be obtained routinely, regardless of the state of the middle ear mechanism. Slight to mild differences in air and bone conduction thresholds (air–bone gap) can exist even when the audiogram and tympanograms are considered "normal." The presence of any air–bone gap of greater than 10 dB suggests some deficit in transduction of the airborne signal through the middle ear system. Maintaining a prospective record of air and bone conduction thresholds helps to document the specific amount of hearing loss resulting from otitis media. Indeed, a baseline air and bone conduction audiogram serves to identify any change in hearing status. Tympanometry should not be considered a substitute for bone conduction audiometry. The former is one means of examining middle ear function; the latter (in conjunction with air conduction responses) provides a means of estimating the effect of middle ear pathology on hearing sensitivity.

A heretofore largely unrecognized sequela of chronic OME in childhood appears to be sensorineural hearing loss affecting high-frequency hearing sensitivity. Hunter and her colleagues (1996) studied the ultra-high-frequency (9,000–20,000 Hz) thresholds of children with documented histories of persistent OME. Figure 1 presents data from their study for both the traditional audiometric range and the ultra-high frequencies. Children with the longest duration OME histories had the poorest thresholds within the ultra-high-frequency range. These results suggest it may be prudent to include the assessment of high-frequency hearing, at least through 8,000 Hz, during routine pure-tone audiometry in order to identify the existence of any impairment in this range. High-

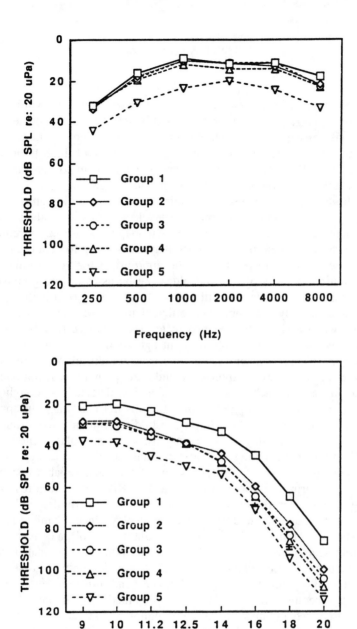

Figure 1. Hearing thresholds plotted as a function of frequency and intensity (in decibels of sound pressure level [dB SPL]) for a control group with no otitis media history and four other groups of children with various amounts of middle ear involvement. Top, Thresholds for the five groups for the conventional audiometric frequency range (250–8,000 Hz). Bottom, Thresholds for the same groups for frequencies from 9,000 through 20,000 Hz. Group 1, controls; Groups 2–5 range from least (Group 2) to most (Group 5) number of OM episodes. (From Hunter, L.L., Margolis, R.H., Rykken, J.R., Le, C.T., Daly, K.A., & Giebink, G.S. [1996]. High frequency hearing loss associated with otitis media. *Ear and Hearing, 17,* 1–11; reprinted by permission.)

frequency hearing loss (in the 4,000- to 8,000-Hz range) can affect the perception of speech sounds whose primary energy is within this spectral region (e.g., /s/, /f/, and /Θ/). Although the cause, course, and functional consequences of Hunter et al.'s findings in the ultra-high-frequency range are still unclear, early detection of high-frequency hearing loss allows the audiologist and the physician to consider the impairment in intervention and follow-up planning.

Clinical procedures used to obtain a pure-tone audiogram are dependent upon the neurodevelopmental level of the child. Although the audiometric test method (e.g., an up–down adaptive staircase procedure) used to establish hearing thresholds may be similar for children and adults, the behavior response must be appropriate for young children. Most children 5 years of age and older can be assessed using conventional response methods. As with adults, hand raising or a button-push response is usually a reliable and efficient means of having the child indicate when a signal has been detected (Northern & Downs, 1991). For younger children (starting at about age 24 months) however, play audiometry techniques, are most appropriate (Wilson & Thompson, 1984). Behavior "play" responses include dropping a block in a bucket or stacking a ring each time the test signal is detected. Although the child's comprehension of spoken directions is not necessary, an appropriate neurodevelopmental level and the child's willingness to participate in testing on a given day are necessary for successful play audiometry.

With infants beginning at about 5 months' developmental age, visual reinforcement audiometry (VRA) is an efficient and reliable test procedure for hearing threshold assessment. In VRA, a head-turn response during, or just after, the presentation of a test signal is reinforced by the illumination of an animated, attractive toy display. Once the infant learns the response contingency (i.e., is under stimulus control), a conventional threshold search procedure can be initiated. Whereas classical unconditioned behavior observation audiometry provides only a gross estimate of auditory function, the conditioned head-turn procedure allows frequency-specific threshold data to be obtained from infants that are similar to those obtained from older children and adults (Nozza & Wilson, 1984). In some infants and children with developmental disabilities (motor or visual impairments), classical VRA may not be appropriate. However, operant audiometry may still be useful in behavioral hearing assessment when a more appropriate behavior response, reinforcer, or both are used. Visual reinforcement audiometry can be used to delineate even mild hearing losses associated with middle ear disorder (Eilers et al., 1991; Ellis, Lee, Gravel, & Wallace, 1995; Gravel, 1989; Hunter, 1995; Nozza & Wilson, 1984).

Auditory Electrophysiologic and Physiologic Methods

Auditory Brainstem Response   The auditory brainstem response (ABR) procedure has proved to be a valuable tool in the estimation of hearing sensitivity in young children. As would be expected, ABR thresholds are influenced by the existence of middle ear involvement. Practically, an ABR cannot be completed each time a child experiences an episode of OME; behavior measures are decidedly more efficient and cost-effective. However, when an ABR is completed on a young child, results must be interpreted with knowledge of the child's middle ear status (determined with tympanometry, pneumatic otoscopy, or both). Usually, all absolute ABR wave latencies are prolonged and the normal latency–intensity function is shifted horizontally by the existence of conductive hearing loss (Mackersie & Stapells, 1994). Indeed, some have suggested that the degree of conductive hearing loss can be estimated based on the absolute value of Wave I (e.g., Fria & Sabo, 1979). However, Mackersie and Stapells (1994) have demonstrated that reliance on Wave I as a means of determining the degree of conductive hearing loss in infants and children is often misleading. Moreover, although the ABR threshold (particularly when frequency specific; Stapells, Gravel, & Martin, 1995) provides a good estimate of hearing sensitivity in children with sensorineural hearing loss, the presence of a conductive impairment can occasionally result in electrophysiologic responses that overestimate behavior thresholds (Gravel & Stapells, 1992; Stapells, 1989). The use of bone-conducted ABR in combination with traditional air-conducted ABR threshold assessment may help to differentiate conductive from cochlear hearing loss and to quantify the degree of conductive involvement (Stapells, 1989). There is some evidence that, when assessed later in childhood, some children with early histories of OME have abnormal suprathreshold ABR recordings (see discussion to follow). The routine referral of children for ABR is, in our opinion, not warranted unless the test is being completed as part of a comprehensive audiologic workup or when the child's neurodevelopmental level precludes reliable behavioral assessment.

Evoked Otoacoustic Emissions   The use of evoked otoacoustic emissions (EOAEs) (Kemp, 1978) assessment has become increasingly widespread in neonatal hearing screening programs (National Institutes of Health, 1993; White, Vohr, & Behrens, 1993). In addition, the use of EOAE as a "cross-check" procedure (Jerger & Hayes, 1976) has also strengthened the pediatric audiologic test armamentarium. Mild hearing losses of cochlear origin are known to eliminate the EOAE (Prieve, 1992). In addition, OME can reduce or eliminate the EOAE; OME attentuates the stimulus available at the cochlea and impedes "reverse transduction" (from the cochlea through the middle ear), reducing or eliminating the emission in the ear canal (Prieve, 1992). The recording of transient EOAEs in children with pressure-equalizing (PE) tubes or active otitis media is directly influenced by the degree of any existing air–bone gap. Figure 2 presents data from Prieve (1992) demonstrating the relationship among middle ear status, the air–bone gap, and the

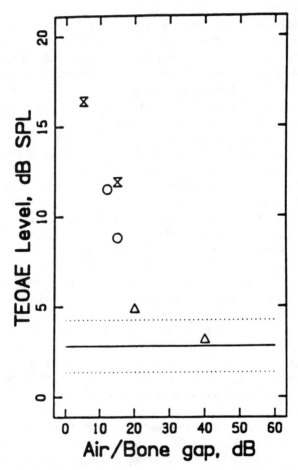

Figure 2.   Level (in dB SPL) of transient evoked otoacoustic emissions (TEOAE) plotted as a function of the degree of air–bone gap (difference [in dB] between air conduction and bone conduction thresholds) for children with patent PE tubes (X), negative (−185 to −330 daPa) tympanometric peak pressure (o), and flat (noncompliant) tympanograms (△). Note that TEOAE level appears to be related to the amount of air–bone gap. The solid line at 3 dB represents the criterion level for judging the presence of a reliable emission. (From Prieve, B.A. [1992]. Otoacoustic emissions in infants and children: Basic characteristics and clinical application. *Seminars in Hearing, 13,* 37–52; reprinted by permission.)

transient EOAE level. It appears that otoacoustic emissions may be useful for both screening and assessment of children at risk for OME.

Acoustic Immittance Assessment Acoustic immittance (tympanometry and acoustic reflex) assessment is undoubtedly our single most valuable tool for the detection of middle ear disorder in infants and children. An assessment of the child's middle ear function should be made at every assessment of hearing sensitivity (ASHA, 1991). Although in the past qualitative typing of tympanogram shape (e.g., Jerger, 1970; Paradise, Smith, & Bluestone, 1976) has been used to describe acoustic immittance findings, quantification of tympanometric variables appears the more accurate means of delineating middle ear status and the most useful method for comparison of findings across clinics and populations (Wiley & Smith, 1995). Tympanometric features frequently quantified are peak compensated static acoustic admittance, tympanometric width (TW), tympanometric peak pressure, equivalent ear canal volume (V_{ec}), and tympanometric gradient. Reports have provided normative data and assessment of the efficiency of specific screening protocols in children for these tympanometric variables (e.g., Margolis & Heller, 1987; Roush, Drake, & Sexton, 1992). Tympanometry, however, cannot predict the degree of hearing loss associated with any middle ear condition, and various degrees and configurations of hearing loss may exist with similar tympanometric findings (Fria et al., 1985).

In order to use acoustic immittance efficiently for the detection of MEE, the specific population to be screened must be well defined (Nozza, 1995). Nozza, Bluestone, Kardatzke, and Bachman (1994) examined the sensitivity, specificity, and predictive accuracy of admittance variables, otoscopy, and their combination in identifying ears with effusion. Tympanometric width was found to have the best performance among all variables for use in the detection of MEE. Importantly, the distribution of TW was examined in three pediatric populations: one with no history of otitis media, one with a positive otologic history but with no fluid found in the middle ear at the time of surgery, and one with MEE present at the time of PE tube placement. As depicted in Figure 3, three distinct distributions of TW were observed. If the clinician were to adopt a TW value of greater than 200 daPa as the "cutoff" for determining fluid-free ears versus ears with MEE, then 99% of ears of children selected from a population considered to have no otologic histories would have correctly been identified as fluid free. Conversely, in the children with no MEE at the time of surgery but with histories of OME, a TW greater than 200 daPa incorrectly identified 53% of the ears as having MEE. However, the same criterion identified

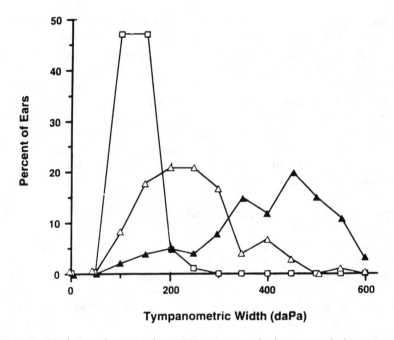

Figure 3.   Distributions of ears according to TW measurements for three groups of subjects: An unselected population, ears with a history of OME but without MEE at surgery, and ears with MEE documented at the time of surgery. (-□- = No MEE [Outpatients]; -△- = No MEE [Surgery group]; -▲- =
MEE [Surgery group].) (Adapted from Nozza, 1995).

89% of the cases of MEE in the surgically confirmed effusion group.
These findings suggest that the accuracy of quantitative acoustic admittance measures is influenced by the characteristics (in this case, previous
middle ear history) of the population under study. The "gold standard"
used for comparison purposes was the presence or absence of fluid in
the middle ear at the time of surgery (for placement of PE/ventilating
tubes). This study provides data that may be useful to clinicians in
selecting the tympanometric or tympanometric/otoscopic criteria for the
detection of MEE best suited for their population and purposes.

Detection of middle ear involvement in very young infants using
acoustic immittance procedures remains somewhat controversial. The
use of higher frequency probe tones (above 220/226 Hz) for obtaining
a tympanogram in infants 4 months and younger has been suggested
(e.g., 660 Hz; Marchant et al., 1986), whereas others found that the
lower frequency may be adequate (Holte, Margolis, & Cavanaugh,
1991). A 660-Hz probe frequency is well established as the frequency
most useful for eliciting the acoustic reflex in this age group (e.g., Marchant et al., 1986).

Measuring V_{ec} is particularly useful in monitoring the viability of PE tubes in infants and young children. One report has provided normative data for determining the patency of PE tubes in young children (Shanks, Stelmachowicz, Beauchaine, & Schulte, 1992). Routine V_{ec} measures in an infant prior to myringotomy and PE tube placement provide a baseline comparison during postsurgical PE tube status evaluation.

Speech Measures
An evaluation of speech reception and speech recognition abilities should be completed in children as soon as it is feasible. Speech audiometry, although useful in estimating the overall influence of OME on auditory function, cannot provide a complete representation of the frequency-specific effects of conductive involvement across the speech frequency range. Indeed, conventional speech measures may actually underestimate the hearing loss association with OME.

The speech recognition threshold (SRT; formerly termed *speech reception threshold*) is the level at which spondees (two-syllable words with equal stress on each syllable, as in *baseball* or *hotdog*) are recognized approximately 50% of the time. To obtain an SRT, the child must either repeat the word or point to a picture depicting the spondee, generally from a limited number (closed set) of test items. Thus, the SRT is dependent upon the child's vocabulary and ability to respond appropriately to a closed-set identification task. The SRT is sometimes considered to be an estimate of the hearing loss for speech (Stool et al., 1994). Unfortunately, the SRT, like the pure-tone average, reflects regions of better sensitivity, such as when hearing is relatively good in the middle frequencies but poor in low- or high-frequency regions. In younger children with immature language, a speech detection threshold or speech awareness threshold may be obtained. The child is taught to respond only to the presence of speech; no recognition of the word is necessary. Both speech measures generally provide little information regarding hearing loss configuration unless, in the detection task, single phonemes that provide some information about low-, mid-, and high-frequency speech regions are used (e.g., vowels and high-frequency consonant sounds).

The word recognition (formerly termed *speech discrimination*) score provides information about the listener's ability to accurately perceive speech. Word recognition measures are traditionally administered at suprathreshold levels, generally at a comfortable listening level (or sensation level) above the SRT. A percent correct score (based on the number of words correctly repeated from a list of 25 or 50 monosyllables) is obtained for each ear. In children, age-appropriate test materials must be used, such as materials that require a picture-point response and incorporate test items that are likely to be within a young child's vocabulary. These features are important when testing children whose speech production accuracy and language competency may not be fully mature or may be impaired.

In the case of conductive hearing loss, administering the word recognition measure at a suprathreshold level most often results in a near-perfect score. Administration of word recognition tests at a comfortable listening level, however, may fail to demonstrate the practical consequences of any existing hearing loss. At comfortably loud intensity levels, the child appears to have no difficulty recognizing speech. However, he or she may actually experience difficulties at speech levels commonly encountered in daily life, such as in the classroom setting. To circumvent this limitation, delineating a performance–intensity function for the speech material may help predict the functional consequences of the hearing loss.

When pure-tone audiometry reveals a conductive hearing loss or when the children presents with a history of recurrent OME, a thorough examination of word recognition ability is in order. Therefore, speech materials that allow the post hoc analysis of perceptual errors are particularly useful. DeMarco and Givens (1989) assessed a 4-year-old boy with a prolonged history of OME before and after insertion of PE tubes. Prior to surgery, they assessed discrimination ability (using word pairs that differed only by a single phoneme) at two intensity levels: one considered normal conversational-level speech (50 dB HL) and the other at a level selected to overcome the child's 20-dB hearing loss (70 dB HL). Some of the errors demonstrated by the child prior to PE tube insertion were clearly the result of the attenuated auditory input; at the higher presentation level these errors were eliminated. However, some of the speech perception errors persisted despite the increased signal intensity. After surgery, speech discrimination was reassessed in the presence of a normal pure-tone audiogram. Interestingly, some speech discrimination errors remained in the presence of normal peripheral hearing. The systematic assessment of speech discrimination/recognition abilities provides insight into any such persistent perceptual errors that may require remediation.

"MILD" HEARING LOSS AND SPEECH PERCEPTION

Clearly, the primary concern of clinicians is that a hearing loss associated with OME results in the degradation of speech input to the young child acquiring language for the first time. In a classic paper by Dobie and Berlin (1979), the influence of "mild" hearing loss on the speech signal was examined. Based on their acoustic analyses, Dobie and Berlin predicted that important speech properties might be absent, distorted, or heard inconsistently when a 20-dB attenuation of the input signal was imposed. These features included grammatic morphemes such as final -*s* or -*ed*, short words, word-final phonemes (particularly those that are voiceless and high frequency in content), and suprasegmental aspects of speech such as inflectional contours.

Nozza and his colleagues have further emphasized that infants and young children require acoustic conditions for the perception of speech that are substantially different than those needed by adult listeners (Nozza, 1987; Nozza, Rossman, & Bond, 1991). They found that infants require a speech signal approximately 20–25 dB more intense than adults in order to achieve maximum speech discrimination performance. Moreover, young children require a more advantageous signal-to-noise ratio than adults in order to discriminate speech sounds in background noise (Nozza et al., 1991). Figure 4 depicts performance–intensity functions for a group of adults and a group of infants, both with normal hearing (Nozza, 1988). The task was the discrimination of a /ba/–/da/ speech contrast. Note that two features characterize the differences between the adult and infant performance–intensity functions. Asymptotic (optimal speech discrimination) performance for adults is reached between 20 and 30 dB HL; acoustic information is sufficiently above threshold for accurate discrimination of the place-of-articulation contrast. However, asymptotic performance for infants with normal hearing occurs when the contrast is presented at 50–60 dB HL. Clearly, infants can discriminate the place contrast at lower intensity levels, because their performance is still significantly better than chance (50%), but they require a greater overall intensity level than adults to achieve optimum perceptual performance (Nozza, 1988).

Also displayed in Figure 4 is a shaded area around 60 dB HL. This represents the approximate level of average conversational speech. Both groups would be expected to discriminate the speech contrast of that overall intensity. The dashed-line area around 40 dB HL represents the level of speech available if a 20-dB attenuation of the 60-dB input signal occurred, such as in the case of a "mild" hearing impairment. Whereas adults would still be functioning optimally in this region, infants would be exposed to an input signal that would reduce their performance to just above chance.

In support of these studies, Eimas and Clarkson (1986) demonstrated that the speech identification and discrimination performance of study groups with early otitis media histories was markedly different from that of children with no known early OME episodes. Gravel and Ellis (1995) reported preliminary data obtained from two groups of 6-

SPEECH-SOUND DISCRIMINATION
/ba/vs/da/

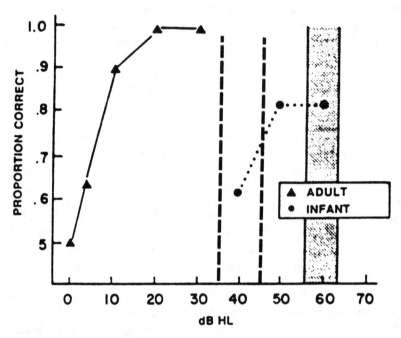

Figure 4. Performance–intensity functions for infants and adults for /ba/–da/ discrimination task. Intensity is depicted in decibels of hearing level; chance is 0.5. The shaded area depicts the intensity of normal conversational-level speech (60 dB HL). The dashed lines around 40 dB HL depict the level of speech within 20 dB of signal attenuation imposed, as in the case of a mild hearing loss. (Adapted from Nozza, 1988).

year-old children; both had normal hearing at the time of word recognition assessment. One group was considered OME positive in the first year of life and the other was essentially free of the condition for the same period. Children in the group with the early middle ear history had more difficulty understanding monosyllabic words at low (30-dB HL) intensity levels than their early otitis media–free peers. At normal conversational speech levels (50 dB HL), however, performance scores were similar for both groups.

Predicting the Effect of
Otitis Media with Effusion on Speech Recognition
It has been important to clinicians to try to convey a clear appreciation of the effect of even a mild hearing loss on a child's speech perception abilities. A simple method used by many pediatric audiologists has been to present the child's hearing threshold levels on the classic pictorial

audiogram developed by Northern and Downs (1978). The value of this method has been to allow the effect of a hearing loss to be visually depicted, particularly "the hearing loss for speech." Speech sounds are depicted at the approximate frequency and intensity at which they occur in normal conversational speech. Figure 5 displays a "typical" mild conductive hearing loss from a child with OME on the Northern and Downs audiogram.

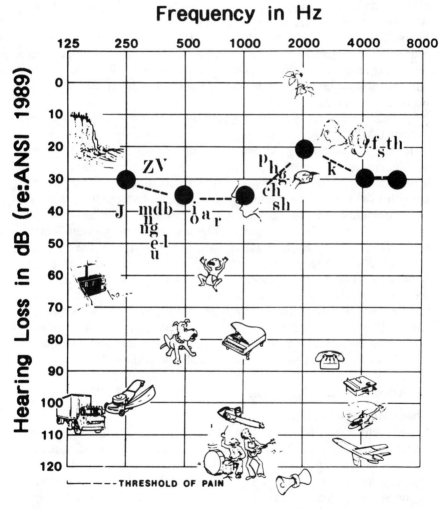

Figure 5.   Typical mild conductive hearing loss associated with otitis media with effusion displayed on the pictorial audiogram originally devised by Northern and Downs (1978) and modified in 1989. (From Northern, J.L., & Downs, M.P. [1991]. *Hearing in children* (4th ed., p. 17). Baltimore:Williams & Wilkins; adapted by permission.)

Perhaps a more useful means of estimating the effect of signal attenuation caused by a hearing loss on speech perception is through the computation of the articulation index (AI). The AI was developed as a means of predicting the efficiency of speech transmission systems such as the telephone. Recently, the AI has been utilized to estimate the effect of signal distortion (attenuation and noise) on adult listeners who hear normally, as well as those with sensorineural hearing loss (Pavlovic, 1991). The AI examines the contribution to speech intelligibility of 16 critical bands of energy ranging from 300 to 6,000 Hz, differentially weighted, with the higher-frequency regions contributing more to the index than the lower-frequency bands. Thus, the AI can provide an estimate of the proportion of the speech signal, weighted for importance in speech recognition, that is audible to the listener (Pavlovic, 1991), and therefore it may be useful to our understanding of the effects of hearing loss associated with OME.

Figure 6 depicts three audiograms obtained from a child with recurrent OME obtained on three separate occasions. For this example, instead of calculating the AI conventionally, it was estimated by using the "count-the-dot" method described by Mueller and Killion (1990). This method provides a means of rapidly calculating the AI by plotting the child's thresholds on the modified audiogram and counting the dots that are audible (i.e., above the child's thresholds). The count-the-dot method weights different frequency regions according to their importance for speech recognition. Calculation of the AI allows the clinician to estimate the "communication handicap" imposed by the hearing loss for normal conversational speech intensity levels. The functional consequences of various AI values are highly dependent upon the speech to be recognized. Note that in our example the child's AI scores varied from 0.32 to 1.0 depending upon the degree of conductive hearing loss present on each day. An AI of 0.32 suggests that intelligibility would be reduced by about two thirds (see Mueller & Killion, 1990).

HIGHER-ORDER (CENTRAL) AUDITORY PROCESSING

Theoretical Background

Usually children with stable, intact hearing and average or above-average cognitive abilities readily learn the auditory-linguistic code of their native language. In theory, the variability associated with having repeated episodes of OME, in combination with the inherent variability of the speech signal and the acoustic conditions of the listening environment, could make attempts at determining the auditory code of language more challenging for some children with persistent or recurrent fluctuating mild hearing loss. Feagans and colleagues have suggested

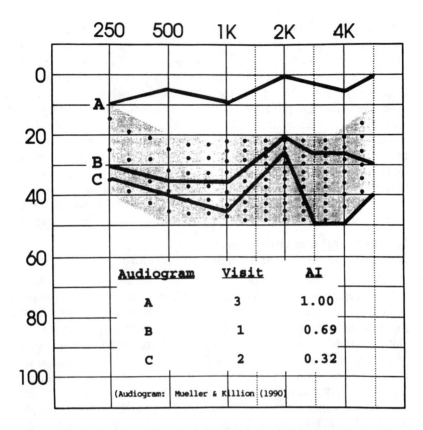

Figure 6.   Threshold values for a child with normal hearing and normal middle ear function (*A*) and the same child with otitis media (*B* and *C*). The articulation index (AI) calculated on the "count-the-dot" audiogram devised by Mueller and Killion (1990). Notations on the audiogram depict the audiogram number, the visit at which the configuration was obtained, and the resultant AI. (From Mueller, H.G., & Killion, M.C. [1990]. An easy method for calculating the Articulation Index. *Hearing Journal, 43*[9], 14, 16–17; reprinted by permission.)

that the motivation for sustained attention to auditory information is also deleteriously influenced by such a hearing loss; essentially, the child "tunes out" or ignores the attenuated auditory input (Feagans, Blood, & Tubman, 1988). These problems are further exacerbated in adverse listening circumstances, such as in situations that require listening to speech in a background of competition. A child who lacks a well-established auditory base cannot refer to it when aural messages are incomplete or lack redundancy (e.g., Feagans et al., 1988; Gravel & Wallace, 1992; Menyuk, 1986; Needleman, 1977; Nozza, 1994; Roberts et al., 1989; Skinner, 1978).

Some theories on the development of OME sequelae suggest directly or indirectly that infants experiencing hearing loss as a result of

MEE may be deprived of the full compliment of auditory cues necessary for optimal language learning during "critical" or "sensitive" periods of auditory development. However, the existence of such crucial periods for auditory development in humans has not, thus far, been demonstrated empirically. (See Chapter 4 for a complete discussion of the literature on early auditory deprivation in animals.) Critics of the auditory deprivation theory suggest that the anatomic, physiologic, and behavioral sequelae demonstrated in animal models differ from the auditory impairments and acoustic environments experienced by children with OME. Some argue that, even if deficits do occur in early life, both neural plasticity and the proportionately greater amount of normal auditory input most children with middle ear histories encounter would serve to reverse any deficits once OME episodes had subsided (Paradise, 1981).

Studies Examining Otitis Media with Effusion and Central Auditory Processing

Behavior Assessments   A relationship between OME and higher-order or central auditory processing problems in school age children has been suggested for some time (e.g., Brandes & Ehinger, 1981; Gottlieb, Zinckus, & Thompson, 1979; Welsh, Welsh, & Healy, 1981; Zinkus & Gottlieb, 1980). These early investigations have been criticized because of various problems with their research designs. However, in some more recent investigations in which children were followed prospectively, auditory-based (listening, academic, attention, and behavior) difficulties have been documented for children with early OME histories (e.g., Feagans et al., 1988; Gravel & Wallace, 1995; Roberts et al., 1989). (Readers are referred to Chapter 7 for a detailed discussion of these topics.)

Of further concern in the educational setting are studies that have demonstrated that speech recognition abilities in demanding listening environments may be associated with the presence or absence of an early otitis media history. Jerger, Jerger, Alford, and Abrams (1983) studied children's word and sentence recognition performance in quiet and in background competition. When the data were examined according to age categories (spanning 2.5–6 years), children with early otitis media histories demonstrated depressed performance in the competition condition relative to peers with normal middle ear histories. Recognition scores for the materials in quiet were no different between the groups. These developmental data suggest that the listening abilities of children who experience otitis media may lag behind those of children without such a history. Moreover, their performance on the monosyllables-in-competition task was poorer than on the sentences-in-competition task. The single-syllable words may have been more difficult because of their reduced acoustic redundancy in comparison to the longer sentence items.

Using the same test materials, Brown (1994) found similar results in a case report of twins, one with and one without an otitis media history.

Gravel and Wallace (1992) studied 4-year-old children whose first-year middle ear status was documented prospectively using pneumatic otoscopy and whose early hearing sensitivity was assessed by ABR during the first year of life. The sentence materials from the Pediatric Speech Intelligibility (PSI) test were presented diotically in an adaptive test paradigm to examine selective attention disabilities. The speech-to-competition ratio that resulted in 50% correct sentence intelligibility was determined for each child. All children had normal hearing and normal tympanograms on the test day. Four-year-old children considered to be otitis media positive in the first year of life required a significantly more advantageous speech-to-competition ratio in order to achieve criterion performance than did their peers without an otitis media history. Moreover, performance on the PSI was related to first-year hearing sensitivity as estimated by the ABR. Children with mild hearing loss in year 1 required a higher signal-to-noise ratio in order to achieve 50% understanding the primary sentence when heard with the competing sentence than those with "normal" hearing histories (Gravel & Wallace, 1995).

Electrophysiologic and Psychoacoustic Assessments Some of the most compelling findings of the effects of early OME and hearing loss on the auditory system are found in the reports of Gunnarson and Finitzo (1991) and Hall and Grose (1993). Gunnarson and Finitzo studied 5- to 7-year-old children whose early otitis media history had been documented prospectively. The children's hearing was estimated with ABR, providing evidence of the status of their hearing sensitivity during early life. Later in childhood, when all children had normal hearing, suprathreshold ABR testing was completed. Differences between children with extensive OME histories and those with no early OME were found in ABR absolute latencies (Waves III and V) and interpeak intervals (I–III and I–V). These authors also examined binaural interaction using the ABR. Significantly more children in the persistent early OME and hearing loss group lacked ABR binaural interaction than in either the control or the infrequent early OME cohort. These findings suggested later brain stem dysfunction in some children with early otitis media histories. The prospective nature of this investigation separates this study from other earlier reports that also demonstrated abnormal ABR findings in children with persistent otitis media histories (Anteby, Hafner, Pratt, & Uri, 1986; Folsom, Weber, & Thompson, 1983; Lenhardt, Shaia, & Abedi, 1985).

Hall and Grose (1993) examined both the masking level difference (MLD) and ABR in children with and without otitis media histories. The MLD paradigm examines the auditory system's capacity to detect subtle interaural phase (time and amplitude) cues. The MLD task examines binaural auditory processing, which is supported by neural elements at the level of the brain stem (Hall & Grose, 1993). Pillsbury, Drake, Hall, and Grose (1991) demonstrated smaller MLDs in children with OME and conductive hearing loss just prior to insertion of PE tubes. Masking level differences for some of the children returned to values considered appropriate for their ages shortly after surgery had restored hearing to normal. Other children, however, continued to demonstrate reduced MLDs (smaller than expected for their age range). Of interest was the finding that for some children reduced MLDs persisted for some time in the presence of normal hearing. After several months, essentially all children's MLD values were within the normal range. Moore and his colleagues have also reported similar findings. MLDs demonstrated by children considered to have early otitis media histories in their study were significantly smaller than MLDs obtained from children of the same age who were free of otitis media in early childhood and from adults (Moore, Hutchings, & Meyer, 1991). Later, Hall and Grose (1993) reported an inverse relationship between the MLD and ABR interaural interwave interval asymmetries. The functional consequences of such electrophysiologic and psychoacoustic findings in children with OME histories remain to be determined. However, the implications for the impact of OME on binaural auditory processes and auditory physiology are provocative. (For a complete discussion of this fascinating literature, readers are referred to Chapter 4.)

SCREENING FOR HEARING LOSS
ASSOCIATED WITH OTITIS MEDIA
WITH EFFUSION IN INFANTS AND CHILDREN

If the hearing loss associated with OME can be detrimental, it is important to identify children who have the condition. Delineating those children who have only occasional or rapidly resolving conditions from those with persistent impairments should be considered the primary goal of early identification initiatives. Because OME is a common condition of early childhood (Gravel et al., 1988; Marchant et al., 1984; Owen et al., 1993; Teele et al., 1980), it is important that the screening techniques utilized for detecting hearing loss and middle ear pathology are both highly sensitive and specific. Measures must identify only children at high risk for persistent conductive hearing loss, as well as indicate those children for whom the condition is transient and infrequent. Valuable intervention resources (medical, audiologic, communicative, and academic) can then be directed at those children who actually need services.

Screening initiatives may be warranted at various points of development because the effects of OME might be manifested differently over the course of childhood. Some children may experience delays in early communication acquisition, whereas other developmental problems (behavior and academic difficulties) may only be apparent at later ages. Language screening may be useful for identifying children at risk for receptive and expressive deficits and referring them for appropriate in-depth assessments. The Early Language Milestone (ELM) scale can be used for this purpose with infants and children ages birth through 36 months (Coplan, 1987). The ELM has been demonstrated to be highly sensitive to receptive and expressive language delays in young children (Walker, Downs, Gugenheim, & Northern, 1989). If a direct screen of language is not completed, information regarding communication development should be obtained from parents or caregivers. In addition to appropriate referrals, suspected or documented delays in language and speech development support the need for audiologic follow-up.

Identification of children at risk for academic deficits, behavior difficulties, or both in the classroom should also be a goal. The Screening Instrument for Targeting Educational Risk (SIFTER; Anderson, 1989) was developed to identify children with hearing loss who are at educational risk through teacher report. Gravel and Wallace (1995) have demonstrated that the SIFTER is sensitive to problems children with OME may experience in the classroom setting. A SIFTER appropriate for preschool-age children will soon be available (Anderson & Matkin, in 1996).

AUDIOLOGIC MANAGEMENT OF INFANTS AND CHILDREN WITH OTITIS MEDIA WITH EFFUSION

Young children experiencing chronic OME during important periods of language development need audiologic evaluation. These tests serve as baseline measures and, importantly, as indices of the stability of auditory sensitivity over time. We would suggest that an assessment of hearing should be considered when the child has had repeated episodes of OME within a 3-month period. Although this recommendation is in keeping with the Agency for Health Care Policy and Research Clinical Practice Guideline (Stool et al., 1994), audiologic assessment should be considered even if the OME has not been present bilaterally for the full 3-month period (Stool et al., 1994). Such practice may identify infants and toddlers who have frequent, fluctuant hearing impairments or long-standing unilateral OME, conditions that in early life could have an impact on emerging expressive and receptive language abilities.

Children with extensive histories of OME but normal hearing at the time of audiologic assessment still require in-depth evaluation. In addition to measures that assess hearing thresholds, tests that examine speech perception abilities are beneficial. The PSI (Jerger & Jerger, 1984) may be a valuable tool in the audiologic test battery for use with young (3- to 9-year-old) children. Performance–intensity functions as well as speech-in-competition abilities for words and sentences may be assessed and compared to normative data. These results, in combination with comprehensive assessments of speech-language and academic abilities, may be useful in recommending intervention strategies in the classroom (see "Specific Management Strategies").

Children who continue to experience OME in the school setting also require aggressive audiologic follow-up. These children often experience periods of time in the classroom when their hearing is depressed. These hearing losses may or may not be detected by current screening programs that test hearing only once during the academic year (ASHA, 1990). Some of these hearing losses may not be readily apparent to teachers. Engaging the cooperation of the school nurse or speech-language pathologist to assist in the periodic screening of a child's hearing throughout the school year can sometimes be beneficial. This information would assist the teacher, therapists, and parents as well as physicians in determining the most appropriate follow-up of such children (see following section).

Children with sensorineural hearing loss, of course, may develop OME, and it is likely that this condition is as prevalent in children with cochlear impairment as in those with normal cochlear function. The effect of conductive hearing loss imposed by OME combined with sensorineural hearing impairment can be particularly devastating. The compounded loss will affect the optimum use of amplification and may require gain adjustments in the hearing instrument. Because of the potential for the development of OME, young children with cochlear hearing loss should be monitored aggressively for middle ear pathology and prompt otologic management should be pursued. In our experience, another group of children requiring particular attention are those who have unilateral sensorineural hearing loss and develop OME. Because a child with unilateral hearing loss already may be at a disadvantage (Bess & Tharpe, 1984), the addition of a conductive hearing loss in the "good" ear can be debilitating.

Specific Management Strategies
Although once advocated for children with OME (Northern & Downs, 1984), the use of conventional hearing aids is no longer considered appropriate unless the middle ear condition cannot be medically or surgically resolved. The problems with recommending the use of personal hearing aids for children with OME are multiple. Conventional hearing aids do not improve the problem of adverse signal-to-noise conditions

in the classroom. Hearing aid settings may also require constant adjustment (often on a daily basis) because of the inherent fluctuations associated with the hearing loss resulting from OME.

FM technology in the educational setting appears to be useful in the audiologic management of children with OME. A personal low-output FM unit coupled to open ear molds or a Walkman-type headset is one fitting option. A sound field FM system, however, may be the optimal recommendation. Increasing numbers of classrooms are finding that sound field FM systems are beneficial to all children, not only those with OME. The sound field FM system provides an enhanced signal-to-noise ratio for all children in the classroom. The teacher wears a lapel microphone coupled to an FM transmitter. The FM signal is delivered to an amplifier that converts the FM signal to AM, which is then delivered through speakers strategically located within the classroom. Thus, the teacher's voice is broadcast throughout the classroom. Because the signal is provided to all children in the classroom, there is no identification of any one child as having "special needs." (See Crandell, Smaldino, & Flexer, 1995, for a complete review of sound field FM technology.)

Providing educators with information about the hearing loss associated with OME and how classroom conditions can affect listening abilities is beneficial. Ultimately, it is also important for children with OME to learn to advocate for their own auditory environment. Edwards (1991) has devised an observation scale useful for focusing a teacher's awareness of children who may be having listening difficulties in the classroom. Completed by the teacher, the scale documents how the child handles information presented through the auditory modality: whether the child misunderstands aural information, frequently asks for repetition, is distracted by background noise, or has difficulty following directions. The scale also determines whether the teacher is already using strategies to modify or improve the listening environment and enhance the child's performance.

Until otherwise documented, children with persistent and significant OME histories, or children who experience OME persistently in the classroom environment, should be followed aggressively. Only when a child is found to be functioning typically with respect to his or her peers should professionals forego their concerns about children with extensive histories of OME.

CONCLUSIONS

Some children with early recurrent OME experience peripheral hearing loss that hinders their optimal development. The relationship between specific attributes (degree, duration, and frequency) of the hearing loss and later outcome has yet to be fully delineated. While research into these sequelae continues, it appears prudent to consider children who have experienced early, chronic conductive hearing loss to be at risk for auditory-based speech, language, behavioral, and academic sequelae. Audiologic, communicative, and educational screening of these children may be warranted in order to identify children who require further assessment. Comprehensive evaluations should then be completed to delineate any deficits that may contribute to difficulties in the academic setting. Simple acoustic modifications of the classroom may serve to overcome some of the potentially detrimental consequences of temporary hearing loss associated with OME. Some children may also require more direct, individualized intervention. Without evidence to the contrary, our current knowledge suggests that it would be premature to dismiss as "inconsequential" the hearing losses experienced by some children with OME.

REFERENCES

American Speech-Language-Hearing Association. (1990). Guidelines for the screening for hearing impairment and middle-ear disorders. *Asha, 32*(Suppl. 2), 17–24.

American Speech-Language-Hearing Association. (1991). Guidelines for the audiologic assessment of children from birth through 36 months of age. *Asha, 33*(Suppl. 5), 37–43.

American Speech-Language-Hearing Association. (1995). Report on audiological screening. *American Journal of Audiology, 5,* 74–82.

Anderson, K.L. (1989). *Screening instrument for targeting educational risk.* Danville, IL: Interstate Printers & Publishers.

Anderson, K.L., & Matkin, N. (1996). Pre-school SIFTER. Manuscript in preparation.

Anteby, I., Hafner, H., Pratt, H., & Uri, A. (1986). Auditory brainstem evoked potentials in evaluating the central effects of middle ear effusion. *International Journal of Pediatric Otorhinolaryngology, 12,* 1–11.

Bess, F.H. (1986). Audiometric approaches used in the identification of middle ear disease in children. In J. Kavanaugh (Ed.), *Otitis media and child development* (pp. 70–82). Parkton, MD: York Press.

Bess, F.H., & Tharpe, A.M. (1984). Unilateral sensorineural hearing loss in children. *Pediatrics, 15,* 206–216.

Brandes, P.J., & Ehinger, D.M. (1981). The effects of early middle ear pathology on auditory perception and academic achievement. *Journal of Speech and Hearing Disorders, 46,* 301–307.

Brown, D.P. (1994). Speech recognition in recurrent otitis media: Results in a set of identical twins. *Journal of the American Academy of Audiology, 5,* 1–6.

Coplan, J. (1987). *The Early Language Milestone Scale (ELM Scale).* Austin, TX: PRO-ED.

Crandell, C., Smaldino, J., & Flexer, C. (1995). *Sound-field FM technology.* San Diego, CA: Singular Publications.

DeMarco, S., & Givens, G. (1989). Speech sound discrimination pre- and posttympanostomy: A clinical case report. *Ear & Hearing, 10,* 64–67.

Dobie, R., & Berlin, C. (1979). Influence of otitis media on hearing and development. *Annals of Otology, Rhinology, and Laryngology, 88,* 48–53.

Edwards, C. (1991). Assessment and management of listening skills in school aged children. *Seminars in Hearing, 12,* 389–401.

Eilers, R.E., Widen, J.E., Urbano, R., Hudson, T., & Gonzales, L. (1991). Optimization of automated hearing test algorithms: A comparison of data from simulations and young children. *Ear and Hearing, 12,* 199–204.

Eimas, P., & Clarkson, R. (1986). Speech perception in children: Are these effects of otitis media? In J. Kavanaugh (Ed.)., *Otitis media and child development* (pp. 139–159). Parkton, MD: York Press.

Ellis, M.A., Lee, W.W., Gravel, J.S., & Wallace, I.F., (1995). *Hearing sensitivity and otitis media in one year old infants.* Paper presented at the Sixth International Symposium on Recent Advances in Otitis Media, Bal Harbor, FL.

Feagans, L., Blood, I., & Tubman, J. (1988). Otitis media: Models of effects and implicaions for intervention. In F. Bess (Ed.)., *Hearing impairment in children.* (pp. 347–374). Parkton, MD: York Press.

Feagans, L., Sanyal, M., Henderson, F., Collier, A., & Applebaum, M. (1987). Relationship of middle ear disease in early childhood to later narrative and attentional skills. *Journal of Pediatric Psychology, 12,* 581–594.

Folsom, R., Weber, B., & Thompson, G. (1983). Auditory brainstem responses in children with early recurrent middle ear disease. *Annals of Otology, Rhinology, and Laryngology, 92,* 249–253.

Fria, T.J., Cantekin, E.I., & Eichler, J.A. (1985). Hearing acuity of children with effusion. *Archives of Otolaryngology, 11,* 10–16.

Fria, T.J., & Sabo, D.L. (1979). Auditory brainstem responses in children with otitis media with effusion. *Annals of Otology, Rhinology, and Laryngology, 89,* 200–206.

Friel-Patti, S., & Finitzo, T. (1990). Language learning in a prospective study of otitis media with effusion in the first two years of life. *Journal of Speech and Hearing Research, 33,* 188–194.

Gottlieb, M.I., Zinckus, P.W., & Thompson, A. (1979). Chronic middle ear disease and auditory perceptual deficits. *Clinical Pediatrics, 18,* 725–732.

Gravel, J.S. (1989). Behavioral assessment of auditory function. *Seminars in Hearing, 10,* 216–228.

Gravel, J.S., & Ellis, M.A. (1995). The auditory consequences of otitis media with effusion: The audiogram and beyond. *Seminars in Hearing 16,* 44–59.

Gravel, J.S., McCarton, C.M., & Ruben, R.J. (1988). Otitis media and NICU graduates: A one-year prospective study. *Pediatrics, 82,* 44–49.

Gravel, J.S., & Stapells, D.R. (1992). Tone-ABR and behavioral threshold concordance in young children. *ASHA, 34,* 208.

Gravel, J.S., & Wallace, I.F. (1992). Listening and language at 4 years of age: Effects of early otitis media. *Journal of Speech and Hearing Research, 35,* 588–595.

Gravel, J.S., & Wallace, I.F. (1995). Early otitis media, auditory abilities, and educational risk. *American Journal of Speech-Language Pathology, 4,* 89–94.

Gunnarson, A.D., & Finitzo, T. (1991). Conductive hearing loss in infancy: Effects on later auditory brainstem electrophysiology. *Journal of Speech and Hearing Research, 34,* 1207–1215.

Hall, J.W., & Grose, J.H. (1993). The effect of otitis media with effusion on the masking-level difference and the auditory brainstem response. *Journal of Speech and Hearing Research, 36,* 210–217.

Holte, L., Margolis, R.H., & Cavanaugh, R.M. (1991). Developmental changes in multifrequency tympanograms. *Audiology, 30,* 1–24.

Hunter, L.L. (1995). Hearing loss in young children with otitis media. Paper presented at the Annual Convention of the American Speech-Language-Hearing Association, Orlando, FL.

Hunter, L.L., Margolis, R.H., Rykken, J.R., Le, C.T., Daly, K.A., & Giebink, G.S. (1996). High frequency hearing loss associated with otitis media. *Ear and Hearing, 17,* 1–11.

Jerger, J. (1970). Clinical experience with impedance audiometry. *Archives of Otolaryngology, 92,* 311–324.

Jerger, J.F., & Hayes, D. (1976). The cross-check principle in pediatric audiometry. *Archives of Otolaryngology, 102,* 614–620.

Jerger, S., & Jerger, J. (1984). *Pediatric Speech Intelligibility Test.* St. Louis: Auditec.

Jerger, S., Jerger, J., Alford, B.R., & Abrams, S. (1983). Development of speech intelligibility in children with recurrent otitis media. *Ear and Hearing, 4,* 138–145.

Kemp, D.T. (1978). Stimulated acoustic emissions from the human auditory systems. *Journal of the Acoustical Society of America, 64,* 1386–1391.

Lenhardt, M., Shaia, F., & Abedi, E. (1985). Brainstem evoked response waveform variation associated with recurrent otitis media. *Archives of Otolaryngology, 111,* 315–316.

Mackersie, C.L., & Stapells, D.R. (1994). Auditory brainstem response wave I prediction of conductive component in infants and young children. *American Journal of Audiology, 3,* 52–58.

Marchant, C.D., McMillan, P.M., Shurin, P.A., Johnson, C.E., Turczyk, V.A., Feinstein, J.C., & Panek, D.M. (1986). Objective diagnosis of otitis media in early infancy by tympanometry and ipsilateral acoustic reflex thresholds. *Journal of Pediatrics, 109,* 590–595.

Marchant, C.D., Shurin, P.A., Turczyk, V.A., Wasikowski, D.E., Tuthasi, M.A., & Kinney, S.E. (1984). Course and outcome of otitis media in early infancy: A prospective study. *Journal of Pediatrics, 104,* 826–831.

Margolis, R.H., & Heller, J.W. (1987). Screening tympanometry: Criteria for medical referral. *Audiology, 26,* 197–208.

Menyuk, P. (1986). Predicting speech and language problems with persistent otitis media. In J. Kavanaugh (Ed.), *Otitis media and child development* (pp. 192–208). Parkton, MD: York Press.

Moore, D.R., Hutchings, M.E., & Meyer, S.E. (1991). Binaural masking level difference in children with a history of otitis media. *Audiology, 30,* 91–101.

Mueller, H.G., & Killion, M.C. (1990). An easy method for calculating the Articulation Index. *Hearing Journal, 43*(9), 14, 16–17.

National Institutes of Health. (1993). Consensus statement. *Early identification of hearing impairment in infants and young children, 11,* 1–24.

Needleman, H. (1977). Effects of hearing loss from early recurrent otitis media on speech and language development. In B. Jaffe (Ed.), *Hearing loss in children* (pp. 640–649). Baltimore: University Park Press.

Northern, J.L., & Downs, M.P. (1978). *Hearing in children* (2nd ed.). Baltimore: Williams & Wilkins.

Northern, J.L., & Downs, M.P. (1984). *Hearing in children* (3rd ed.). Baltimore: Williams & Wilkins.

Northern, J.L., & Downs, M.P. (1991). *Hearing in children* (4th ed.). Baltimore: Williams & Wilkins.

Nozza, R. (1988). Auditory deficits in infants with otitis media with effusion: More than a "mild" hearing loss. In D.J. Lim, C.D. Bluestone, J.O. Klein, & J.D. Nelson (Eds.), *Recent advances in otitis media with effusion* (pp. 376–379). Philadelphia: B.C. Decker.

Nozza, R.J. (1987). Infant speech-sound discrimination testing: Effects of stimulus intensity and procedural model on measures of performance. *Journal of the Acoustical Society of America, 81,* 1928–1939.

Nozza, R.J. (1994). The effects of mild hearing loss on infant auditory function. *Infant-Toddler Intervention, 4,* 285–298.

Nozza, R.J. (1995). Critical issues in acoustic-immittance screening for middle-ear effusion. *Seminars in Hearing, 16,* 86–98.

Nozza, R.J., Bluestone, C., Kardatzke, D., & Bachman, R.N. (1994). Identification of middle ear effusion by aural acoustic admittance and otoscopy. *Ear and Hearing, 15,* 310–323.

Nozza, R., Rossman, R., & Bond, L. (1991). Infant–adult differences in unmasked thresholds for the discrimination of consonant-vowel–syllable pairs. *Audiology, 30,* 102–112.

Nozza, R., Rossman, R., Bond. L., & Miller, S. (1990). Infant speech-sound discrimination in noise. *Journal of the Acoustical Society of America, 87,* 339–350.

Nozza, R.J., & Wilson, W.R. (1984). Masked and unmasked pure-tone thresholds of infants and adults: Development of auditory frequency selectivity and sensitivity. *Journal of Speech and Hearing Research, 27,* 613–622.

Owen, M.J., Baldwin, C.D., Luttman, D., & Howie, V.M. (1993). Universality of otitis media with effusion detected by tympanometry on frequent home visits in Galveston, Texas. In D.J. Lim, C.D. Bluestone, J.O. Klein, J.D. Nelson, & P.L. Ogra (Eds.), *Recent advances in otitis media* (pp. 17–20). Toronto, Ontario, Canada: Decker Periodicals.

Paradise, J.L. (1981). Otitis media in early life: How hazardous to development? A critical review of the evidence. *Pediatrics, 68,* 869–873.

Paradise, J.L., Smith, C., & Bluestone, C.D. (1976). Tympanometric detection of middle ear effusion in infants and young children. *Pediatrics, 58,* 198–206.

Pavlovic, C.D. (1991). Speech recognition and five Articulation Indexes. *Hearing Instruments, 42*(9), 20, 22–23.

Pillsbury, H.C., Drake, A.F., Hall, J.W., & Grose, J.H. (1991). The masking-level difference in children having a history of otitis media with effusion. *Archives of Otolaryngology, 117,* 718–723.

Prieve, B.A. (1992). Otoacoustic emissions in infants and children: Basic characteristics and clinical application. *Seminars in Hearing, 13,* 37–52.

Pukander, J.S., & Karma, P.H. (1988). Persistence of middle ear effusion and its risk factors after an acute attack of otitis media with effusion. In D.J. Lim, C.D. Bluestone, J.O. Klein, & J.D. Nelson (Eds.), *Recent advances in otitis media with effusion* (pp. 8–11). Philadelphia: B.C. Decker.

Roberts, J.E., Burchinal, M.R., Collier, A.M., Ramey, C.T., Coch, M.A., & Henderson, F.W. (1989). Otitis media in early childhood and cognitive, academic and classroom performance of the school-aged child. *Pediatrics, 83,* 477–485.

Roush, J., Drake, A., & Sexton, J.E. (1992). Identification of middle ear dis-
function in young children: A comparison of tympanometric screening procedures. *Ear and Hearing, 13,* 63–69.

Shanks, J.E., Stelmachowicz, P.G., Beauchaine, K.L., & Schulte, L. (1992).
Equivalent ear canal volumes in children pre- and post-tympanostomy tube
insertion. *Journal of Speech and Hearing Research, 35,* 936–941.

Skinner, M. (1978). The hearing of speech during language acquisition. *Otolaryngologic Clinics of North America, 11,* 631–650.

Stapells, D.R. (1989). Auditory brainstem response assessment of infants and
children. *Seminars in Hearing, 10,* 229–251.

Stapells, D.R., Gravel, J.S., & Martin, B.A. (1995). Thresholds for auditory brain
stem responses to tones in notched noise from infants and young children
with normal hearing or sensorineural hearing loss. *Ear and Hearing, 16,*
361–371.

Stool, S.E., Berg, A.O., Berman, S., Carney, C.J., Cooley, J.R., Culpepper, L.,
Eavey, R.D., Feagans, L.V., Finitzo, T., Friedman, E.M., Goertz, J.A., Goldstein, A.J., Grundfest, K.M., Long, D.G., Macconi, L.L., Melton, L., Roberts,
J.E., Sherrod, J.L., & Sisk, J.E. (1994). *Otitis media with effusion in young
children: Clinical practice guideline No. 12* (AHCPR Publication No. 94-
0622). Rockville, MD: Agency for Health Care Policy and Research.

Teele, D., Klein, J., & Rosner, B. (1980). Epidemiology of otitis media in children. *Annals of Otology, Rhinology, and Laryngology. Supplement, 89,* 5–6.

Ventry, I., & Weinstein, B. (1983). Identification of elderly people with hearing
problems. *ASHA, 25,* 37–42.

Walker, D., Downs, M.P., Gugenheim, S., & Northern, J.L. (1989). Early Language Milestone scale and language screening of young children. *Pediatrics,
83,* 284–288.

Wallace, I.F., Gravel, J.S., McCarton, C.M., Stapells, D.R., Bernstein, R.S., &
Ruben, R.J. (1988). Otitis media, auditory sensitivity, and language outcomes
at 1 year. *Laryngoscope, 98,* 64–70.

Welsh, L., Welsh, J., & Healy, M. (1981). Effect of sound deprivation on central
hearing. *Laryngoscope, 93,* 1569–1575.

White, K.R., Vohr, B.R., & Behrens, T.R. (1993). Universal newborn hearing
screening using transient evoked otoacoustic emissions: Results of the Rhode
Island Hearing Assessment project. *Seminars in Hearing, 14,* 18–29.

Wiley, T.L., & Smith, P.S.U. (1995). Acoustic-immittance measures and middle-
ear screening. *Seminars in Hearing, 16,* 60–79.

Wilson, W.R., & Thompson, G. (1984). Behavioral audiometry. In J. Jerger
(Ed.), *Pediatric Audiology* (pp. 1–44). San Diego: College-Hill Press.

World Health Organization. (1980). *International classification of impairments,
disabilities, and handicaps: A manual of classification relating to consequences of disease.* Geneva: Author.

Zinkus, P.W., & Gottlieb, M.I. (1980). Patterns of perceptual and academic defects related to early chronic otitis media. *Pediatrics, 66,* 246–253.

4

Effects of Otitis Media with Effusion on Auditory Perception

Joseph W. Hall, III,
John H. Grose, and Amelia F. Drake

In children with a history of chronic otitis media with effusion (OME), audiometric detection thresholds typically return to normal soon after the restoration of adequate middle ear ventilation. However, deficits in more complex auditory processing may persist long after the audiogram has returned to normal limits. For example, it appears that binaural hearing (the coordinated processing of the inputs to the two ears for sound localization and sound detection/recognition in noisy or reverberant environments) and certain aspects of monaural hearing in noise can show deficits, even in the face of normal audiometric thresholds. At this point, such effects found in psychoacoustic studies are probably less controversial than possibly related effects that have been reported for speech, language, and psychological development (Brandes & Ehinger, 1981; Holm & Kunze, 1969; Kessler & Rudolph, 1979; Sak & Ruben, 1982; Teele et al., 1984, 1990). This chapter reviews the effect of chronic OME on the development of some basic auditory abilities and considers the ramifications that the psychoacoustic data may have for hearing in real-world environments.

Preparation of this chapter was supported by a grant (R01DC00397) from the National Institute on Deafness and Other Communication Disorders, National Institutes of Health.

TYPICAL AUDITORY DEVELOPMENT

Before examining effects of OME on hearing, it is worthwhile first to consider some general aspects of typical auditory development. Although the characterization of typical auditory development in children is by no means straightforward, certain broad statements concerning development milestones are possible. A few aspects of hearing, particularly those depending almost exclusively upon cochlear function, appear to be adultlike in infancy. For example, frequency selectivity (the ability to process one frequency component in the presence of other simultaneously present frequency components) is adultlike by age 6 months (Olsho, 1985). This finding is in accord with the fact that otoacoustic emissions from the cochlea are essentially adultlike in infants (e.g., Norton & Widen, 1990). Furthermore, many relatively complex auditory abilities are present in infancy, but most appear to require several years before adultlike levels of performance are reached. For example, the ability to detect a temporal gap (e.g., a short interruption in an ongoing sound) is present in infants ages 3 months to 1 year (Werner, Marean, Halpin, Spetner, & Gillenwater, 1992) but continues to improve until age 6 years or later (Irwin, Ball, Kay, Stillman, & Bosser, 1985; Wightman, Allen, Dolan, Kistler, & Jamieson, 1989). A similar situation pertains to the ability to localize sound; gross localization abilities are apparent in infants ages 6–18 months (Ashmead, Clifton, & Perris, 1987; Morrongiello, 1988; Morrongiello & Rocca, 1987, 1990), with small developmental differences remaining between adults and children ages 7–12 years (Besing & Koehnke, 1995). In general, auditory performance often continues to show improvement over the years that are associated with a relatively high incidence of OME. It is therefore important to separate effects that are related to OME from effects that may be related to changes in typical auditory development.

THEORETICAL CONSEQUENCES
OF CONDUCTIVE HEARING LOSS

Conductive hearing loss is often modeled as a simple, linear attenuation—that is, the conductive loss acts to "turn down" the level of the sound. In this model, it is assumed that the conductive loss has essentially no effect on the structure and function of sensorineural elements. Interestingly, some results from tests of auditory perception are not entirely consistent with this simple, but reasonable, model. For example, Florentine (1976) found that adult listeners chronically fitted with a unilateral earplug experienced changes in auditory localization ability that, over time, largely accommodated to the distorted binaural difference cues that resulted from the unilateral attenuation. Following removal of the earplug, localization abilities gradually returned to normal. In a similar vein, studies investigating binaural hearing abilities of adults with long-standing conductive hearing loss (Hall & Derlacki, 1986; Hall, Grose, & Pillsbury, 1990; Magliulo, Gagliardi, Muscatello, & Natale, 1990) show that normal binaural hearing is not always established immediately following surgical correction of the conductive loss (see later). Such results suggest that a conductive hearing loss may sometimes be associated with some form of neural adaptation or reorganization.

Studies on adults indicating perceptual effects associated with chronic conductive hearing loss raise interesting questions regarding the effect of conductive hearing loss on auditory development in children. For example, animal studies of visual perception (e.g., Weisel & Hubel, 1965) show that visual disability resulting from abnormal visual input is substantially greater (and more likely to be enduring) in young than in old animals. Animal research in the auditory modality has suggested a similar age effect for some forms of sound deprivation (e.g., Knudsen, Knudsen, & Esterly, 1984). These studies support the notion that abnormal sensory input occurring within a "critical period" of development may be associated with chronic perceptual disability. Next we consider evidence for reduced auditory perceptual capabilities in children having a history of OME.

PSYCHOACOUSTIC STUDIES OF
THE EFFECTS OF OTITIS MEDIA WITH EFFUSION

Psychoacoustic Terminology

- **Binaural hearing** refers to auditory processes that depend upon a comparison of information (usually interaural time and interaural level differences) from the two ears. This information can be used to aid the detection of signals in noise and the localization of sound sources.
- **Virtual localization** refers to the situation in which localization cues are presented over headphones such that the perception is similar to that which would occur in the free field. This is usually accomplished by placing microphones in the ear canals of a mannequin placed in a free field, and recording sounds that emanate from various locations around the mannequin. The recordings are then played back to a listener who is wearing earphones.
- **Masking level difference** (MLD) refers to a psychoacoustic test that measures the ability of the auditory system to take advantage of small interaural time and level differences in detecting signals in noisy backgrounds.

- **Comodulation masking release** (CMR) refers to a psychoacoustic test that measures the ability of the auditory system to take advantage of the correlation of temporal fluctuations across frequency in detecting signals in noisy backgrounds.
- **Otoacoustic emissions** are minute sounds that are generated by the normally functioning sensory organ of hearing (the cochlea). These sounds are either spontaneously emitted or are "evoked" by stimulating the ear with a sound.

Binaural Hearing

The binaural hearing skills of children with a history of OME have received considerable attention in the 1990s. Part of the interest in binaural hearing abilities sprang from the research on adult listeners mentioned earlier. This research showed that adults with histories of acquired conductive hearing loss often showed reduced binaural hearing capabilities, even in some cases in which normal audiograms had been restored through middle ear surgery. One explanation of these results is that the auditory system is unable to process normal binaural cues effectively following prolonged experience with diminished or abnormal binaural input. It was therefore of considerable interest to determine whether binaural effects in children might be more dramatic, given the possibility that effects related to diminished/abnormal sensory input might be particularly great during auditory development. Another factor stimulating interest in possible effects of OME on binaural hearing abilities was related to physiologic research using laboratory animals. For example, research on the developing ferret (Moore, Hutchings, King, & Kowalchuk, 1989) indicated that, whereas effects of auditory deprivation were not apparent at the level of the cochlear nucleus, abnormal neural connectivity was evident in inferior colliculus neurons receiving binaural input.

Several studies have employed the masking level difference (MLD) (Hirsh, 1948) to investigate the effect of OME on binaural hearing. Although this test is highly constrained and somewhat artificial, it is a powerful indicator of the sensitivity of the auditory system to minute interaural differences in time and amplitude. Because these cues are critical for the localization of sound and for the detection and understanding of signals in background noise, the MLD can potentially provide important information about the ability of the listener to hear effectively in complex acoustic environments. The conditions used to derive the MLD are summarized in Figure 1. In the baseline condition, both the signal and noise are presented interaurally in phase (S_0 and N_0, respectively). There are no interaural difference cues available for detection in this condition. In the second condition, the noise is again

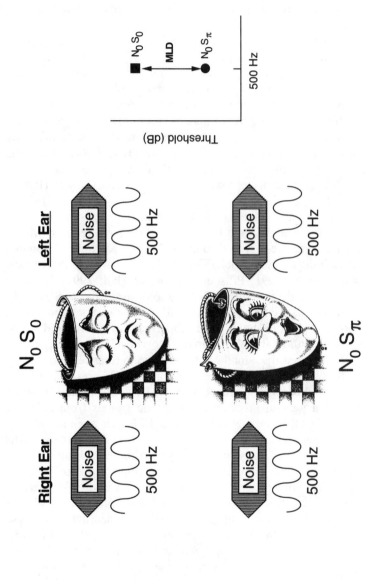

Figure 1. Schematic summary of MLD stimuli. For N_0S_0 stimulation, the signal waveform and the noise waveform are both presented interaurally in phase. For N_0S_π stimulation, the noise waveform is presented interaurally in phase, but the signal is presented with an interaural phase shift of 180°.

presented interaurally in phase (N_0), but the signal is presented 180° out of phase (S_π). In adult, normal-hearing listeners, the N_0S_π threshold is often about 15 dB lower (better) than the N_0S_0 threshold because of the sensitivity of the auditory system to interaural differences of time and amplitude. The improvement in threshold (in decibels) is referred to as the MLD.

Developmental effects have been found for the MLD in the normal-hearing population. For example, Nozza (1987) found significantly smaller pure-tone MLDs for normal-hearing infant listeners as contrasted with an adult control group. Similarly, Hall and Grose (1990) found that MLDs for pure tones presented in wide-band noise were smaller in children age 4–5 years than in adults. However, MLDs for wide-band noise maskers generally have been found to be adultlike by age 5–6 years (Hall & Grose, 1990; Roush & Tait, 1984). When the masking noise is narrow band (e.g., 20–40 Hz wide), adultlike MLDs may not be achieved until approximately age 9 years (Grose, Hall, & Mendoza, 1995).

The available data suggest that children having a history of OME (but normal hearing at the time of testing) often have reduced MLDs when compared with age-matched controls (Besing, Koehnke, & Goulet, 1993; Hall & Grose, 1993; Hall, Grose, & Pillsbury, 1995; Moore, Hutchings, & Meyer, 1991; Pillsbury, Grose, & Hall, 1991). Because the MLD is a derived measure (N_0S_0 threshold minus the N_0S_π threshold), it is critical to specify whether a small MLD appears to be related to an abnormal N_0S_0 threshold, to an abnormal N_0S_π threshold, or to abnormalities in both of these thresholds. Most results in children with OME histories suggest that small MLDs are due to relatively poor N_0S_π thresholds (N_0S_0 thresholds are generally normal). This result is important because it indicates that a history of OME does not appear to be associated with a general problem in extracting signals from noise, at least when the signal is simple and binaural difference cues are absent. The pure-tone detection results indicate that the MLD deficit in the OME groups is confined specifically to the analysis of binaural cues.

A prospective study (Hall et al., 1995) attempted to determine the longitudinal effects of OME on binaural hearing. Children 5 years of age or older were identified who were scheduled for pressure-equalizing (PE) tube surgery because of a history of OME with hearing loss. These listeners were tested on the MLD task before surgery and then at various intervals after surgery in order to characterize the long-term effects of OME on binaural hearing. The results of the presurgery test and a test 1 month following surgery were highly similar, both tests indicating reduced MLDs in many of the children with OME history. Follow-up testing over a 4-year period indicated a slow recovery of the MLD, with most children showing normal MLDs 2 years after surgery (see Figure 2).

Work by Besing and Koehnke (1995) indicated that a history of OME may also be associated with a reduced ability to localize the position of a sound source. These investigators used a virtual localization method to assess the acuity of listeners to changes in apparent location of target stimuli. In this method, targets having cues for localization are presented through headphones rather than in an actual free field, allowing precise experimental control over stimuli. The results of this research indicated that the spatial acuity was significantly poorer in children with a history of OME than in a normally hearing control group.

Monaural Hearing

As noted earlier, previous results have indicated that, for N_0S_0 stimuli, the detection of a signal in noise was not deleteriously affected by a history of OME. One interpretation of this result is that impairments in hearing associated with OME may be restricted to stimuli possessing binaural difference cues. However, the N_0S_0 conditions examined were

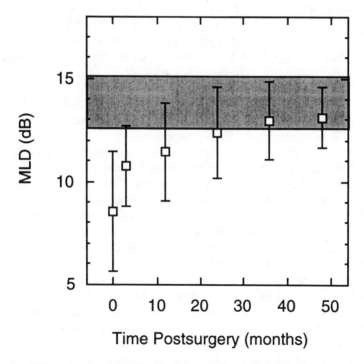

Figure 2.   MLD as a function of time after PE tube surgery. The stippled region is the normal mean ± 1 standard deviation. Error bars around data symbols show ± 1 standard deviation for the OME history group.

extremely simple, involving the detection of a single pure tone in random masking noise. This, of course, leaves open the possibility that effects of OME might exist for more complex forms of monaural auditory perception. With this in mind, Hall and Grose (1994) tested children with a history of OME in a more complex monaural task, one that might be thought of as a monaural analog of the MLD.

The task investigated by Hall and Grose was comodulation masking release (Buus, 1985; Carlyon, Buus, & Florentine, 1989; Cohen & Schubert, 1987; Grose & Hall, 1989; Hall, Haggard, & Fernandes, 1984; McFadden, 1986; Moore & Shailer, 1991). The results of many masking experiments using random noise maskers can be explained by assuming that only the masking noise components within a relatively restricted bandwidth around the frequency of a signal contribute to the masking of the signal. This simple model does not hold, however, when noise components well away from the signal frequency have a fluctuation pattern similar to that of the noise components centered on the signal frequency. The presence of such comodulated noise energy results in an *improvement* in detection threshold (see Figure 3). This improvement in threshold is referred to as CMR. It is generally held that CMR depends upon some form of across-frequency analysis of envelope information. Whereas the binaural MLD depends upon a comparison of information across the two ears, monaural CMR depends upon a comparison of information across separate frequency channels in the same ear.

Hall and Grose (1994) investigated the effects of OME in a longitudinal study, measuring CMR in children having OME with hearing loss, and then obtained follow-up data on two separate occasions following PE tube surgery. In the baseline condition of the experiment, the masking noise was a single, 20-Hz wide-noise band centered on the pure-tone signal frequency. The task of the listener was simply to detect the signal in the masking noise. In the main experimental condition, several additional 20-Hz wide-noise bands were added at frequencies relatively remote from the signal frequency. The noise bands were generated such that their fluctuations were identical to the fluctuations of the on-signal noise band; that is, all bands were comodulated. Because the envelopes of the noise bands were comodulated across frequency, it was expected that the detection threshold would be lower in the experimental condition than in the baseline condition. A dichotic CMR condition was also used. In this condition, the comodulated flanking bands were presented to one ear, and the signal and the on-signal masking band were presented to the other ear. The dichotic condition was included to determine whether impairments associated with a history of OME may be restricted to conditions involving analysis of information across the two ears.

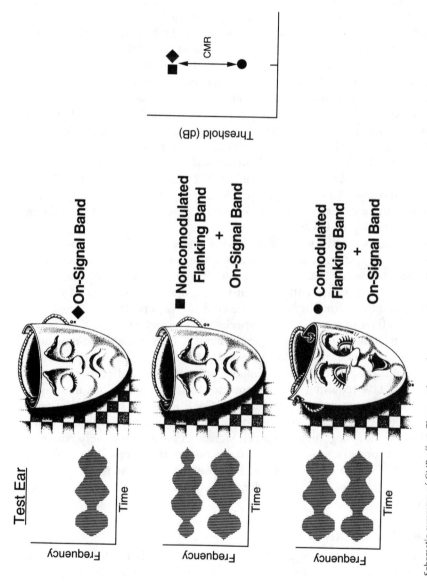

Figure 3. Schematic summary of CMR effect. The waveforms demonstrate the envelopes of the various noise stimuli used in the CMR paradigm. Schematic thresholds are for pure tones presented in the three different types of masking noise.

101

The presurgery test indicated that the monaural CMR values of the children with histories of OME were significantly smaller than normal. Of greater interest was the fact that CMR remained significantly reduced 1–3 months after PE tube surgery, even though audiometric thresholds were normal. This effect occurred because the thresholds in the presence of comodulated noise were relatively poor in the OME group. The baseline thresholds (on-signal band alone) did not differ from normal in the postsurgery test. This means that, whereas the monaural task of detecting a tone in a single narrow band of noise would not appear to be compromised in the postsurgery test, a more complex monaural process based upon an across-frequency analysis of envelope information is apparently reduced, even 1–3 months after restoration of normal hearing thresholds. When retested 4–8 months after surgery, the children with a history of OME showed monaural CMR values that were not different from those of the control group. Thus, compared with recovery of the MLD, the recovery of monaural CMR was relatively rapid in children with a history of OME.

Unexpectedly, the children having histories of OME did not show significantly reduced dichotic CMR on any of the three occasions on which they were tested. However, the variability of results among the control group was relatively great for the dichotic condition. It is possible that this variability among the control listeners served to mask any actual effect that may have been related to history of OME.

In summary, the limited psychoacoustic data available on monaural signal analysis in noise indicate no effect of OME for the simple detection of a pure-tone signal in random noise but reduced performance in a CMR task requiring across-frequency analysis. This raises the possibility that monaural effects related to OME may be likely to exist only for relatively complex auditory processes. In agreement with this point of view, the recognition of speech signals in noise, a relatively complex auditory process, also appears to be poorer than normal in listeners having histories of OME (Gravel & Wallace, 1992; Jerger, Jerger, Alford, & Abrams, 1983; Schilder, Snik, Straatman, & van den Broek, 1994).

CRITICAL PERIOD

It is interesting to note that the reductions of MLD in children with a history of OME were similar to those found in adults whose conductive hearing losses had been corrected with stapedectomy (Hall & Derlacki, 1986; Hall et al., 1990; Magliulo et al., 1990). This may perhaps be seen as evidence against a "critical period" for the development of binaural hearing. This view should be tempered by the fact that it is not clear what magnitude of deprivation effect should be expected in cases of OME. That is, because OME is usually a fluctuating, relatively mild condition, the affected child will usually develop with some degree of exposure to normal binaural cues. The deficits in binaural hearing that do occur may therefore reflect the sequelae of only partial or intermittent deprivation. It is interesting that children with surgically corrected unilateral atresia also show reduced binaural performance (Wilmington, Jahrsdoerfer, & Gray, 1994). Furthermore, the results of these subjects did not always reach normal values even 2 years following corrective surgery. However, even these listeners, having stable, congenital unilateral hearing losses over several years' duration, had postsurgical binaural impairments that were comparable in magnitude to those seen in posttapedectomy adults. Overall, therefore, psychoacoustic evidence for a clearly defined critical period for the development of binaural hearing is not particularly strong. Any role that binaural stimulation via bone conduction (e.g., a listener's own voice) may have on ameliorating effects on auditory deprivation resulting from conductive hearing loss is currently unknown.

INTERPRETATION OF PSYCHOACOUSTIC EFFECTS

At this time, interpretation of psychoacoustic effects of OME must be regarded as somewhat speculative. It is possible to interpret reduced binaural function in terms of the kind of abnormal brain stem neural connectivity that has been found previously in animals developing with conductive hearing loss (Moore et al., 1989). However, it is also possible that brain stem processing is essentially normal but more central auditory structures are relatively inefficient in processing binaural auditory information. A study by Hall and Grose (1993) may provide a clue to the possible role of brain stem involvement in the abnormal MLDs found in many children with OME history. Hall and Grose examined both the MLD and the auditory brain stem response (ABR) in the same group of children. In the ABR component of the study, separate ABRs were determined for each ear. Previous studies (Anteby, Hafner, Pratt, & Uri, 1986; Chambers, 1989; Folsom, Weber, & Thompson, 1983) had indicated that certain aspects of the ABR were often abnormal in children with a history of OME. Specifically, Wave III is often delayed, resulting in a prolonged Wave I–III interwave interval (Anteby et al., 1986; Chambers, 1989). Studies of the binaural interaction component of the ABR also indicate abnormal response in listeners with histories of OME (Dobie & Berlin, 1979; Gunnarson & Finitzo, 1991).

In agreement with previous ABR studies, Hall and Grose (1993) found that the Wave I–III interval was significantly prolonged in children having a history of OME. Significantly reduced MLDs were also found in the listeners with a history of OME. The relation between the MLD and the ABR was not completely straightforward, however. For example, there was no relation between the MLD and aspects of the ABR for either ear alone, either in terms of absolute wave latencies or in terms of interwave intervals. However, significant correlations were obtained between the MLD and measures of ABR asymmetry, including the interear difference in the I–III and I–V interwave intervals. The correlations were in the direction such that small MLDs were associated with large inter-ear asymmetries in ABR. These results are consistent with an interpretation that reduced MLDs in children having a history of OME may be related to abnormal brain stem function. However, further work is called for to better establish whether there are tight relations between OME effects that have been noted separately in psychoacoustic and electrophysiologic paradigms.

RAMIFICATIONS FOR
PERFORMANCE IN REAL-WORLD SETTINGS

Although psychoacoustic tests on children with OME history involve the presentation of highly constrained stimuli over headphones, the results may provide important clues about hearing difficulties that children may face in real-world environments. For example, it is well known that auditory localization and the ability to hear signals at unfavorable signal-to-noise ratios depend critically upon the processing of interaural difference cues. Because the processing of these cues is compromised in children with histories of OME, it is reasonable to assume that such children would potentially be at a disadvantage in noisy classroom situations. For example, consider a situation in which a child is trying to hear the teacher (with the teacher directly in front of the child) when a sound emanating from a second location (e.g., fellow student or other nontarget sound source) is also present. In such a situation, binaural differences provide important cues that could potentially be used to separate the competing sound sources from each other. If such cues were utilized, the child would then have the potential to selectively attend to the signal of choice (we hope, the teacher). If the usefulness of binaural cues is diminished, the ability of the child to attend selectively is likely to be reduced.

Similar assumptions can be made regarding monaural results from the CMR paradigm. It has been argued that CMR reflects an auditory process that contributes to the perceptual separation of simultaneously present auditory sources. When the auditory system is presented with multiple sound sources, each composed of multiple frequency components, a crucial task is to sort out which frequency components go with which auditory source. Again, once auditory sources have been effectively sorted, it becomes possible for the listener to attend to a particular source. One cue that may help the auditory system to assign particular frequency components to particular sources is amplitude comodulation among the frequency components. That is, frequency components that covary in amplitude envelope over time would be assigned to the same source. Once auditory sources have been sorted in terms of comodulation, the listener would be able to selectively attend to the desired sound. A reduction in this auditory ability could again pose difficulties for sound analysis in noisy backgrounds.

POSSIBLE DIRECTIONS FOR FUTURE RESEARCH

Although it is known that deficits in certain basic auditory skills are associated with a history of OME, there is relatively little information about the relation between the age over which hearing loss was present and the outcome for auditory function. For example, it is unclear at this time whether hearing loss over the ages of birth to 2 years is any more deleterious than comparable hearing loss over the interval from, for example, 2 to 4 years. Along similar lines, it remains of interest to settle the issue of whether the lingering auditory perception deficits experienced by children with a history of OME differ in any substantial way from the deficits experienced by adults with acquired conductive hearing losses.

The limited work examining monaural hearing suggests that, for a very simple task such as the detection of a pure tone in a random masking noise, a history of OME has no effect, but for a more complex task, such as CMR, OME is associated with reduced performance. This raises the possibility that the most substantial effects of OME may be associated with very complex types of auditory analysis. An example of such an analysis might involve the ability to selectively process particular auditory targets in the presence of complex interfering stimuli. An advantage of research along these lines is that the stimuli called for begin to approach the complexity that characterizes the auditory sources that the listener must deal with in real-life environments. Research along these lines will therefore allow us to draw firmer conclusions about the effect of OME on hearing in real-life environments.

REFERENCES

Anteby, I., Hafner, H., Pratt, H., & Uri, N. (1986). Auditory brainstem evoked potentials in evaluating the central effects of middle ear effusion. *International Journal of Pediatric Otorhinolaryngology, 12,* 1–11.

Ashmead, D.H., Clifton, R.K., & Perris, E.E. (1987). Precision of auditory localization in human infants. *Developmental Psychology, 23,* 641–647.

Besing, J.M., & Koehnke, J. (1995). A test of virtual auditory localization. *Ear and Hearing, 16,* 220–229.

Besing, J.M., Koehnke, J., & Goulet, C. (1993). *Binaural performance associated with a history of otitis media in children.* Paper presented at the 15th Midwinter Research Meeting of the Association for Research in Otolaryngology, St. Petersburg Beach, FL.

Brandes, P.J., & Ehinger, D.M. (1981). The effects of early middle ear pathology on auditory perception and academic achievement. *Journal of Speech and Hearing Research, 24,* 301–307.

Buus, S. (1985). Release from masking caused by envelope fluctuations. *Journal of the Acoustical Society of America, 78,* 1958–1965.

Carlyon, R.P., Buus, S., & Florentine, M. (1989). Comodulation masking release for three types of modulators as a function of modulation rate. *Hearing Research, 42,* 37–46.

Chambers, R. (1989). Auditory brain-stem responses in children with previous otitis media. *Archives of Otolaryngology—Head and Neck Surgery, 115,* 452–457.

Cohen, M.F., & Schubert, E.D. (1987). Influence of place synchrony on detection of a sinusoid. *Journal of the Acoustical Society of America, 81,* 452–458.

Dobie, R.A., & Berlin, C.I. (1979). Influence of otitis media on hearing and development. *Annals of Otology, Rhinology, and Laryngology. Supplement, 88,* 48–53.

Florentine, M. (1976). Relation between lateralization and loudness in symmetrical hearing losses. *Journal of the American Audiological Society, 1,* 243–251.

Folsom, R.C., Weber, B.A., & Thompson, G. (1983). Auditory brainstem responses in children with early recurrent middle ear disease. *Annals of Otology, Rhinology, and Laryngology, 92,* 249–253.

Gravel, J.S., & Wallace, I.F. (1992). Listening and language at 4 years of age: Effect of early otitis media. *Journal of Speech and Hearing Research, 35,* 588–595.

Grose, J.H., & Hall, J.W. (1989). Comodulation masking release using SAM tonal complex maskers: Effects of modulation depth and signal position. *Journal of the Acoustical Society of America, 85,* 1276–1284.

Grose, J.H., Hall, J.W., & Mendoza, L. (1995). Developmental effects in complex sound processing. In G.A. Manley, G.M. Klump, C. Koppl, H. Fastl, & H. Oekinghaus (Eds.), *Proceedings of the 10th International Symposium on Hearing* (pp. 97–104). Singapore: World Scientific Publishers.

Gunnarson, A.D., & Finitzo, T. (1991). Conductive hearing loss during infancy: Effects on later brain stem electrophysiology. *Journal of Speech and Hearing Research, 34,* 1207–1215.

Hall, J.W., & Derlacki, E.D. (1986). Binaural hearing after middle ear surgery. *Journal of Otology, Rhinology, and Laryngology, 95,* 118–124.

Hall, J.W., & Grose, J.H. (1990). The masking-level difference in children. *Journal of the American Academy of Audiology, 1,* 81–88.

Hall, J.W., & Grose, J.H. (1993). The effect of otitis media with effusion on the masking level difference and the auditory brainstem response. *Journal of Speech and Hearing Research, 36,* 210–217.

Hall, J.W., & Grose, J.H. (1994). The effect of otitis media with effusion on comodulation masking release in children. *Journal of Speech and Hearing Research, 37,* 1441–1449.

Hall, J.W., & Grose, J.H., & Pillsbury, H.C. (1990). Predicting binaural hearing after stapedectomy from pre-surgery results. *Archives of Otolaryngology, 116,* 946–950.

Hall, J.W., Grose, J.H., & Pillsbury, H.C. (1995). Long-term effects on chronic otitis media on binaural hearing in children. *Archives of Otolaryngology, 121,* 843–852.

Hall, J.W., Haggard, M.P., & Fernandes, M.A. (1984). Detection in noise by spectro-temporal pattern analysis. *Journal of the Acoustical Society of America, 76,* 50–56.

Hirsh, I.J. (1948). Binaural summation and interaural inhibition as a function of the level of the masking noise. *Journal of the Acoustical Society of America, 20,* 205–213.

Holm, V.A., & Kunze, L.H. (1969). Effect of chronic otitis media on language and speech development. *Pediatrics, 43,* 833–839.

Irwin, R.J., Ball, A.K., Kay, N., Stillman, J.A., & Bosser, J. (1985). The development of auditory temporal acuity in children. *Child Development, 56,* 614–620.

Jerger, S., Jerger, J., Alford, B.R., & Abrams, S. (1983). Development of speech intelligibility in children with recurrent otitis media. *Ear and Hearing, 4,* 138–145.

Kessler, M.E., & Rudolph, K. (1979). The effects of early middle ear disease on the auditory abilities of third grade children. *Journal of the Academy of Rehabilitative Audiology, 12,* 6–20.

Knudsen, E.J., Knudsen, P.F., & Esterly, S.D. (1984). A critical period for the recovery of sound localization accuracy following monaural occlusion in the barn owl. *Journal of Neuroscience, 4,* 1012–1020.

Magliulo, G., Gagliardi, M., Muscatello, M., & Natale, A. (1990). Masking level difference before and after surgery. *British Journal of Audiology, 24,* 117–121.

McFadden, D. (1986). Comodulation masking release: Effects of varying the level, duration, and time delay of the cue band. *Journal of the Acoustical Society of America, 80,* 1658–1667.

Moore, B.C.J., & Shailer, M.J. (1991). Comodulation masking release as a function of level. *Journal of Acoustical Society of America, 90,* 829–835.

Moore, D.R., Hutchings, M.E., King, A.J., & Kowalchuk, N.E. (1989). Auditory brainstem of the ferret: Some effects of rearing with unilateral ear plug on the cochlea, cochlear nucleus, and projections to the inferior colliculus. *Journal of Neuroscience, 9,* 1213–1222.

Moore, D.R., Hutchings, M.E., & Meyer, S.E. (1991). Binaural masking level differences in children with a history of otitis media. *Audiology, 30,* 91–101.

Morrongiello, B.A. (1988). Infants' localization of sound along the horizontal axis: Estimates of minimum audible angle. *Developmental Psychology, 24,* 8–13.

Morrongiello, B.A., & Rocca, P.T. (1987). Infants' localization of sounds in the horizontal plane: Effects of auditory and visual cues. *Child Development, 58,* 918–927.

Morrongiello, B.A., & Rocca, P.T. (1990). Infants' localization of sounds within hemifields: Estimates of minimum audible angle. *Child Development, 61,* 1258–1270.

Norton, S.J., & Widen, J.E. (1990). Evoked otoacoustic emissions in normal-hearing infants and children: Emerging data and issues. *Ear and Hearing, 11,* 121–127.

Nozza, R.J. (1987). The binaural masking level difference in infants and adults: Developmental change in binaural hearing. *Infant Behavior and Development, 10,* 105–110.

Olsho, L.W. (1985). Infant auditory perception: Tonal masking. *Infant Behavior and Development, 8,* 371–384.

Pillsbury, H.C., Grose, J.H., & Hall, J.W. (1991). Otitis media with effusion in children: Binaural hearing before and after corrective surgery. *Archives of Otolaryngology, 117,* 718–723.

Roush, J., & Tait, C.A. (1984). Binaural fusion, masking level differences, and auditory brainstem responses in children with language-learning disabilities. *Ear and Hearing, 5,* 37–41.

Sak, R.J., & Ruben, R.J. (1982). Effects of recurrent middle ear effusion in preschool years on language and learning. *Journal of Developmental and Behavioral Pediatrics, 3,* 7–11.

Schilder, A.G.M., Snik, A.D.M., Straatman, H., & van den Broek, P. (1994). The effect of otitis media with effusion at preschool age on some aspects of auditory perception at school age. *Ear and Hearing, 15,* 224–231.

Teele, D.W., Klein, J.O., Chase, C., Menyuk, P., Rosner, B.A., & the Greater Boston Otitis Media Study Group. (1990). Otitis media in infancy and intellectual ability, school achievement, speech and language at age 7 years. *Journal of Infectious Disease, 162,* 685–694.

Teele, D.W., Klein, J.O., Rosner, B.A. & the Greater Boston Otitis Media Study Group. (1984). Otitis media with effusion during the first three years of life and the development of speech and language. *Pediatrics, 74,* 282–287.

Weisel, T.N., & Hubel, D.G. (1965). Comparison of the effects of unilateral and bilateral eye closure on cortical unit responses in kittens. *Journal of Neurophysiology, 28,* 1029–1040.

Werner, L.A., Marean, G.C., Halpin, C.F., Spetner, N.B., & Gillenwater, J.M. (1992). Infant auditory temporal acuity: Gap detection. *Child Development, 63,* 260–272.

Wightman, F., Allen, P., Dolan, T., Kistler, D., & Jamieson, D. (1989). Temporal resolution in children. *Child Development, 60,* 611–624.

Wilmington, D., Jahrsdoerfer, R., & Gray, L. (1994). Binaural processing after corrected congenital unilateral conductive hearing loss. *Hearing Research, 74,* 99–114.

5

Phonological Acquisition and Otitis Media

Speech Perception and Speech Production

Richard G. Schwartz,
Maria Mody, and Kakia Petinou

Phonology is the component of language that underlies speech perception and production. The components of phonology are features (e.g., whether a sound is produced with vocal fold vibration or not), segments (consonants and vowels), syllables, words, phrases, and a small set of rules or constraints that govern the form of these components as well as the relationships among them. Phonology serves as a link between abstract representations of these components and their production or perception. Phonology also is the bridge to the expression and comprehension of semantic (i.e., sentence and word meaning), syntactic (i.e., sentence structure), and morphological (i.e., word inflections such as past tense and plural endings as well as derived forms such as -*ly*) information. In order to acquire phonology, a child must be able to perceive, store, and analyze the characteristics (e.g., consonants, vowels, stress patterns, pauses) of the speech and language to which he or she is exposed. Thus, any impairment in speech perception and speech pro-

Preparation of this chapter was supported by a PHS grant from the National Institute on Deafness and Other Communicative Disorders (DC00223).

duction is likely to have its most immediate effect on phonological acquisition. It is also important to understand that such impairments have a secondary effect on the acquisition of other aspects of language, such as morphology and syntax. This chapter focuses on the development of speech perception and production of children with and without histories of otitis media with effusion (OME). Because certain features of morphology (e.g., inflections such as plural and tense markers, freestanding words such as articles that are unstressed) may be directly affected by perception and production abilities, they may be particularly vulnerable to impairment. Our aim is to examine the effects of limitations in perception on the acquisition of phonology and morphology.

The relationship between OME and development of language remains unknown. Parents of children with various types of speech and language impairments frequently report histories of chronic ear infections. However, there are also many children with reported histories of chronic middle ear disease who develop language typically, as well as children who have speech and language impairments and do not have a reported history of chronic OME.

There are many reasons why the potential relationship between OME and speech-language development is complex. It is reasonable to expect that a loss of hearing sensitivity, transient though it may be, would have some negative effect on speech and language development at certain critical points. One question is whether the effect itself might be transitory. For example, if a child spends 15 weeks of her first year of life with middle ear effusion and elevated hearing thresholds and 37 weeks with normal ears, it seems likely that the process of language acquisition and the input upon which it depends should be sufficiently robust that it would withstand the interruption represented by the period of effusion.

To date, there have been a number of large-scale investigations of the speech and language abilities of children with histories of chronic OME. These investigations have yielded conflicting results; some suggest that children with positive histories exhibit general language deficits (see Chapter 6); some reveal more specific deficits, and others have found that there are no differences from children without this history. Most puzzling are findings of speech and language deficits in production but not in perception or comprehension.

The hearing impairment associated with OME poses a different problem for the developing child than other types of hearing impairment. The magnitude of the hearing loss is in the mild to moderate range, with an average hearing level of 25 dB (range from 0 to 50 dB). The hearing loss is conductive and, despite previous assumptions of its effect on lower frequencies, there is evidence of higher frequency loss. Furthermore, the loss is fluctuating and transitory. Gravel and Nozza (Chapter 3) provide a more detailed account of the audiometric profiles associated with OME. Unlike a more stable, more severe hearing loss, the hearing loss associated with OME does not preclude auditory input during an active episode or after resolution of the effusion.

The central question is what aspects of language are most likely to be affected by this type of transient hearing loss. One obvious place to look is in the domain of phonological acquisition. Although phonology is sometimes equated with the acquisition of segments, recent theories of phonology and phonological acquisition have changed this perspective. This chapter reviews these theories of phonological acquisition, those aspects of phonological acquisition we believe to be relevant in studying the effects of OME, and investigations of speech acquisition in children with OME.

PHONOLOGICAL THEORIES

Phonological theories have played an important role in describing normal and disordered phonological acquisition. All of these theories propose some form of abstract mental representation (i.e., the information that is stored about the consonants, vowels, syllables, words, and larger units of an individual's language) and some mechanism for transforming that representation into a surface form (the form that is produced or perceived). Generative phonology (Chomsky & Halle, 1968) and Natural Phonology (Stampe, 1972) are among the earliest theories that have been used in this way. In generative phonology, abstract mental representations were transformed by both universal and language-specific rules to phonetic output (i.e., speech). Generative theories assumed that children have accurate representations that would be altered by reduction and substitution rules. A subsequent, less formal proposal called natural phonology (Stampe, 1972) suggested that abstract representations of words were transformed into output by simplification processes (i.e., phonological processes) that reflect limitations of the human speech mechanism. For example, there is a natural tendency to produce certain voiced consonants (/b/, /d/, /g/, /z/) as their voiceless counterparts (/p/, /t/, /k/, /s/). Stampe (1972) believed that children began development with a full set of simplification processes and, through some unspecified mechanism, eliminated processes that are not permissible in their language.

New theories of phonology offer a radically different approach, considering units of varying size and complexity from features (e.g., voicing) to segments (i.e., consonants and vowels) to syllables (e.g., sequences such as consonant–vowel–consonant) to sequences of syllables (e.g., feet, words, phrases); hierarchical relationships among these units, described as tiers (e.g., words consist of syllables that, in turn, consist of segments that, in turn, consist of features); and the pattern of stress that occurs within and across words (see Figures 1 and 2). The emphasis is on the nature of the representation, with a small number of general rules or constraints. These theories, termed *nonlinear phonology* (see Bernhardt, 1992; Bernhardt & Gilbert, 1992; Bernhardt & Stoel-Gammon, 1994; Schwartz, 1992b; for reviews), include four theories that address different aspects of phonology: autosegmental phonology, lexical phonology, feature geometry, and metrical phonology (see Schwartz, 1992b). Autosegmental phonology describes the tier structure of phonology; lexical phonology deals with, among other things, elaborations to word roots (i.e., inflectional and derivational morphology); feature geometry describes the representation of features; and metrical phonology addresses the rhythmic (i.e., stress) pattern of words and phrases.

Several related approaches to development have been proposed along with these theoretical advances. One is an elaboration of nativist or innatist proposals. In this view, language can be described as a relatively small set of characteristics called parameters. One example is the syllable structure of a language—whether a language predominantly

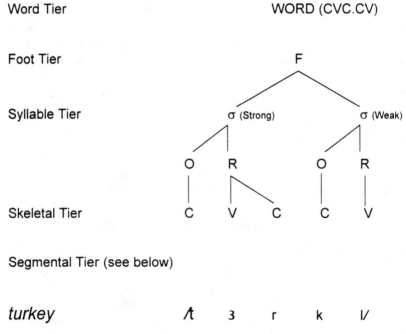

Figure 1. Tier structure in English phonology.

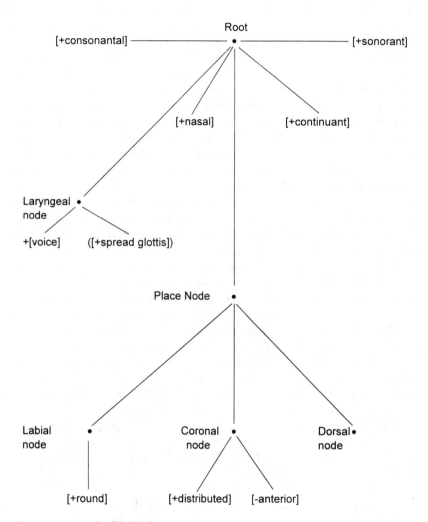

Figure 2. An example of English feature geometry.

has a closed (e.g., consonant–vowel–consonant) or an open (consonant–vowel) syllable structure. These parameters are like the switches in a computer printer. They have default or initial settings so that, if a Russian tourist purchases a printer in the United States, the switches are set to print English characters. To print Cyrillic characters, the settings of these switches must be changed. Similarly, a young child at the beginning of phonological acquisition has initial parameter settings. If the initial setting for syllable structure is open syllables and the child is acquiring Italian (a language with open syllables), the setting does not need to be changed. However, if the child is acquiring English, in which closed syllables predominate, the setting must be changed in response to the input.

An alternative view, termed *optimality theory* (Prince & Smolensky, in press) is that phonology is a set of constraints (e.g., syllables must have beginnings or onsets). In a given language, some constraints are extremely important and cannot be violated, whereas violations of others can be tolerated. The prioritizing of these constraints differs from language to language and must be learned by the child. This suggests a more gradual course of acquisition with greater variability both within and across children than the binary-parameter-setting view. Optimality theory shares some common characteristics with a more general theory of development called a *dynamic system*. Dynamic system theory (see Schwartz, 1992a, for a review) suggests that organisms (including developing children) are self-organizing within the general constraint of a biologic envelope. The self-organization is driven by the input and is reflected in behavior as transitions from the absence of a given pattern, to a period of instability, to a new stable pattern. This may be true for categories of consonants and vowels, sylllables, words, and larger units.

In summary, theories of phonology have expanded our scope of interest beyond consonants and vowels to include larger units (i.e., syllables, words, and phrases) and suprasegmentals (i.e., the stress pattern of words and phrases). They have also clarified relationships between phonology and other aspects of language, particularly morphology and syntax. These theories point the way for broader investigations of phonological acquisition in children developing typically, in children with phonological disorders, and in children at risk for phonological disorders. Importantly, they all characterize input as having a major role in acquisition. In children with OME, this is the key issue: whether their access to input is compromised.

Although theoretical models provide a general framework for describing the nature of phonological acquisition, they do not specify the psychological mechanisms involved. One such attempt is the two-lexicon model (Menn & Matthei, 1992; Schwartz 1988). This model attempts to describe the relationship between perception and production as separable but linked levels of representation. Within the context of such models, it is possible to explain the fact that the child has an underlying representational structure that has been formed from a combination of some initial state and input and that the formed representation may be differentially accessible from perception and production. Importantly, the child's representations, as well as perception access and production access to these representations, at a given point in development may be different from those of an adult and may be influenced by a lower level deficit (i.e., a deficit in speech perception and speech production) (see Figure 3).

PHONOLOGICAL ACQUISITION

Early Speech Perception and Production

Despite earlier held beliefs that phonological acquisition begins with the emergence of meaning, the bases for phonological acquisition can be traced to speech perception and production of young infants. Researchers have shown that infants have remarkable capabilities to discriminate a wide range of speech contrasts that ultimately will be important in the acquisition and use of language (see Kuhl, 1987, for a review). In recent years, investigators have also revealed significant developmental changes in infants' perceptual behavior that indicate the beginning of acquiring the ambient language. Specifically, 6-month-old infants are able to discriminate consonant contrasts that are part of their native language as well as contrasts from other languages that are not present in their native language. By 10–12 months of age, infants can no longer discriminate the nonnative contrasts (Werker, Gilbert, Humphrey, &

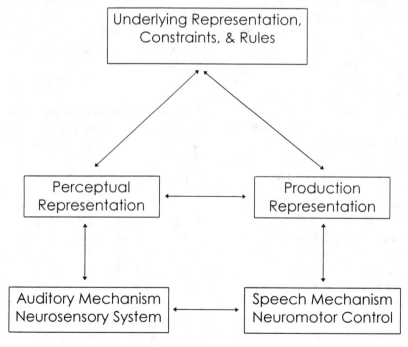

Figure 3. Two-lexicon model of phonological acquisition.

Tees, 1981; Werker & Lalonde, 1988; Werker & Tees, 1984). This is particularly true for those contrasts close to contrasts in their native language (Best, McRoberts, & Sithole, 1988; Best et al., 1990). Sensitivity to the structure of vowel categories and prosodic patterns of the native language appear even earlier. Some language-specific vowel category information seems to be acquired by 6 months of age (e.g., Griesser & Kuhl, 1989). Polka and Werker (1991) found that 10- to 12-month-olds discriminated an English contrast but not a nonnative contrast. Unlike the consonant studies, most of the 6- to 8-month-olds discriminated the English vowel contrast but not the nonnative contrast. This suggests an earlier shift for vowels than for consonants.

Perceptual specialization for prosody may appear even earlier. For example, 4-day-old infants prefer listening to passages from their native language when contrasted to passages of a foreign language but do not discriminate between two foreign languages (Mehler et al., 1988). Jusczyk, Friederici, Wessells, Svenkerud, and Jusczyk (1993) have demonstrated another developmental change in speech perception. Six-month-olds exposed to English showed no preference for English or Dutch words, whereas 9-month-olds did exhibit a preference for the English words. The effect of differential preference in the 9-month-olds disappeared when the speech was filtered so as to remove segmental content (consonants and vowels and their sequences). Because Dutch and English have similar prosodic patterns, this suggests that the children relied on the segmental characteristics of words to distinguish them. In a follow-up experiment, Jusczyk and his colleagues (1993) found that 6-month-olds were able to distinguish English and Norwegian words that had markedly different prosodic patterns. Two related findings concern a change from 4½ to 6 months of age in English-exposed infants' sensitivity to clause boundaries in English and in a nonnative language (Hirsh-Pasek et al., 1987) as well as a change in sensitivity to word boundaries in their native language from 9 to 11 months of age (Woodward et al., 1995). Thus, there are important developmental changes in speech perception during the first year of life that depend directly upon the child's auditory access to the language of the environment.

There are significant changes in children's production during the first year of life that parallel some of the changes in perception. For example, at approximately 6 months of age, children's vocalizations expand to encompass a wide variety of sounds, including sounds that are not part of their native language (Oller, 1980; Stark, 1980). As children begin babbling between 8 and 10 months of age, their vocalizations increasingly resemble the ambient language in the environment (de Boysson-Bardies et al., 1992). Specifically, beyond individual differences and universal trends (e.g., labials and dentals occur more frequently than velars, stops and nasals are more frequent than fricatives and liquids), the babbling of children exposed to French, English, Japanese, or Swedish reflected the relative frequencies of the phonetic inventories of their languages. Thus, the auditory input to infants shapes their emerging speech production characteristics. If infants are deprived of all or part of this input, they will not follow a typical course of early vocal development.

Besides cross-linguistic investigations, another source of evidence for the importance of input in shaping these early vocalizations is the early speech of children with hearing impairments. Young children with hearing impairments are different from their hearing peers in a number of early speech characteristics: 1) reduced frequency of babbling, 2) simpler syllable structures, 3) limited production of multisyllabic utterances, and 4) a limited phonetic repertoire (e.g., Kent, Osberger, Netsell, & Hustedde, 1978; Oller, Eilers, Bull, & Carney, 1980; Stark, 1983; Stoel-Gammon & Otomo, 1986). Thus, the form, the nature, and the variety of babbling is strongly influenced by the input to the child. The accessibility of the input is also a critical factor in the development of children's babbling repertoire; a sensory impairment such as the hearing loss associated with OME may restrict the child's access to that critical input.

Early Words Children's earliest words are often considered as a separable period of phonological acquisition (Ingram, 1976). Although there is a great deal of information regarding this early period of phonological development that begins with children's earliest words and ends approximately 8 months later with the acquisition of the 50th word in production, two characteristics are particularly noteworthy. The first concerns the relationship between the characteristics of babbling and children's earliest words. There is now ample evidence of a close relationship between the phonetic characteristics of babbling and of children's earliest words (e.g., de Boysson-Bardies et al., 1992; Vihman, Macken, Miller, Simmons, & Miller, 1985). Given a child whose babbling repertoire is restricted in comparison to that of a typically developing child, we would expect comparable limitations in the child's early vocabulary. In children with OME and an associated hearing loss during their first year of life, we might expect to see parallel limitations in early vocabulary. A second related phenomenon is referred to as phonological selectivity (see Schwartz, 1988, for a review). In their early production vocabularies, some universal tendencies aside, children tend to select words with certain phonological characteristics and fail to select others. For example, one child may prefer bilabials (e.g., /p/, /b/) and produce few words that begin with alveolars (e.g., /t/, /d/) or velars (e.g., /k/, /g/), whereas another child may have a preference for velars and alveolars. A series of experimental studies suggest that once such patterns are established they are not influenced by asymmetries in input (Schwartz, 1988). They do appear to reflect the preferences first exhibited in babbling. This phenomenon is important because it reflects the earliest stage of the phonological organization of the lexicon, which becomes better established later in development and plays a role in lexical processing by adults.

Early Phonological Acquisition Much of the current work on phonological acquisition has added more detail to the large-scale studies of consonant and vowel acquisition that provided us with commonly used consonant and vowel acquisition data (see Vihman, 1993). The large-scale studies indicated that children generally produce vowels accurately by 2 years of age. Stop consonants, glides, and nasals tend to be acquired earlier than fricatives, affricates, and liquids. In terms of place of articulation, alveolar and labial consonants tend to be acquired earlier than palatal and velar consonants. These normative data provided no information concerning the types of errors children make. The application of phonological processes to describe the course of typical development led to the description of the error patterns and their disappearance (Ingram, 1976). In general, patterns involving the omission of segments (e.g., /dʌ/ for *duck*) tend to disappear before those involving substitutions of one consonant for another. Substantial individual differences were also revealed. Unlike the earlier data that focused only on single consonants, information on phonological processes also led to the examination of context-based errors such as assimilation, in which the error reflects the influence of another consonant in the word (e.g., /kʌk/ for *cut*). All of these normative studies also revealed inter- and intrachild variability that was not readily described in any existing framework.

The newer theories of phonology reviewed earlier provide some new approaches to the description of phonological acquisition during this period (e.g., Bernhardt, 1992; Bernhardt & Gilbert, 1992; Bernhardt & Stoel-Gammon, 1994; Schwartz, 1992a, 1992b). These theories allow a more systematic description of errors that might entail a number of phonological processes. For example, a child may substitute /t/ for a number of targets, leading to assumptions that a child is stopping (/t/ for /s/), fronting (/t/ for /k/), and backing (/t/ for /p/). Using a feature geometry (see Figure 3), one might say instead that place and continuacy are not yet specified and so the child produces what is called a default, in this case the consonant /t/. Autosegmental phonology permits the description of positional constraints for a child who produces certain consonants in only one syllable or word position, instead of describing the substitutions in other positions as variable processes. Similarly, a pattern limiting the variety of consonants to final position can be described. Finally, patterns such as final consonant omission can be explained in terms of an underlying representation that has only consonant–vowel syllables.

One phenomenon that has received a great deal of attention is children's well-documented tendency to omit unstressed syllables (e.g., Ingram, 1976). The pattern of omission is more complex; children are more likely to omit weak or unstressed syllables that occur in the initial position of words or a larger phonological unit called a foot (i.e., a word or phrase consisting of a sequence of stressed and unstressed syllables). There are two types of feet: iambic, which have a weak syllable followed by one or more strong syllables, and trochaic, which have a strong syllable followed by zero or more syllables. English has a dominant troachaic pattern, whereas other languages may follow other patterns. For example, in words, the initial syllable of the word *balloon* is more likely to be omitted than the second unstressed syllable of the word *bottle*. In noun phrases such as *the dog*, children are most likely to omit the article. Some investigators have suggested that a trochaic bias is universal because children's productions of words reflected a bias toward a trochaic metrical pattern, whereas others have suggested that the pattern reflects the pattern of the ambient language (see Schwartz & Goffman, 1995, for a recent review). Another controversy concerning children's omission of unstressed syllables is whether these omissions are attributable to limitations in children's perception of these syllables (Echols, 1993; Echols & Newport, 1992) or some limitation in the production of these syllables or foot types (Gerken, 1991; Gerken, Landau, & Remez, 1990). It is difficult to come to a final determination regarding these two possible sources, in part because most of the studies to date have relied on production data to infer children's perceptual abilities.

Another significant development during this period is the emergence of inflectional morphology. Between ages 20 and 36 months, children acquiring English develop productive use of morphological markers such as final -*s* for plurals, third person singular, and possessives; -*ing* for present progressive; *a* and *the* for indefinite and definite articles; auxiliary and copula *to be*; and regular past tense -*ed* (e.g., Brown, 1973; de Villiers & de Villiers, 1973). Although there are widespread individual variations in the rate of acquisition, the order of acquisition remains relatively consistent: Present progressive, regular plural, and regular past tense are among the first acquired, followed by third person singular, articles, auxiliary *to be,* and copula *to be*. This aspect of language acquisition is important because it reflects underlying syntactic knowledge (e.g., subject–verb agreement in person and number) and because it involves inflectional endings. As mentioned earlier, inflectional morphology and function words are vulverable to omission early in the course of normal acquisition because they tend to be unstressed syllables or final consonants and consequently are brief and low in intensity. As a result, they are not as salient as the content words that tend to be maintained in early utterances. Consequently, some investigators have attributed their vulnerability in typically developing children and in children with language impairment to the potential difficulty they pose in perception (see Schwartz & Goffman, 1995).

Later Phonological Acquisition

By 4 years of age, children have acquired a great deal of the phonology of their language (Ingram, 1976). From 4 to 7 years of age, children complete the acquisition of their phonetic inventory. This involves the correct production of consonants and consonant clusters across contexts, and the correct production of multisyllabic words. During this period, children for the first time can successfully perform active perception tasks such as identification (e.g., judging whether a given stimulus is a /b/ or a /p/) and discrimination (e.g., judging whether two stimuli are the same or different, judging which of two stimuli most closely resembles a third stimulus). During and beyond this period, children's productions are increasingly refined (Kent, 1976). Specifically, children's abilities to match the timing and coarticulation of adults develop gradually. This aspect of development continues beyond this period through 12 years of age. Various abilities that appear to be related to later reading skills also emerge during this period. Among these abilities are a group of skills called phonological awareness, such as identifying the segments at the beginnings and the ends of words, segmenting words, and providing rhyming words (e.g., Bradley, 1992; Trieman & Zukowski, 1991).

Children in this age range are also able to perform successfully, for the first time, tasks that reflect phonological working memory (see Gathercole & Baddeley, 1993, for a review). Among the tasks that have been examined is the ability to repeat nonsense words of increasing length. A number of investigators have observed a similarity or interference effect exhibited when children make more errors in repeating a list of words that are phonologically similar than in repeating a list of words that are phonologically dissimilar. Such tasks are thought to reflect children's ability to code and hold or represent words in a short-term memory and to make reference to the phonological characteristics of their existing lexicon. Another potentially relevant set of findings from children in this age range comes from work on spoken word recognition (e.g., Walley, 1988). Walley found that children's word recognition was dependent on segmental information throughout the word, whereas adults rely more heavily on word-initial segments. She attributed this difference to changes in lexical representation and organization. Young children may not yet have the well-established representation and organization that adults can use for recognition, relying on partial information from the beginnings of words. In summary, this period of development is a rich one in which children's phonological development and task performance abilities advance in a number of areas. Particularly because of their ability to perform complex tasks, it is possible to examine subtle aspects of speech production and speech perception.

IMPACT OF OTITIS MEDIA
WITH EFFUSION ON PHONOLOGICAL ACQUISITION

Speech Perception in Children with Otitis Media with Effusion

Despite the fact that speech perception is the most likely locus of deficit in children with histories of OME, it has received limited investigative attention. Dobie and Berlin (1979) suggested some possible effects of OME on speech perception. Interestingly, even with a filtered signal designed to resemble a 20-dB hearing loss, adult listeners were inconsistent in their misperception of phrases. Dobie and Berlin predicted that word-final voiceless fricatives, short unstressed syllables, or words (i.e., function words or inflectional endings) were most likely to be affected. Unfortunately, they did not address the potential effects on consonant discrimination or identification.

The speech perception of children with OME has been examined in two investigations, both of which have focused on children over 5 years of age. Eimas and Clarkson (1986) showed that 6-year-old children with histories of OME (i.e., an average of 3.4 infections per year up to the time of testing) had difficulty in discriminating and identifying synthetic (/da/ versus /ta/) and natural (*bath* versus *path*) stimuli differing in voicing dimensions. Specifically, the children with a history of OME (OME positive) were less consistent in assigning the stimuli to their respective phonetic categories, required longer voice onset time intervals before perceiving a change in voicing, and had lower levels of discrimination compared with their counterparts without a history of OME (OME negative; i.e., an average of 0.21 infections per year). A second investigation involved a comparison of three groups of children with different durations of effusion (Menyuk, 1986) in their performance across a number of standardized and nonstandardized tasks. The three groups were children who had experienced 32 days of effusion, children with 32–108 days of effusion, and children with more than 108 days of effusion. At 7 years of age, the children in the high-effusion group made more errors on contrasts involving voiced and voiceless plosives and voiceless continuants on a standardized test of minimal-pair discrimination.

In another experiment, 9-year-old children with and without histories of OME were compared in their abilities to identify and to make temporal order judgments about syllable pairs varying in degree of acoustic phonetic contrast (Mody et al., in press). The otitis-positive children had bilateral OME at 30% or more of six visits during the first year of life, as confirmed by otoscopic examination. The otitis-free children were OME free at 80% or more of their first-year visits. Although the groups did not differ in their overall identification of syllables or in their overall abilities to make temporal order judgments, the OME-positive children had more difficulty with the syllable pairs differing by a single feature than with those differing by more than one feature. This finding suggests that the disruption of input caused by the early occurrence of OME has a subtle but long-term effect on speech perception. The resultant perceptual deficits may also have a subtle impact on subsequent phonological acquisition and on more general aspects of development, such as language acquisition and academic performance. One issue that has yet to be investigated concerns the timing of OME. There may be sensitive periods in language acquisition during which disruptions in input have a more serious and a longer-lasting impact.

Speech Production in Otitis Media with Effusion
To date, two investigations have examined the early speech production of children with OME (Luloff, Menyuk, & Teele, 1991; Petinou, Mody, Schwartz, Gravel, & Wallace, in press). In both of these investigations, the OME-positive and OME-negative children, identified by OME status in the first year of life, exhibited differences in the diversity of their babbling. In the investigation conducted by Petinou and her colleagues, both the OME-positive (OME bilaterally by otoscopy or tympanometry at 30% or more of six first-year visits) and the OME-negative bilaterally OME free at 100% of the visits) children exhibited increasing productivity of babbling from 10 to 14 months. However, the diversity of the inventory was greater for the OME-negative than for the OME-positive children. This parallels the findings concerning the babbling inventories of subjects with hearing impairment (Stark, 1983; Stoel-Gammon, 1988; Stoel-Gammon & Otomo, 1986) and would be expected to be reflected in these children's first words. Only one published report (Donahue, 1993) has focused on the early words of a child with chronic OME (i.e., six episodes within the first 10 months of life). This was a diary study in which the data were the author's broad phonetic transcription of her daughter's lexical acquisition from the onset of first words to the fre-

quent use of multiword utterances. From 9 to 22 months, the child's phonology consisted only of vowels, nasals, glottal stops, and intonation. This could be easily described using the feature geometry discussed earlier. In the next stage, her phonology involved consonant harmony (all consonants in a word are similar or identical). When stop consonants first emerged, there was a strong emphasis on bilabials. This child ultimately proved to have a phonological disorder. The limitation of such a case is that it is difficult to determine whether this is an example of individual variation or a pattern that might be attributed to OME. Although group studies continue to offer important insights into this relationship, more case studies, particularly from this period, would add significantly to our understanding of the early effects of OME on the acquisition of phonology.

The phonological abilities of older children with histories of OME have been extensively investigated (see Roberts & Clarke-Klein, 1994, for an extensive review). The vast majority of these investigations have focused on individual consonant errors and on error patterns in children 3 years of age or older. The investigations have been quite mixed in the number and diversity of subjects, ranging from single-case studies (e.g., Donahue, 1993) to large-scale, cross-sectional studies with cohorts (e.g., Roberts, Burchinal, Koch, Footo, & Henderson, 1988). In the nature of information regarding the occurrence of OME, the studies have ranged from retrospective studies relying on parent report or medical records for the period from birth to 3 years of age (e.g., Bishop & Edmundson, 1986; Paden, Novak, & Beiter, 1987; Shriberg & Smith, 1983) to prospective studies in which episodes of OME are documented through tympanometry or ostoscopy (e.g., Teele, Klein, & Rosner, 1984; Roberts et al., 1988). The dependent measures have varied both in the data source (e.g., standardized articulation tests, spontaneous samples) and in the analysis of samples (counting absolute numbers of consonant errors or the frequency of phonological processes). The results have been quite mixed, with some investigations (e.g., Bishop & Edmundson, 1986; Teele et al., 1984) showing no difference in speech production between children with a history of chronic OME and children with no history of chronic OME. Other investigations (e.g., Roberts et al., 1988) have demonstrated general differences between OME-positive and OME-negative children. Notably, in a carefully designed, prospective study, Roberts and her colleagues (1988) found that phonological processes disappeared more slowly from the speech of OME-positive children than from the speech of OME-negative children after 4½ years of age. Several studies have found specific patterns of deficit associated with a positive history of OME. However, there is little consistency in the error patterns identified with OME. For example, Shriberg and Smith

(1983) found errors in word-initial consonants and in nasals; Paden and her colleagues (1987) found errors on velars, postvocalic consonants, and liquids; and, in a separate study, Paden and her colleagues (1987) and Paden (1994) found errors on velars and cluster reductions. The only thing that can be concluded from this body of literature is that we do not yet know whether there is a phonological effect of OME or, if there is such an effect, what other associated variables might play a role.

IMPACT OF OTITIS MEDIA
WITH EFFUSION ON MORPHOLOGICAL ACQUISITION

The acquisition of function words (e.g., articles; auxiliary and copula verbs *to be*) and inflectional endings (e.g., third person singular, plurals, possessives) are of great interest in studying the effects of OME on language acquisition. These elements are unstressed or occur in word-final position with limited intensity. As Dobie and Berlin (1979) noted, this aspect of language may be particularly vulnerable to the hearing loss associated with OME. One of the hallmarks of specific language impairment (SLI) is an impairment in the production of function words and inflectional morphemes that is greater than impairments in other areas of language. Leonard (1989) hypothesized that children with SLI experience difficulties in perceiving these elements because they have low phonetic substance. Further support for this notion came from cross-linguistic studies of SLI (Leonard, 1994). In children with SLI acquiring languages in which function words and inflectional endings have characteristics that might make them more readily perceptible, these difficulties are not present.

It is difficult to parcel out morphological deficits in most investigations of OME because of the use of standardized tests that include only a few relevant items or the use of mean length of utterance derived from spontaneous samples in which morphology is only one of several factors. A retrospective study by Weber (1982) focused on children's ability to repeat morphological endings presented at normal and attenuated speech presentation levels. The dependent variable was the number of verbs repeated correctly by the subjects. Children with histories of otitis media performed similarly to their relatively otitis-free peers at a 65-dB presentation level. At the lowest presentation level of 35 dB, the OME population had difficulty repeating regular past tense (*-ed*) and third person singular (*-s*) verb markers. In the study reviewed by Menyuk (1986), persistent OME also had a significant effect on morphological development. The paradigms used by both investigators are limited by the fact that inferences about perception are based on production data. Logically, if a child is asked to repeat a particular item and he or she does so correctly, it can be assumed that the child accurately perceived the target. However, if the child does not repeat correctly, then it is impossible to make inferences about the source of error and the child's underlying representation of the target item unless perception is examined directly.

ISSUES AND FUTURE DIRECTIONS

The literature is somewhat frustrating in that the relationship between OME and phonological acquisition remains unknown. We continue to suspect that some children with a history of OME will not exhibit the typical course or timing of phonological acquisition, whereas other children with this history will not exhibit deficits. However, the group studies appear to have led us to a dead end in which we cannot predict the phonological outcome of OME for an individual child. There are several reasons this may be true: 1) Group studies may conceal individual differences; 2) measures without sufficient sensitivity may fail to reveal deficits; 3) most investigations to date may have focused on later periods of development, whereas relationships between the course of OME and subsequent phonological acquisition may only be observable earlier in development; and 4) the resultant hearing loss may be the key variable rather than the OME itself.

Investigators have long noted the individual differences among children in the general course and sequence of phonological acquisition (see Vihman, 1993). When one considers that typically developing children exhibit a range of individual differences and then adds the variation introduced by OME, the effects of OME may be masked. This does not mean that group studies are not viable. Instead, it means that group studies must include within-subject (i.e., repeated measure) comparisons, some type of item analysis, or individual subject data. One example of the kind of data that an individual analysis can yield was presented by Donahue (1993).

Children with a history of OME eventually acquire the phonology of their native language. There are no reports of children with a history of OME who fail to accomplish this. They produce phrases, consonants, vowels, and prosodic patterns that appear to be characteristic of their native language. The measures that have been used to date may not be sufficiently sensitive to reveal subtle deficits in speech production or in the phonological organization of the lexicon. Furthermore, in the absence of specific hypotheses regarding the impact of OME on phonological acquisition, most investigators have taken more global approaches to comparing speech production across groups. With more focused sampling techniques and more focused analyses using the theoretical approaches described earlier, it might be possible to identify more focal deficits. The deficits exhibited by these children might be too subtle to be detected by listener-perceived transcription and counting of errors or phonological processes. Instead, more detailed analysis of individual children's phonologies or acoustic analyses examining temporal and spectral aspects of speech may be more revealing. Research to date has focused almost exclusively on speech production, with occasional production-based influences regarding speech perception. The Eimas and Clarkson (1986) study does suggest that there are speech perception deficits not unlike those seen in children with SLI (e.g., Sussman, 1993). Given that we expect perception to be the primary locus of deficit, it is surprising that there has not been more work done in this area. Other experimental paradigms such as the tasks that assess phonological working memory or the phonological organization of the lexicon may reveal other deficits that are not revealed by standardized tests or by nonstandardized assessments of spontaneous speech.

The third potential limitation of the existing body of research is the period of development that has been examined. It is likely that the most visible effects of early episodes of OME occur during early periods of phonological acquisition, before 3 years of age. These periods of development in children with OME remain largely unexplored. It is indeed possible, as Menyuk (1986) suggested, that by later ages many of the deficits attributable to OME are no longer or are only inconsistently apparent. We disagree with Menyuk in that we believe children may compensate for these developments without truly resolving them. At these later ages, then, it may require measures of increasing sensitivity to reveal these residual deficits.

The final concern and direction for future research concerns the primary variable of interest, the occurrence of OME. It may well be the case that this is not the critical variable of interest. Instead, it may be the degree, the pattern, and the duration of hearing loss (see Chapter 3) that determines the effect of OME on phonological acquisition. The preliminary experiment reported by Dobie and Berlin (1979) suggests that this is true.

A significant amount of work remains ahead in speech perception, speech production, and morphological acquisition if we are to understand the impact of OME on phonological acquisition. Until such work is begun, we can only speculate about its effect on phonological acquisition by any individual child or about what preventive measures might be taken.

In the meantime, practitioners are faced with children who exhibit speech and language disorders that might be the result of earlier histories of OME. There is no reason to assume that the procedures that have been shown to be effective in the remediation of speech and language impairments would not be effective for children with histories of OME (see Fey, 1986, for a review). Several additional considerations may be warranted, however. First, early intervention using language stimulation techniques may be advisable for children who, by 1 year of age, have a significant history of OME. This can take the form of parent training to provide an enriched language environment. Such preventative intervention might be provided to all such children. Alternatively, given limited resources, this type of intervention might be reserved for children who have a positive history of OME and are already exhibiting slow speech and language development between 18 and 24 months of age. Second, careful consideration should be given to the fluctuating hearing losses exhibited by young children with a history of OME. This may involve providing these children with FM systems for use in therapy, in preschool, and in school settings to provide amplification that will improve the speech signal that serves as input for language acquisition. It may also require a greater emphasis on speech production and speech perception than is typically provided in intervention. A clearer understanding of the relationship between OME and speech perception and speech production will naturally lead to intervention techniques that will ameliorate the effects of this common childhood disease on phonological acquisition.

REFERENCES

Bernhardt, B. (1992). Developmental implications of nonlinear phonology. *Clinical Linguistics and Phonetics, 6,* 259–281.

Bernhardt, B., & Gilbert, J. (1992). Applying linguistic theory to speech-language pathology: The case for nonlinear phonology. *Clinical Linguistics and Phonetics, 6,* 123–145.

Bernhardt, B., & Stoel-Gammon, C. (1994). Nonlinear phonology: Introduction and clinical application. *Journal of Speech and Hearing Research, 37,* 123–143.

Bernstein, L., & Stark, R. (1985). Speech perception development in language-impaired children: A 4-year follow-up study. *Journal of Speech and Hearing Disorders, 50,* 21–30.

Best, C., McRoberts, G., Goodell, E., Womer, J., Insabella, G., Klatt, L., Luke, S., & Silver, J. (1990). *Infant and adult perception of nonnative speech contrasts differing in relation to the listeners' native phonology.* Paper presented at the International Conference on Infant Studies, Montreal.

Best, C., McRoberts, G., & Sithole, N. (1988). Examination of the perceptual reorganization for speech contrasts: Zulu click discrimination by English-speaking adults and infants. *Journal of Experimental Psychology: Human Perception and Performance, 14,* 345–360.

Bishop, D., & Edmundson, A. (1986). Is otitis media a major cause of specific developmental language disorders? *British Journal of Communication Disorders, 21,* 321–338.

Bradley, L. (1992). Rhymes, rimes, and learning to read and learning to spell. In C. Ferguson, L. Menn, & C. Stoel-Gammon (Eds.), *Phonological development: Models, research, implications* (pp. 539–553). Timonium, MD: York Press.

Brown, R. (1973). *A first language: The early stages.* Cambridge, MA: Harvard University Press.

Chomsky, N., & Halle, M. (1968). *The sound pattern of English.* New York: Harper & Row.

de Boysson-Bardies, B., Vihman, M., Roug-Hellichius, L., Durand, C., Landberg, I., & Arao, F. (1992). Material evidence of infant selection from target language: A crosslinguistic phonetic study. In C. Ferguson, L. Menn, & C. Stoel-Gammon (Eds.), *Phonological development: Models, research, implications* (pp. 369–391). Timonium, MD: York Press.

de Villiers, J.G., & de Villiers, P.A. (1973). A cross-sectional study of the acquisition of grammatical morphemes in child speech. *Journal of Psycholinguistic Research, 2,* 267–278.

Dobie, R., & Berlin, C. (1979). Influence of otitis media on hearing and development. *Annals of Otolaryngology, 88,* 48–53.

Donahue, M. (1993). Early phonological and lexical development and otitis media. *Journal of Child Language, 20,* 489–501.

Echols, C. (1993). A perceptually-based model of children's earliest productions. *Cognition, 46,* 245–296.

Echols, C., & Newport, E.L. (1992). The role of stress and position in determining first words. *Language Acquisition, 2,* 189–220.

Eimas, P., & Clarkson, R. (1986). Speech perception in children: Are there effects of otitis media? In J. Kavanagh (Ed.), *Otitis media and child development* (pp. 139–159). Timonium, MD: York Press.

Fey, M. (1986). *Language intervention with young children.* Austin, TX: PRO-ED.

Gathercole, S., & Baddeley, A. (1993). *Working memory and language.* Hillsdale, NJ: Lawrence Erlbaum Associates.

Gerken, L.A. (1991). The metrical basis for children's subjectless sentences. *Journal of Memory and Language, 30,* 431–451.

Gerken, L.A., Landau, B., & Remez, R. (1990). Function morphemes in young children's speech perception and production. *Developmental Psychology, 26,* 204–216.

Grieser, D., & Kuhl, P. (1989). Categorization of speech by infants: Support for speech-sound prototypes. *Developmental Psychology, 25,* 577–588.

Hirsh-Pasek, K., Kemler Nelson, D., Jusczyk, P., Wright Cassidy, K., Druss, B., & Kennedy, L. (1987). Clauses are perceptual units for young infants. *Cognition, 26,* 269–286.

Ingram, D. (1976). *Phonological disability in children.* London: Edward Arnold.

Juscyzk, P., Friederici, A., Wessels, J., Svenkerud, V., & Jusczyk, A. (1993). Infants' sensitivity to the sound patterns of native language words. *Journal of Memory and Language, 32,* 402–420.

Kent, R. (1976). Anatomical and neuromuscular maturation of the speech mechanism: Evidence from acoustic studies. *Journal of Speech and Hearing Research, 19,* 421–447.

Kent, R., Osberger, M.J., Netsell, R., & Hustedde, C. (1978). Phonetic development in identical twins differing in auditory function. *Journal of Speech and Hearing Disorders, 52,* 64–75.

Kuhl, P. (1987). Perception of speech and sound in early infancy. In P. Salapatek & L. Cohen (Eds.), *Handbook of infant perception* (Vol. 2, pp. 275–381). New York: Academic Press.

Leonard, L. (1989). Language learnability and specific language impairment in children. *Applied Psycholinguistics, 10,* 179–202.

Leonard, L. (1994). Some problems facing accounts of morphological deficits in children with SLI. In R.V. Watkins & M.L. Rice (Eds.), *Communication and language intervention series: Vol. 4. Specific language impairments in children* (pp. 69–89). Baltimore: Paul H. Brookes Publishing Co.

Luloff, A., Menyuk, P., & Teele, D. (1991). Effects of persistent otitis media on the speech sound repertoire of infants. In D.J. Lim, C.D. Bluestone, J.O. Klein, & J.D. Nelson (Eds.), *Recent advances in otitis media* (pp. 531–533). Philadelphia: Decker Periodicals.

Mehler, J., Jusczyk, P., Lambertz, G., Halsted, N., Bertoncini, J., & Amiel-Tison, C. (1988). A precursor of language acquisition in young infants. *Cognition, 29,* 143–178.

Menn, L., & Matthei, E. (1992). The "two-lexicon" account of child phonology: Looking back, looking ahead. In C. Ferguson, L. Menn, & C. Stoel-Gammon (Eds.), *Phonological development: Models, research, implications* (pp. 211–248). Timonium, MD: York Press.

Menyuk, P. (1986). Predicting speech and language problems in children with persistent otitis media. In Kananagh, J. (Ed.), *Otitis media and child development* (pp. 83–98). Timonium, MD: York Press.

Mody, M., Schwartz, R., Gravel, J., Wallace, I., Ellis, M., & Lee, W. (in press). *Speech perception and verbal memory in children with OME.* Paper presented at the sixth International Symposium on Recent Advances in Otitis Media, Fort Lauderdale, FL.

Oller, D.K. (1980). The emergence of the sounds of speech in early infancy. In G. Yeni-Komshian, J. Kavanagh, & C. Ferguson (Eds.), *Child phonology: Vol. 1. Production* (pp. 93–112). New York: Academic Press.

Oller, D.K., Eilers, R., Bull, D.H., & Carney, A. (1980). Prespeech vocalizations of a deaf infant: A comparison with normal metaphonological development. *Journal of Speech and Hearing Research, 28,* 47–63.

Paden, E. (1994). Otitis media and disordered phonologies: Some concerns and cautions. *Topics in Language Disorders, 14,* 72–83.

Paden, E., Novak, M., & Beiter, A. (1987). Predictors of phonological inadequacy in young children prone to otitis media. *Journal of Speech and Hearing Disorders, 52,* 232–242.

Petinou, K., Mody, M., Schwartz, R., Gravel, J., & Wallace, I. (in press). *Vocal development in children with otitis media.* Paper presented at the sixth International Symposium on Recent Advances in Otitis Media, Fort Lauderdale, FL.

Polka, L., & Werker, J.F. (1991). *Developmental changes in cross-language vowel perception.* Paper presented at the biennial meeting of the Society for Research in Child Development, Seattle, WA.

Prince, A., & Smolensky P. (in press). *Optimality theory: Constraint interaction in generative grammar.* Cambridge, MA: MIT Press.

Roberts, J., Burchinal, M., Koch, M., Footo, M., & Henderson, F. (1988). Otitis media in early childhood and its relationship to later phonological development. *Journal of Speech and Hearing Disorders, 53,* 416–424.

Roberts, J., & Clarke-Klein, S. (1994). Otitis media. In J. Bernthal (Ed.), *Articulatory and phonological disorders* (pp. 182–198). New York: Thieme Medical Publishers.

Schwartz, R.G. (1988). Phonological factors in early lexical acquisition. In M. Smith & J. Locke (Eds.), *The emergent lexicon* (pp. 185–222). New York: Academic Press.

Schwartz, R.G. (1992a). Clinical applications of recent advances in phonological theory. *Language, Speech, and Hearing Services in the Schools, 23,* 269–276.

Schwartz, R.G. (1992b). Non-linear phonology as a framework for acquisition. In R. Chapman (Ed.), *Childtalk: Processes in language acquisition and disorders* (pp. 876–888). St. Louis: Mosby-Yearbook.

Schwartz, R.G., & Goffman, L. (1995). Metrical patterns of words and production accuracy. *Journal of Speech and Hearing Research, 38,* 108–124.

Shriberg, L., & Smith, A. (1983). Phonological correlates of middle-ear involvement in speech delayed children: A methodological note. *Journal of Speech and Hearing Research, 26,* 293–297.

Stampe, D. (1972). *A dissertation on natural phonology.* Unpublished Ph.D. dissertation, University of Chicago.

Stark, R.E. (1980). Stages of speech development in the first year of life. In G. Yeni-Komshian, J. Kavanagh, & C. Ferguson (Eds.), *Child phonology: Vol. 1. Production* (pp. 73–92). New York: Academic Press.

Stark, R.E. (1983). Phonatory development in young normally hearing and hearing-impaired children. In I. Hochberg, H. Levitt, & M.J. Osberger (Eds.), *Speech of the hearing impaired: Research, training and personnel preparation* (pp. 251–266). Baltimore: University Park Press.

Stoel-Gammon, C. (1988). Prelinguistic vocalizations of the hearing-impaired and normally hearing subjects: A comparison of consonantal inventories. *Journal of Speech and Hearing Disorders, 53,* 302–315.

Stoel-Gammon, C., & Otomo, K. (1986). Babbling development of hearing-impaired and normally hearing infants. *Journal of Speech and Hearing Disorders, 51,* 33–41.

Sussman, J.E. (1993). Perception of formant transition cues to place of articulation in children with language impairments. *Journal of Speech and Hearing Research, 36,* 1286–1299.

Teele, D., Klein, J., & Rosner, B. (1984). Otitis media with effusion during the first three years of life and development of speech and language. *Pediatrics, 74,* 282–287.

Trieman, R., & Zukowski, A. (1991). Levels of phonological awareness. In S. Brady & D. Shankweiler (Eds.), *Phonological processes in literacy* (pp. 67–84). Hillsdale, NJ: Lawrence Erlbaum Associates.

Vihman, M. (1993). Early phonological development. In J. Bernthal & N. Bankson (Eds.), *Articulation and phonological disorders* (pp. 63–111). Englewood Cliffs, NJ: Prentice-Hall.

Vihman, M., Macken, M., Miller, R., Simmons, H., & Miller, J. (1985). From babbling to speech: A reassessment of the continuity issue. *Language, 61,* 395–443.

Walley, A. (1988). Spoken word recognition by children and adults. *Cognitive Development, 3,* 137–165.

Weber, S. (1982). *The perception of grammatical morphemes in attenuated speech by children with histories of recurrent otitis media.* Unpublished doctoral dissertation, University of Minnesota.

Werker, J.F., Gilbert, J.H.V., Humphrey, K., & Tees, R.C. (1981). Developmental aspects of cross-language speech perception. *Child Development, 6,* 349–355.

Werker, J., & Lalonde, C. (1988). Cross-language speech perception: Initial capabilities and developmental change. *Developmental Psychology, 24,* 672–683.

Werker, J.F., & Tees, R.C. (1984). Speech perception in severely disabled and average reading children. *Canadian Journal of Psychology, 41,* 48–96.

Woodward, A., Kemler Nelson, D., Jusczyk, P., Hirsh-Pasek, K., Kennedy, L., & Jusczyk, A. (1995). *Infants' sensitivity to word boundaries in fluent speech.* Unpublished manuscript, State University of New York at Buffalo.

6

Language and Otitis Media

Joanne E. Roberts and Ina F. Wallace

The extent to which a history of persistent otitis media with effusion (OME) causes later language difficulties is an important issue for health care professionals, educators, and families. The relationship between language difficulties and moderate and severe permanent hearing loss is well established (Levitt, McGarr, & Geffner, 1987; Northern & Downs, 1991). There is evidence that the earlier the onset and the greater the severity of hearing loss, the greater the impact on language. Yet the effects of a mild to moderate fluctuating hearing loss associated with persistent and recurrent OME during the formative years of language learning are not clear (Paradise & Rogers, 1986; Roberts, Burchinal, Davis, Collier, & Henderson, 1991; Ruben et al., 1989; Stool et al., 1994). This raises many questions for the educational and medical management of young children. Will repeated or persistent episodes of otitis media during early childhood cause a child to have later language difficulties? If language difficulties occur, do they cause general language delays or are they domain specific? Will these language difficulties then affect a child's learning skills in school? If there are effects on language, is there a certain period of development (i.e., infancy, preschool, or school age) when OME sequelae are more evident? Will tympanostomy

This chapter was supported by grants from the Maternal and Child Health Program (MCJ-370599 and 370649; Title V, Social Security Act), Health Resources and Services Administration, Department of Health and Human Services, and U.S. Department of Education (H029K20342).

133

tubes to drain the fluid in the middle ear or other strategies that caregivers use alleviate the possibility of language difficulties?

This chapter examines the current literature on language sequelae of OME and then suggests strategies for the management of young children with frequent and persistent OME. First milestones in the language development of young children are discussed, then the role of hearing in language development is reviewed, and next a model of how a history of OME can cause later language difficulties is presented. In the next section, the literature on language sequelae of OME is reviewed, and finally strategies for the management of young children with a history of OME are presented.

DEVELOPMENT OF LANGUAGE

Otitis media with effusion occurs most frequently during the developmental period when children are acquiring the fundamentals of language. In order to examine how a history of otitis media may affect the acquisition of language, it is important to first review the milestones of language development. Figure 1 on pages 136 and 137 highlights some of the major milestones in language comprehension compared with language production.

Milestones in Language Development

Birth to 1 Year Infants' interactions with people and things in their environment during the first year of life provide the foundations for the development of language. In the first few months of life, infants orient to sounds, learn to recognize familiar voices, "coo" and "gurgle," and produce some single syllables such as "ba." Caregivers then respond to infants' eye gaze, body movements, and sounds as if the infants are purposefully communicating. For example, crying is often interpreted as a purposeful indication of a desire to be picked up. By 4 months of age, infants can localize to sounds. At 6 months, infants typically begin to babble using consonant–vowel combinations (e.g., "mamma," "dada") and produce nonspeechlike vocalizations such as raspberries and squeals. At about 9–10 months of age, a change typically occurs that marks the beginning of intentional communication, such that the infant's communication now has a planned effect on the behavior of others. For example, if a child wants a cookie from the cookie jar, the child will pick up an adult's hand and lead the adult to the cookie jar. By the end of the first year, the child uses wordlike sounds consistently and gestures to request (e.g., child points to a desired truck and says "ah"), protest (e.g., child pushes adult's hand away and says "na"), and comment on objects and actions (e.g., child holds up toy car, looks at adult, and giggles).

Age 1–2 Years During the second year, children's communication becomes more frequent, consistent, and clear, resulting in greater success in getting needs met. Along with gestures and vocalizations, children's first words emerge around 12–13 months. These early words are those that have the most meaning for the child and express the same intentions that were previously conveyed through gestures and vocalizations. Children also begin to make consistent responses to simple, familiar action words. Between 12 and 18 months, acquisition of new words is slow and unstable, with some words dropping out of the vocabulary. At 18 months, two major shifts in development occur. First, vocabulary begins to expand dramatically, particularly word comprehension. Whereas children may have a productive vocabulary of about 50 words, they may understand as many as 300 words. Toddlers also begin to combine two or more words into multiword utterances (e.g., "Doggie bark," "Mommy eat cookie"). Children now are able to request information (e.g., "What's that?") and answer simple questions (e.g., "juice" in response to "What do you want?") as well as naming and describing objects and events (e.g., "dog," "cat"). They also show increasing ability to participate in a conversation, although interactions are generally short and focused on observable events that the child is experiencing. Other linguistic achievements include following directions, finding familiar objects, and identifying body parts.

Age 2–3 Years Between 2 and 3 years, children acquire basic sentence grammar and syntax, expand their vocabulary, produce sounds correctly more of the time, and use language in a more precise and descriptive fashion. Although 2-year-old children tend to speak in utterance of two to three words (e.g., "I like cake," "block on chair"), they also still use single-word utterances and occasionally produce ones that are six words long. As children begin to use three-word utterances, they typically add morphologic markers to their utterances. These include -*s* for plural (e.g., "hats"), -*'s* or possessive (e.g., "Sue's"), -*ed* for past tense (e.g., "walked"), and -*ing* for present progressive (e.g., "running"). There is considerable variation in the rate of acquisition of morphemes; however, the order of acquisition remains generally constant across children. By age 2, children generally produce vowels and many types of sounds. However, the words children produce often fail to match the sound of the words produced by adults. For example, the 2-year-old may say "nana" for "banana." At the same time, children's word knowledge expands greatly. Children at 2½ years frequently have a vocabulary of 500 words and can comprehend as many as 1,000 words. During this same time period, their understanding of abstract relations also increases dramatically. Children usually can understand and talk about spatial, temporal, quantity, and color concepts. They begin to use

check one ✓ YES NO	Hearing and understanding	Child's age	Talking	check one ✓ YES NO
	Does your child hear and understand most of what is said at home and in school? Does everyone who knows your child think he or she hears well (teacher, baby sitter, grandparent, etc.)? Does your child pay attention to a story and answer simple questions about it?	4½–5 Years	Does your child communicate easily with other children and adults? Does your child say all sounds correctly except maybe one or two? Does your child use the same grammar as the rest of the family? Does your child's voice sound clear like other children's? Does your child use sentences that give lots of details (e.g., "I have two red balls at home")? Can your child tell you a story and stick pretty much to the topic?	
		4–4½ Years		
	Does your child hear you when you call from another room? Does your child hear television or radio at the same loudness level as other members of the family? Does your child answer simple "who," "what," "where," and "why" questions? Does your child undestand differences in meaning ("go–stop," "in–on", "big–little," "up–down")? Does your child continue to notice sounds (e.g., telephone ringing, television sound, knocking at the door)? Can your child follow two requests (e.g., "get the ball and put it on the table")?	3–4 Years	Does your child talk about what he or she does at school or at friends' homes? Does your child say most sounds correctly except a few, like r, l, th and s? Does your child usually talk easily wtihout repeating syllables or words? Do people outside your family usually understand your child's speech? Does your child use a lot of sentences that have four or more words?	
		2–3 Years	Does your child have a word for almost everything? Does your child use two- to three-word "sentences" to talk about and ask for things? Do you understand your child's speech most of the time? Does your child often ask for or direct your attention to objects by naming them?	
	Can your child point to pictures in a book when they are named? Does your child point to a few body parts when asked? Can your child follow simple commands and understand simple questions (e.g., "Roll the ball," "Kiss the baby," "Where's your shoe?")? Does your child listen to simple stories, songs, and rhymes?	1–2 Years	Is your child saying more and more words every month? Does your child use some one- to two-word questions (e.g., "where kitty?" "go bye-bye?" "what's that"?)? Does your child put 2 words together (e.g., "more cookie," "no juice," "mommy block")? Does your child use many different consonant sounds at the beginning of words?	

(continued)

Figure 1. Milestones of communiation development. Instructions: Read each question through your child's age group and check *yes* or *no*. Add the total and see below. ALL YES: Good. Your child is developing hearing, speech, and language normally. 1–2 NO: CAUTION! Your child may have delayed hearing, speech, and language development. 3 or more NO: ACTION! Take your child for professional help. (Adapted with permission from the brochure *How Does Your Child Hear and Talk?* © American Speech-Language-Hearing Association.)

Figure 1. (continued)

check one ✓ YES NO	Hearing and understanding	Child's age	Talking	check one ✓ YES NO
	Does your child recognize words for common items like "cup," "shoe," and "juice"? Has your child begun to respond to requests (e.g., "Come here," "Want more?")?	7 Months–1 Year	Does your child have one or two words (e.g., bye-bye, dada, mama, no), although they may not be clear?	
	Does your child enjoy games like peekaboo and pat-a-cake? Does your child turn or look up when you call his or her name? Does your child listen when spoken to?		Does your child's babbling have both long and short groups of sounds such as "tata upup bibibibi"? Does your child imitate different speech sounds? Does your child use speech or non-crying sounds to get and keep your attention?	
	Does your child respond to "no"? Changes in your tone of voice? Does your child look around for the source of new sounds (e.g., the doorbell, vacuum, dog barking)? Does your child notice toys that make sound?	4–6 Months	Does your child's babbling sound more speech-like with lots of different sounds, including p, b, and m? Does your child tell you (by sound or gesture) when he or she wants you to do something again? Does your child make gurgling sounds when left alone? When playing with you?	
	Does your child turn to you when you speak? Does your child smile when spoken to? Does your child seem to recognize your voice and quiet down if crying?	0–3 Months	Does your child repeat the same sounds a lot (cooing, gooing)? Does your child cry differently for different needs? Does your child smile when he or she sees you?	
	Does your child listen to speech? Does your child startle or cry at noises? Does your child awaken at loud sounds?	Birth	Does your child make pleasure sounds? When you play with your child, does he or she look at you, look away, and then look again?	
	Total		Total	

words referring to objects or people not in their immediate environment, including past and future events.

Age 3–5 Years Between 3 and 5 years, growth and fine tuning in all aspects of language occur. At about age 3 years, children begin to use complex sentences in which clauses are conjoined and embedded into one another. Now sentences sound like "My mommy says that the stove is hot" and "Why don't you like jelly on it?" Errors in children's speech sounds decrease dramatically after 3½ years, and by 4 years of age children can produce accurately most of the sounds of their native language, although some errors persist. Continued refinements of sounds in words with constant clusters and multisyllable words take place over the next few years. The 3½-year-old is a more skilled conversationalist, displaying the ability to maintain and elaborate on a topic of conversation a majority of the time.

By 4 years, children shift from a focus on the here and now to talk about events and people more distant in time. The 4-year-old is able to report on present and past events, imagine situations, identify his or her own and others' feelings, plan events, anticipate what will happen, and respond appropriately to requests for clarifications in conversations. Around 4 years, children also develop metalinguistic knowledge (i.e., the competence to focus on the form and content of language). Metalinguistic skills include the ability to identify correctly versus incorrectly produced sounds and utterances, segment words into phonemes and sentences into words, recognize word beginnings and endings, judge whether two sounds or words are the same, and define words. The 4-year-old is also sensitive to the language skills of the listener, can modify language to the age and knowledge of the listener, and can tell jokes, tease, and provide warnings.

Age 5–8 Years   Between 5 and 8 years of age, children further enhance their grammar, vocabulary, conversational, and metalinguistic skills and make the greatest strides in learning to read and write. The typical 5-year-old speaks in utterances that sound very much like those of adults. During the next few years, children expand many of the forms that they began developing in the preschool years, such as irregular past tense (e.g., "went") and embedding to join clauses (e.g., "The watch that I want is broken"). They also go on to learn new forms such as passives (e.g., "The boy is asked by the girl to leave") and prefixes (e.g., *un-, dis-*). Children's vocabulary increases as they further acquire spatial and temporal concepts (e.g., "right," "left") and other abstract words (e.g., "remember"); sharpen their definitions; and learn metaphors, idioms, and proverbs (e.g., "go fly a kite"). Between 5 and 8 years, metalinguistic skills improve, as does speech sound accuracy, so by 8 years children can produce all speech sounds correctly. Children also become more effective conversationalists and can talk about a larger number of topics in a conversation, take more turns on a particular topic, and clarify their conversation when it is unclear. Children also can use more ideational language that is abstract, not tied to the present context ("The reason why I need that is . . ."), and narratives that are long spans of utterances focused on a common theme ("Yesterday at my birthday party I was so excited. First, I . . ."). However, the major achievement of children between 5 and 8 years of age is in the development of literacy skills: learning to read, write, and spell. Children's ability to learn to read is to a large extent a function of their linguistic abilities, and the development of literacy skills helps further the development of children's language.

Role of Hearing in Language Learning
Although language acquisition often appears to be effortless, there are many underlying prerequisites for it to develop smoothly. For instance,

cognitive achievements such as object permanence and symbolic thought are tied to the emergence of language. Information acquired through sight, hearing, touch, and taste contributes to the cognitive structures from which language develops. Yet of all of the sensory systems involved in acquiring the knowledge base, hearing plays the pivotal role in language development. A young child acquires language through listening and interacting with people in the environment. From the continuous flow of surrounding speech, the child learns to detect and organize speech into units, categorize these units, attach meaning to them, and then abstract the rules for language.

However, conversational speech is not always a consistent and clear source of information because it often occurs so rapidly that words may be glossed over. The precision of producing sounds varies greatly among speakers and even within the same speaker. Adjacent speech sounds, stress patterns, a speaker's style, and the environment all affect a speaker's articulation of speech and consequently the ability of a listener to understand a message. Environmental influences include the distance between the talker and the listener and the level of background noise. Average conversational speech at 3 feet is 45 dB hearing level (HL), yet as the distance between the talker and listener increases there is a corresponding decrease in the intensity of the speech signal (e.g., 6 feet = 39 dB HL, 12 feet = 33 dB HL). To hear clearly, background noise should ideally be 10–15 dB less than the intensity level of speech, but it is often more, making speech hard to understand.

The typical challenges experienced by a listener with an intact auditory system are magnified for children with an impairment in the auditory system resulting from OME. Moveover, hearing loss may place an additional burden on children in the early stages of language learning. Young children do not have the same ability as older children and adults to use contextual cues or previous experience to decipher a message, even when the message is clear. Thus, segmenting communication, categorizing it into units of meaning, and acquiring rules may be particularly difficult for a young child with a hearing loss caused by frequent and persistent OME. The next section describes a model of how OME may affect children's language development.

Hypothesized Linkage of Otitis Media with Effusion to Language Development

Several causal mechanisms have been offered to explain the relationship between language difficulties and persistent or recurrent OME during early childhood (see Figure 2). These mechanisms are consistent with the transactional model of development (Sameroff, 1983), which hypothesizes that children's learning is influenced by the interaction of a child with his or her environment (i.e., home, caregivers, community).

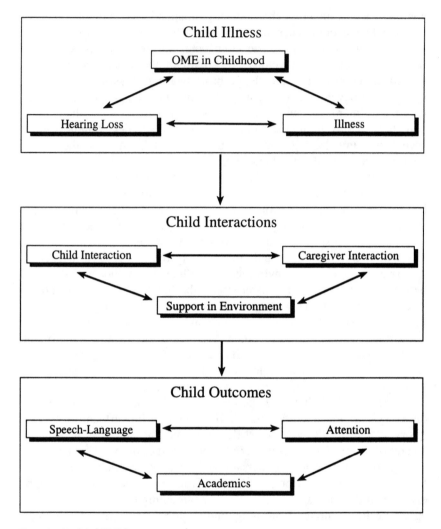

Figure 2. Model of OME language sequelae.

First, a child with OME may experience a mild to moderate fluctuating hearing loss and thus receive a partial or inconsistent auditory
signal. The hearing loss is usually mild (26 dB HL, equivalent to the
loss experienced when the ears are plugged with the fingers), although
it can range from no loss to a moderate loss (50 dB HL). The hearing
loss is conductive and generally returns to normal when the fluid resolves. A mild hearing loss might diminish important auditory signals,
making the speech signal more difficult to filter from background noise.

As a consequence, the child might appear distracted and disorganized. Persistent (prolonged) or frequent (and varied) disruptions in auditory input may impede the discrimination and processing of speech and thus cause the child to encode information incompletely and inaccurately into the database from which language develops.

In addition to the hearing loss, the illness associated with OME (i.e., the stuffy, congested feeling and general malaise) may affect a child's interactions in and responsiveness to the environment. Frequent experience with illness may diminish the quality of interactions with both people and objects. Depending somewhat on the age of the child, the illness experience itself may cause tiredness, withdrawal, lethargy, distractibility, protest, or clinging behavior as the child seeks familiarity and decreases his or her willingness to explore the surrounding away from a caregiver (Parmelee, 1993). Thus, the child may then have fewer opportunities to establish a knowledge base from which language develops.

Second, the fluctuating hearing loss associated with OME and its associated illness symptoms (congestion, malaise) may cause the child to restrict or change his or her interactions with caregivers. This may then lead to a less responsive pattern of interaction from the caregivers themselves and less support. Less responsive caregiving has been associated with poorer language development (Bruner, 1978; Garvey, 1984; Snow, 1984), as caregivers provide less contingent and less meaningful stimulation for the child.

Third, prolonged or frequent OME may affect child outcomes in attention, speech-language, and academics. It could lead to difficulties in attending to auditory-based communication. Children may experience frequent changes in the intensity of signals, learn to tune out, and therefore develop attention difficulties specifically to auditory-based information. This may be manifested in the school setting as distractibility and difficulty working independently, further reducing the chances that the child will receive important auditory information in the classroom.

In addition, a child with frequent hearing loss resulting from OME may then be at a disadvantage for learning the rules of language for its sounds (phonology), meanings (semantics), grammar (syntax), and uses (pragmatics). Children's phonology may be affected by the hearing loss associated with OME because certain sounds (e.g., /t/, /k/, /s/, /sh/), unstressed syllables (e.g., /ba/ in "banana"), and final consonants (e.g., /t/ in "hat") are brief and of low intensity, making them difficult to hear. Perception of morphologic markers (e.g., -s to mark plurality or possessive) and short words (e.g., "is," "the") can be affected by the hearing loss from OME because they are spoken rapidly and softly, and occur at ends of words or in an unstressed position. Semantic development may be affected by the hearing loss resulting from OME, which may cause a child to misperceive words and thus be less successful in storing a catalog of words. Pragmatic development may be affected because children may miss subtle nuances of language (e.g., intonation marks, questions), disrupting their ability to follow conversation topics. Finally, these attentional and language difficulties may in turn negatively influence later academic achievement, particularly in reading and other language-based subjects. Linguistic-based impairments in phonologic or syntactic skills have been found often in children with reading disabilities. Thus, when OME results in language difficulties, it can have a secondary affect on academic skills that require language skills.

DOES OTITIS MEDIA CAUSE LANGUAGE SEQUELAE?

Studies Examining the Otitis Media–Language Linkage

Variations in Study Design   Over 75 original studies since the mid-1960s have examined whether persistent OME in early childhood influences children's language skills. These studies have varied greatly in their populations, study design, documentation procedures, and outcome measures. The populations of children in these studies were from the United States (e.g., Teele et al., 1984), Canada (e.g., Pearce, Saunders, Creighton, & Sauve, 1988), Denmark (e.g., Lous, Fiellau-Nikolajsen, & Jeppeson, 1988), the Netherlands (e.g., Rach, Zielhuis, & van den Broek, 1988), and New Zealand (e.g., Silva, Kirkland, Simpson, Stewart, & Williams, 1982). The ethnic groups included children who were Caucasian (e.g., Friel-Patti & Fintizo, 1990), African American (e.g., Roberts, Burchinal, et al., 1991), Eskimos (e.g., Kaplan, Fleshman, Bender, Baum, & Clarke, 1973), and Native Americans (e.g., Fischler, Todd, & Feldman, 1985). The populations studied included children with learning disabilities (e.g., Gottleib, Zinkus, & Thompson, 1979), language disorders (e.g., Lonigan, Fischel, Whitehurst, Arnold, & Valdez-Menchaca, 1992), cleft palate (e.g., Hubbard, Paradise, McWilliams, Elster, & Taylor, 1985), cerebral palsy (van der Vyver, van der Merwe, & Tesner, 1988), and Down syndrome (e.g., Whiteman, Simpson, & Compton, 1986). It also included children who were at risk for learning problems because of low birth weight (e.g., Wallace, Gravel, McCarton, & Ruben, 1988) or socioeconomic status (e.g., Roberts, Burchinal, et al., 1991). Children were recruited from a general population sample (e.g., Lous et al., 1988), medical practices (e.g., Teele et al., 1984), child care centers (e.g., Roberts, Burchinal, et al., 1991), and vaccine studies (e.g., Wright et al., 1988).

Study designs varied from cohort (i.e., groups of children at risk for OME were followed and OME status and language monitored) (e.g.,

Wright et al., 1988) to case–control (i.e., subjects were chosen based on whether they had language problems, and children with OME and language problems were compared with children without OME and language problems) (e.g., Zinkus & Gottleib, 1980) to cross-sectional (i.e., OME and language experienced are measured at the same time) (e.g., Silva et al., 1982). Data on OME were collected either prospectively, whereby the data were collected longitudinally from early infancy at specified sampling intervals (e.g., Roberts, Burchinal, et al., 1991), or retrospectively, whereby the data were obtained through recall of past events or review of medical records (e.g., Black et al., 1988).

Children's middle ear status was documented using parent recall (e.g., Zinkus & Gottleib, 1980), review of medical records (e.g., Black et al., 1988), or examinations during routine medical visits (e.g., Teele et al., 1990). Ears were assessed with otoscopy only (e.g., Wallace, Gravel, McCarton, & Ruben, 1988), tympanometry only (e.g., Grievink, Peters, van Bon, & Schilder, 1993), or both otoscopy and tympanometry (e.g., Roberts, Burchinal, et al., 1991). Documentation of OME occurred during a short period of time in infancy (e.g., Wallace, Gravel, Mc-Carton, & Ruben, 1988), in the preschool years (e.g., Grievink et al., 1993), at school age (e.g., Silva, Chalmers, & Stewart, 1986), or for a longer period of time over infancy and the preschool years (e.g., Teele et al., 1990). The index of OME was the amount of OME (e.g., Teele et al., 1990) and in some studies it is unclear if it was OME or otitis media (e.g., Zinkus & Gottleib, 1980) because these studies did not differentiate between otitis media and OME, often using parent report to establish a diagnosis. In other studies, OME was quantified as the number of episodes a child experienced (e.g., Friel-Patti & Finitzo, 1990) or the number of days of OME a child experienced (e.g., Roberts, Burchinal, et al., 1991). Children's hearing status in addition to OME status was examined in a few studies (e.g., Friel-Patti & Finitzo, 1990). The language outcomes were assessed during infancy (e.g., Wallace, Gravel, McCarton, & Ruben 1988), preschool years (e.g., Pearce et al., 1988), or school-age years (e.g., Fischler et al., 1985) using standardized tests (e.g., Teele et al., 1984), language samples (e.g., Roberts, Burchinal, et al., 1991) or parental recall of language milestones (e.g., Zinkus & Gottleib, 1980).

Findings of Studies In brief, the findings indicate that, in comparison with children who infrequently experienced otitis media, children with a history of OME score lower on tests of speech production (Paden, Novak, & Beiter, 1987; Roberts, Burchinal, Koch, Footo, & Henderson, 1988; Teele et al., 1984), receptive language (Friel-Patti & Finitzo, 1990; Pearce et al., 1988; Teele et al., 1984), and expressive language (Friel-Patti & Finitzo, 1990; Rach et al., 1988; Wallace,

Gravel, McCarton, & Ruben, 1988) than children without such a history. In addition to the studies conducted with typically developing populations (Friel-Patti & Finitzo, 1990; Silva et al., 1982; Teele, Klein, & Rosner, 1989; Teele et al., 1984), language sequelae as a function of OME has also been reported for children from special populations, including children with Down syndrome (Whiteman et al., 1986), cerebral palsy (van der Vyver et al., 1988), learning disabilities (Gottlieb et al., 1979; Hagerman & Falkenstein, 1987; Secord, Erickson, & Bush, 1988), and language disorders (Lonigan et al., 1992).

Despite the large body of research that has shown a significant relationship between OME and later measures of language, many studies have not supported this association. These studies have failed to find a significant relationship between a history of OME in early childhood and later measures of speech production (Bishop & Edmundson, 1986; Lous, 1990; Teele et al., 1984), receptive language (Feagans, 1986; Rach et al., 1988; Teele et al., 1990; Wallace, Gravel, McCarton, & Rubens, 1988; Wright et al., 1988), and expressive language (Feagans, Hannan, & Manlove, 1992; Gravel & Wallace, 1992; Pearce et al., 1988; Roberts, Burchinal, et al., 1991; Wright et al., 1988).

In addition to these conflicting findings, the relationship between OME and later language remains controversial because serious concerns have been raised about the validity of some studies in which a significant relationship between OME and later development was reported (Paradise & Rogers, 1986; Ruben et al., 1989). In particular, the methods of research design, the timing of the data collection, and the OME documentation procedures have been challenged. For example, in many of the studies, the OME data were collected retrospectively rather than prospectively. Retrospective OME data collection generally has been done through recall of past events or review of medical records and thus has been more likely to contain measurement error. In contrast, data collected prospectively examine the natural course of children's OME experience longitudinally and are likely to have greater objectivity and accuracy over time. (See Ruben et al., 1989; Paradise, 1980, and Roberts, Burchinal, et al., 1991, for a discussion of the methodologic problems in previous OME studies.)

Prospective Studies

Criteria for Study Review   Because the literature as previously described is contradictory and has methodologic problems, a study review of the most methodology-rigorous studies was undertaken. In order to evaluate the nature of the findings for the present review, we used criteria similar to the 1994 review of the literature published in the otitis media Clinical Practice Guidelines (Stool et al., 1994). The following studies were excluded: ones that were retrospective in design; those selecting children with language disorders and learning disabilities or children with a biologic condition that increased the risk of otitis media; research that used parental report to document otitis media; studies in which otitis media was not documented before 2 years of age; and studies that were published in conference papers, proceedings, and book chapters. Consequently, we included only original peer-reviewed published studies of nonspecial populations that were prospective in design in which OME documentation was initiated before 2 years of age. Although this may seem limiting, we believe it was necessary to adhere to these criteria in order to rigorously evaluate whether a history of otitis media in early childhood affects children's language development.

A total of 15 studies were examined. Table 1 describes the results of studies examining how OME or associated hearing loss in early childhood relates to later language outcomes. These outcomes are grouped under the headings of receptive language (i.e., the ability to receive and comprehend language), expressive language (i.e., the ability to produce language), phonology (i.e., speech sounds of language), semantics (i.e., meanings of words), syntax (i.e., grammar and word order), and pragmatics (i.e., use of language).

Receptive and Expressive Language Twelve studies examined the relationship of OME to later receptive and expressive language. The results were analyzed first according to the test instrument and then the assessment ages: infancy (birth to 2) and preschool (3–5). There were no prospective studies examining receptive and expressive language for children above the age of 6 years. As can be seen in Table 1, a variety of test instruments were used to examine receptive and expressive language, the most common being the Sequenced Inventory of Communication Development–Revised (SICD–R). However, the test results varied even when using the same test instrument. For example, for receptive language on the SICD–R, significant results were reported in four studies (Friel-Patti & Finitzo, 1990; Friel-Patti, Finitzo-Hieber, Conti, & Brown, 1982; Pearce et al., 1988; Roberts et al., 1995) and nonsignificant results were reported in four studies (Feagans, Kipp, & Blood, 1994; Friel-Patti & Finitzo, 1990; Gravel & Wallace, 1992; Wallace, Gravel, McCarton, & Rubens, 1988; Wallace, Gravel, McCarton, Stapells, et al., 1988). (The reports by Wallace and colleagues come from the same study.) Looking at receptive language, three of the studies of infants reported significance (Friel-Patti et al., 1982; Friel-Patti & Finitzo, 1990; Roberts et al., 1995) while one did not (Wallace, Gravel, McCarton, & Ruben, 1988; Wallace, Gravel, McCarton, Stapells, et al., 1988), and two of the studies of preschoolers reported significance (Pearce et al., 1988; Teele et al., 1984) while six did not (Feagans et

Table 1. Prospective studies examining early OME or hearing loss and later language sequelae

Group	Reference	Subjects (N)	Population	Age OME documented (years)	Age outcome assessed (years)	Receptive language		Expressive language		Phonology		Syntax		Semantics		Pragmatics	
						S	NS	S	NS	S	NS	S	NS	S	NS	S	NS
Alberta, Canada	Pearce et al. (1988)	43	Preterm	1–2	2–4	SICD			SICD								
Boston, MA	Teele et al. (1984)	205	Medical practice; Low & mid SES	Birth–3	3	PLS[e]		PLS[e]						PPVT			
	Teele et al. (1990)	194	Medical practice; Low & mid SES	Birth–7	7					GFTA		Morphol. (LS)	Grammar (LS), WUG		PPVT, BOSTON, Voc. diversity (LS)		
Bronx, NY	Wallace et al. (1988)[b]	27	Low birth weight & high risk	Birth–1	1		SICD	SICD[c]									
	Gravel & Wallace (1992)	23	Low birth weight & high risk	Birth–1	4		SICD		SICD								
Chapel Hill, NC	Feagans et al. (1987)	44	Low SES, attend child care	6 wks–3	5–7							MLU (LS)				Para-phrase (LS)	
	Roberts et al. (1988)	55	Low SES, attend child care	6 wk–3	2.5–8					GFTA >4.5 yr	GFTA <4.5 yr						
	Roberts, Burchinal, et al. (1991)	63	Low & mid SES, attend child care	6 wk–3	4.5–6		CELF		CELF			MLU (LS), MY, Depend. clauses (LS)		PPVT, BLST, Voc. diversity (LS)			
	Roberts et al. (1995)	61	Low & mid SES, attend child care	6 mo–1	1	SICD[c,d]		SICD[c,d]								CSBS[c,d] Total	

146

Location	Study	N	Sample						
Dallas, TX	Friel-Patti et al. (1982)	35	Low birth weight, intensive care infants	6 wk–2	1–2	REEL, SICD	REEL, SICD		
	Friel-Patti & Finitzo (1990)	483	Mid SES, medical practice	6 mo–1.5	1–2	SICD[c] 1 yr	SICD[c] 1.5 yr	SICD 1&2 yr	
Nashville, TN	Wright et al. (1988)	156	Low SES, enrolled in vaccine study	Birth–2	2–4	PLS, REEL, BOONE	PLS, REEL, BOONE		PPVT
Nijmegen, Netherlands	Rach et al. (1988)	65	Residents of a Netherland municipality	2–4	2–4	Reynell	Reynell		
	Rach et al. (1991)	102	Residents of a Netherland municipality	2–4	2–4	Reynell	Reynell		
	Grievink et al. (1993)	270	Residents of a Netherland municipality	2–4	7		Reynell	Reynell	Word forms (LTC), Meanings (LTC)
State College, PA	Feagans et al. (1994)	46	Mid SES, attend child care	1–2	2	SICD	SICD		
Tucson, AZ	Fischler et al. (1985)	167	Residents of Apache reservations	Birth–2	6–8	SICD			Grammar (TOLD), Vocabulary (TOLD)

[a] BLST, Bankson Language Screening Test; BOONE, Boone Infant Speech and Language Development; BOSTON, Boston Name Test; CELF, Clinical Evaluation of Language Functions; CSBS, Communication and Symbolic Behavior Scales; GFTA, Goldman-Fristoe Test of Articulation; LS, Language sample; LTC, Language Testing for Children; MLU, mean length of utterance; MY, Miller-Yoder Language Comprehension Test; PLS, Zimmerman Preschool Language Scale; PPVT, Peabody Picture Vocabulary Test; REEL, Receptive-Expressive Emergent Language Scale; Reynell, Reynell Developmental Language Scale; SICD, Sequenced Inventory of Communication Development; TOLD, Test of Language Development–Revised; WUG, WUG Test; S, significant; NS, nonsignificant; SES, socioeconomic status.

[b] Wallace, Gravel, McCarton, and Ruben (1988) and Wallace, Gravel, McCarton, Stapells, et al. (1988).

[c] Significantly correlated with hearing loss.

[d] Home environment predicted relation between hearing loss and language outcomes.

[e] Significant for mid SES, not low SES.

al., 1994; Gravel & Wallace, 1992; Rach, Zielhuis, van Baarle, & van den Broek, 1991; Rach et al., 1988; Roberts, Burchinal, et al., 1991; Wright et al., 1988). For expressive language, all four studies in infancy reported significant findings (Friel-Patti, & Finitzo, 1990; Friel-Patti et al., 1982; Roberts et al., 1995; Wallace, Gravel, McCarton, & Ruben, 1988; Wallace, Gravel, McCarton, Stapells, et al., 1988), yet for the preschool age significance was found in two studies (Rach et al., 1988; Teele et al., 1984) and not in five studies (Feagans et al., 1994; Gravel & Wallace, 1992; Rach et al., 1991; Roberts, Burchinal, et al., 1991; Wright et al., 1988). For receptive language, the effects ranged from correlations of .16 (Friel-Patti & Finitzo, 1990) to .42 (Roberts et al., 1995). For expressive language, the effects ranged from $r = .13$ (Friel-Patti & Finitzo, 1990), to $r = -.56$ in the study by Wallace, Gravel, McCarton, and Ruben (1988). In summary, the findings from these studies of receptive and expressive language are mixed. However, there is a pattern showing more of an association between an early history of OME and language skills during infancy, particularly in the expressive domain.

In order to understand the potential impact of OME on language learning, it is important not only to consider global indices of receptive and expressive language, but also to look at how children's acquisition of the four domains of language (phonology, syntax, semantics, and pragmatics) are related to the history of OME.

Phonology The Goldman-Fristoe Test of Articulation was used in two studies to examine the relationship between a history of OME and later speech development. There were no significant findings for preschoolers (Roberts et al., 1988); however, for school-age children, speech errors occurred more often ($r = .22$) (Teele et al., 1990) and phonologic processes dropped out more slowly ($r = .35$) (Roberts et al., 1988) for children with a history of OME as compared with children who did not have a history of OME. (See Chapter 5 for more discussion of the effects of OME on phonology.) Thus, interpretation of these results is limited given the very small number of studies. Yet the data suggest that associations between OME and phonological skills are more apparent during the school-age years, when most children no longer display speech error, than during the preschool years.

Syntax and Morphology Five studies examined the relationship between syntax/morphology and OME history; all were in school-age children. In one study in which a language sample was analyzed, significant results were found in the number of morphological markers used ($r = .32$) (Teele et al., 1990). The other studies reported nonsignificant findings for tests of morphology and syntax (Fischler et al., 1985; Grievink et al., 1993; Roberts, Burchinal, et al., 1991; Teele et al., 1990), mean length of utterance (Feagans, Sanyal, Henderson, Collier, & Applebaum, 1987; Roberts, Burchinal, et al., 1991; Teele et al., 1984), and grammar usage on a language sample (Teele et al., 1990; Roberts, Burchinal, et al., 1991). Although based on a small number of studies, interpretations of these findings do not appear to lend much support for an association between a history of early OME and later development of syntax and morphology.

Semantics   Three studies of preschool children and three studies of school-age children examined children's semantic skills. The Peabody Picture Vocabulary Test–Revised (Roberts, Burchinal, et al., 1991; Teele et al., 1984, 1990; Wright et al., 1988) was used most often, and other assessments of semantics were done using the Boston Naming Test (Teele et al., 1990), the Test of Language Development (vocabulary subtest) (Fischler et al., 1985), the Language Test for Children (concepts subtest) (Grievink et al., 1993), and vocabulary diversity on a language sample (Roberts, Burchinal, et al., 1991; Teele et al., 1990). Significant findings were obtained only for preschool children on the Peabody Picture Vocabulary Test (Teele et al., 1984) ($r = .45$); the other study results were not significant. These results do not support the possibility that aspects of semantic development are affected by a history of OME in early childhood.

Pragmatics   Only two studies have looked at children's pragmatic skills in relation to OME history. One study examined children's pragmatic skills during infancy using the standardized Communication and Symbolic Behavior Scales (Roberts et al., 1995), and the other looked at school-age children's ability to paraphrase on a narrative task (Feagans et al., 1987). Results were significant in both investigations (effect sizes of OME or hearing in isolation are not reported). These two studies do support the notion that an early OME history may have an impact on children's pragmatic skills; however, given the small number of studies in this area, this linkage should be interpreted cautiously.

Summary   The results of the prospective studies are not conclusive regarding the extent and nature of the language sequelae of OME. The most support is present for sequelae in expressive language in infancy and in children's pragmatic skills (use of language). Even for the studies that reported significant findings, the effect size is generally very small, accounting for only about 8% of the variance (range, 2%–30%). Thus, these data suggest that a history of OME in early childhood may be one of many variables that can have an impact on children's language development, yet these linkages merit further scrutiny.

Research Needs
Because findings relating OME and communicative outcomes have not allowed the research community to reach a consensus, the nature of the relationship continues to be controversial (Paradise & Rogers, 1986;

Ruben et al., 1994; Stool et al., 1994). However, it is clear that, in order to adequately examine this issue, more attention must be directed toward the following areas.

Study Design There is a need for prospective, cohort studies of children followed from infancy. In addition to naturalistic studies, experimental research designs in which children are randomly assigned to treatment or nontreatment conditions (see Pittsburgh-Area Child Development/Otitis Media Study described in Chapter 12) would contribute complimentary information. The field would be greatly helped if research were hypothesis driven and predictions were made about how OME might affect specific language skills and at what ages children might be most vulnerable.

Populations There is a need to include samples that are large and diverse enough so that subgroup analyses can be made. Inclusion of a sufficient number of individuals from both lower- and middle-class backgrounds will permit comparisons of the sequelae of OME among children of different socioeconomic groups. Additional studies of children who may be at added risk, such as those with Down syndrome, would be useful.

Independent Variables There is a need to document OME progressively beginning in infancy. This documentation must be made using reliable, valid procedures such as tympanometry or pneumatic otoscopy. In addition, documentation of the child's illness experience can help sort out "silent" episodes from those episodes in which the child has active symptoms. Most important of all is the concurrent assessment of hearing; only with such assessment will it be possible to adequately test hypotheses that postulate hearing as the mediating variable.

Dependent Variables There is a need to measure specific language competencies in the domains of phonology, syntax, semantics, and pragmatics on which OME is thought to have an impact, in addition to more general receptive and expressive skills. For instance, it might be hypothesized that the morpheme "*-s*" would be negatively affected by recurrent OME but that the morpheme "*-ed*" would not. Tests of the comprehension and expression of these markers as well as examination of naturalistic samples for the presence of these forms would provide theoretically motivated measurement. It would also be useful to adopt a developmental approach by examining language longitudinally beginning in infancy. Such an approach may help uncover whether there are specific periods that are more sensitive to the effects of OME. By the same token, children's language should continue to be assessed at school age. Use of multiple sources of language data, such as standardized tests, experimental paradigms, language samples, and parent and teacher reports, can offer the opportunity to achieve convergent findings. All of the measures must be reliable and valid.

Covariates It is necessary to study other important variables that may affect the development of language skills. Both factors relating to the child (e.g., general cognitive abilities) and those relating to the child's multiple environments (e.g., quality of child care, parent interaction style, family support) should be examined. The examination of a combination of variables (e.g., history of OME and unresponsive child-rearing environments) may help elucidate which children are most vulnerable to potential adverse developmental consequences of OME.

Summary Clearly, there continues to be the need for methodologically rigorous studies to examine OME sequelae. Until future research provides consistent evidence of a consensus about whether such a relationship exists as well as the nature of the relationship, knowledge about OME will be useful in assessing young children and developing intervention programs.

MANAGEMENT STRATEGIES FOR
CHILDREN WITH OTITIS MEDIA WITH EFFUSION

Although the review of the current literature does not provide sufficient evidence that a history of OME is related to later language difficulties, there are indications that some children experiencing recurrent and persistent OME during the first few years of life may be at increased risk for later language difficulties. In addition, a history of OME and hearing loss may further contribute to language difficulties of children from special populations (e.g., children with Down syndrome or Apert syndrome, low birth weight children) who are generally at higher risk for language problems. Until the nature of this relationship is determined, guidelines for the management of children with OME are necessary.

The Agency for Health Care Policy and Research (AHCPR) of the U.S. Department of Health and Human Services (Stool et al., 1994) published a Clinical Practice Guideline for the management of otitis media with effusion in young children that include recommendations for medical management and hearing testing (see the appendix at the end of this book). The American Academy of Pediatrics (1984) and the American Academy of Audiology (1992) reported their positions on the management of OME and stressed the importance of early identification and assessment of children with OME and associated hearing loss. Recommendations from these guidelines are discussed in this section.

Guidelines for management of OME and its sequelae from a developmental perspective are available for specific groups of professionals, including teachers and other early childhood educators (Watt,

Roberts, & Zeisel, 1993), speech-language pathologists (Roberts & Medley, 1995), early childhood special educators (Medley, Roberts, & Zeisel, 1995), families and health care professionals (Roberts & Zeisel, 1996), and physicians (Roberts & Roush, 1992).

Identify Otitis Media–Associated Hearing Loss
Because of the role of audition in learning language, it is important to identify when children who experience OME have a hearing loss, as well as the degree (e.g., mild, moderate) and the laterality (e.g., one or both ears) of the hearing loss. Hearing screening should occur after children experience 3 months of bilateral OME (Stool et al., 1994). A hearing screening is also recommended for children who experience 3 months of unilateral OME because of the potential effects of unilateral hearing loss (see Chapter 4), as well as for children who experience recurrent episodes of OME. The hearing of special populations of children who are at increased risk for OME and language difficulties (e.g., children with Down syndrome or fetal alcohol syndrome) should be routinely screened, particularly during the winter months. Guidelines for screening hearing of preschool and school-age children and for the identification of hearing loss in infants, preschoolers, and school-age children have been reported (American Academy of Audiology, 1992; ASHA, 1990, 1991a). Children who fail a screening should be rescreened and children who fail a rescreening should be referred for an audiologic assessment. (See Chapters 4 and 5 for a discussion of procedures for the identification of and screening for OME and hearing loss.)

Monitor for Early Evidence of Language Delays
The language skills of children with persistent OME should be monitored to determine if a child is showing a language delay. The American Academy of Audiology (1992) recommends screening communication development with every hearing screening. The American Academy of Pediatrics (1984) recommends monitoring the development of communication skills in any child with OME persisting for longer than 3 months. The AHCPR Guideline did not include recommendations for screening communication because of the conflicting information about language sequelae associated with OME. Despite these differences, it is recommended that speech and language screenings occur after 3 months of persistent OME, whenever hearing loss is present, and/or when families or caregivers express concerns regarding a child's development. Children's language skills can be screened as young as 6 months of age with tests such as the Early Language Milestone Scale (Coplan, 1993) or a parent report form such as the one in Figure 1. Children's language should be rescreened when OME, hearing loss, or concerns persist. Chil-

dren who do not pass a communication or developmental screen should be referred to a speech-language pathologist, a psychologist, or a developmental pediatrician. The language assessment should follow standard practices, examine all domains of language (i.e., phonology, syntax, semantics, and pragmatics), and include assessments in both standardized contexts (e.g., tests) and nonstandardized contests (e.g., language sample in a classroom). (For additional information on screening and assessing children's language, see Crais & Roberts, 1996, and Paul, 1995.)

Share Information with Caregivers About Otitis Media, Hearing, and Language Learning

Families and other caregivers (e.g., child care providers) of young children who experience recurrent or persistent OME need current, understandable, and accurate information in order to make decisions about managing young children who experience OME. Information about the signs and symptoms of OME and hearing loss in young children should be provided. Families and other caregivers who interact daily with a young child may detect behavior changes and be the first to recognize the signs of OME or hearing loss. However, many children with OME and hearing loss do not exhibit any obvious symptoms, and the effects of OME, hearing loss, or illness may be hard to distinguish from other day-to-day behavior changes. Consequently, increasing caregivers' awareness of these signs and symptoms, along with middle ear and hearing screenings as described earlier, may best identify children who are experiencing OME and associated hearing loss. Information can also be provided about the role of hearing in language development, language development milestones and indicators of development delay, possible language sequelae of a history of OME, and intervention strategies for children experiencing frequent or persistent OME. (See Chapter 8 and Roberts & Zeisel, 1996, for additional suggestions of how professionals can work with families in managing children with OME.)

Provide an Optimal Listening Environment

Children who have hearing loss as a result of otitis media and children who experience OME frequently need listening environments that optimally facilitate language. It is important to examine the child's classroom environment to determine what changes should be made to improve listening skills. Two types of strategies can be used in all settings to increase the saliency of the speech signal and minimize background noise. First, the saliency of the speech signal can be increased by techniques such as talking to the child in face-to-face interaction, seating or having the child close (i.e., within 6 feet) to the person speaking, getting the child's attention before speaking, speaking clearly using natural intonation, repeating important words, and checking with children frequently to see if they comprehend instructions or new material. Second, background noise should be minimized so speech can be heard clearly. Background noise should be at most 15 dB less than speech in the environment. Strategies to decrease background noise include fixing noisy air conditioners, fans, heaters, clocks, and other appliances and reducing or eliminate background sounds from televisions, videocassette recorders, radios, and record players. Other approaches include hanging washable drapes, closing windows and doors when it is noisy outside, and using partitions for creating smaller spaces within the classroom.

For a child with ongoing OME or a history of OME who is experiencing hearing or attention difficulties, an open classroom or a large group setting with background noise may be particularly difficult. In addition to the techniques described here, incorporating one-to-one or small-group activities into the classroom will allow the child to be in close proximity to speakers and to pick up facial and other cues from communication partners. See Table 2 for suggestions for working with a child with a mild hearing loss associated with OME.

Provide a Responsive Language Environment
Children who frequently experience OME will benefit from a highly responsive language environment using strategies that have been shown to facilitate language in young children. An environment rich in interesting pictures, toys, and materials often will provide the stimulus for children to comment and ask questions. Techniques to initiate interactions with children include modeling desired verbal and nonverbal behavior using gestures, vocalizations, words, phrases, and sentences the child would typically use. For example, one can describe one's own or the child's actions during daily activities (e.g., as the child gets dressed, say "Kendra puts on socks; now Kendra puts on shoes"). Participating with infants and preschoolers in back-and-forth interactive games (e.g., peekaboo, "I'm gonna get you") provides opportunities for the child to take turns in conversational exchanges. For example, the adult holds up a blanket and asks, "Where's Matthew?" Matthew responds "Here" as he pushes away the blanket, and giggles. Older children should also be given frequent opportunities to take a turn in a conversation by asking open-ended questions about their interests. Having children explain how to do something, such as building a house with Legos, or describe a favorite movie can offer practice in using connected discourse. Once the child takes a turn in an interaction, it is important to keep the interactions going. Approaches include consistently responding to children's communication attempts even if they are unclear or not linguistically correct, revising a child's communication attempt on the next turn (e.g., child: "See go"; mother: "See the car go"), pausing to allow children

Table 2.   Listening and language strategies for a child with frequent otitis media

Make speech louder or clearer

- Get down on the child's eye level to talk whenever possible. Get close (no more than 3 feet away) and face the child to provide clear visual and auditory information.
- Gain the child's attention before speaking to make sure that the child is listening. Remind the child to listen when necessary.
- Speak clearly and repeat important words, but use a natural speaking intonation or pattern.
- When possible, use visual support to help the child understand what he or she is hearing. For a young child, point to objects, pictures, or people and gesture when talking. For an older child, give written as well as verbal instructions.
- When there is a speaker in a classroom, seat the child close to the speaker but where the child also can see other children (e.g., at the side of the room).

Minimize background noise

- Turn off record players, radios, recorders, and television playing in the background, which can interfere with children hearing ongoing conversation.
- Repair noisy appliances (e.g., air conditioners, heaters, fans, vacuum cleaners) that make it hard to hear speech clearly.
- Reduce distractions by using movable barriers (e.g., bookshelves, flannel boards) to create small areas in a classroom where small-group and one-to-one interactions can take place.
- Hang washable draperies over windows to absorb sound, and close doors and windows if there is noise that makes it hard to hear.

Promote language learning

- Show an interest in what the child is talking about and in things that interest the child, and follow the child's topic.
- Play interactive games with children to encourage turn taking (e.g., peekaboo).
- Model desired language by describing ongoing activities.
- Respond immediately and consistently to a child's communication attempts.
- Pause to give the child time to talk.
- Check with the child to see if directions and new information are understood.
- Give positive feedback for language attempts.
- Elaborate on what the child says by adding words to the child's utterances.
- For older preschoolers, encourage discussions that explain things, predict what will happen next, describe feelings, and refer to children's own experiences.

Increase children's attention to language

- Sing simple songs with repeated words and phrases (e.g., The Wheels on the Bus).
- Play word and listening games (e.g., I Spy) in which children listen to familiar patterns and fill in words.
- For older preschool children, play rhyming games (e.g., cat, fat, bat).
- Read frequently with children, labeling and describing pictures and referring to children's own experiences.

to take their next turn in a conversation, and expanding and elaborating on children's topics. (See Girolametto, 1988; Roberts, Bailey, & Nychka, 1991; and Snow, 1984, for procedures that caregivers and families can use to facilitate conversational interactions with young children.)

Increase Children's Attention to Language

Many activities can be used to increase children's skills in attending to language. Activities that accentuate auditory information and reinforce it with visual information should greatly enhance children's attention. Verbal explanations for new concepts can be enhanced with visual support (e.g., pictures, models). Games that include repetition of important words (e.g., Simon Says), songs with repeated words and phrases (e.g., The Wheels on the Bus), and stories with repeated words (e.g., Jump Frog Jump) can give the child both multiple models of the words and opportunities for the child to repeat speech when most of the phrase is familiar and the new information is limited. These games often have hand and face movements that visually reinforce what the child hears and anticipates. Book-reading activities can be used to augment listening and pictures can be used for visual support, while also introducing early literacy concepts.

Other activities can also heighten children's attention to language and listening skills. For preschoolers, games in which a child listens for his or her name or a sound before responding (e.g., Red Rover, Simon Says) and rhyming games (e.g., cat, fat, bat) are effective. For older children, activities that require the child to repeat what he or she has heard to other people (e.g., telephone, Whispering down the Lane) and barrier games in which the child must follow directions given only auditory cues (e.g., "put the red block on the square") to create something (e.g., building games, drawing games) can be used. Daily routines can also be used to highlight new auditory information by keeping most of the activity familiar (i.e., not demanding much attention from the child), thus making new information more salient. Additional suggestions for encouraging attention to language for children with OME can be found in the literature (Davis, 1989; Feagans et al., 1992; Roberts & Medley, 1995).

Provide Intervention Programs
Some children with a history of OME may exhibit language difficulties and thus need to be enrolled in speech-language therapy. Although the literature suggests some areas that may be more affected by OME than others (e.g., phonology, pragmatic aspects of language), each child's language profile as well as family and caregiver concerns must determine the nature of an intervention plan. The recommendations described earlier for optimizing children's language and attention to language will be useful in such an intervention program.

In some cases, children who experience persistent hearing loss associated with OME or processing/attention difficulties because of a past history of OME may benefit from acoustic amplification. FM sound field amplification (amplified sound transmitted through speakers in a room) has been recommended for children in settings such as preschools during book reading or circle time and in elementary school during instructional lessons to enhance the speaker's voice over background noise (ASHA, 1991). (For discussions of the use of FM amplification for children with a history of OME, see Chapter 4 and ASHA's position statements [ASHA, 1991b, 1994] on use of FM amplification.)

In accordance with the Individuals with Disabilities Education Act Amendments of 1991 (PL 102-119), children under 3 years of age with developmental delays and children with a diagnosed mental or physical condition that likely will result in developmental delay are eligible for early intervention services. Some states also provide services to children birth to 2 years who do not meet these criteria but who are at risk of having substantial developmental delay. It is necessary to consult a particular state's eligibility guidelines to determine whether or not children under 3 years of age with frequent or persistent OME in early childhood can be considered for services under this special "at risk" clause of PL 99-457.

CONCLUSIONS

Otitis media with effusion is highly prevalent in young children, yet its effects on children's acquisition of language continue to be controversial. There is some support in the literature that OME may be one of multiple risk factors that influence the development of language. Until further research can clarify whether there is such a relationship and what aspects of language are affected, the status of children's hearing and language must be considered in the medical management of and educational decision making for young children with histories of OME. Furthermore, families, caregivers, and professionals must take preventative measures as early as possible to minimize any possible adverse language developmental consequences of OME in early childhood.

REFERENCES

American Academy of Audiology. (1992). Public meeting on clinical practice guidelines for the diagnosis and treatment of otitis media in children. *Audiology Today, 4,* 23–24.

American Academy of Pediatrics. (1984). *Middle ear disease and language development: Policy statement.* Elk Grove Village, IL: Author.

American Speech-Language-Hearing Association. (1990). Guidelines for screening for hearing impairments and middle-ear disorders. *Asha, 32*(Suppl. 2), 17–24.

American Speech-Language-Hearing Association. (1991a). Guidelines for the audiologic assessment of children from birth through 36 months of age. *Asha, 33*(Suppl. 5), 37–43.

American Speech-Language-Hearing Association. (1991b). The use of FM amplification instruments for infants and preschool children with hearing impairment. *Asha, 33*(Suppl. 5), 1–2.

American Speech-Language-Hearing Association. (1994). Guidelines for fitting and monitoring FM systems. *Asha, 36*(Suppl. 12), 1–9.

Bishop, D.V.M., & Edmundson, A. (1986). Is otitis media a major cause of specific developmental language disorders? *British Journal of Disorders of Communication, 21,* 321–338.

Black, M.M., Gerson, L.F., Freeland, C.A.B., Nair, P., Rubin, J.S., & Hutcheson, J.J. (1988). Language screening for infants prone to otitis media. *Journal of Pediatric Psychology, 13*(3), 423–433.

Bruner, J. (1978). The role of dialogue in language acquisition. In A. Sinclair, R.J. Jarvella, & W.M. Lervet (Eds.), *The child's conception of language,* (pp. 241–255). Berlin: Springer-Verlag.

Coplan, J. (1993). *The Early Language Milestone Scale* (2nd ed.). Austin, TX: PRO-ED.

Crais, E.R., & Roberts, J.E. (1996). Assessing communication skills. In M. Mc-Lean, D.B. Bailey, & M. Wolery (Eds.), *Assessing infants and preschoolers with special needs,* (2nd ed., pp. 334–397). Columbus, OH: Charles E. Merrill Press.

Davis, D.S. (1989). *Otitis media: Coping with effects in the classroom.* Stanhope, NJ: Hear You Are, Inc.

Education of the Handicapped Act Amendments of 1986, PL 99-457, 20 U.S.C. §1400 et seq.

Feagans, L. (1986). Otitis media: A model for long-term effects with implications for intervention. In J.F. Kavanagh (Ed.), *Otitis media and child development* (pp. 192–208). Parkton, MD: York Press.

Feagans, L.V., Hannan, K., & Manlove, E. (1992). An ecological and developmental/contextual approach to intervention with children with chronic otitis media. In F.H. Bess & J.W. Hall (Eds.), *Screening children for auditory function* (pp. 435–461). Nashville, TN: Bill Wilkerson Center Press.

Feagans, L.V., Kipp, E., & Blood, I. (1994). The effects of otitis media on the attention skills of day-care-attending toddlers. *Developmental Psychology, 30,* 701–708.

Feagans, L., Sanyal, M, Henderson, F., Collier, A., & Appelbaum, M. (1987). Relationship of middle ear disease in early childhood to later narrative and attention skills. *Journal of Pediatric Psychology, 12*(4), 581–594.

Fischler, R.S., Todd, N.W., & Feldman, C.M. (1985). Otitis media and language performance in a cohort of Apache Indian children. *American Journal of Diseases of Children, 139,* 355–360.

Friel-Patti, S., & Finitzo, T. (1990). Language learning in a prospective study of otitis media with effusion in the first two years of life. *Journal of Speech and Hearing Research, 33,* 188–194.

Friel-Patti, S., Finitzo-Hieber, T., Conti, G., & Brown, K.C. (1982). Language delay in infants associated with middle ear disease and mild, fluctuating hearing impairment. *Pediatric Infectious Disease, 1*(2), 104–109.

Garvey, C. (1984). *Children's talk.* Cambridge, MA: Harvard University Press.

Girolametto, L.E. (1988). Improving the social-conversational skills of developmentally delayed children: An intervention study. *Journal of Speech and Hearing Disorders, 53*(2), 156–167.

Gottlieb, M.I., Zinkus, P.W., & Thompson, A. (1979). Chronic middle ear disease and auditory perceptual deficits: Is there a link? *Clinical Pediatrics, 18,* 725–732.

Gravel, J.S., & Wallace, I.F. (1992). Listening and language at 4 years of age: Effects of early otitis media. *Journal of Speech and Hearing Research, 35,* 588–595.

Grievink, E.H., Peters, S.A.F., van Bon, W.H.J., & Schilder, A.G.M. (1993). The effects of early bilateral otitis media with effusion on language ability: A prospective cohort study. *Journal of Speech and Hearing Research, 36*(5), 1004–1012.

Hagerman, R.J., & Falkenstein, A.R. (1987). As association between recurrent otitis media in infancy and later hyperactivity. *Clinical Pediatrics, 26,* 253–257.

Hubbard, T.W., Paradise, J.L., McWilliams, B.J., Elster, B.A., & Taylor, F.H. (1985). Consequences of unremitting middle-ear disease in early life: Otologic, audiologic and developmental findings in children with cleft palate. *New England Journal of Medicine, 312*(24), 1529–1534.

Individuals with Disabilities Education Act Amendments of 1991, PL 102-119, 20 U.S.C. §1400 *et seq.*

Kaplan, G.J., Fleshman, J.K., Bender, T.R., Baum, C., & Clarke, P.S. (1973). Long-term effects of otitis media: A ten-year cohort study of Alaskan Eskimo children. *Pediatrics, 52,* 577–585.

Levitt, H., McGarr, N., & Geffner, D. (Eds.), (1987). *Development of language and communication skills in hearing impaired children* (ASHA monographs, #26). Rockville, MD: American Speech-Language-Hearing Association.

Lonigan, C.J., Fischel, J.E., Whitehurst, G.J., Arnold, D.S., & Valdez-Menchaca, M.C. (1992). The role of otitis media in the development of expressive language disorder. *Development Psychology, 28*(3), 430–440.

Lous, J. (1990). Secretory otitis media and phonology when starting school. *Scandinavian Audiology, 19,* 215–222.

Lous, J., Fiellau-Nikolajsen, M., & Jeppeson, A.L. (1988). Secretory otitis media and verbal intelligence: A six-year prospective case control study. In D.J. Lim, C.D. Bluestone, J.O. Klein, & J.D. Nelson (Eds.), *Recent advances in otitis media with effusion* (pp. 393–395). Philadelphia: B.C. Decker.

Medley, L.P., Roberts, J.E., & Zeisel, S.A. (1995). *Hear to listen & learn: A language approach for children with ear infections.* Baltimore: Paul H. Brookes Publishing Co.

Northern, J.L., & Downs, M.P. (Eds.). (1991). *Hearing in children* (4th ed.). Baltimore: Williams & Wilkins.

Paden, E.P., Novak, M.A., & Beiter, A.L. (1987). Predictors of phonologic inadequacy in young children prone to otitis media. *Journal of Speech and Hearing Disorders, 52,* 232–242.

Paradise, J.L. (1980). Otitis media in infants and children [review article]. *Pediatrics, 65*(5), 917–943.

Paradise, J.L., & Rogers, K.D. (1986). On otitis media, child development, and tympanostomy tubes: New answers or old questions? *Pediatrics, 77,* 88–92.

Parmelee, A.H. (1993). Children's illness and normal behavioral development: The role of caregivers. *Zero to Three, 13*(4), 1–9.

Paul, R. (1995). *Language disorders from infancy through adolescence: Assessment and intervention.* St. Louis: Mosby–Year Book.

Pearce, P.S., Saunders, M.A., Creighton, D.E., & Sauve, R.S. (1988). Hearing and verbal-cognitive abilities in high-risk preterm infants prone to otitis media with effusion. *Developmental and Behavioral Pediatrics, 9,* 346–351.

Rach, G.H., Zielhuis, G.A., van Baarle, P.W., & van den Broek, P. (1991). The effect of treatment with ventilating tubes on language development in preschool children with otitis media with effusion. *Clinical Otolaryngology, 16,* 128–132.

Rach, G.H., Zielhuis, G.A., & van den Broek, P. (1988). The influence of chronic persistent otitis media with effusion on language development of 2- to 4-year-olds. *International Journal of Pediatric Otorhinolaryngology, 15,* 253–261.

Roberts, J.E., Bailey, D.B., Nychka, H.B. (1991). Teachers' use of strategies to facilitate the communication of preschool children with disabilities. *Journal of Early Intervention, 15,* 369–376.

Roberts, J.E., Burchinal, M.R., Davis, B.P., Collier, A.M., & Henderson, F.W. (1991). Otitis media in early childhood and later language. *Journal of Speech and Hearing Research, 34,* 1158–1168.

Roberts, J.E., Burchinal, M.R., Koch, M.A., Footo, M.M., & Henderson, F.W. (1988). Otitis media in early childhood and its relationship to later phonological development. *Journal of Speech and Hearing Disorders, 53,* 416–424.

Roberts, J.E., Burchinal, M.R., Medley, L.P., Zeisel, S.A., Mundy, M., Roush, J., Hooper, S., Bryant, D., & Henderson, F.W. (1995). Otitis media, hearing sensitivity, and maternal responsiveness in relation to language during infancy. *Journal of Pediatrics, 126*(3), 481–489.

Roberts, J.E., & Medley, L.P. (1995). Otitis media and speech-language sequelae in young children: Current issues in management. *American Journal of Speech-Language Pathology, 4,* 15–24.

Roberts, J.E., & Roush, J. (1992). Otitis media. In M.D. Levine, W.B. Carey, & A.C. Crocker. (Eds.), *Developmental behavioral pediatrics* (2nd ed., pp. 309–316). Philadelphia: W.B. Saunders Company.

Roberts, J.E., & Zeisel, S.A. (1996). *A language approach for children with ear infections.* Chapel Hill, NC: Frank Porter Graham Child Development Center.

Ruben, R.J., Bagger-Sojback, D., Chase, C., Feagans, L.B., Friel-Patti, S., Gravel, J.S., Haggard, M.P., Iino, Y., Klein, J.O., Menyuk, P., Morizono, T., Paparella, M.M., van Cauwenberge, P., & Wallace, I. (1994). Complications and sequelae. *Recent Advances in Otitis Media, 103*(8, Pt. 2. Suppl. 164), 67–80.

Ruben, R.J., Bagger-Sjoback, D., Downs, M.P., Gravel, J.S., Karakashian, M., Klein, J.O., Morizono, T., & Pararella, M.M. (1989). Complications and sequelae. *Annals of Otology, Rhinology, and Laryngology, 98*(Suppl. 139), 46–55.

Sameroff, A.J. (1983). Developmental systems: Contexts and evolution. In W. Kessen (Ed.), *Handbook of child development: Vol. 1. History, theories, and methods* (P.H. Mussen, Gen. Ed.) (pp. 237–254). New York: John Wiley & Sons.

Secord, G.J., Erickson, M.T., & Bush, J.P. (1988). Neuropsychological sequelae of otitis media in children and adolescents with learning disabilities. *Journal of Pediatric Psychology, 13*(4), 531–542.

Silva, P.A., Chalmers, D., & Stewart, I. (1986). Some audiological, psychological, educational and behavioral characteristics of children with bilateral otitis media with effusion: A longitudinal study. *Journal of Learning Disabilities, 19*(3), 165–169.

Silva, P.A., Kirkland, C., Simpson, A., Stewart, I.A., & Williams, S.M. (1982). Some developmental and behavioral problems associated with bilateral otitis media with effusion. *Journal of Learning Disabilities, 15*(7), 417–421.

Snow, C.E. (1984). Parent-child interaction in the development of communicative ability. In R.L. Schiefelbusch & J. Pickar (Eds.), *The acquisition of communicative competence* (pp. 69–107). Baltimore: University Park Press.

Stool, S.E., Berg, A.O., Berman, S., Carney, C.J., Cooley, J.R., Culpepper, L., Eavey, R.D., Feagans, L.V., Finitzo, T., Friedman, E.M., Goertz, J.A., Goldstein, A.J., Grundfast, K.M., Long, D.G., Macconi, L.L., Melton, L., Roberts, J.E., Sherrod, J.L., & Sisk, J.E. (1994). *Otitis media with effusion in young children: Clinical practice guideline, No. 12* (AHCPR Publication No. 94-0622). Rockville, MD: Agency for Health Care Policy and Research, Public Health Service, U.S. Department of Health and Human Services.

Teele, D.W., Klein, J.O., Chase, C., Menyuk, P., Rosner, B.A., & the Greater Boston Otitis Media Study Group. (1990). Otitis media in infancy and intellectual ability, school achievement, speech, and language at age 7 years. *Journal of Infectious Diseases, 162,* 685–694.

Teele, D.W., Klein, J.O., & Rosner, B.A. (1989). Epidemiology of otitis media during the first seven years of life in children in greater Boston. *Journal of Infectious Diseases, 160,* 83–94.

Teele, D.W., Klein, J.O., Rosner, B.A., & the Greater Boston Otitis Media Study Group. (1984). Otitis media with effusion during the first three years of life and development of speech and language. *Pediatrics, 74*(2), 282–287.

van der Vyver, M., van der Merwe, A., & Tesner, H.E.C. (1988). The effect of otitis media on articulation in children with cerebral palsy. Brief research report. *International Journal of Rehabilitation Research, 11*(4), 386–389.

Wallace, I.F., Gravel, J.S., McCarton, C.M., & Ruben, R.J. (1988). Otitis media and language development at 1 year of age. *Journal of Speech and Hearing Disorders, 53,* 245–251.

Wallace, I.F., Gravel, J.S., McCarton, C.M., Stapells, D.R., Bernstein, R.S., & Ruben, R.J. (1988). Otitis media, auditory sensitivity, and language outcomes at one year. *Laryngoscope, 98*(1), 64–70.

Watt, M.R., Roberts, J.E., & Zeisel, S. (1993). Ear infections in young children: The role of the early childhood educator. *Young Children, 49*(1), 65–72.

Whiteman, B.C., Simpson, G.B., & Compton, W.C. (1986). Relationship of otitis media and language impairment in adolescents with Down syndrome. *Mental Retardation, 24*(6), 353–356.

Wright, P.F., Sell, S.H., McConnell, K.B., Sitton, A.B., Thompson, J., Vaughn, W.K., & Bess, F.H. (1988). Impact of recurrent otitis media on middle ear function, hearing, and language. *Journal of Pediatrics, 113,* 581–587.

Zinkus, P.W., & Gottleib, M.I. (1980). Patterns of perceptual and academic deficits related to early chronic otitis media. *Pediatrics, 66*(6), 246–253.

7

Otitis Media and Its Impact on Cognitive, Academic, and Behavioral Outcomes

A Review and Interpretation of the Findings

Ina F. Wallace and Stephen R. Hooper

It has been suggested that children who have experienced recurrent otitis media (OM) or persistent otitis media with effusion (OME) are more likely to display learning and behavioral difficulties. In a survey (Byrd & Weitzman, 1994) of almost 10,000 children ages 7–17 years, 22.7% were found to have had frequent ear infections, and children with ear infections were more likely to have repeated kindergarten or first grade (odds ratio: 1.3; 95% confidence interval: 1.1–1.7). Given the incidence of OM (Schappert, 1992), this finding has important public health implications. Although Byrd and Weitzman did not set out to examine this particular association, there is an ample body of research that has assessed the relationship between OM and cognitive and behavioral outcomes. However, there has been little consensus regarding the possible effects of OM on developmental outcomes. This chapter synthesizes the findings from these studies, attempts to resolve discrepancies between

Support for this chapter was provided by National Institute on Deafness and Other Communication Disorders Center Grant (DC 00223).

the studies by examining methodologic factors, and discusses the theoretical rationale for the association between OM and cognitive and behavioral outcomes. Finally, some suggestions for intervention techniques are offered for children who have had recurrent OM and have been found to have learning and behavior problems.

REVIEW OF TERMINOLOGY

In this review, standard epidemiologic terms are used to classify studies. Studies are classified as *prospective* if the cohort is followed from the outset of the study with regard to OM. In the present chapter, only those cohort studies in which OM is independently documented (i.e., not by parental report) as the study progresses are classified as prospective; in other words, such studies are those in which a group of individuals are followed and their OM status and developmental outcomes are measured over time. Studies are classified as *retrospective* when the participants' OM occurred prior to the initiation of the study. *Case–control* research designs are one type of retrospective study in which cases, either those with histories of OM or with some developmental disability identified prior to the study, are compared with controls who do not have a history of OM or the developmental disorder. In some case–control designs, comparisons of outcomes such as IQ scores or rates of academic failure are made between children with different OM histories. Studies involving comparisons of OM histories for children with different academic histories, such as learning disabilities versus no learning disabilities, also are classified as retrospective case–control designs. *Cross-sectional* studies are those in which both OM and developmental outcomes are measured at the same point. If the investigators continue to follow the sample, the later follow-up is classified as prospective.

Studies have varied not only in when they documented OM, but in how OM was documented and in what form the data were used in analyses. Both pneumatic otoscopy and tympanometry have been used, with some researchers using a combination of both methods for documentation. Some researchers have treated OM as a continuous variable and have derived measures, such as the number of days with effusion (e.g., Roberts, Burchinal, & Campbell, 1994; Roberts et al., 1986, 1989; Teele et al., 1990) or the number of episodes (e.g., Roberts et al., 1994). Others have dichotomized groups by their OM histories into OM positive and OM free (e.g., Wallace, Gravel, McCarton, & Ruben, 1988) or into chronic OM and nonchronic OM (e.g., Feagans, Kipp, & Blood, 1994). Furthermore, classification criteria were often different from study to study. For instance, Wallace, Gravel, McCarton, and Ruben (1988) classified as OM positive those children in whom 30% or more of health care visits were bilaterally positive for OM, whereas Pearce, Saunders, Creighton, and Sauve (1988) included as OM cases those children who had abnormal tympanometry assessments on two or more visits or who had myringotomy tubes inserted before age 3 years. In this chapter, distinctions between studies relating to documentation methods and procedures for treating OM data are not made; however, a review of these procedures is available in Chapter 2. Finally, because in many studies no distinction was made between acute OM and OME, outcomes of children experiencing both forms are included.

For the purposes of brevity, multiple studies involving the same cohort by the same investigator or investigative group are treated together. All attempts were made to include every cohort in which cognitive, academic, and behavioral outcomes were assessed, although not every published report by an investigator may have been indicated. When an investigative group examined more than one cohort, each is included separately; if there were discrepant results, these are noted. For the purposes of this chapter, school-age outcomes include those of children who were either in first grade or higher or who were at least 6 years of age. Investigations involving samples of children at high risk for developmental disorders, such as those who were born prematurely, are included, whereas those with known anomalies, such as children born with Down syndrome or cleft palate, are not included because the applicability of findings from such populations to the general population is limited. A cross section of ethnic groups and populations is also included to examine some generalizability issues.

OTITIS MEDIA AND COGNITION
Since 1970, 18 study groups have examined the association between OM and intellectual functioning. Silva's Dunedin group is listed as both cross-sectional (Silva, Kirklang, Simpson, Stewart, & Williams, 1982) and prospective (Silva, Chalmers, & Stewart, 1986). Unlike research examining academic outcomes, cognitive outcomes of infants and toddlers are available. Table 1 provides a summary of the investigators, the participants, the population from whom the sample was drawn, how and when OM was documented, and the outcomes measured. Documentation of hearing status is also noted. Studies are listed by type of design.

Retrospective Studies
There have been nine cohorts in which investigators have employed retrospective sampling designs, two of which (Black & Sonnenshein, 1993; Knishkowy, Palti, Adler, & Tepper, 1991) examined outcomes through the preschool years. In these two studies, cognitive outcomes were examined prospectively during the preschool years, but the inves-

Table 1. Otitis media and cognitive status

Group reference	Participants[a]	Population[b]	Hearing assessed	History OM/age OM documented, method	Age cognition assessed	Outcome measures[c] Significant	Outcome measures[c] Nonsignificant
Retrospective							
1a. Black et al. (1988)	48 (27 OM+ cases, 21 OM− controls)	Lower SES; Maryland	No	History of OM during first year with documentation of otoscopy	8–22 months		Bayley MDI
1b. Black & Sonnenshein (1993)	31 (21 OM+ cases, 10 OM− controls)		No	5 years			McCarthy GCI
2. Brandes & Ehinger (1981)	30 (15 OM+ cases, 15 OM− controls)	Mid-SES; Canada	Yes	History of OM during first 2 years from parent report and failure on hearing screen	8 years		Raven's Progressive Matrices
3. Freeark et al. (1992)	56	Mid-SES; Michigan	No	History of OM during first 3 years from medical records	3–4 years		McCarthy Verbal Scale Index
4. Kaplan et al. (1973)	489 (207 OM+ cases, 76 OM− controls)	Lower SES Eskimos; Alaska	Yes	History of OM with otorrhea during first 4 years from parent report	9–10 years	WISC VIQ and PIQ	

Study	N	Sample	Hearing controlled	OM criteria	Age	Measures	Measures
5. Knishkowy et al. (1991)	207 (25 high OM, 182 low OM)	Lower and mid-SES; Israel	Yes	History of OM during first 3 years from parent report	2 and 3 years	B-L DQ; S-B IQ	
6. Sak & Ruben (1982)	36 (18 OM+ cases, 18 OM− sibling controls)	Mid-SES; New York	Yes	History of OM during first 5 years from medical records and normal hearing	8–11 years	WISC–R VIQ	Full-scale IQ; PIQ
7. Secord et al. (1988)	84 (49 OM+ cases, 35 OM− controls)	Mid-SES, learning disabilities; Virginia	No	History of OM during first 5 years	5–16 years	WISC–R IQ; Spatial factor> Sequential factor in cases	
8. Webster et al. (1989)	20 (10 OM+ cases, 10 OM− controls)	Great Britain	Yes	History of OM during first 5 years with some otoscopic or impedance documentation	7–11 years		WISC–R IQ, VIQ, PIQ
9. Zinkus et al. (1978)	40 (18 severe OM, 22 mild OM)	Mid-SES, academic underachievers; Tennessee	No	History of OM during first 3 years from medical records and parent reports	6–11 years	WISC–R IQ VIQ, PIQ	

(continued)

Table 1. (continued)

Group reference	Participants[a]	Population[b]	Hearing assessed	History OM/age OM documented, method	Age cognition assessed	Outcome measures[c] Significant	Outcome measures[c] Nonsignificant
Cross-Sectional							
Silva et al. (1982)	404 (47 OM+ cases, 357 OM− controls)	Mid-SES; New Zealand	Yes	Tympanometry at 5 years	5 years	S-B IQ	
Prospective							
1. Fischler et al. (1985)	167 (33 high OM, 63 high OM infancy only, 71 low OM)	Apache Native Americans; Arizona	Yes	Otoscopy during first 6–8 years	6–8 years		WISC–R Block Design Subtest
2. Lous et al. (1988)	52 26 OM+ cases, 26 OM− controls)	Denmark	Yes	Tympanometry at 3–4 years	8 years		WISC–R VIQ
3. Pearce et al. (1988)	42 (23 OM+ cases, 19 OM− controls)	Mid-SES Preterms; Canada	Yes	Tympanometry during first 3 years or PE tubes	8 months to 4 years	Bayley or McCarthy Verbal–Nonverbal Difference	
4. Peters et al. (1994)	270 (151 OM+ cases without PE tubes, 37 OM+ cases with PE tubes, 82 OM− controls)	Varied SES; Netherlands	Yes	Tympanometry from 2 to 4 years	7–8 years		Raven's Progressive Matrices
5a. Roberts et al. (1986)	61	Lower SES children in child care; North Carolina	No	Otoscopy during first 3 years	3½, 4, 4½, and 5 years		McCarthy GCI; S-B IQ; WPPSI IQ, VIQ, PIQ

Study	N	Sample	[a]	Method	Age	Measures
5b. Roberts et al. (1989)	44		No	Otoscopy during first 5 years	8 years	WISC–R VIQ
5c. Roberts et al. (1994)	55		No	Otoscopy during first 5 years	3, 3½, 4, 4½, 5, 6½, and 8 years	S-B IQ; McCarthy GCI; WPPSI IQ, VIQ, PIQ; WISC–R IQ, VIQ, PIQ
5d. Roberts, Burchinal, & Clarke-Klein (1995)	56		No	Otoscopy during first 3 years	12 years	WISC–R IQ, VIQ, PIQ
6. Roberts, Burchinal, Medley, et al. (1995)	61	Lower and mid-SES African Americans in child care; North Carolina	Yes	Otoscopy with tympanometry at 6–12 months	1 year	Bayley MDI
7. Silva et al. (1986)	352 (41 OM+ cases, 311 OM– controls)	New Zealand	Yes	Tympanometry at 5 years	5, 7, 9, and 11 years	S-B IQ; WISC–R IQ
8. Teele et al. (1990)	207	Lower and mid-SES; Massachusetts	No	Otoscopy during first 3 years	7 years	WISC–R IQ, VIQ, PIQ
9. Wallace, Gravel, McCarton, & Ruben (1988)	27 (12 OM+ cases, 15 OM– controls)	Lower SES NICU graduates and healthy full terms; New York	Yes	Otoscopy during first year	1 year	Bayley MDI

[a]OM+, OM-positive; OM–, OM-negative; PE, pressure-equalizing.

[b]NICU, neonatal intensive care unit; SES, socioeconomic status.

[c]Bayley MDI, Bayley Mental Developmental Index; B–L, Brunet-Lezine; DQ, developmental quotient; McCarthy GCI, McCarthy General Cognitive Index; PIQ, Performance IQ; S-B, Stanford-Binet Intelligence Scale; VIQ, Verbal IQ; WISC, Wechsler Intelligence Scale for Children; WISC–R, Wechsler Intelligence Scale for Children–Revised; WPPSI, Wechsler Preschool and Primary Scale of Intelligence.

tigators did not examine all the children's middle ear status at regular intervals. Therefore, these studies are classified with the retrospective studies. Two of the nine study groups (Secord, Erickson, & Bush, 1988; Webster, Bamford, Thyer, & Ayles, 1989) did not examine overall cognitive functioning as their outcome measure but rather examined patterns of scores on the Wechsler Intelligence Scale for Children–Revised (WISC–R). A third study (Brandes & Ehinger, 1981) used a nonverbal measure of reasoning, Raven's Coloured Progressive Matrices. In five of the studies, hearing was measured (Brandes & Ehinger, 1981; Kaplan, Fleshman, Bender, Baum, & Clark, 1973; Knishkowy et al., 1991; Sak & Ruben, 1982; Webster et al., 1989) either concurrently or at an earlier time.

The conclusions of four studies (Kaplan et al., 1973; Knishkowy et al., 1991; Secord et al., 1988; Zinkus, Gottlieb, & Shapiro, 1978) were that children with recurrent OM, irrespective of how defined, displayed lower cognitive test scores, a different pattern of cognitive abilities, or both. In one additional study (Sak & Ruben, 1982), overall IQ and performance IQ scores did not distinguish children grouped on the basis of OM, although verbal IQ scores did. In the studies with significant findings, the mean full-scale IQ difference was between 5 and 12 points (0.33–0.8 standard deviation [SD]); the mean verbal IQ difference was 5 to 9 points (0.33–0.66 SD). In the one study that examined cognition in relation to both OM and hearing (Kaplan et al., 1973), the relationship was due to lower IQ scores in the OM group with a hearing loss as compared to the OM group with no hearing loss.

Prospective and Cross-Sectional Studies

There was one cross-sectional study (Silva et al., 1982) in which IQ and OM status were each examined at 5 years; the group with bilateral OM scored 7 points lower than the children with normal otologic examinations. In addition, there were nine investigative groups that both followed their samples prospectively and documented otitis media independently. In most studies, documentation of OM began before children were 3 years. However, in addition to the cohort followed by Silva et al. (1986), Lous, Fiellau-Nikolajsen, and Jeppesen (1988) did not initiate tympanometry until the cohort was 3 years old. There were three cohorts who were only followed through infancy or preschool years, two cohorts who were followed up during both the infancy/preschool and school-age years, and four who were examined only during school-age years. It should be noted that, with one exception (Fischler, Todd, & Feldman, 1985), middle ear status was not monitored beyond the preschool period. Hearing was examined in seven of the nine studies, oftentimes only at one point in time.

The overall findings in these retrospective studies were essentially negative. That is, irrespective of whether outcomes were assessed in infancy, in preschool, or at school age, the investigators failed to detect a relationship between OM and cognitive test scores, with only two exceptions. An association between early OM and subsequent IQ scores at 7 years was found in the Boston collaborative group (Teele et al., 1990). Their strongest correlation ($r = -.29$) was between the estimated time spent with OM in the first year and full-scale IQ, accounting for less than 10% of the variance in IQ. Modest correlations were also found between time spent with middle ear effusion during the first 3 years of life and full-scale, verbal, and performance IQ scores. In this cohort, the maximum difference in intellectual abilities was 8 points in the full-scale WISC–R IQ (i.e., a little more than 0.5 *SD*), found between children who were estimated to have spent less than 30 days and those who spent more than 130 days with OM during the first 3 years of life. The only other investigative group to find a cognitive difference was Pearce and colleagues (1988), who found a greater nonverbal–verbal discrepancy in cognitive test scores in OM-negative compared with OM-positive children; in other words, children with positive OM histories performed relatively better on nonverbal than verbal items on the Bayley Mental Development Index. In addition, the difference in IQ scores that Silva and colleagues (1982) found at 5 years was not maintained when the children were followed at 7, 9, and 11 years of age (Silva et al., 1986). Although hearing was examined in most of the studies (seven of the nine), it was generally not included as an explanatory variable. One exception was the study of Roberts, Burchinal, Medley, et al. (1995) in which hearing, as well as OM, was unrelated to cognitive status.

In contrast to retrospective studies, the preponderance of evidence from prospective studies is that OM is not associated with global cognitive status during infancy or throughout childhood. Some of the significant associations found between parent reports of OM and IQ could be a spurious artifact of parents having a better memory for OM episodes in children who have developmental difficulties. Although the evidence suggests that OM during early childhood is not related to global measures of cognition, it is not known whether OM is related to more specific aspects of cognitive functioning, such as verbal reasoning, attention, and memory.

OTITIS MEDIA AND ACADEMIC ACHIEVEMENT

There are 19 study groups reviewed in which the relationship between OM and academic outcomes was assessed. In these reports, academic outcomes include standardized test scores, discrepancies between expected and actual test scores, learning disability or reading disability classifications made by the school or clinic, and teacher ratings of academic progress. Some studies have included multiple outcomes. Table 2 provides a summary of these studies.

Retrospective Studies

Eight studies used retrospective designs to assess the impact of OM on academic outcomes. Two of these studies (Zinkus et al., 1978; Zinkus & Gottlieb, 1980) included only children referred because of academic failure. The remainder of the studies compared academic outcomes in children with histories of OM, as indicated by records, parental report, or current middle ear pathology indicative of past episodes. The majority of investigators (five) had at least one assessment of hearing.

In the studies conducted by Zinkus and colleagues (Zinkus et al., 1978; Zinkus & Gottlieb, 1980), children with a history of OM had a greater discrepancy between reading/spelling achievement and grade level than a similar group of children without histories of OM. These differences were found in children referred for academic difficulties as well as children with academic problems who had auditory processing problems. Although Sak and Ruben (1982) found that children with histories of OM had a greater discrepancy between academic achievement and grade level placement than their siblings without histories of OM, there were no differences between the groups in mean reading, spelling, or arithmetic scores; moreover, both groups were above grade level. Of the remaining five studies, a history of OM was linked to at least one indicator of academic difficulties in three of them.

Cross-Sectional Studies

Three investigations used cross-sectional designs, in two of which children with learning impairments were compared with typically achieving children (Bennett, Ruuska, & Sherman, 1980; Freeman & Parkins, 1979). The outcome in these studies was the prevalence of middle ear pathology as assessed by concurrent tympanometry with or without otoscopy. Both found that children diagnosed with learning difficulties were more likely to have abnormal tympanograms. In addition, Bennett et al. (1980) found that a greater percentage of children with learning disabilities had positive OM histories. The third cross-sectional study (Scaldwell, 1989) found that Native Indian children in Canada with present OM or signs of past OM had lower reading scores than children with normal otologic exams.

Prospective Studies

In eight cohorts the link between OM and academic outcomes was investigated in a prospective fashion. In three of the study groups OM

Table 2. Otitis media and academic status

Group and reference	Participants[a]	Population[b]	Hearing assessed	History OM/age OM documented, method	Age/grade academics assessed	Outcome measures[c] Significant	Outcome measures[c] Nonsignificant
Retrospective							
1. Brandes & Ehinger (1981)	30 (15 OM+ cases, 15 OM− controls)	Mid-SES; Canada	Yes	History of OM during first 2 years from parent report and failure of hearing screen	8 years		PIAT Reading Comprehension; WRAT Reading, Arithmetic
2. Howie, Jensen, Fleming, Peeler, & Meigs (1979)	144 (72 OM+ cases, 72 OM− controls)	Alabama	No	History of OM during first 3 years from physicians' records	Unknown—school age	SRA academic composite	SRA Reading, Language Arts, Spelling
3. Kaplan et al. (1973)	489 (201 OM+ cases, 74 OM− controls)	Lower SES Eskimos; Alaska	Yes	History of OM with otorrhea during first 4 years from parent report	9–10 years	Grade level (below expectation)	
4. Sak & Ruben (1982)	36 (18 OM+ cases, 18 OM− control siblings)	Mid-SES; New York	Yes	History of OM during first 5 years from medical records and normal hearing	8–11 years	WRAT Spelling	WRAT Reading, Arithmetic
5. Updike & Thornburg (1992)	48 (24 OM+ cases, 24 OM− controls)	Indiana	Yes	History of OM during first 3 years from medical records and normal hearing	6–7 years	CRI	

(continued)

Table 2. (continued)

Group and reference	Participants[a]	Population[b]	Hearing assessed	History OM/age OM documented, method	Age/grade academics assessed	Outcome measures[c] Significant	Outcome measures[c] Nonsignificant
6. Webster et al. (1989)	20 (10 OM+ cases, 10 OM− controls)	Great Britain	Yes	History of OM during first 5 years with some otoscopic or impedance documentation	7–11 years		NPRT; SST; DPT
7. Zinkus et al. (1978)	40 (18 severe OM, 22 mild OM)	Mid-SES academic underachievers; Tennessee	No	History of OM during first 3 years from medical records and parent report	6–11 years	WRAT Reading, Spelling	WRAT Arithmetic
8. Zinkus & Gottlieb (1980)	60 (20 OM+/AP+, 20 OM−/AP+, 20 OM−/AP−)	Mid-SES academic underachievers; Tennesse	No	History of OM during first 3 years from medical records and parent report	7–11 years	WRAT Reading, Spelling, Arithmetic	
Cross-Sectional							
1. Bennett et al. (1980)	109 (53 cases w/LD, 56 controls w/o LD)	Mid-upper SES; Washington	Yes	History of OM during first 6 years from parent report, concurrent tympanometry	7–12 years	Greater % of LD with history of OM and abnormal tympanograms	
2. Freeman & Parkins (1979)	82 (50 cases w/LD, 32 controls w/o LD)	No information	Yes	Concurrent tympanometry and otoscopy	6–14 years	Greater % of LD with abnormal tympanograms	Concurrent otoscopy
3. Scaldwell (1989)	524 (147 present OM+, 112 past OM+, 265 OM− controls)	Native Indian; Canada	No	Concurrent otoscopy and tympanometry	School-aged—unspecified	G-M, Reading	

174

Prospective							Academic Ratings
1. Brooks (1986)	64	Varied SES; Great Britain	Yes	Tympanometry from ages 5 to 7 years	16–18 years		
2. Gravel & Wallace (1995)	14 (7 OM+ cases, 7 OM– controls)	Low SES NICU graduates and healthy full terms; New York	Yes	Otoscopy during first year of life	6 years	SIFTER total; W-J-R Reading	W-J-R Math
3. Lous et al. (1988)	56 (28 OM+ cases, 28 OM– controls)	Denmark	Yes	Tympanometry from 3 to 4 years	8 years		OS-400 Silent Reading
4. Lous (1993)	366 (76 OM+ cases, 290 OM– controls)	Varied SES; Denmark	Yes	Tympanometry and otoscopy during the first year of school	8 years	OS-400 Silent Reading	
5. Peters et al. (1994)	270 (151 OM+ cases w/o PE tubes, 37 OM+ cases w/PE tubes, 82 OM– controls)	Varied SES; Netherlands	Yes	Tympanometry from 2 to 4 years	7–8 years	Spelling; teacher ratings of writing	OMRT; WRT; SVT; Grapheme Test; teacher ratings of reading and arithmetic

(continued)

Table 2. (continued)

Group and reference	Participants[a]	Population[b]	Hearing assessed	History OM/age OM documented, method	Age/grade academics assessed	Outcome measures[c]	
						Significant	Nonsignificant
6a. Roberts et al. (1986)	55	Lower SES in child care; North Carolina	No	Otoscopy during first 3 years	Kindergarten		PIAT
b. Roberts et al. (1989)	44		No		2nd grade		W-J Reading, Mathematics
c. Roberts et al. (1994)	55		No	Otoscopy during first 5 years	8–9 years		W-J Reading, Mathematics
b. Roberts, Burchinal, & Clarke-Klein (1995)	56		No	Otoscopy during first 3 years	12 years		W-J Reading, Mathematics, Knowledge, Written Language
7. Silva et al. (1986)	367 (44 OM+ cases, 323 OM− controls)	New Zealand	Yes	Tympanometry at age 5 years	7, 9, and 11 years	Burt Word Reading Test	
8. Teele et al. (1990)	207	Lower and mid-SES; Massachusetts	No	Otoscopy during first 3 years	7 years	MAT Mathematics, Reading	

[a]AP+, auditory processing problems; AP−, no auditory processing problems; LD, learning disabilities; OM+, OM-positive; OM−, OM negative; PE, pressure-equalizing.

[b]NICU, neonatal intensive care unit; SES, socioeconomic status.

[c]CRI, Classroom Reading Inventory; DPT, Domain Phonic Test; G-M, Gates-MacGinitie Reading Tests; MAT, Metropolitan Achievement Test; NPRT, Nelson Primary Reading Test; OMRT, One-Minute Test (Reading); PIAT, Peabody Individual Achievement Test; SIFTER, Screening Instrument for Targeting Educational Risk; SRA, Science Research Associates; SST, Schonell Spelling Test; SVT, Sentence Verification Test (Reading); W-J, Woodcock-Johnson Psychoeducational Battery; W-J-R, Woodcock-Johnson Revised Psychoeducational Battery; WRAT, Wide Range Achievement Test; WRT, Word Recognition Test.

was documented beginning in infancy, in three of the cohorts OM was documented during the preschool years, and in the remaining two cohorts OM was documented during the early school years. Most of the studies evaluated outcomes during the elementary school years, although one study (Brooks, 1986) linked OM during the first 2 years of school to academic outcomes at the end of secondary school. In all but one of the studies, hearing was examined at some point during the follow-up.

The results of the prospective studies were not as clear-cut, although a relationship was found in the majority (five of eight). In two of the three cohorts in which OM was documented beginning in infancy (Gravel & Wallace, 1995; Teele et al., 1990), children with recurrent OM were found to have lower achievement scores in one or more academic areas. Differences in reading in the Gravel and Wallace cohort were 17 points (a little more than 1 *SD*) and in the Teele et al. cohort were 38 points (1.25 *SD*). Teele and colleagues also found a difference of 31 points in mathematics achievement (about 1 *SD*). In addition, the OM-positive children followed by Gravel and Wallace received lower ratings by their teachers across several areas of academic functioning. In contrast, Roberts and colleagues (Roberts, Burchinal, & Campbell, 1994; Roberts, Burchinal, & Clarke-Klein, 1995; Roberts, Burchinal, Collier, et al., 1989; Roberts, Sanyal, et al., 1986) found no association between OM and academic achievement at either kindergarten, 8, or 12 years of age.

Results were also inconsistent for samples whose OM status was documented during the preschool years. In the follow-up of the Nijmegan cohort, Peters, Grievink, van Bon, and Schilder (1994) found a 6-point difference in spelling between a group of children with OM who had not received ventilation tubes and a group without OM. They also found a difference in teachers' ratings of writing skills, but no differences in reading, arithmetic, or grade repetition. Silva et al. (1986) found differences in reading achievement measured at 7, 9, and 11 years between the children with and without OM (measured at age 5 years). Finally, in the two studies examining OM during the school years, only one found an association with OM. Lous (1993) found that children who had normal tympanograms at every assessment had reading scores that were 20 points higher than children with at least one abnormal tympanogram. However, there was no association with reported histories of OM, nor was there an association with hearing at school age.

These results suggest that there may be a modest effect of OM on academic skills, with the effect somewhat stronger for language-based skills such as reading, spelling, and written language. Few of these studies included other variables that could further explain the relationship between OM and academic achievement, such as parental education and intelligence or the quality of the home environment. Nor have investigators considered whether there is a different pattern of effects for children whose OM was resolved by age 3, in contrast to those who continued to have OM through the preschool or early school years or both.

OTITIS MEDIA AND BEHAVIOR

Since the 1980s, there has been more interest in the association between OM and behavior, particularly attention, attention deficit disorder (ADD), and attention-deficit/hyperactivity disorder (ADHD). Since 1982, there have been eight study groups (see Table 3) in which investigators considered the associations in this domain. Most of these studies were of school-age children, although two reports (Arcia & Roberts, 1993; Feagans et al., 1994) included data from toddlers and preschoolers. This outcome area is broadly defined, including parent and teacher ratings of attention and behavior as well as performance-based measures of attention. In addition, case–control studies of children classified with ADHD have also been made. Unlike intellectual outcomes, attention and behavior are more likely to be situation specific, so that knowledge of the source of the data becomes vitally important.

Retrospective / Cross-Sectional Studies

Four investigative groups employed retrospective or cross-sectional designs. Two of these were case–control studies (Adesman, Altshuler, Lipkin, & Walco, 1990; Hagerman & Falkenstein, 1987), comparing children with hyperactivity (ADHD) with children with learning problems (either learning disabilities or school failure), all of whom were referred to child development clinics. The other two studies (Black & Sonnenshein, 1993; Webster et al., 1989) compared ratings on children with and without histories of OM. Hearing was assessed only in the Webster et al. investigation.

Both study groups who compared children with ADHD with other children with school difficulties found an association between reports of OM and a diagnosis of hyperactivity; that is, children with a diagnosis of hyperactivity were more likely to have been reported as having OM. In contrast, Webster et al. (1989) did not detect any differences in teacher ratings of behavior between children who were referred for surgery because of OM and children with no histories of OM. Nor were there any differences in parent ratings as a function of OM in the Black and Sonnenshein study (1993).

There was one cross-sectional study conducted by Silva, Kirklang, et al. (1982). They included ratings of a variety of maladaptive behaviors (e.g., fearfulness, dependency, restlessness, being quarrelsome) that were

Table 3. Otitis media and behavior outcomes

Group and reference	Participants[a]	Population[b]	Hearing assessed	History OM/age OM documented, method	Age/behavior assessed	Outcome measures[c]	
						Significant	Nonsignificant
Retrospective							
1. Adesman et al. (1990)	66 (45 w/LD, 21 w/ ADHD)	Mid-SES psychoeducational clinic referrals; New York	No	History of OM from parental report	5–13 years	More ear infections in ADHD in the past year	Total number of ear infections since birth
2. Black & Sonnenshein (1993)	31 (21 OM+ cases, 10 OM− controls)	Lower SES; Maryland	No	History of OM during first year from medical records with documentation of otoscopy	5 years		CBCL
3. Hagerman & Falkenstein (1987)	67 (27 cases w/ADHD, 40 controls w/o ADHD)	Mixed SES school learning problems; Colorado	No	History of OM from parent report and medical records	6–13 years	More OM in ADHD	
4. Webster et al (1989)	20 (10 OM+ cases, 10 OM− controls)	Great Britain	Yes	History of OM during first 5 years with some otoscopic or impedance documentation	7–11 years		CBQT
Cross-Sectional							
1. Silva et al. (1982)	404 (47 OM+ cases, 357 OM− controls)	Mid-SES; New Zealand	Yes	Tympanometry at 5 years	5 years	Attentional behaviors	Other behaviors

(continued)

179

Table 3. (*continued*)

Group and reference	Participants[a]	Population[b]	Hearing assessed	History OM/age OM documented, method	Age/behavior assessed	Outcome measures[c] Significant	Outcome measures[c] Nonsignificant
Prospective							
1. Feagans et al. (1994)	46 (28 high OM, 18 low OM)	Mid-SES in child care; Pennsylvania	Yes	Otoscopy and tympanometry from 6 months to 3 years	12 or 18 months	Ratings of nonattention	Ratings of negative affect
2. Gravel & Wallace (1995)	14 (7 OM+ cases, 7 OM− controls)	Lower SES NICU graduates & healthy full terms; New York	Yes	Otoscopy during first year of life	6 years		CPRS; CTRS; SIFTER Behavior, Attention
3a. McGee et al. (1982)	853 (123 OM+ cases, 730 OM− controls)	Mid-SES; New Zealand	Yes	Tympanometry at 5 years	7 years	Rutter Child Scales A and B	
b. Silva et al. (1986)	337 (39 OM+ cases, 298 OM− controls)		Yes		5, 7, 9, and 11 years	Rutter Child Scale B (Teachers)	Rutter Child Scale A (Parents)

Study		Lower SES/sample	OM measure	Otoscopy/OM assessment	Age at outcome	Outcome measures
4a. Roberts et al. (1989)	44	Lower SES in child care; North Carolina	No	Otoscopy during first 3 years	2nd grade	CBI Independence, Task Orientation
b. Arcia & Roberts (1993) (2 studies)	1) 35–55 2) 24		1) No 2) Yes		1) 2, 3, and 4 years 2) 52–84 months	1) TBI Attention Cooperativeness 2) CPT attention
c. Roberts et al. (1994)	51		No	Otoscopy during first 5 years	8–9 years	CBI Task Orientation
d. Robert, Burchinal, & Clarke-Klein (1995)	56		No	Otoscopy during first 3 years	12 years	WISC–R Freedom from Distractibility; CBCL Externalizing and Internalizing Problems

[a] ADHD, attention-deficit/hyperactivity disorder; LD, learning disabilities; OM+, OM-positive; OM−, OM-negative.

[b] NICU, neonatal intensive care unit; SES, socioeconomic status.

[c] CBCL, Child Behavior Checklist; CBI, Classroom Behavior Inventory; CBQT, Children's Behavior Questionnaire for Teachers; CPRS, Conners' Parent Rating Scales; CPT, Continuous Performance Test; CTRS, Conners' Teacher Rating Scales; SIFTER, Screening Instrument for Targeting Educational Risk; TBI, Test Behavior Inventory; WISC–R, Wechsler Intelligence Scale for Children–Revised.

observed by assessors during a psychological evaluation and were reported by parents. Differences at 5 years between OM-positive and OM-negative children were found in ratings of motivational, attentional, and hyperactive behaviors, such as short attention span, weak goal orientation, restlessness, destructiveness, and disobedience.

Prospective Studies

The prospective studies included two follow-up reports from the Dunedin study group (McGee, Silva, & Stewart, 1982; Silva et al., 1986), several reports of children from Chapel Hill research child care programs (i.e., Arcia & Roberts, 1993; Roberts, Burchinal, Clarke-Klein, 1995; Roberts et al., 1989, 1994), and two other studies assessing behavior. In two of these reports (Arcia & Roberts, 1993; Feagans et al., 1994), behavior was measured using direct assessments of the children by either ratings- or performance-based measures. The remainder used either parent or teacher ratings of the child's behavior. Hearing was assessed in all the cohorts at least once during the study period.

The conclusions of this group of prospective studies are also mixed, although there is somewhat more evidence that there is an association between OM and attention, hyperactivity, and the diagnosis of ADHD. In three of the four cohort studies, relationships were found between OM and at least one behavioral outcome at one time period. In one of these positive studies, which included young children, Feagans et al. (1994) found that the percentage of time toddlers had OM was associated with their nonattending behaviors during a book-reading task. In contrast, Arcia and Roberts (1993) did not find an association between duration of OM and either assessor ratings of preschoolers' behaviors during testing or the sustained attention of 4- to 7-year-old children on a continuous performance task. However, many of these same children were included in the reports of Roberts and colleagues (Roberts, Burchinal, & Campbell, 1994; Roberts, Burchinal, & Clarke-Klein, 1995; Roberts, Burchinal, Collier, et al., 1989). They found that the duration of OM during the first 3 years of life was related to teachers' ratings of both independence and task orientation at 5 years, whereas the duration of OM during the first 5 years of life was related to teachers' ratings of task orientation at 8 years. However, no overall relationship was found with attention/behavior problems at 12 years. Although the OM-positive sample of Silva, Chalmers, and Stewart (1986) was no longer rated differently by their parents at the school-age follow-up, their teachers continued to rate this group as having more behavior problems throughout the elementary school years. Gravel and Wallace (1995) found that children with positive histories of OM were rated as participating less by their teachers than children free of OM, but no differences were found in either parent or teacher ratings of attention or behavior.

SYNTHESIS OF FINDINGS

Previous investigators (Paradise, 1981; Ventry, 1980) who have discussed the diverse findings in the outcome literature have pointed to the differences and deficiencies in many research designs. The greatest limitation has been the failure to examine OM prospectively. Conclusions deriving from retrospective studies are unclear because an association between OM and an outcome may have been due to bias in recall of episodes. Likewise, the failure to find an association may have been due to the presence of "silent" episodes among those participants who were considered otitis free. Aside from the retrospective design difficulty, no two studies employed the same OM classification. In those studies that included both OM-positive and OM-negative groups, designation of a positive status was made for children with two or more episodes in the first year (Black & Sonnenshein, 1993; Black et al., 1988), six or more episodes in the first 3 years (Knishkowy et al., 1991), two or more abnormal tympanograms or tube placement before age 3 (Pearce et al., 1988), 30% or more of the first-year otoscopic examinations being positive (Wallace, Gravel, McCarton, & Ruben, 1988), and four abnormal tympanograms during a 6-month period when the children were 3 years of age (Lous et al., 1988). Because these studies varied tremendously in the period of OM documentation as well as the age when documentation began, it is not possible to achieve consensus regarding the age of greatest impact. In addition, few investigators considered other variables that could mediate cognitive, academic, and behavioral outcomes, limiting the kinds of conclusions that can be drawn from this body of research.

With these methodologic limitations in mind, it appears that some conclusions can be reached. Global cognitive status appears relatively less related to either early or late OM than are academic skills and behavioral adjustment. There are few consistent differences between children with greater and fewer episodes of OM in intellectual functioning. However, there appears to be a modest association between recurrent/persistent OM and both academic skills and the presence of behavior problems, particularly in the area of attention. The reasons for this pattern of findings remain largely speculative. However, some explanations are offered based on theories regarding early learning, compensatory mechanisms, and the role of audition in cognitive abilities. Insights acquired from children with profound hearing loss are also considered.

EXPLANATION OF FINDINGS

Although infants learn about their environments in a multiplicity of ways, it has been thought that much of early learning is visual (Thompson, Fagan, & Fulker, 1991). Within the early months of life, visual acuity improves, the ability to smile in response to a smile occurs, and guided reaching is attained. Through these early achievements the infant learns about important objects in his or her environment. With maturation, the visual system develops and provides input enabling recognition, memory, and classification skills to develop. Long before they use language productively, infants exhibit the capacity to process, discriminate, and remember complex visual stimuli (Fagan, 1970; Fantz, 1964) as well as to transfer information across modalities (Gottfried, Rose, & Bridger, 1977). (See Colombo, 1993, for a thorough discussion of all of these abilities.) As Piagetian models of child development have borne out, by 2 years of age most infants are able to anticipate events, imitate behaviors, and indicate an understanding that objects have invariant properties. Although such skills largely develop as a result of visually acquired information, these abilities have been shown to underlie later cognitive, linguistic, and memory processes.

One explanation for these accomplishments is that, as sensorimotor abilities develop, the infant is better able to interact with the environment. Feldman and Gelman (1986) discussed several theories of cognitive development in relation to OM that amplify this notion, and they deemed the rational-constructionist theory as the one most in accord with available data. According to this position, which is based on Piagetian theories, children not only use their innate capacities to interpret and process environmental input but play an active role in developing their abilities. From this position it is predicted that, when auditory stimuli are degraded, the infant can actively seek out alternative sources of input to support cognitive development.

For example, it has been shown that congenitally deaf individuals without brain damage can compensate for their loss of auditory input. Research using event-related potential (ERP) electrophysiology has shown differences in the visual abilities of congenitally deaf and normally hearing adults. Neville, Schmidt, and Kutas (1983) reported that congenitally deaf adults who were deprived of auditory stimulation from birth had greater visual ERPs than adults without hearing impairments. These results and others suggested to Neville (1990) that there are areas within the left hemisphere, normally involved in speech and auditory language comprehension in hearing adults, that are active in attention to and perception of movement in the peripheral visual fields in deaf subjects. Other research involving deaf children indicates that, as a group, they may utilize different learning strategies than children without hearing impairments, as evidenced by how memory processes are organized (Marschark, 1993).

These results are consonant with several of the investigations of children with OM showing stronger visual-spatial abilities. For instance,

Pearce et al. (1988) showed that, beginning in infancy, there was a greater discrepancy between verbal and visuomotor abilities. Moreover, Secord et al. (1988) reported that children with learning disabilities and positive histories of OM performed better on nonverbal spatial tasks than children with learning disabilities without histories of OM and that they performed worse on sequential verbal tasks. The investigators hypothesized that the hearing loss secondary to OM might have led to permanent auditory–cortical processing deficits in the OM-positive children, who compensated by using visual channels to acquire information about the world.

This body of research suggests that young children who are deprived of typical auditory input are nevertheless acquiring a great deal of information about their world. Moreover, if the deprivation is severe enough (as in the case of congenitally deaf children), brain functions may be reorganized to take advantage of other avenues of information processing (e.g., visual-perceptual processes). Although many of these studies have used the example of children who are deaf or have hearing impairment, there may be some lessons to be learned for children with OM. As a consequence of OM, there may be some lasting effects in the form of brain stem and central auditory processing deficits (see Chapter 4), that may not affect global intellectual skills. Although the level of hearing loss that usually results from OM is in the mild to moderate range, there is some evidence that it could interfere with some linguistic-based skills, particularly in the area of phonology (see Chapter 5), during a sensitive developmental period for these skills. According to Feldman and Gelman (1986), the rational-constructionist theory suggests that only some abilities would be affected by OM, and language-dependent abilities would seem to be more vulnerable to the impact of OM than non-language-based abilities.

It is not surprising that, even when there are disruptions in the auditory environment as often occur during episodes of OM, young children continue to learn about their environments and acquire the skills that are assessed on standard measures of intellectual functioning. In contrast, achievement in academic domains, such as reading and spelling, is predicted to be more affected by OM. This prediction rests on the critical importance of linguistic skills in both reading and spelling (Perfetti, 1985; Vellutino, 1979). In particular, there has been ample research demonstrating the relationship between children's phonological skills and achievement in reading (Stanovich, 1988; Wagner & Torgeson, 1987) and spelling (Bryant, MacLean, Bradley, & Crossland, 1990). In a review of several studies, Brady (1986) concluded that children with documented reading disabilities are less accurate at phonetic encoding than are children without such disabilities. At the same time, there is some evidence that school-age children with a history of recurrent OM display phonological deficits. For instance, there have been reports that a positive history of OM is associated with difficulties in aspects of speech perception, such as the discrimination and identification of stimuli varying in phonemic characteristics (Eimas & Clarkson, 1986; Menyuk, 1986; Mody et al., in press; see Chapter 5 for a discussion). In addition, in one cohort (Wallace, Gravel, McCarton, & Stapells, et al., 1988) in which early OM history was related to elevations in concurrent hearing sensitivity as measured by the auditory brain stem response (ABR), the average ABR threshold from the first year of life was related to a measure tapping higher-order phonological skills at early school age. Thus, it is hypothesized that conductive hearing loss secondary to OM can affect the acquisition of phonological processing skills that underlie reading and spelling. Moreover, this effect would appear to be independent of more global measures of intellectual functioning, particularly in the early school-age years.

The link between OM and behavior is less obvious, although recent research models have suggested that hearing loss is the mediating factor. Feagans et al. (1994) found that toddlers in child care with chronic OM were less attentive during a book-reading activity and were rated by their mothers as more distractible and nonattentive than toddlers with nonchronic OM. There were no differences in hearing loss between toddlers with chronic and nonchronic OM (i.e., both groups displayed a 10-dB loss during OM episodes). However, these investigators speculated that the behavior of the chronic OM group was affected because they experienced a hearing loss for a much greater period of time than the nonchronic OM group. Results of other studies by Feagans, Sanyal, Henderson, Collier, and Applebaum (1987) and Roberts, Burchinal, Collier, et al. (1989) indicate that the frequency of OM during the first 3 years of life was associated with off-task behaviors and teacher ratings of task orientation. Feagans (1986) proposed the attention-to-language model to account for these relationships. In brief, it hypothesizes that the mild hearing loss secondary to OM tends to make affected children less attentive to language, especially to lengthy language sequences. As a result, such children may learn to "tune out" language during periods of hearing loss, a pattern that may become habitual even when hearing is unimpaired. It is further suggested that noise that is typical in many classrooms could interfere with children's already impaired ability to attend to verbal instruction (Gravel & Wallace, 1992). In addition, it is not hard to imagine that children who find it difficult to attend would be prone to distractions and problematic behaviors in the classroom setting. In fact, it is precisely these behaviors that contribute to the academic and social difficulties of children diagnosed with ADD/ADHD (Barkley, 1990).

IMPLICATIONS OF THE RESEARCH

Although we and others have speculated why OM tends to display the observed pattern of associations with cognitive, academic, and behavioral outcomes, there is a critical need for researchers to test specific models based on these hypotheses. In fact, Feldman and Gelman (1986) made just such a suggestion. Some progress has been made. Ongoing investigations of OM now include measures that will elucidate both hearing status and a more complete range of auditory capacities that are thought to underlie complex cognitive and behavioral processes. There has also been some movement toward obtaining greater specificity in the kinds of cognitive and behavioral outcomes that are being assessed. In addition, most of the ongoing research is guided by the importance of prospective documentation of OM. However, until the results of these research endeavors are available, consensus about the effects of OM is limited.

In addition, future research must build on the theoretical models of how OM is thought to operate and must consider other factors that can moderate OM's effect. For instance, some investigators have now begun to include measures of the child-rearing environment in studies of the sequelae of OM (i.e., Black et al., 1988; Black & Sonnenshein, 1993; Freeark et al., 1992; Roberts, Burchinal, Medley, et al., 1995; Wallace, Gravel, Schwartz, & Ruben, 1996). Inclusion of measures that assess the teaching style of parents, parental communicative interactions, and general quality of the home environment along with affective measures (e.g., attachment, temperament, mastery motivation) could provide more ecologically valid approaches to examining developmental outcomes. Moreover, techniques such as ERP electrophysiology and functional magnetic resonance imaging could be used to examine the impact of hearing loss secondary to OM on brain function. The combination of measures of brain activity and structure with more precise measures of neurolinguistic competence in these children may provide additional insights into the impact of OM on developmental outcomes.

RECOMMENDATIONS FOR EDUCATORS

The fact that there is no one-to-one correspondence between a history of OM and the presence of specific cognitive, academic, and behavioral sequelae offers challenges for individuals who work with children with histories of OM. Despite this lack of a clear connection between OM and later outcomes, the research to date does provide clues for working with these children during the preschool as well as the school-age years. Furthermore, a number of organizations (e.g., American-Speech-Language-Hearing Association, 1990) and investigators (Roberts &

Medley, 1995) have provided general guidelines for intervening with these children. Consequently, in addition to the medical management of children with OM, additional educational strategies can be proffered from the literature.

For example, Roberts and Medley (1995) noted that the tasks of the speech-language pathologist when working with prekindergarten children who have a positive OM history include 1) monitoring for hearing loss and early evidence of developmental delays, 2) sharing information with caregivers about possible developmental sequelae of OM, 3) working with caregivers to provide an optimal health and learning environment, 4) consulting in the medical management of OM, and 5) developing intervention programs that are natural extensions of the speech and language evaluation. More specifically, these tasks may include using multiple modalities in language-learning situations, increasing attention to language across all activities, encouraging keen listening skills, and capitalizing on familiar learning routes when introducing new information. Additionally, considerations for providing acoustic amplification (e.g., low-gain hearing aids, FM sound field amplification) for children who experience persistent hearing loss or attention difficulties because of a past history of OM may prove fruitful, particularly given the emergent findings related to such treatments of children with phonological disorders (Gordon-Brannan, Hodson, & Wynne, 1992) and academic problems (Sarff, Ray, & Bagwell, 1981).

In a similar vein, Wallach and Miller (1988) noted the importance of adapting interventions and teaching strategies to meet each child's individual and unique learning needs. Thus, educational interventions for the child with OM should be no different than interventions for any child with special needs (e.g., children with learning disabilities) (Hooper, Willis, & Stone, 1996). One of the key findings that has emerged in the literature to date is that children with OM may show stronger visual-perceptual abilities and weaker auditory-verbal abilities (Secord et al., 1988), and instructional strategies should target these strengths. For example, the liberal use of visual prompts (e.g., pictures) and cues (e.g., written outlines) may serve to increase learning efficiency for children with OM. Furthermore, given the relative weaknesses in the auditory-verbal domain, any instruction tapping this learning modality should routinely be accompanied by materials that tap other modalities. This does not imply that the weaker modality should be ignored or avoided but, rather, that it should not be used as the primary vehicle for learning. Indeed, specific remediation efforts may be in order.

Another key finding that has emerged from the educational outcomes of children with OM is that academic skills of these children may be vulnerable to the effects of OM, particularly language-based skills. More specifically, phonological deficits in children with early OM have been described by a number of investigators (e.g., see Chapter 5). It is likely that, if such deficits are present, they contribute to the reading and spelling problems found in early elementary schoolchildren with histories of OM. Indeed, phonological processing deficits have come to be viewed as one of the core problems contributing to developmental reading and spelling disorders (e.g., Brady, 1986; Vellutino, Scanlon, & Tanzman, 1994; Wagner & Torgeson, 1987), and the need for phonological process training may be inherent for many of these children.

Given the emergent effectiveness of such treatment strategies for preschool children at risk for reading disabilities (e.g., Ball & Blachman, 1988; Korkman & Peltomaa, 1993), early intervention and prevention could be provided to children with OM using these treatment vehicles. As suggested by Hooper and colleagues (1986), the kinds of tasks used to assess phonological awareness abilities could be modified for remedial uses. An intervention designed to train children in phonological awareness might begin with one of the earlier tasks, recognition and production of rhyming. After mastering rhyming, more difficult tasks such as discrimination and matching of sounds could be introduced. Thereafter, phoneme segmentation and phoneme deletion tasks could be added. Another strategy is to arrange individual phonological awareness tasks hierarchically. For instance, segmentation tasks could be introduced at the compound word or syllable level before progressing to segmentation at the phoneme level. Phonological awareness could be enhanced by associating plastic letters (i.e., the visual symbols) with letter sounds. A technique to facilitate the acquisition of phonological awareness as suggested by Lindamood and Lindamood (1975) and Stone (1990) is to provide articulation awareness training, which focuses on how sounds are produced. Such training helps children explicitly attend to speech sounds and identify the motor characteristics in the production of the speech sounds.

Despite the equivocal findings with respect to the presence of inattention, it would be prudent to include frequent attentional checks for these children during new learning tasks. This would seem particularly critical during learning situations requiring rapid or dense language comprehension and, perhaps, during the preschool and early elementary school years when core academic skills are being formed. It remains unclear, however, if the attention problems described in children with OM mirror these evidenced by children with various manifestations of ADD/ADHD and, subsequently, whether they would respond to various types of pharmacologic treatments (e.g., stimulant medications).

CONCLUSIONS

As health surveys have indicated, OM is a nearly universal disease in young children (Schappert, 1992). Although there has been extensive research examining the sequelae of middle ear disease, there is no firm consensus regarding the consequences of early OM on cognitive and behavioral outcomes. Nevertheless, it is suspected that the mild conductive hearing loss often accompanying OM may result in some primary linguistic and attention deficits that may affect the acquisition of skills such as reading and spelling and on the ability to function in a classroom. Future research must delineate more specific models for testing these associations. When the mechanisms of how OM affects outcomes are better understood, it may be possible to prevent some of the sequelae.

REFERENCES

Adesman, A.R., Altschuler, L.A., Lipkin, P.H., & Walco, G.A. (1990). Otitis media in children with learning disabilities and in children with attention deficit disorder with hyperactivity. *Pediatrics, 85,* 442–446.

American Speech-Language-Hearing Association. (1990). Guidelines for screening for hearing impairments and middle-ear disorders. *Asha, 32*(Suppl. 2), 17–24.

Arcia, E., & Roberts, J.E. (1993). Otitis media in early childhood and its association with sustained attention in structured situations. *Journal of Developmental and Behavioral Pediatrics, 14,* 181–183.

Ball, E.W., & Blachman, B.A. (1988). Phoneme segmentation training: Effect on reading readiness. *Annals of Dyslexia, 38,* 208–225.

Barkley, R.A. (Ed.). (1990). *Attention deficit-hyperactivity disorder: A handbook of diagnosis and treatment* (2nd ed.). New York: Guilford Press.

Bennett, F.C., Ruuska, S.H., & Sherman, R. (1980). Middle ear function in learning-disabled children. *Pediatrics, 66,* 254–260.

Black, M.M., Gerson, L.F., Freeland, C.A.B., Nair, P., Rubin, J.S., & Hutcheson, J.J. (1988). Language screening for infants prone to otitis media. *Journal of Pediatric Psychology, 13,* 423–433.

Black, M.M., & Sonnenschein, S. (1993). Early exposure to otitis media: A preliminary investigation of behavioral outcome. *Journal of Developmental and Behavioral Pediatrics, 14,* 150–155.

Brady, S. (1986). Short-term memory, phonological processing, and reading ability. *Dyslexia, 36,* 138–153.

Brandes, P.J., & Ehinger, D.M. (1981). The effects of early middle ear pathology on auditory perception and academic achievement. *Journal of Speech and Hearing Disorders, 46,* 301–307.

Brooks, D.N. (1986). Otitis media with effusion and academic attainment. *International Journal of Pediatric Otorhinolaryngology, 12,* 39–47.

Bryant, P.E., MacLean, M., Bradley, L.L., & Crossland, J. (1990). Rhyme and alliteration, phoneme detection, and learning to read. *Developmental Psychology, 26,* 429–438.

Byrd, R.S., & Weitzman, M.L. (1994). Predictors of early grade retention among children in the United States. *Pediatrics, 93,* 481–487.

Colombo, J. (1993). *Infant cognition: Predicting later intellectual functioning.* Newbury Park, CA: Sage Publications.

Eimas, P., & Clarkson, R. (1986). Speech perception in children: Are there effects of otitis media? In J.F. Kavanaugh (Ed.), *Otitis media and child development* (pp. 139–159). Parkton, MD: York Press.

Fagan, J.F. (1970). Memory in the infant. *Journal of Experimental Child Psychology, 9,* 217–226.

Fantz, R.L. (1964). Visual experience in infants: Decreased attention to familiar patterns relative to novel ones. *Science, 146,* 668–670.

Feagans, L. (1986). Otitis media: A model for long term effects with implications for intervention. In J.F. Kavanaugh (Ed.), *Otitis media and child development* (pp. 192–208). Parkton, MD: York Press.

Feagans, L.V., Kipp, E., & Blood, I. (1994). The effects of otitis media on the attention skills on day-care-attending toddlers. *Developmental Psychology, 30,* 701–708.

Feagans, L., Sanyal, M., Henderson, F., Collier, A., & Applebaum, M.I. (1987). The relationship of middle ear disease in early childhood to later narrative and attention skills. *Journal of Pediatric Psychology, 12,* 581–594.

Feldman, H., & Gelman, R. (1986). Otitis media and cognitive development: Theoretical perspectives. In J.F. Kavanaugh (Ed.), *Otitis media and child development* (pp. 27–41). Parkton, MD: York Press.

Fischler, R.S., Todd, N.W., & Feldman, C.M. (1985). Otitis media and language performance in a cohort of Apache Indian children. *American Journal of Diseases of Children, 139,* 355–360.

Freeark, K., Frank, S.J., Wagner, A.E., Lopez, M., Olmsted, C., & Girard, R. (1992). Otitis media, language development, and parental verbal stimulation. *Journal of Pediatric Psychology, 17,* 173–185.

Freeman, B.A., & Parkins, C. (1979). The prevalence of middle ear disease among learning impaired children. *Clinical Pediatrics, 18,* 205–212.

Gordon-Brannan, M., Hodson, B.W., & Wynne, M.K. (1992). Remediating unintelligible utterances of a child with a mild hearing loss. *American Journal of Speech-Language Pathology, 1,* 28–38.

Gottfried, A.W., Rose, S.A., & Bridger, W.H. (1977). Cross-modal transfer in human infants. *Child Development, 48,* 118–123.

Gravel, J.S., & Wallace, I.F. (1992). Listening and language at 4 years of age: Effects of early otitis media. *Journal of Speech and Hearing Research, 35,* 588–595.

Gravel, J.S., & Wallace, I.F. (1995). Early otitis media, auditory abilities, and educational risk. *American Journal of Speech-Language Pathology, 4,* 89–94.

Hagerman, R.J., & Falkenstein, A.R. (1987). An association between recurrent otitis media in infancy and later hyperactivity. *Clinical Pediatrics, 26,* 253–257.

Hooper, S.R., Willis, W.G., & Stone, B.H. (1996). Issues and approaches in the neuropsychological treatment of children with learning disabilities. In E.S. Batchelor, & R.S. Dean (Eds.), *Pediatric neuropsychology: Interfacing assessment and treatment for rehabilitation* (pp. 211–247). Boston: Allyn & Bacon.

Howie, V.M., Jensen, N.J., Fleming, J.W., Peeler, M.B., & Meigs, S. (1979). The effect of early onset of otitis media on educational achievement. *International Journal of Pediatric Otorhinolaryngology, 1,* 151–155.

Kaplan, G.J., Fleshman, J.K., Bender, T.R., Baum, C., & Clark, P.S. (1973). Long term effects of otitis media: A ten-year-cohort study of Alaskan Eskimo children. *Pediatrics, 52,* 577–585.

Kirkwood, C.R., & Kirkwood, M.E. (1983). Otitis media and learning disabilities: The case for a causal relationship. *Journal of Family Practice, 17,* 219–227.

Knishkowy, B., Palti, H., Adler, B., & Tepper, D. (1991). Effect of otitis media on development: A community-based study. *Early Human Development, 26,* 101–111.

Korkman, M., & Peltomaa, A.K. (1993). Preventive treatment of dyslexia by a preschool training program for children with language impairments. *Journal of Clinical Child Psychology, 22,* 277–287.

Lindamood, C.H., & Lindamood, P.C. (1975). *The A.D.D. Program: Auditory Discrimination in Depth.* (2nd ed.). Columbus OH: SRA Division, Macmillan-McGraw-Hill.

Lous, J. (1993). Silent reading and secretory otitis media in school children. *International Journal of Pediatric Otorhinolaryngology, 25,* 25–38.

Lous, J., Fiellau-Nikolajsen, M., & Jeppesen, A.L. (1988). Secretory otitis media and verbal intelligence: A six-year prospective case control study. In D.J. Lim, C.D. Bluestone, J.O. Klein, & J.D. Nelson (Eds.), *Recent advances in otitis media: Proceedings of the fourth international symposium* (pp. 393–395). Toronto, Ontario, Canada: B.C. Decker.

Marschark, M. (1993). *Psychological development of deaf children.* New York: Oxford University Press.

McGee, R., Silva, P.A., & Stewart, I.A. (1982). Behaviour problems and otitis media with effusion: A report from the Dunedin Multidisciplinary Child Development Study. *New Zealand Medical Journal, 95,* 655–657.

Menyuk, P. (1986). Predicting speech and language problems in children with persistent otitis media. In J.F. Kavanaugh (Ed.), *Otitis media and child development* (pp. 83–98). Parkton, MD: York Press.

Mody, M., Schwartz, R., Gravel, J., Wallace, I., Ellis, M., & Lee, W. (in press). *Speech perception and verbal memory in children with OME.* Paper presented at the sixth International Symposium on Recent Advances in Otitis Media, Ft. Lauderdale, FL.

Neville, H.J. (1990). Intermodal competition and compensation in development: Evidence from studies of the visual system in congenitally deaf adults. *Annals of the New York Academy of Sciences, 608,* 71–91.

Neville, H.J., Schmidt, A., & Kutas, M. (1983). Altered visual evoked potentials in congenitally deaf adults. *Brain Research, 266,* 127–132.

Paradise, J.L. (1981). Otitis media during early life: How hazardous to development? A critical review of the evidence. *Pediatrics, 68,* 869–873.

Pearce, P.S., Saunders, M.A., Creighton, D.E., & Sauve, R.S. (1988). Hearing and verbal-cognitive abilities in high-risk preterm infants prone to otitis media with effusion. *Journal of Developmental and Behavioral Pediatrics, 9,* 346–351.

Perfetti, C.A. (1985). *Reading ability.* New York: Oxford University Press.

Peters, S.A.F., Grievink, E.H., van Bon, W.H.J., & Schilder, A.G.M. (1994). The effects of early bilateral otitis media with effusion on educational attainment: A prospective cohort study. *Journal of Learning Disabilities, 27,* 111–121.

Roberts, J.E., Burchinal, M.R., & Campbell, F. (1994). Otitis media in early childhood and patterns of intellectual development and later academic performance. *Journal of Pediatric Psychology, 19,* 347–367.

Roberts, J.E., Burchinal, M.R., & Clarke-Klein, S.M. (1995). Otitis media in early childhood and cognitive, academic, and behavior outcomes at 12 years of age. *Journal of Pediatric Psychology, 20,* 645–660.

Roberts, J.E., Burchinal, M.R., Collier, A.M., Ramey, C.T., Koch, M.A., & Henderson, F.W. (1989). Otitis media in early childhood and cognitive, academic, and classroom performance of the school-aged child. *Pediatrics, 83,* 477–485.

Roberts, J.E., Burchinal, M.R., Medley, L.P., Zeisel, S.A., Mundy, M., Roush, J., Hooper, S., Bryant, D., & Henderson, F.W. (1995). Otitis media, hearing sensitivity, and maternal responsiveness in relation to language during infancy. *Journal of Pediatrics, 126,* 481–489.

Roberts, J.E., & Medley, L.P. (1995). Otitis media and speech-langue sequelae in young children: Current issues in management. *American Journal of Speech-Language Pathology, 4,* 15–24.

Roberts, J.E., Sanyal, M.A., Burchinal, M.R., Collier, A.M., Ramey, C.T., & Henderson, F.W. (1986). Otitis media in early childhood and its relationship to later verbal and academic performance. *Pediatrics, 78,* 423–430.

Sak, R.J., & Ruben, R.J. (1982). Effects of recurrent middle ear effusion in preschool years on language and learning. *Journal of Developmental and Behavioral Pediatrics, 3,* 7–11.

Sarff, L.S., Ray, H., & Bagwell, C. (1981). Why not amplification in every classroom? *Hearing Aid Journal, 34,* 47–52.

Scaldwell, W.A. (1989, January). Effect of otitis media upon reading scores of Indian children in Ontario. *Journal of American Indian Education,* pp. 32–39.

Schappert, S.M. (1992). *Office visits for otitis media: United States, 1975–90* (Advance Data from Vital and Health Statistics of the National Center for Health Statistics, No. 214). Hyattsville, MD: National Center for Health Statistics.

Secord, G.J., Erickson, M.T., & Bush, J.P. (1988). Neuropsychological sequelae of otitis media in children and adolescents with learning disabilities. *Journal of Pediatric Psychology, 13,* 531–542.

Silva, P.A., Chalmers, D., & Stewart, I. (1986). Some audiological, psychological, educational and behavioral characteristics of children with bilateral otitis media with effusion: A longitudinal study. *Journal of Learning Disabilities, 19,* 165–169.

Silva, P.A., Kirklang, C., Simpson, A., Stewart, I.A., & Williams, S.M. (1982). Some developmental and behavioral problems associated with bilateral otitis media with effusion. *Journal of Learning Disabilities, 15,* 417–421.

Stanovich, K.E. (1988). Explaining the differences between the dyslexic and the garden-variety poor reader: The phonological-core variable-difference model. *Journal of Learning Disabilities, 21,* 590–604.

Stone, B.H. (1990). *Phonological processing abilities: Their interrelations in the presence and absence of phonological awareness training.* Unpublished manuscript, University of Rhode Island, Kingston.

Teele, D.W., Klein, J.O., Chase, C., Menyuk, P., Rosner, B.A., & the Greater Boston Otitis Media Study Group (1990). Otitis media in infancy and intellectual ability, school achievement, speech, and language at age 7 years. *Journal of Infectious Diseases, 162,* 685–694.

Thompson, L.A., Fagan, J.F., & Fulker, D.W. (1991). Longitudinal prediction of specific cognitive abilities from infant novelty preference. *Child Development, 62,* 530–538.

Updike, C., & Thornburg, J.D. (1992). Reading skills and auditory processing ability in children with chronic otitis media in early childhood. *Annals of Otology, Rhinology, and Laryngology, 101,* 530–537.

Vellutino, F. (1979). *Dyslexia: Theory and research.* Cambridge, MA: MIT Press.

Vellutino, F.R., Scanlon, D.M., & Tanzman, M.S. (1994). Components of reading ability: Issues and problems in operationalizing word identification, phonological coding, and orthographic coding. In G.R. Lyon (Ed.), *Frames of reference for the assessment of learning disabilities: New views on measurement issues* (pp. 279–332). Baltimore: Paul H. Brookes Publishing Co.

Ventry, I.M. (1980). Effects of conductive hearing loss: Fact or fiction. *Journal of Speech and Hearing Disorders, 45,* 143–156.

Wagner, R.K., & Torgeson, J.K. (1987). The nature of phonological processing and its causal role in the acquisition of reading skills. *Psychological Bulletin, 101,* 192–212.

Wallace, I.F., Gravel, J.S., McCarton, C.M., & Ruben, R.J. (1988). Otitis media and languge development at 1 year of age. *Journal of Speech and Hearing Disorders, 53,* 245–251.

Wallace, I.F., Gravel, J.S., McCarton, C.M., Stapells, D.R., Bernstein, R.S., & Ruben, R.J. (1988). Otitis media, auditory sensitivity, and language outcomes at one year. *Laryngoscope, 98,* 64–70.

Wallace, I.F., Gravel, J.S., Schwartz, R.G., & Ruben, R.J. (1996). Otitis media, communication style of primary caregivers, and language skills of 2 years old: A preliminary report. *Journal of Development and Behavioral Pediatrics, 17,* 27–35.

Wallach, G., & Miller, L. (1988). *Language intervention and academic success.* Boston: College-Hill Press.

Webster, A., Bamford, J.M., Thyer, N.J., & Ayles, R. (1989). The psychological, educational and auditory sequelae of early, persistent, secretory otitis media. *Journal of Child Psychology and Psychiatry, 30,* 529–546.

Zinkus, P.W., & Gottlieb, M.I. (1980). Patterns of perceptual and academic deficits related to early chronic otitis media. *Pediatrics, 66,* 246–253.

Zinkus, P.W., Gottlieb, M.I., & Shapiro, M. (1978). Developmental and psychoeducational sequelae of chronic otitis media. *American Journal of Diseases of Children, 132,* 1100–1104.

8

Family–Professional Partnerships in Managing Otitis Media

Pamela J. Winton, Joanne E. Roberts, and Susan A. Zeisel

Janis Peters sighed with relief and exhaustion as she lowered her sleeping 2-year-old son Andy into his crib. With some luck Andy would sleep for a couple of hours, and Janis could decide whether to sleep herself or haul her bulging briefcase out of the back seat of the car and try to get some work done. After her all-night stint of trying to treat Andy's ear ache and fever, her morning at the doctor's office and the pharmacy, her calls to Andy's child care provider, and her calls to work trying to cancel important meetings, she was dead tired and figured sleep was the only possibility. Her work, once again, would have to wait. The pediatrician had said that Andy had acute otitis media and that fluid was present in both ears. Janis is to bring Andy back in 4 weeks to see if the fluid has resolved. "With all the medical research and technology in this country, why can't we figure out how to prevent ear aches . . . or at least develop a consistent approach to treating them?" thought Janis. The accumulation of missed work, lost sleep, conflicting information from health care professionals and friends, and worry over Andy had taken its toll on Janis, her husband Rick, Andy, and his 5-year-old sister Amy.

This chapter was supported by Maternal and Child Health Program (MCJ-370599 and 370649), Health Resources and Services Administration, Department of Health and Human Services.

The Peters family scenario is not a rare or unusual one. Millions of families deal with the challenges and frustration that occur when young children experience chronic otitis media with effusion (OME). According to data reported by Schappert (1992), otitis media is the most common diagnosis made by physicians in the United States, accounting for approximately 18% of office visits in children birth to 5 years old. Some groups of children are at even greater risk for experiencing otitis media than the general population (Bluestone & Klein, 1990). These include children with cleft palate, Down syndrome, or other craniofacial abnormalities that affect the middle ear; Native American or Eskimo children; children with a family history of otitis media; and children exposed to certain environmental risks, such as cigarette smoke, group child care, and bottle feeding in a reclined position. Age also poses a risk, with younger children being at greater risk than older children for otitis media.

There are two types of otitis media: acute otitis media (AOM; commonly called an ear infection), which is an acute infection in the middle ear; and OME (commonly called middle ear fluid), which occurs when fluid is present in the middle ear but the ear is not infected. Fluid in children's ears (OME) may persist for weeks or even months after the onset of AOM. Fluid that persists for more than 3 months is called chronic OME. Children may alternate between AOM and OME, and, although the focus of this chapter is on OME management, the issues are similar in managing children with AOM.

RATIONALE FOR A FAMILY-CENTERED APPROACH

Although the child is the identified patient in cases of OME, the impact on the family can be pervasive and often significant. The fact that there are so many controversial issues related to OME adds to the challenges that families face as they deal with managing and preventing OME. Families and professionals alike often struggle with decision making related to OME treatment and management because many times there is no one best course of action. There is increasing recognition that the most effective approach is for families and professionals to work in partnership in determining effective treatment. In this way, an individual aproach tailored to meet each unique child and family situation can be developed. Indeed, consumer and family involvement in decisions related to health care and education of children is increasingly recognized as a critical and important approach to effectively managing and preventing many problems, such as OME, that are complex and require a problem-solving, individualized approach. Often referred to as family-centered care (Hanson, Johnson, Jeppson, Thomas, & Hall, 1994;

Shelton & Stepanek, 1994), this approach includes the following components:

- Working in partnership with families in developing treatment plans
- Providing care that is culturally sensitive and respectful of the individual differences in family lifestyle, communication patterns, and routines
- Respecting family priorities and preferences for treatment and allowing families to be the ultimate decision makers in which course of treatment to follow
- Providing families with clear and concise information so that they can be informed decision makers in promoting and maintaining the health of their children

The purpose of this chapter is twofold: 1) to outline specific ways that OME affects families, highlighting those areas in which there is controversy over appropriate treatment; and 2) to provide guidelines and strategies for professionals related to taking a family-centered approach. Strategies for the different types of professionals (medical, educational, or therapeutic) who may have contact with families or who may be asked for help, information, or support related to OME are discussed.

POTENTIAL IMPACT OF
OTITIS MEDIA WITH EFFUSION ON THE FAMILY

Financial Costs to Families

Stool and colleagues (1994) estimated that the cost for OME treated medically is $406 per patient per episode. This includes costs of medical visits, antibiotics, other drugs, hearing tests, and time off from work. For patients treated surgically (i.e., myringotomy, tympanostomy tube insertion), costs increase to $2,174 per patient (Stool et al., 1994). The financial burdens of OME for some families, especially those who do not have adequate insurance, may preclude children from receiving adequate treatment and families from receiving adequate attention to the partnership aspects of care. For instance, families who have no insurance sometimes resort to emergency room treatment, simply because they cannot be denied care in that setting. This is not a context in which attention to ongoing problem solving and monitoring of OME is likely to take place.

Emotional Costs

The emotional costs of OME, especially when it is a chronic condition, can be many-faceted. Worry and distress over the child's acute condition and concern about the short-term and long-term impact of OME on the child can be common costs for parents. Parents may be fatigued from dealing with children who do not feel well, although children with OME may not have any acute signs of illness. They also may be worried why their child does not respond consistently to them. Other concerns may relate to whether a child has a hearing loss and, if he or she does, how this might affect the child's later language and learning. A further concern is whether fluid is still present in a child's ears and if and when return visits to a health care professional are necessary to determine if the fluid has resolved. Families may also experience stress from related factors, such as getting behind at work and disruption of family life and normal routines. For families with additional children, parents may worry about directing so much attention toward the sick child, with less time available for siblings. Another source of stress for many families is related to the burden of interacting with the health care system. For example, parents may need to contact their medical insurers to determine what fees their insurance would cover for hearing tests and medical treatment, and this may often require numerous phone calls and much correspondence.

Cross-cultural research emphasizes the importance of attending to individual differences in each child and family situation when considering emotional costs and providing family support. Wuest and her colleagues (Wuest, 1991; Wuest & Stern, 1990) studied Native American and non–Native American families of children with OME and found differences in what families viewed as the worst thing about dealing with persistent middle ear disease. Non–Native American families were most likely to identify their frustration with the health care system and its inability to cure their child. Native American families reported that the worst thing was having to listen to their children cry.

Uncertainty and Confusion Over Treatment

Related to emotional costs, but deserving of a category of its own, is the uncertainty and confusion concerning management strategies. These controversies, which are covered in more detail in other chapters of this book, include the following:

- Use of antibiotics (effectiveness and different types, when to use, length of treatment, side effects, developing immunity, possible drawbacks and benefits)
- Surgical procedures (myringotomy and tube insertion, efficacy, timing, drawbacks and benefits)
- Physician monitoring (when to respond to symptoms, when and how often to follow up, role of specialists)
- Hearing assessment (when and how often to follow up)
- Speech and language assessment (when and how often to follow up)

Unfortunately, there are no simple, clear-cut "truths" about treatment, or standard recommended procedures that have been proven effective in every situation. In an attempt to summarize and clarify for professionals and for families what is known about treatment and management of OME, a Clinical Practice Guideline has been developed under the auspices of the Agency for Health Care Policy and Research of the Public Health Service (Stool et al., 1994). Although extremely helpful from the point of view of summarizing the available research on OME, the Guideline reinforces the degree to which there are no definitive answers to many of the questions that many parents have about OME, including what causes it, how to prevent it, how to treat it, and what are its long- and short-term impacts on children.

IMPACT ON CHILD'S HEARING, BEHAVIOR, LANGUAGE, AND LEARNING

An additional potential impact of OME is the possibility of long-term adverse language and learning sequelae resulting from the chronic hearing loss associated with OME. Whether such sequelae exist is highly controversial, as described later (Roberts, Burchinal, Davis, Collier, & Henderson, 1991; Stool et al., 1994). A hearing loss may affect a child in a variety of ways that, in turn, affects the family.

Impact on Hearing

The average hearing loss resulting from OME is mild, 26-dB hearing level (HL); however, loss can range from none to as much as 50-dB HL, which is considered a moderate hearing loss. A 26-dB HL is equivalent to the amount of sound you hear when you put your fingers in both your ears. A child with even a mild hearing loss may have trouble hearing some sounds, some grammatical forms, and the subtle nuances of language, such as the intonation used to indicate a question. Once the fluid resolves, hearing returns to normal. The following vignette illustrates the impact of a mild hearing loss on listening.

John, a 3-year-old, has had fluid in his ears for the past 2 months. His mother reported that he often seems not to listen. For example, when she asked him to get his hat, he brought his mother his bat. When she called him, even when he was facing her, he did not respond. His mother thought he just seemed to have trouble listening.

Impact on Behavior

A child with a hearing loss may have difficulty participating in ongoing activities in the classroom, the playground, or at home. Misunderstandings and miscommunications may occur. For instance, following instructions, engaging in interactive play, and relating positively to peers and siblings could be compromised by the inability to hear. Furthermore, parents may be confused about the level or extent of a hearing loss. One reason for this is that a child may respond at some times and not at others, in part because of how much contextual information is available to support what someone is saying. For example, at one point in time someone may say "Give me your shoe" as he or she points to the shoe. The next time the request is made, he or she may not point to the shoe, thus providing less contextual support for the request. A further point of confusion relates to fluctuation that may occur in the level of hearing loss during an episode of OME. Often, level of loss is greater during the first 2 weeks and improves gradually during the episode. In addition, parents often wonder to what extent a child's behavior can be attributed to the hearing loss or to what extent a child is being uncooperative and stubborn. A child with a mild loss may understand what is said when the speaker is standing close but not hear enough to understand when the speaker is across the room. It may be unclear if a child has a hearing loss or if the behaviors are just characteristic of a typical preschool child. The following vignette illustrates this kind of challenge for families.

José and Marie Miranda are parents of 2-year-old twin daughters, Carmen and Margarita. The twins were born prematurely. At 2 years of age, the twins are active; however, José and Marie have some concerns about Margarita's behavior and language development. They have noticed that she is not able to imitate the animal sounds that Carmen can so readily make. They also think she is willful and disobedient at times. They wonder if these differences between the twins could be related to Margarita's frequent ear infections or to possible hearing loss. They have had her hearing tested, and the audiologist detected a moderate hearing loss. However, their relatives believe Margarita just needs time to catch up and be loved. The Mirandas are not sure what to do or whom to believe. They are not sure how to interpret Margarita's behavior.

Long-Term Impact on Language and Learning

Concern over the possible long-term developmental impact on a child of short- or long-term hearing loss resulting from chronic OME is a cause of anxiety for parents. Research does not provide a straightforward and unequivocal answer to parents who have this question. Some studies have shown associations between OME in early childhood and academic and language achievement in later childhood; other studies have not demonstrated these associations (Roberts et al., 1991; Stool et al., 1994). As a result, parents such as José and Marie often find themselves surrounded by conflicting opinions and recommendations about the need for remediation or intervention. Will a child who is difficult to understand because of many speech errors outgrow it, or should the parents pursue speech therapy? Will a child's inability to concentrate lessen as the child matures and language develops, or should the child be tested for attention deficit disorder? These are the kinds of questions that parents frequently have. Trying to find answers often entails interacting with a new range of intervention specialists (special educators, speech–language pathologists, social workers, etc.). These new relationships take time and money, and the costs for families of children with OME can continue to escalate.

Margarita, the twin with the ear infection, was also seen by a speech-language pathologist, who diagnosed a language delay. The speech-language pathologist then referred the family to a community-based clinic for preschoolers with language impairment. This program had an excellent reputation for providing state-of-the-art center-based services to young children with language impairments. Within a week of the referral, an intake specialist had made arrangements to meet with José and Marie in their home in order to introduce them to the program. Although José and Marie listened quietly and respectfully to the presentation, they had not followed up by scheduling a visit to the clinic. The intake specialist was concerned when she followed up with a phone call and was told by Marie that they were not interested.

Why would a family who was lucky enough to have a model program in their community not respond positively to the opportunity that this program afforded their child? The next section of this chapter explores strategies for building family–professional partnerships that are designed to ensure that families like the Mirandas and the Peters are supported by professionals in their attempts to effectively deal with their children's chronic OME.

STRATEGIES FOR SUPPORTING FAMILIES AND WORKING AS PARTNERS IN THE TREATMENT AND MANAGEMENT OF OTITIS MEDIA WITH EFFUSION

Building on Family Strengths and Natural Coping Strategies

An overarching theme in the research on family adaptation to chronic illness is the importance of recognizing and supporting each family's unique coping style (Affleck & Tennen, 1993; Gallimore, Weisner, Kaufman, & Bernheimer, 1989; Turnbull et al., 1993). The ecocultural model developed by Gallimore and his associates provides a useful theoretical framework for understanding the unique aspects of each family's adaptation to a chronic condition. According to this model, families strive to maintain their normal routines, even when faced with circumstances and events that create crises or change. One of the ways that families cope with these external demands that accompany crises is by developing strategies that allow them to maintain their usual patterns and roles as much as possible. These patterns, roles, and everyday behaviors are adaptive and reflect underlying values and beliefs about lifestyle, parenting, and the like. These adaptations convey important messages about what is valued by families. Therefore, it is important that professionals who become involved in working with a child or family understand, appreciate, and build on family adaptations, rather than imposing recommendations or interventions that may be impossible to implement or run counter to the adaptational strategies that families have developed.

Qualitative research on families of children with chronic OME by Wuest and Stern (1990) provides more specific information on patterns of family responses in this population. They define family adaptation to chronic OME as a continuum of passive to active behaviors that fall under the umbrella term "learning to manage" (Wuest & Stern, 1990, p. 25). They defined "learning to manage" as having four major dimensions: acquiescing, helpless floundering, becoming an "expert," and managing effectively. Acquiescing is basically considered to be a family's first reaction to OME, and this approach is characterized by trust in professionals to cure the problem. When parents begin to realize that a cure may not be in sight and that their child's problem is ongoing, they enter the helpless floundering phase. In this phase, families find that there are many confusing and conflicting opinions about how to treat and manage OME. At some point, families realize that there are no simple answers and that they, rather than the professionals, must ultimately become experts in learning about the options for managing their child and negotiating the health care system. Finally, parents develop the knowledge and skills to effectively manage and work within the health care system for their child.

Three variables were identified by Wuest and Stern that affect a family's progression on this continuum: 1) the effects of the disease on the child, 2) the amount of disruption in family life, and 3) the family's relationship with the health care system. Other factors also have an impact, such as birth order of the child. Families who already have been through chronic OME with an older child may move directly to a management role. Helping families view their child as essentially healthy individuals supports strategies that foster normal development.

The role that differences in cultural background have on coping strategies was explored by Wuest (1991) in a subsequent study that she conducted with Canadian Native American families with a child with OME. Using a qualitative methodology similar to the one used by Wuest and Stern in their 1990 study with Caucasian Canadian families, she discovered important differences in the management styles of these two groups of families. Caucasian families largely sought out ways to direct and control the situation, whereas Native American families tried to manage by harmonizing or integrating the situation into the family life-style. Native Americans were less likely to be upset with the health care system and less likely to develop adversarial relationships with professionals. Wuest speculated on how these adaptational differences correspond to basic value differences in the two cultures.

An important point to make about family adaptation and cross-cultural research is that it is dangerous to generalize findings from a research study to mean that all members of a certain group respond according to the patterns of response identified in the research. The point that should be made is that each family brings its own unique cultural history, values, and traditions to any situation or crisis. Being aware of and sensitive to differences in regard to beliefs about illness and the health care system is important for professionals who desire to effectively support and assist families and children with OME. Recognizing and accepting what parents are doing to cope, providing information and intervention in ways that fit or mesh with existing strategies, and acknowledging parents as valid and reliable information sources and managers are all important strategies for building family–professional partnerships. These strategies are explored in more depth throughout the rest of this chapter.

Sharing Accurate and Up-to-Date Information in Ways that Empower Families

Research studies with families whose children are experiencing health problems or developmental delays have consistently shown that families want accurate, honest, straightforward information about their child's condition and about intervention and treatment that will ameliorate the condition (Able-Boone, Sandall, Loughry, & Frederick, 1990; Sontag & Schacht, 1994; Summers et al., 1990). If parents do not have current and relevant information, they cannot possibly be expected to serve as equal partners in treatment decisions about their child's health care and management. Professionals who operate out of a family-centered paradigm place a high priority on addressing parents' informational needs in an individualized and sensitive fashion. Table 1 provides a list of some of the common questions that parents have in relationship to persistent OME. Appendix A at the end of this chapter contains references that provide the needed information to address these questions.

The challenge for professionals is to provide the needed information in ways that are clearly understood and accepted by families. What

Table 1.   Questions that families may ask related to OME

Otitis Media
- What are causes of OME?
- What are symptoms? How do I know if my child has OME?
- How can I prevent OME?
- What are treatment approaches?

Hearing Loss
- What is hearing loss?
- What are symptoms of hearing loss?
- What are treatment approaches?

Speech and Language
- What are symptoms of speech and language delay?
- What are management approaches?

follows is a discussion of strategies related to providing information in ways that families will find useful.

Written Information   Written information on topics related to management of OME is available to families from a number of sources. This includes information on OME and its management, hearing loss, and speech and language development and intervention. The types of materials available include booklets, checklists, journal articles, magazine articles, and books. The chapter appendix includes examples of these kinds of materials. Professionals could use the information in these resources as a guide for assembling information for parents related to questions that parents ask. Professionals can obtain copies of the written information and provide copies to parents in response to specific questions. This allows for an individualized system for sharing information depending on the needs of a particular family. It is useful to have a variety of materials available to meet the learning needs and styles of parents. Please note that some of these written materials in Appendix A (e.g., "Middle Ear Fluid in Children: Parent Guide") are also available in Spanish.

Other Strategies for Sharing Information   As mentioned earlier, not all families will be able to relate to written information. A survey of parents of young children by Gowen, Christy, and Sparling (1993) indicated that differences in maternal education level are associated with where parents seek information about child rearing. Mothers with less than a high school education surveyed in this study were more likely to turn to family and friends for information. With increasing education, family and friends were selected less frequently and reading materials more frequently as the preferred sources for information on child-rearing topics. Some families may appreciate a verbal explanation with pictures and diagrams that they can take home and examine at their leisure. Wuest (1991) pointed out that storytelling is a tradition in Native

American cultures and that this medium might be used for sharing information with some Native American families. Sharing information by videotape is another strategy that is becoming increasingly possible because of the growing number of home and office videocassette recorders (VCRs). An annotated list of relevant videotapes is also available in the chapter appendix. Professionals may want to share videos with families in their offices or let families check them out for a period of time so that the information can be shared with their children's care providers or relatives.

A rapidly expanding source of information on all kinds of health-related topics is the Internet and World Wide Web. There are numerous "bulletin boards" and "forums" that provide people with a chance to share information across a broad range of topics, including otitis media, hearing loss, early intervention, and language development. Some families may appreciate information about how to access this opportunity for information exchange and networking with other families who have experienced similar challenges and frustrations.

In some situations, professionals may want to enlist the assistance of extended family, community leaders, or other agencies such as schools to assist in providing information. Providing information sessions on OME at school or community meetings, in parent publications or newsletters, on public awareness slots available through public television, or in newspaper articles are all ways of educating the broader population about the health and education issues related to OME. A successful public awareness approach taken in one community was to send a van equipped with hearing screening equipment and health professionals to community child care and preschool settings to conduct free screenings and distribute educational information to child care providers and parents. The project was jointly funded and sponsored by a private university and a large corporation. Creating an awareness in the business community of the costs of OME for families and businesses in terms of lost time on the job and stress for families is an important role for health care professionals who wish to address the problem at the community level.

An important professional skill entails being able to ascertain exactly what informational format is most appealing to each individual family or target audience. For instance, a strategy that a practicing audiologist found helpful was to create a lending library of videotapes, printed information, models, and pictorial representations of the ear in her office. This area included a portable VCR. The audiologist could select materials that seemed to address parents' questions and introduce several options. It was possible to gauge parent interest in different media and formats so that a match could be made between the information options and the family's preferences. In addition, the audiologist used these materials to make presentations in the community on hearing loss, utilizing different media for different audiences.

Supporting Families in Their Decision-Making Role
One of the most challenging aspects of a family-centered approach for many professionals is sharing the decision-making role and, in fact, allowing families to have the final say in decisions made about the care and treatment of their children. A study by Giangreco (1990) on the topic of professional–family decision-making authority provided evidence that professionals do not accept this premise. In this study, occupational therapists, physical therapists, and speech-language pathologists working in the public schools were asked who should retain final decision-making authority regarding provision of related services. The professionals believed they should retain the final authority; in contrast, the parents surveyed in the study predominantly thought final authority belongs to the child's parents.

A major reason why this is a challenge for professionals is because most health care professionals have received specialized training that has emphasized the importance of their expertise and decision-making authority. Giving up that authority is difficult. Likewise, parents often come to professionals in hopes of a "cure" or easy solution to their children's health problems. In situations in which there is widespread professional consensus on recommended treatments, parent–professional relationships regarding decision making are less problematic. Professionals can provide straightforward, uniform, and noncontroversial advice; parents are likely to hear the same advice from other informational sources and are likely to follow this advice. As described in earlier sections of this chapter and other chapters in this text, the treatment and management of OME are not straightforward and there are few standard recommendations, making decision making much harder. A key role for the health care professional is providing information about the possible courses of action in a manner that is easy for families to understand so that parents can make a truly informed decision.

What about situations in which families decide upon a course of action that is not what the health care professional has recommended? These situations are most challenging for professionals. It is easier for health care professionals to respect and honor the decisions of parents when the parents' perspectives are similar or identical to the professional's. When parents make decisions that do not match recommendations, professionals have a much more difficult time accepting their right to do so and may even question whether it is ethically responsible to let parents make decisions that, from the professional's perspective, are not in the best interest of children. The word "perspective" is critical here. Families are in the best position to evaluate the treatment and management options from the perspective of what recommendations are most realistic and workable, given their resources and constraints. For families, this is sometimes an unconscious and therefore hard-to-explain process that involves family values, beliefs, traditions, and lifestyles.

Thomasina was a 3-year-old who had experienced a total of 5 months of persistent OME. Her pediatrician referred the family to an ear, nose, and throat specialist, who recommended that Thomasina receive tubes to drain the fluid in her ears. The surgery was recommended to eliminate her hearing loss. Thomasina's parents were upset because Thomasina would have to go into the hospital for an operation and be sedated. Although they understood that the fluid would be gone after the surgery, they did not want to incur any risk from sedation. They were also concerned about the medical costs. After considerable discussion, they decided they were not interested in Thomasina getting tubes.

In those rare cases in which family decisions lead to neglect or abuse, professionals are obligated to notify the proper authorities and to tell parents that they are jeopardizing their child's welfare and must be reported. However, these situations are not the norm. It is of utmost importance that professionals have some understanding of the broader aspects of a family's situation and that they present information in ways that reflect this understanding. For instance, recommending that the family embark upon an expensive round of antibiotics without some attention to the family's ability to pay for the drugs does not make sense. Recommending that a family remove their child from a child care situation to reduce the risk of further episodes of OME is unrealistic if both parents must work and home care options are limited.

Another important consideration is the manner in which information is conveyed to families. A study by Cadman, Shurvell, Davies, and Bradfield (1984) identified several factors that increased the likelihood that parents complied with professional recommendations: time and care spent in listening to parents, parental agreement with professional recommendations, parental belief that they had the skill to implement the recommendation, and parental belief that the recommendation was feasible. These data support the data collected by Gallimore and his associates (1989) described earlier, which indicated that, unless recommendations are meaningful and sustainable within a family's daily routine, they are likely to be ineffective and ignored. Additional support for the importance of listening to and respecting family perspectives is provided in a qualitative study by Kalyanpur and Rao (1991) with a small number of low-income African American families whose children were being served through an early intervention program. These families reported that, if they were not respected and their cultural values and situations were not understood, they did not seek out and follow the advice of the professional community nor were they satisfied with their interactions with the professional community. What families often say when confronted with confusing and conflicting advice is that they simply sort through all of the information and try to make the decision that makes sense to them. If a professional believes that he or she has important information to share with families, then it is of the utmost importance that families receive that information in ways that they can understand and incorporate within their existing values and knowledge base. Questions that have been identified as being helpful in terms of gathering information from families in ways that acknowledge and respect their perspectives, past experiences, and expertise are shown in Table 2.

In summary, the following guidelines relate to supporting families in their decision-making role in the treatment and management of OME:

- Provide complete, clear, jargon-free information on all treatment options in a manner that is individualized in terms of each family's preference for receiving information.
- In making specific recommendations, take into account family values, beliefs, and the potential costs and benefits for the family in implementing the recommendations.
- Recognize the family's expertise and experience in dealing with the child's previous bouts of OME and other illnesses; acknowledge and validate their frustrations in dealing with OME.

Table 2. Collaborative questions for early interventionists and families regarding a child's OME

- What information have you been given about your child's ear status?
- What information have you been given about your child's hearing loss?
- How does that information fit with what you know and believe about your child?
- How do you think your child's illness or hearing loss has affected you and your family?
- What kinds of advice have you been given?
- How has that advice been helpful or not helpful?
- Are there areas you would like more information or advice about?
- What ideas do you have about how we might find those things out?

From Medley, L.P., Roberts, J.E., & Zeisel, S.A. (1995). At-risk children and otitis media with effusion: Management issues for the early childhood special educator. *Topics in Early Childhood Special Education, 15,* p. 58; reprinted by permission with modifications made in Winton (1991) and Winton & Bailey (1993).

- If families do not follow professional recommendations, do not blame or give up on the family; consider the following strategies for maintaining a positive relationship.
- Suggest a time frame and strategies for monitoring the outcomes or effectiveness of the family's treatment decision.
- Suggest a backup plan that might be considered if the first decision is not effective.
- Convey ongoing interest and support for the child and the family.

Addressing Service Coordination Needs

In situations in which families have been working with a variety of professionals, often what is most needed is for someone to take on the role of service coordinator. The term *service coordinator,* as used here, means someone who assists the family in accessing and integrating information and resources related to the child's health condition. If a child is under 3 and qualifies for early intervention services, then service coordination is a guaranteed service that will be provided by the early intervention lead agency in the community (Individuals with Disabilities Education Act of 1990). States that participate in this federal program (all 50 states and all jurisdictions are currently participating) must provide services to two groups of children: those who are experiencing developmental delays and those who have a diagnosed mental or physical condition that has a high probability of resulting in developmental delay. In addition, states may, if they choose, serve children who are at risk of having substantial developmental delay if early intervention services are not provided (U.S. Department of Education, 1989; see section 303.300). However, most children with a history of OME do not qualify for early intervention services; therefore, families must rely on the willingness of health care providers to recognize when families need this kind of assistance and to respond appropriately. In many cases, by choice or by default, families serve as their own service coordinators. There is a growing body of information from the early intervention field available to assist families in this role. (See the chapter appendices for some of the materials available.) It is important to recognize that all parents need support from professionals in linking and integrating services and information, even those who opt to serve as their own service coordinators. It should also be noted that many families feel uncomfortable taking a leadership role in this regard and desperately want professionals to take the lead in coordinating what is often a complex set of information, systems, and people. Again, the emphasis should be on choices and individualization.

CONCLUSIONS

Providing emotional, informational, and instrumental support to families and encouraging and promoting family competence and expertise is the heart of a family-centered approach. If professionals approach each family from the perspective of what can be learned first from families about their children, their situation, and their interests and priorities for treatment and management before providing the advice and recommendations that families hope to obtain, then a family-centered approach is being implemented. In spite of the frustrations and challenges for families inherent in dealing with chronic OME, children who have this condition in early childhood are often healthy and are highly likely to emerge without problems or delays. The health care professional's primary role is to reinforce the family's positive coping in managing OME, to foster and build confidence in the family's capacity to deal with the intermittent but persistent crises that accompany the condition, and to reinforce the family's ability to foster the child's positive development.

REFERENCES

Able-Boone, H., Sandall, S., Loughry, A., & Frederick, L. (1990). An informed, family-centered approach to Public Law 99-457: Parental views. *Topics in Early Childhood Special Education, 10*, 100–111.

Affleck, G., & Tennen, H. (1993). Cognitive adaptation to adversity: Insights from parents of medically fragile infants. In A.P. Turnball, J.M. Patterson, S.K. Behr, D.L. Murphy, J.G. Marquis, & M.J. Blue-Banning (Eds.), *Cognitive coping, families, and disability* (pp. 135–150). Baltimore: Paul H. Brookes Publishing Co.

Bluestone, C.D., & Klein, J.O. (1990). Otitis media, atelectasis and eustachian tube dysfunction. In C.D. Bluestone, S.E. Stool, & M.D. Scheetz (Eds.), *Pediatric otolaryngology* (pp. 320–486). Philadelphia: W.B. Saunders Company.

Cadman, D., Shurvell, B., Davies, P., & Bradfield, S. (1984). Compliance in the community with consultants' recommendations for developmentally handicapped children. *Developmental Medicine and Child Neurology, 26*, 40–46.

Gallimore, R., Weisner, T., Kaufman, S., & Bernheimer, L. (1989). The social construction of ecocultural niches: Family accommodation of developmentally delayed children. *American Journal of Mental Retardation, 94*, 216–230.

Giangreco, M.F. (1990). Making related service decisions for students with severe disabilities: Roles, criteria, and authority. *Journal of The Association for Persons with Severe Handicaps, 15*, 22–31.

Gowen, J.W., Christy, D.S., & Sparling, J. (1993). Informational needs of parents of young children with special needs. *Journal of Early Intervention, 17*, 194–210.

Hanson, J.L., Johnson, B.H., Jeppson, E.S., Thomas, J., & Hall, J.H. (1994). *Hospitals moving forward with family-centered care.* Bethesda, MD: Institute for Family-Centered Care.

Individuals with Disabilities Education Act of 1990, PL 101-476, 20 U.S.C. § 1400 *et seq.* (Supp. 2).

Kalyanpur, M., & Rao, S. (1991). Empowering low-income black families of handicapped children. *American Journal of Orthopsychiatry, 61*, 523–532.

Medley, L.P., Roberts, J.R., & Zeisel, S.A. (1995). At-risk children with otitis media with effusion: Management issues for the early childhood special educator. *Topics in Early Childhood Special Education, 15*(1), 44–64.

Roberts, J.E., Burchinal, M.R., Davis, B.P., Collier, A.M., & Henderson, F.W. (1991). Otitis media in early childhood and later language. *Journal of Speech and Hearing Research, 34,* 1158–1168.

Schappert, S.M. (1992). *Office visits for otitis media: United States, 1975–90.* (Advance Data from Vital and Health Statistics of the National Center for Health Statistics, No. 214). Hyattsville, MD: National Center for Health Statistics.

Shelton, T.L., & Stepanek, J.S. (1994). *Family-centered care for children needing specialized health and developmental services* (3rd ed.). Bethesda, MD: Association for the Care of Children's Health.

Sontag, J., & Schacht, R. (1994). An ethnic comparison of parent participation and information needs in early intervention. *Exceptional Children, 60,* 422–433.

Stool, S.E., Berg, A.O., Berman, S., Carney, C.J., Cooley, J.R., Culpepper, L., Eavey, R.D., Feagans, L.V., Finitzo, T., Friedman, E.M., Goertz, J.A., Goldstein, A.J., Grundfast, K.M., Long, D.G., Macconi, L.L., Melton, L., Roberts, J.E., Sherrod, J.L., & Sisk, J.E. (1994). *Otitis media with effusion in young children: Clinical practice guideline, No. 12* (AHCPR Publication No. 94-0622). Rockville, MD: Agency for Health Care Policy and Research.

Summers, J., Dell'Oliver, C., Turnbull, A., Benson, H., Santelli, E., Campbell, M., & Siegel-Causey, E. (1990). Examining the individualized family service plan process: What are family and practitioner preferences? *Topics in Early Childhood Special Education, 10,* 78–99.

Turnbull, A.P., Patterson, J.M., Behr, S.K., Murphy, D.L., Marquis, J.G., & Blue-Banning, M.J. (Eds.). (1993). *Cognitive coping, families, and disability.* Baltimore: Paul H. Brookes Publishing Co.

U.S. Department of Education. (1989, June 22). 34 CFR Part 303: Early Intervention program for infants and toddlers with handicaps; final regulations. *Federal Register, 54*(119), 26306–26348.

Winton, P. (1991). *Communicating with families in early intervention: A training module.* Chapel Hill: University of North Carolina, Frank Porter Graham Child Development Center.

Winton, P., & Bailey, D. (1993). Communicating with families: Examining practices and facilitating change. In J. Paul & R. Simeonsson (Eds.), *Understanding and working with parents of children with special needs* (2nd Ed., pp. 210–230). New York: Holt, Rinehardt & Winston.

Wuest, J. (1991). Harmonizing: A North American Indian approach to management of middle ear disease with transcultural nursing implications. *Journal of Transcultural Nursing, 3*(1), 5–14.

Wuest, J., & Stern, P.N. (1990). Childhood otitis media: The family's endless quest for relief. *Issues in Comprehensive Pediatric Nursing, 13,* 25–39.

Appendix A

Information Resources
Related to Otitis Media
for Families and Practitioners

The following annotated bibliography provides an overview of materials available on otitis media and where to obtain them.

OTITIS MEDIA

"Middle Ear Fluid in Children: Parent Guide"; "Otitis Media with Effusion in Young Children: Clinical Practice Guideline"
Authors and Date Published: S.E. Stool et al. (1994)
Format: Pamphlets include guidelines for managing young children with OME; also available in Spanish
Source: Agency for Health Care Policy and Research Publications Clearinghouse, P.O. Box 8547, Silver Spring, MD 20907
Cost: Parent Guide: free; Clinical Practice Guideline: $6.00

Ear Infections in Your Child
Authors and Date Published: K.M. Grundfast and C.J. Carney (1987)
Format: Book for families about managing young children with OME
Source: Warner Books, Inc., 666 5th Avenue, New York, NY 10103
Cost: $12.95

"Otitis Media: A Children's Story . . . for Parents"
Author and Date Published: Lederle Laboratories (1992)
Format: Video, 12 minutes; illustrates effects of OME on hearing
Source: Lederle Laboratories, 280 King of Prussia Road, St. Davids, PA 19087
Cost: Free

"Hear to Listen and Learn"
Authors and Date Published: L. Medley, J. Roberts, & S. Zeisel (1994)
Format: Video, 20 minutes; describe OME and what caregivers can do to help children with OME hear, listen, and learn
Source: Paul H. Brookes Publishing, P.O. Box 10624, Baltimore, MD 21285-0624 (1-800-638-3775)
Cost: $38.00

Understanding Ear Infections
Author and Date Published: P. Allen (1993)
Format: Book; primary function is to help educate patients about their ear problems
Source: Hear You Are, Inc., 4 Musconetcong Avenue, Stanhope, NJ 07874, (201-347-7662)
Cost: $24.95

SPEECH-LANGUAGE-HEARING
(SEE ALSO OTITIS MEDIA)
"How Does Your Child Hear and Talk?"
Author and Date Published: American Speech-Language-Hearing Association (1988)
Format: Brochure that is a checklist of speech and language milestones
Source: American Speech-Language-Hearing Association, 10801 Rockville Pike, Rockville, MD 20852
Cost: Free

"Answers to Questions about Otitis Media, Hearing, and Language Development"
Author and Date Published: American Speech-Language-Hearing Association (1989)
Format: Brochure that covers common questions about OME, hearing, and language
Source: American Speech-Language-Hearing Association, 10801 Rockville Pike, Rockville, MD 20852
Cost: Free

SERVICE COORDINATION
"Parents and Professionals: Partners in Co-Service Coordination"
Authors and Date Published: P. Rosin, A. Whitehead, L. Tuckman, G. Jesien, & A. Begun (1993)
Format: Videotape and print companion guide

Source: The Early Intervention Program, Waisman Center, Room 231, 1500 Highland Avenue, Madison, WI 53705-2280
Cost: $39.00

Pathways: A Training and Resource Guide for Enhancing Skills in Early Intervention and Service Coordination
Authors and Date Published: P. Rosin, M. Green, L. Hecht, L. Tuckman, & S. Robbins (1993)
Format: Notebook
Source: The Early Intervention Program, Waisman Center, Room 231, 1500 Highland Avenue, Madison, WI 53705-2280
Cost: $35.00

Family-Centered Service Coordination: A Manual for Parents
Authors and Date Published: I. Zipper, N. Hinton, C. Weil, & K. Rounds (1993)
Format: Book
Source: Brookline Books, P.O. Box 1046, Cambridge, MA 02238 (1-800-666-2665; Fax 617-868-1772)
Cost: $7.00

FAMILY-CENTERED CARE

Caring for Children and Families: Guidelines for Hospitals
Authors and Date Published: B. Johnson, E.S. Jeppson, & L. Redbum (1992)
Format: Monograph
Source: Association for the Care of Children's Health, 7910 Woodmont Avenue, Suite 300, Bethesda, MD 20814-3015 (301-654-1205, Fax 301-986-4553)
Cost: $125.00 plus shipping and handling

Families, Professionals and Exceptionality: A Special Partnership
Authors and Date Published: A.P. Turnbull & H. Rutherford Turnbull III (1990)
Format: Book
Source: Charles E. Merrill Publishing Company, P.O. Box 508, Columbus, OH 43216 (1-800-257-5755)
Cost: $38.00

"Family-Centered Care"
Author and Date Published: Association for the Care of Children's Health (1988)
Format: Videotape with brief accompanying discussion guide

Source: Association for the Care of Children's Health, 7910 Woodmont Avenue, Suite 300, Bethesda, MD 20814-3015 (301-654-6549)
Cost: $85.00 plus shipping and handling

"Heart to Heart"
Author and Date Published: T. Fullerton (1992)
Format: Videotape that provides information and interviews with families and professionals about what a family-centered approach means
Source: Robin Sims, Developmental Disabilities Planning Council, 275 East Main Street, Frankfort, KY 40621 (1-800-928-6583)
Cost: $10.00

A Practical Guide to Embedding Family-Centered Content into Existing Speech-Language Pathology Coursework
Author and Date Published: E. Crais (1991)
Format: Book
Source: Frank Porter Graham Child Development Center, CB#8180, The University of North Carolina, Chapel Hill, NC 27599-8180 (919-966-4221, Fax 919-966-7532)
Cost: $10.00

"Seasons of Caring"
Author and Date Published: Association for the Care of Children's Health (1986)
Format: Videotape with accompanying curriculum guides
Source: Association for the Care of Children's Health, 7910 Woodmont Avenue, Suite 300, Bethesda, MD 20814-3015 (301-654-6549)
Cost: $140.00 plus shipping and handling

Working with Families in Early Intervention: An Interdisciplinary Preservice Curriculum
Author and Date Published: P.J. Winton (1991)
Format: Book
Source: Frank Porter Graham Child Development Center, CB#8180, The University of North Carolina, Chapel Hill, NC 27599-8180, (919-966-4221, Fax 919-966-7532)
Cost: $15.00

Appendix B

Web Links for Parents: Health and Education Information

PARENTS AND FAMILIES

Internet Resources for Urban/Minority Families
  http://eric-web.tc.columbia.edu/families/other.html

The Electronic Schoolhouse-The Parent Connection
  http://www/niagara.com/~eschool/default.html

PACER Center: The Parent Advocacy Coalition for Educational Rights
  http://freenet.msp.mn.us.ip/family/PACER

Baby Web: The Internet Parenting Resource
  http://www/netaxs.com/~iris/infoweb/baby.html

MEDICAL/HEALTH

Med Web: Disabilities
  http://www.cc.emory.edu/WHSCL/medweb.disabled.html

Med Help International
  http:medhlp.netusa.net

MedWeb: Pediatrics
  http://www.cc.emory.edu/WHSCL/medweb.pediatrics.html

III

MEDICAL AND
SURGICAL
MANAGEMENT

9

Medical Management of Otitis Media

Frederick W. Henderson

The most frequent therapeutic decision a primary care physician evaluating preschool children must make concerns the selection of an antibiotic treatment program for patients with a clinical diagnosis of acute otitis media (AOM) of presumed bacterial etiology. This diagnosis is made in approximately 30%–40% of all acute illness assessments performed in children less than 5 years of age (Teele, Klein, Rosner, & the Greater Boston Otitis Media Study Group, 1989). The antibiotic selection process is becoming more complex as common otitis pathogens demonstrate, with increasing frequency, either high-level resistance or significantly reduced susceptibility to commonly employed antibiotics. In the case of beta-lactam antibiotics (penicillins and cephalosporins), antibiotic sensitivity occurs along a continuum. Thus, the clinician must understand the relative degree of susceptibility of specific organisms to a number of different antibiotics to make the most informed treatment decisions.

Much of our knowledge of the clinical and microbiologic efficacy of antibiotics was obtained in an era when antibiotic resistance was a relatively minor problem among isolates of *Streptococcus pneumoniae* (pneumococci). Because pneumococci routinely account for close to 50% of isolates from bacteriologically proven cases of AOM, the recent emergence of resistance to multiple antibiotics in these organisms has substantial implications for otitis management. Continued monitoring of the efficacy of drugs currently in use and newly developed agents will be required as drug susceptibility patterns among otitis pathogens change. This chapter includes 1) a review of the microbiology and pathogenesis of otitis media, 2) the microbiologic and pharmacologic data upon which antibiotic treatment decisions should be based, and 3) a summary of the evidence for the efficacy of antibiotics in bacterial otitis media. In addition, the chapter provides 4) an examination of the microbiology of AOM in children with persisting symptoms after antibiotic treatment, 5) a discussion of an approach to the child with treatment-resistant otitis in the era of antibiotic-resistant pneumococci, 6) a survey of options for managing recurrent suppurative AOM, and 7) a review of the roles of antibiotics and corticosteroids in management of persistent nonsuppurative otitis media with effusion (OME).

MICROBIOLOGY AND PATHOGENESIS OF ACUTE OTITIS MEDIA

Viral Infections and Otitis Media

Parents, grandparents, and even physicians have long recognized the temporal relationship between the occurrence of viral respiratory infections and the development of otitis media. Since the 1980s, the role of respiratory viral infection in otitis media pathogenesis has been the focus of substantial research attention. Viral respiratory infections establish the pathophysiologic conditions (mucus hypersecretion, mucosal edema, altered eustachian tube ventilatory function, and altered mucociliary clearance) in the upper respiratory tract that are permissive for the development of middle ear effusion and acute bacterial otitis media (Sanyal, Henderson, Stempel, Collier, & Denny, 1980). Using prospective surveillance of children in group child care, Henderson and colleagues (1982) documented the occurrence of AOM among children with culture-proven viral respiratory illnesses (Table 1). Acute otitis media was observed in approximately 30%–40% of children with respiratory illnesses caused by respiratory syncytial virus, influenza viruses,

Table 1. Occurrence of AOM in children with documented viral infections

Viral infection	Henderson et al. (1982)	Ruuskanen & Heikkinen (1994)
Respiratory syncytial virus	28/71 (.39)[a]	510/945 (.54)[a]
Influenza A and B viruses	12/43 (.28)	80/280 (.29)
Adenoviruses	41/128 (.32)	115/413 (.28)
Parainfluenza viruses	24/155 (.15)	77/295 (.26)
Rhinoviruses	5/48 (.10)	nr[b]
Enteroviruses	21/131 (.16)	nr

[a]Proportion with AOM.
[b]nr, not reported.

and adenoviruses. In contrast, the incidence of AOM averaged approximately 15% among children with antecedent upper respiratory infection (URI) caused by parainfluenza viruses, rhinoviruses, or enteroviruses. A similar pattern was observed by Ruuskanen and Heikkinen (1994), who documented the occurrence of AOM among children hospitalized with documented viral respiratory infections in Finland (Table 1). Whereas early attempts to isolate viruses from middle ear fluids were frequently unsuccessful, more recent work using viral antigen or nucleic acid detection together with virus isolation has demonstrated that evidence for viral infection of middle ear fluid can be obtained regularly; this is particularly true of respiratory syncytial virus. Even these observations are likely to underestimate the association of viral infection with the development of otitis media because this can be a relatively late consequence of the alterations in upper respiratory tract physiology initiated by viral infection. Of additional significance, Chonmaitree and colleagues (1992) have observed that there is an increased risk of poor response to antibacterial therapy for otitis when there is concurrent viral infection. Recurrent viral respiratory infections are probably intimately involved in the maintenance of OME, particularly in infants and toddlers, although research to document this relationship has not been conducted. It is likely that ultimate control of OME will require not only reduction in the incidence of bacterial OM but prevention of the viral respiratory infections that are the frequent antecedents of both purulent (containing a neutrophilic exudate [pus]) and nonpurulent middle ear effusions.

Bacterial Infections of the Middle Ear Space
The bacteria that infect the middle ear space are routinely found in the nasopharyngeal mucus of healthy children. Cross-sectional studies of healthy toddlers have demonstrated that, at any point in time, 45%–55% are carrying *S. pneumoniae,* 20%–35% *Haemophilus influenzae,* and 30%–50% *Moraxella catarrhalis* in nasopharyngeal secretions. These organisms gain access to the middle ear space and establish localized infection when conducive pathophysiologic alterations occur in the mucosa of the upper respiratory tract. Studies documenting the bacteria recovered from middle ear fluid samples of patients with AOM have been conducted throughout this century. In the early 1950s, Lahikainen (1953) and Rudberg (1954) reviewed bacteriologic data published between 1906 and 1954; much of the work had been performed in Scandinavia. In 25 studies involving 8,483 otitis cases, *Streptococcus pyogenes* (group A beta-hemolytic streptococci) routinely accounted for 20%–40% of bacterial isolates from middle ear fluids obtained from patients with AOM. In four studies that used direct aspiration of middle

Table 2. Bacterial isolates from patients with otitis media in Scandinavia: 1945–1954

| Author | Year | N | Proportion of samples yielding pathogen[a] | | | |
			S. pyo.	S. pn.	H. inf.	np/ng[b]
Nielson	1945	811	.26	.47	.16	.11
Bjuggren	1952	134	.21	.50	.17	.11
Lahikainen	1953	734	.24	.38	.15	.22
Rudberg	1954	1,365	.19	.39	.07	.35

Data from Lahikainen (1953) and Rudberg (1954).
[a]S. pyo., Streptococcus pyogenes; S. pn., Streptococcus pneumoniae; H. inf., Haemophilus influenza.
[b]np/ng, no pathogen or no growth.

ear fluids and appropriate bacteriologic methods for isolation of *H. influenzae*, group A beta-hemolytic streptococci were recovered from an average of approximately 25% of middle ear fluid samples (Table 2). Although *S. pyogenes* was responsible for a substantial fraction of total AOM isolates in the 1930s and 1940s, these organisms were recovered most frequently from older preschool and school-age children. In children less than 2 years of age, *S. pneumoniae* and *H. influenzae* were the predominant isolates.

Beginning in the late 1940s and continuing through the 1950s, the role of *S. pyogenes* in the etiology of AOM waned progressively and markedly. In a large number of studies conducted since the 1960s, the bacteria isolated from middle ear fluids of children with AOM have been strikingly similar from year to year (Table 3). A bacterial pathogen can be cultured from 65%–85% of middle ear fluid samples obtained from children with the clinical diagnosis of AOM. *Streptococcus pneumoniae* is recovered from approximately 35% of ears examined and accounts for approximately 50% of all bacterial isolates, as it did in the first half of this century. Nontypable *H. influenzae* accounts for 30%–35% of bacteria recovered from middle ear fluid aspirates and *M. catarrhalis* for 10%–15%. Since the early 1960s *S. pyogenes* has accounted for only 3%–7% of bacteria isolated from middle ear fluids of children with AOM. *Staphylococcus aureus, Staphylococcus epidermidis, Pseudo-*

Table 3. Bacteria recovered from middle ear exudates in AOM: Contemporary studies

| Reference | N | Proportion of samples yielding pathogen[a] | | | | |
		S. pn.	H. inf.	M. cat.	S. pyo.	np/ng[b]
Coffey et al. (1966)	267	.37	.30	.05	.02	.28
Howie et al. (1970)	858	.38	.24	.08	.03	.30
Shurin et al. (1983)	145	.31	.20	.20	.01	.34
Bluestone et al. (1992)	2,807	.35	.23	.14	.03	nr
Ruuskanen & Heikkinen (1994)	523	.29	.19	.15	nr[c]	nr

[a]S. pn., Streptococcus pneumoniae; H. inf., Haemophilus influenzae; M. cat., Moraxella catarrhalis; S. pyo., Streptococcus pyogenes.
[b]np/ng: no pathogen or no growth.
[c]nr: not reported.

monas aeruginosa, and diphtheroids are all common colonizers of the external auditory canal. Whereas *S. aureus* and *P. aeruginosa* are both recovered from children with chronic draining otitis media, the organisms recovered from the external auditory canal and anaerobic upper respiratory bacteria have no significant role in the etiology of uncomplicated AOM in healthy children (Bluestone, Stephenson, & Martin, 1992; Coffey, Booth, & Martin, 1966; Howie, Ploussard, & Lester, 1970; Ruuskanen & Heikkinen, 1994; Shurin et al., 1983).

Otitis Media During the First 3 Months of Life

Although the incidence of AOM is highest between 3 months and 2 years of age, the disease is occasionally diagnosed in children less than 3 months of age. There have been several studies of the bacterial etiology of AOM in this age group. Initially, Bland (1972) described 21 children less than 6 weeks of age with otitis media. Symptoms of URI were observed in 70% of infants, 19% were febrile, and 33% had been born prematurely. Bacteria were isolated from 18 middle ear aspirates, and gastrointestinal organisms (predominantly *Escherichia coli* or *Klebsiella*) were recovered from 13 of 18 culture-positive samples (72%). In contrast to these findings, subsequent studies (Berman & Lauer, 1983; Shurin, Howie, Pelton, Ploussard, & Klein, 1978; Tetzlaff, Ashworth, & Nelson, 1977) demonstrated typical otitis pathogens of later infancy (*S. pneumoniae, H. influenzae, M. catarrhalis*) in the majority of children less than 12 weeks of age with positive middle ear fluid cultures. In these studies, gastrointestinal bacteria were isolated from only 12 of 154 middle ear fluid samples (8%). Fever was observed in 10%–40% of children, and blood cultures were positive in only 4 of 94 children studied (4%). Although the etiology of otitis media is variable in very young infants, typical otitis pathogens are isolated most frequently; however, gram-negative gastrointestinal bacteria must be considered as potential etiologic agents, particularly during the first 6 weeks of life.

MANAGEMENT OF ACUTE OTITIS MEDIA

Although control of the viral infections that are the antecedents of many episodes of otitis media and middle ear effusion is likely to prove to be an integral component of effective strategies for prevention of both AOM and OME, there are no antiviral therapies known to influence the course of established AOM. Presently, the sole intervention known to have a direct bearing on the clinical course of AOM is effective antibiotic treatment.

Antimicrobial Susceptibility of Otitis Pathogens

To select an appropriate antibiotic for treatment of bacterial infections, one must understand the antibacterial potency of the drugs that might be employed against the bacteria most likely to be the cause of infection. This information is provided for common otitis pathogens in Table 4 (Barry, Pfaller, Fuchs, & Packer, 1994; Fung-Tomc et al., 1995; Linares et al., 1992; Spangler, Jacobs, Pankuch, & Appelbaum, 1993). Data tabulated reflect the range of typical median minimum inhibitory concentration (MIC) values (the lowest concentration of antibiotic that inhibits growth of the organism) for specific antibiotics against different otitis pathogens. Data for *S. pneumoniae* are presented in Table 4 according to level of sensitivity of the organism to penicillin G. Pneumococci with penicillin MICs of 0.06 μg/ml or less are classified as sensitive, those with MICs ranging from 0.12 to 1.0 μg/ml are classified as intermediately (or relatively) resistant, and those with MICs of 2.0 μg/ml or more are classified as resistant.

Achievable Concentrations of Antibiotics in Serum and Middle Ear Fluid

The clinical efficacy of an antibiotic is related to both its antibacterial potency and the effective drug concentration achieved at the site of

Table 4. In vitro susceptibility (range of median MICs) of otitis pathogens to commonly employed antibiotics

| Antibiotic | S. pneumoniae | | | H. influenzae (BL− or +)[a] | M. catarrhalis (BL+)[a] |
	Sensitive	Intermediate	Resistant		
Amoxicillin	0.015	0.12–0.25	2.0	0.5 (BL−)	N/A
Amoxicillin and					
clavulanate	0.015	0.12–0.25	2.0	0.5 (BL −/+)	0.25
Ceftriaxone	0.015	0.12	1.0[b]	0.03	0.25
Cefpodoxime	0.03	0.25–0.5	4.0	0.06	0.5
Cefuroxime	0.03	0.25–0.5	4.0	0.5	0.5
Cefprozil	0.12–0.25	0.5–1.0	8.0	4.0	1.0
Cefaclor	0.50–1.0	2.0–4.0	>16.0	4.0	1.0
Loracarbef	0.50–1.0	2.0–4.0	>16.0	1.0–2.0	1.0
Cefixime	0.25	2.0–4.0	>16.0	0.06	0.25
Ceftibuten	2.0	8.0	>16.0	0.12	0.25
Erythromycin[c]	0.03	0.03	2.0–>16.0	8.0	0.06
Clarithromycin[c]	0.03	0.03	2.0–>16.0	8.0/4.0[d]	0.06
Azithromycin[c]	0.03	0.03	2.0–>16.0	0.5	0.06
Trimethoprim–					
sulfamethoxazole[e]	0.12/2.4	0.12/2.4	>4.0/76	0.12/2.4	0.25/4.8

Data from Barry et al. (1994), Fung-Tomc et al. (1995), Linares et al. (1992), and Spangler et al. (1993).
[a]BL−, beta-lactamase negative; BL+, beta-lactamase producing.
[b]Occasionally the MIC for ceftriaxone or cefotaxime can be four-fold or more higher than penicillin MIC.
[c]Approximately 40% of highly penicillin-resistant strains of *S. pneumoniae* are resistant to erythromycin; strains resistant to erythromycin are also resistant to clarithromycin and azithromycin. Erythromycin-resistant strains may be susceptible to clindamycin. Typically, less than 5% of penicillin-susceptible and up to 15% of penicillin-intermediate *S. pneumoniae* isolates are resistant to the macrolides.
[d]Clarithromycin/14-hydroxyclarithromycin.
[e]MIC greater than or equal to μg/ml 1/19, for approximately 30% of penicillin-susceptible and intermediate *S. pneumoniae* strains.

bacterial replication in the host. The peak serum concentrations and approximate peak middle ear fluid concentrations of antibiotics commonly employed in otitis treatment are shown in Table 5. Middle ear fluid levels of antibiotics are difficult to measure with great precision because the small volume of middle ear fluid obtained is frequently difficult to measure accurately, and errors are introduced in preparing dilutions of the sample for assay. For beta-lactam antibiotics, middle ear fluid concentrations are approximately 30%–40% of peak serum concentrations. Newer macrolides are concentrated in phagocytes and may preferentially accumulate at sites of neutrophilic inflammation. Peak serum levels of orally administered antibiotics are usually achieved approximately 90 minutes after ingestion, and peak middle ear fluid concentrations occur approximately 30–45 minutes later.

Assessing the Efficacy of Antibiotics in Bacterial Otitis Media

In recent years there has been interest in critically evaluating the role of antibiotics in the treatment of AOM and in limiting the inappropriate use of antibiotics in pediatric respiratory infections. This concern is attributable primarily to the relatively rapid emergence of antibiotic resistance among strains of S. pneumoniae. Because the majority of antibiotic prescriptions written for preschool children are for treatment of AOM, careful use of antibiotics for this condition could have a substantial impact on antibiotic utilization in pediatrics.

Antibiotic effectiveness in bacterial AOM can be measured by 1) an increased likelihood of sterilization of middle ear fluid, 2) a substantial reduction in the concentration of bacteria in middle ear fluid, 3) termination of drainage of purulent fluid from the middle ear space,

Table 5. Range of expected peak serum and middle ear fluid (MEF) concentrations of antibiotics commonly employed in treatment of AOM

Antibiotic (dose [mg/kg])	Peak serum conc.[a]	Peak MEF conc.[a]
Amoxicillin (15)	6–9	2.0–3.0
Cefuroxime (15)	4–6	1.0–1.5
Cefpodoxime (10)	1.5–3	0.5–0.7[c]
Cefixime (10)	1.5–3	0.5–0.7[c]
Cefaclor (15)	11–15	3.0–5.0
Loracarbef (15)	11–15	3.0–5.0
Cefprozil (15)	11–15	3.0–5.0
Ceftibutin (9)	11–15	3.0–5.0
Erythromycin ES (12.5)	1.0–1.5	0.75
Clarithromycin (7.5)	1.7/0.8[b]	2.5/1.3[b]
Azithromycin (5.0)	0.8–1.2	5.0–7.0[c]
Trimethoprim–sulfamethoxazole (4/20)	3.0/50	1.5/15

Source: Klimek et al. (1980) and Krause et al. (1982) for MEF concentrations.
[a]Antibiotic concentrations in micrograms per milliliter.
[b]Clarithromycin/14-hydroxyclarithromycin.
[c]Azithromycin is concentrated in phagocytes; its higher concentration in middle ear fluid relative to serum reflects its presence in infiltrating neutrophils.

4) prevention of progression of otitis media to mastoiditis, 5) clearance of purulent middle ear effusion or conversion of middle ear fluid from purulent to nonpurulent, or 6) resolution of acute clinical symptoms. These outcomes are purposefully ordered from the ones providing the most direct and convincing evidence of microbiologic efficacy to the least directly informative. Although sterilization of middle ear fluid has been used as an outcome in a substantial number of clinical investigations, many clinical trials comparing the efficacy of different antibiotics or comparing antibiotic treatment with placebo administration have relied on the combination of outcomes 5 and 6 to provide evidence for treatment efficacy. It is clear that clinical symptoms associated with AOM frequently resolve or improve substantially when placebos are administered or when sterilization of middle ear fluid is not achieved following antibiotic administration. Resolution of the neutrophilic exudate in the middle ear space has usually been encompassed in clinical trials by the phrase "improvement in otoscopic appearance," which may or may not accurately reflect clearance of the suppurative exudate. Thus, improvement in clinical symptoms and otoscopic appearance could encompass a wide range of microbiologic outcomes. Whereas improvement in the symptoms of clinical otitis media may not be dramatically influenced by antibiotic administration, the favorable outcomes 1, 2, and 3 are all substantially enhanced with effective antibiotic treatment in patients with proven bacterial infections of the middle ear space. The data that substantiate these statements can be found in the following sections.

Sterilization of Middle Ear Fluid   Using an investigative strategy introduced by Howie and Ploussard (1969), several researchers have assessed antibiotic efficacy in otitis media by performing repeat middle ear fluid cultures 3–6 days after initiating antibiotic treatment for proven bacterial otitis media. Klein (1993) compiled and reviewed studies that had used this investigative strategy. Results from these studies, expressed as proportion of middle ear fluids not sterilized 4–6 days after initiation of antibiotic therapy, are presented in Table 6 and reflect the differences in the in vitro potency of the antibiotics against common otitis pathogens and the pharmacokinetics of the drugs. Thus, amoxicillin failed to sterilize over 60% of infections caused by beta-lactamase–producing strains of *H. influenzae,* and erythromycin was no more effective than placebo in clearance of *Haemophilus* infections. Similarly, among beta-lactam antibiotics, the lowest rate of sterilization of pneumococcal infection was observed with cefixime, which is less active than amoxicillin against the pneumococcus and achieves lower concentrations in middle ear fluid than many orally administered beta-lactams. Similarly, failure to sterilize *Haemophilus* infections was highest with

Table 6.   Failure to sterilize middle ear fluid within 4–6 days of initiating antibiotic treatment as documented by repeat tympanocentesis

Antibiotic	S. pneumoniae	H. influenzae[a]	M. catarrhalis[a]
Amoxicillin	10/199 (.05)[b]	6/60 (.10)[c] (BL−)[c]	0/10 (.00)[b] (BL−)
		7/11 (.64) (BL+)[c]	4/19 (.21) (BL+)
Amoxicillin and clavulanate	See amoxicillin	11/58 (.19)	2/30 (.07)
Cefaclor	16/88 (.18)	27/82 (.33)	2/17 (.12)
Cefixime	16/61 (.26)	4/66 (.06)	3/30 (.10)
Cefprozil	1/13 (.08)	8/14 (.57)	
Cefpodoxime	4/24 (.17)	1/22 (.05)	4/15 (.27)
Cefuroxime	0/11 (.00)		
Trimethoprim–sulfamethoxazole	6/51 (.12)	15/61 (.25)	
Erythromycin	1/15 (.07)	17/20 (.85)	
Clarithromycin	0/12 (.00)	12/15 (.80)	
Placebo/inactive	46/52 (.88)	51/70 (.73)	

Modified from Klein, J.O. (1993). Microbiologic efficacy of antibacterial drugs for acute otitis media. *Pediatric Infectious Disease Journal, 12,* 973–975.
[a]Sample sizes less than 10 omitted.
[b]Proportion culture positive 4–6 days after initiation of antibiotic treatment; proportion not calculated if sample size less than 10.
[c]BL−, beta-lactamase negative; BL+, beta-lactamase producing.

cefaclor and cefprozil, the beta-lactam drugs with the highest MICs for *Haemophilus* isolates.

Most of these results were obtained in an era when pneumococci demonstrating reduced susceptibility to penicillin and cephalosporins were infrequent causes of infection. As the prevalence of penicillin resistance in pneumococci increases, antibiotics with borderline or marginal efficacy against fully penicillin-susceptible organisms will be less effective in treatment of pneumococcal otitis media.

Termination of Purulent Drainage from the Middle Ear Space   This outcome was commonly reported in placebo-controlled studies conducted during the early years of the antibiotic era. Typically myringotomy was performed to obtain a middle ear specimen for culture, and the patient was randomly assigned to antibiotic or placebo treatment. The primary outcome was days to termination of purulent drainage from the myringotomy incision. The data of Lahikainen (1953) and Rudberg (1954) are representative and informative (Table 7). The duration of discharge in placebo recipients is an underestimate of total duration because subjects designated as nonresponders were switched to active antibacterial therapies. With effective antibiotic treatment, the duration of purulent drainage from the myringotomy incision site in streptococcal otitis media (group A streptococcus or pneumococcus) was reduced from an average of 10 days to an average of 3 days.

Prevention of Mastoiditis   Acute and chronic mastoiditis have become infrequent complications of otitis media in the antibiotic era. This change could be attributable to differences in the virulence of otitis

Table 7. Mean duration of purulent aural discharge (days) after myringotomy in relation to antibiotic treatment (placebo-controlled trials)

Author (year)	Treatment	S. pyogenes	S. pneumoniae	H. influenzae	No pathogen
Lahikainen	Penicillin	3.8 (69)[a]	3.9 (76)	5.1 (9)	3.2 (20)
(1953)	Placebo	12.4 (102)[a]	11.5 (147)	5.8 (72)	4.1 (106)
Rudberg	Penicillin	4.2 (119)	4.1 (228)	5.1 (44)	3.3 (117)
(1954)	Sulfonamide	9.0 (43)	4.2 (109)	4.5 (16)	2.9 (45)
	Pen + sulfa	4.5 (49)	3.8 (95)	4.0 (13)	2.7 (41)
	Placebo	10.0 (54)	7.8 (95)	8.4 (23)	5.3 (48)

[a]Mean duration of discharge in days (number in treatment group).

pathogens, changes in host resistance to invasive infection, or the effectiveness of antibiotics. Again placebo-controlled studies from the late 1930s, when sulfonamides were introduced, to the middle and late 1940s, when penicillin became available, are informative. Data regarding penicillin treatment are provided in Table 8. These data leave little doubt that use of effective antibiotics in AOM has contributed to the reduction in occurrence of mastoid disease in the antibiotic era.

These findings provide convincing evidence that antibiotics can attenuate substantially the duration and severity of bacterial AOM. One should consider these observations when attempting to place in perspective the findings of a recent meta-analysis (see next section) concerning the effect of antibiotics on the clinical course of AOM.

Resolution of Clinical Symptoms and Otoscopy Evidence that antibiotic treatment modifies the course of *clinical* otitis media (clinical diagnosis, without requiring culture proof of bacterial infection) was critically reviewed in a meta-analysis (Rosenfeld et al., 1994). The authors of that report concluded that almost 80% of children with the clinical diagnosis of AOM would have a satisfactory course without antibiotic treatment, or, alternatively, that only 1 in 7 children could be expected to benefit from antibiotic treatment. This topic had been previously addressed by Marchant, Carlin, Johnson, and Shurin (1992) when they described the unexpectedly good clinical results obtained

Table 8. Effects of penicillin on the occurrence of acute mastoiditis in patients with OM

Author	Year	Treatment	N	Mastoiditis (%)
Gulsvik	1949	Conservative	57	30
		Penicillin	186	2
Riskaer	1949	Conservative	177	11
		Penicillin	175	0
Jersild	1950	Conservative	66	30
		Penicillin	144	4
Rudberg	1950	Conservative	240	14
		Penicillin	272	2

Adapted from Rudberg (1954).

with partially effective antimicrobial agents as the "Pollyanna phenomenon." Two factors contribute to the outcomes of these investigations. First, only 70%–80% of children with a clinical diagnosis of AOM have culture-proven active bacterial infections of the middle ear space at the time the diagnosis is made. Antibiotics are unlikely to have an impact on the 20%–30% of cases without bacterial isolates. To the extent that participants in a clinical otitis study had a higher rate of culture-negative effusions, the differences in favorable outcome associated with antibiotic treatment would be reduced. Second, the natural history of clinical symptoms in children with proven bacterial otitis media can be rather benign, even when bacterial infection of the middle ear space is untreated or only partially suppressed by antibiotic treatment. Rosenfeld et al. included in their meta-analysis four studies that included placebo-treated otitis patients; only 1 of these studies involved patients with culture-proven bacterial otitis media (Halstead, Lepow, Balassanian, Emmerich, & Wolinsky, 1968). In that study, 70% of 19 placebo recipients with positive initial middle ear fluid cultures improved clinically within 72 hours of diagnosis. Although bacterial cultures of middle ear fluids were not performed at the 72-hour follow-up, it is likely that resolution of clinical symptoms occurred without a significant change in middle ear fluid bacteriology.

Marchant et al. (1992) reviewed the data on 293 children with culture-confirmed bacterial AOM who had participated in antibiotic treatment trials. Among 40 children who continued to have positive middle ear fluid cultures 3–6 days after beginning antibiotic treatment, clinical signs and symptoms had improved in over 60% despite ongoing bacterial infection of the middle ear space. It is likely that the incompletely effective antibiotics had reduced the concentration of organisms in middle ear fluid among children whose follow-up cultures were not sterile, but this was not measured in those studies.

Engelhard and colleagues (1989) conducted a randomized trial of amoxicillin–clavulanate versus myringotomy only versus myringotomy plus amoxicillin–clavulanate in 105 infants with AOM. Clinical improvement as reflected by resolution of fever or irritability occurred equally frequently and rapidly in all treatment groups. However, persistent middle ear infection was judged to be present at 10 days in 63% of ears of children treated with myringotomy and placebo compared with 9% of ears of children receiving amoxicillin–clavulanate. Purulent drainage continued from the myringotomy site in 56% of ears of placebo recipients at days 3–6 and in 17% of ears at days 9–11.

In a similar investigation, Kaleida and co-workers (1991) compared amoxicillin only, myringotomy only (in children >2 years old), or the combination of amoxicillin plus myringotomy in 536 infants and children with AOM. Episodes were categorized by the severity of symptoms before randomization; bacteriologic data were not obtained at illness onset. In mild cases (75% of total cases) clinical outcome was good in both amoxicillin and placebo recipients; only 4% and 7% of amoxicillin and placebo recipients, respectively, were deemed treatment failures ($p = .007$ favoring amoxicillin treatment). Among children more than 2 years old with more severe AOM, children treated with myringotomy and placebo had a substantially higher rate of treatment failure (24%) than children given amoxicillin with or without myringotomy (4%). Children less than 2 years of age with more severe otitis were not randomized to the combination of myringotomy and placebo. The prevalence of middle ear effusion at the 6-week observation (observed in 35%–55% of subjects) did not differ by the AOM severity classification or by treatment assignment.

Thus it is clear that antibiotic treatment can have a favorable impact on the microbiology and clinical course of otitis media. However, resolution of fever, irritability, and ear discomfort frequently occur within 3–5 days with placebo treatment or treatment with incompletely effective antibiotics, which limits the usefulness of these markers of treatment efficacy. The proportion of children with clinical otitis media who will benefit from antibiotic treatment depends on 1) the proportion of children with clinical otitis who have bacterial otitis media, 2) the organism causing infection, and 3) the severity of infection, which may be a reflection of the concentration of organisms in infected middle ear fluid. Data from the early years of antibiotic use leave no doubt that children with bacterial otitis media can benefit dramatically from antibiotic treatment. With the emergence middle ear infections caused by highly penicillin-resistant and multidrug-resistant pneumococci, the importance of the availability of effective antibiotics for treatment of these infections may once again become more apparent.

Management of Otitis Media in
Children Less than 6 Weeks of Age

As noted earlier, enteric gram-negative bacteria can be important causes of otitis media during the first 6 weeks of life, although the usual bacterial pathogens of otitis media in older infants are isolated most frequently. Because many febrile children less than 8 weeks of age are evaluated comprehensively for serious bacterial infections and treated with broad-spectrum intravenous antibiotics pending culture results, it is perhaps not surprising that most children in these studies have benign clinical outcomes. For afebrile children less than 6 weeks of age with purulent otitis media, outpatient management with oral antibiotics can be satisfactory (Berman & Lauer, 1983), but these children should be followed closely. The results of multiple studies of serious bacterial infections during the first 8–12 weeks of life suggest that otitis is not commonly an initiating focus for invasive bacterial disease (bacteremia or meningitis) in this age group.

Microbiologic Findings in Children with Continuing Symptoms After Initiating Antibiotic Treatment

As noted previously, fever (when present), ear ache, and irritability frequently resolve within 72 hours of the diagnosis of AOM, regardless of the effectiveness of treatment. However, up to 10% of effectively treated patients and 30% of placebo- or ineffectively treated patients will have ongoing symptoms 3–6 days after starting antibiotic treatment. In the individual patient who manifests continuing symptoms on antibiotic treatment, the clinician must address the question of whether treatment modification is warranted. In one of the first reports to examine this issue, Teele, Pelton, and Klein (1981) studied 42 infants and toddlers who continued to manifest symptoms (fever, irritability, or ear discomfort) 2 to more than 6 days after initiation of antibiotic treatment for AOM. Fifty-seven percent had negative bacterial cultures of middle ear fluid, and bacteria sensitive to the treatment being employed were isolated from 5 of 42 cases (12%). Antibiotic-resistant organisms were recovered from 31% of children (five with *S. aureus*, seven with *H. influenzae*, and one with *S. pneumoniae*).

Subsequently, Arola, Ziegler, and Ruuskanen (1990) studied 22 infants and toddlers with persistent symptoms a mean of 5 days after initiating antibiotic treatment for AOM. Bacteria were recovered from middle ear fluid in only four (22%), but evidence of acute viral respiratory infection was obtained in 68% (32% had virus identified in middle ear fluid). The bacteria isolated were resistant to the initial antibiotic treatment in two cases and borderline susceptible in two others; however, all children with bacterial isolates also had evidence of concurrent viral infection. Ongoing infection caused by overtly antibiotic-resistant bacteria was implicated as possibly contributing to continuing symptoms in a minority of subjects. In support of this observation, Chonmaitree and colleagues identified concurrent viral infection in 46% of children with AOM and observed that children with bacterial otitis media and concurrent viral infection were less likely to have resolved clinical symptoms or to have sterile middle ear fluid after antibiotic treatment than children without documented viral infection (Sung et al., 1993). Thus, ongoing fever and malaise can be attributable to concurrent viral infection in a meaningful proportion of children under treatment for AOM. Conversely, true bacteriologic failures can be demonstrated in a subset of cases, and the proportion of true bacteriologic failures is likely to increase as the prevalence of drug-resistant organisms increases, as demonstrated by the following observations.

Brook and Yocum (1995) studied 12 children who had continuing symptomatic bilateral AOM following 5–10 days of amoxicillin therapy. Only 5 of 24 ear aspirates (21%) revealed no bacterial growth, and no child had negative cultures from both ears. Beta-lactamase–producing *H. influenzae* or *M. catarrhalis* were isolated from 18 ears, including all 5 that yielded amoxicillin-susceptible *S. pneumoniae*. Thus, as expected, beta-lactamase–producing organisms can have an important role in culture-proven bacteriologic treatment failures following amoxicillin administration.

These studies were conducted in an era when antibiotic resistance among isolates of *S. pneumoniae* occurred relatively infrequently. As highly and multiply resistant pneumococci become more prevalent, the proportion of children with ongoing symptoms who are infected with resistant pneumococci will also increase. Pichichero and Pichichero (1995) reported results of tympanocenteses in children deemed clinical antibiotic treatment failures. They obtained no growth from 53% of 200 middle ear fluid samples. *Streptococcus pneumoniae* was the single most prevalent isolate, recovered from 52 specimens (26%). It accounted for 21 of 44 isolates from amoxicillin-treated patients (48%), 4 of 16 isolates from trimethoprim–sulfamethoxazole recipients (25%), and 8 of 10 isolates from children receiving cefixime (80%). *Haemophilus influenzae* (7%) and *M. catarrhalis* (6.5%) were recovered less frequently. Only 11 of the 50 *S. pneumoniae* isolates were subjected to antibiotic susceptibility testing; 2 demonstrated reduced penicillin sensitivity. Block and colleagues (1995) studied AOM in a community in Kentucky where the prevalence of drug-resistant *S. pneumoniae* was unusually high. Penicillin-resistant *S. pneumoniae* (PRSP) accounted for 17% of 283 isolates from all children with AOM. Fifty percent of the PRSP strains were highly resistant to penicillin. Most children with highly PRSP strains had experienced three or more episodes of otitis in the previous 4 months (87%), had been treated with antibiotics within the 7 days before the culture that revealed highly PRSP strains (91%), and had received an average of 5.5 prior courses of antibiotic therapy. PRSP accounted for 44% of isolates from 63 children who had tympanocentesis because of treatment-refractory otitis media, whereas beta-lactamase–producing organisms accounted for only 11% of isolates. Resolution of clinical otitis occurred with either 5–8 days of intramuscular ceftriaxone or with high-dose amoxicillin (80–100 mg/kg/day). Clinical failures were observed with ceftriaxone administered for less than 4 days and with alternate-day ceftriaxone. No pneumococcal isolates with high-level ceftriaxone resistance (MIC >4 μg/ml) were encountered in the Kentucky study.

Nasopharyngeal Culture as a Guide to Possible Otitis Media Etiologies and to Antibiotic Selection

The "gold standard" for selecting antibiotic therapy for children with bacterial AOM is to base treatment on the results of culture and sensitivity data obtained by direct sampling of middle ear fluid by tympanocentesis (needle aspiration of middle ear fluid through the tympanic membrane). This procedure has not been warranted in routine cases of AOM because empiric therapy has usually continued to result in a satisfactory clinical success rate. In complex AOM cases, however, tympanocentesis should be employed to determine etiology and therapy.

An additional source of information relevant to treatment decisions is the nasopharyngeal culture. The nasopharyngeal culture has generally been maligned as noninformative in predicting the etiology of otitis media. The following discussion demonstrates the inaccuracy of this perception. This point of view is counterintuitive because the nasopharynx is the portal of entry of bacteria in all cases of uncomplicated AOM. In culture-proven bacterial otitis media, the organism isolated from aspirated middle ear fluid is recovered by concurrent nasopharyngeal culture in 95% of cases (Mortimer & Watterson, 1956). The 5% of cases in which the organism isolated from the middle ear is not found by nasopharyngeal culture represent examples of sampling error. At a minimum, then, the nasopharyngeal culture can be regarded as a good method for identifying potential causes of bacterial AOM ("rounding up the suspects"). The principal limitations of the nasopharyngeal culture are 1) its low positive predictive value for organisms commonly carried by children without AOM and 2) the isolation of multiple potential otitis pathogens from nasopharyngeal secretions. The difference between the pretest probability of a specific etiologic diagnosis and the posttest probability of that diagnosis increases progressively as the prevalence of carriage of the potential pathogen by healthy children decreases. The nasopharyngeal culture always carries an informative negative predictive value (low probability that an agent is the cause of otitis if it is not recovered from nasopharyngeal mucus). The following example demonstrates the utility of the nasopharyngeal culture in clinical otitis media management.

A clinician wants to estimate the likelihood that a child with clinical otitis media is infected with a highly penicillin-resistant strain of *S. pneumoniae*. The child lives in a community where the prevalence of high-level penicillin resistance among pneumococcal isolates from the upper respiratory tracts of preschool children averages 20%. The nasopharyngeal culture is obtained before antibiotic treatment is initiated. The pretest probability of highly PRSP otitis media is 8% (0.8 [the probability that the middle ear fluid culture is positive for bacteria] × 0.5 [the probability that the bacterium isolated is a pneumococcus] × 0.2 [the probability of high-level penicillin resistance if the organism is a pneumococcus] = 0.08). If the nasopharyngeal culture is negative for highly PRSP strains, then the posttest probability of highly PRSP otitis media is 0.5%. If the nasopharyngeal culture is positive for highly PRSP strains, the posttest probability of highly penicillin-resistant pneumococcal infection is 45%. Both of these predictive estimates are substantially more informative than the estimate without nasopharyngeal culture data.

PREVENTION OF RECURRENT ACUTE OTITIS MEDIA

Several investigators have studied continuous oral antibiotic prophylaxis as a strategy for preventing recurrent otitis media among susceptible (otitis-prone) children. The results of selected studies are provided in Table 9. Perrin et al. (1974) reported successful prophylaxis of recurrent AOM among otherwise healthy otitis-prone children attending a general pediatric practice. Using a randomized crossover design, sulfisoxazole or placebo was given twice daily to children who had experienced two or more episodes of AOM in a 6-month period of time and either five or more episodes of lifetime otitis media or at least three episodes in the 18 months before study participation. During 6 months of follow-up, there was an 86% reduction in AOM incidence during periods of sulfonamide administration (1.05 episodes/6 months versus 0.15 episodes/6 months). Other investigators have also observed a significant reduction in AOM incidence during daily administration of sulfonamides (Schwartz, Puglise, & Rodriguez, 1982; Liston, Foshee, & Pierson, 1983). Similarly, amoxicillin has been demonstrated to reduce the frequency of AOM in susceptible children (Casselbrant et al., 1992; Maynard, Fleshman, & Tschopp, 1972). Antibiotic administration at the onset of URI may be a partially effective strategy, but not as effective as continuous prophylaxis (Berman et al. 1992).

We demonstrated that sulfonamide-resistant pneumococci were readily selected in a child care setting when sulfonamide-containing antibiotics were employed in otitis treatment or prophylaxis (Henderson,

Table 9. Suppression of AOM with antibiotic prophylaxis

Reference	N	Observation period	Treatment	Incidence AOM
Maynard et al. (1972)	191	12 months	Placebo	.79/child-year
	173		Amoxicillin	.42/child-year
Perrin et al. (1974)	54	6 months	Placebo	1.05/6 mo
	54		Sulfisoxazole	0.15/6 mo
Berman et al. (1992)	22[a]	4 months	Amoxicillin with URI	0.80/4 mo
	28		Amoxicillin daily	0.23/4 mo
Casselbrant et al. (1992)	80	2 years	Placebo	1.08/child-year
	86		Amoxicillin	0.60/child-year
	77		Tympanostomy tubes	1.02/child-year

[a]Data for children over 12 months of age.

Gilligan, Wait, & Goff, 1988). Similarly, treatment with beta-lactam antibiotics is a risk factor for infection with penicillin-resistant pneumococci (Block et al. 1995; Ford, Mason, Kaplan, Lamberth, & Tillman, 1991). If antibiotic suppression is to be considered, sulfonamides alone should probably be employed, acknowledging their limitations with respect to preventing pneumococcal disease. The risk of increasing the prevalence of colonization with penicillin-resistant pneumococci by long-term use of beta-lactam antibiotics is probably greater than the risk of facilitating spread of sulfonamide-resistant strains. Recurrent episodes attributable to *Haemophilus* and *Moraxella* can probably be reduced with sulfonamide administration. Currently, the rapid dissemination of drug-resistant *S. pneumoniae* in many communities has produced a climate in which prophylactic antibiotic administration, if employed at all, must be used in a highly restricted manner.

PATHOGENESIS AND MEDICAL MANAGEMENT OF PERSISTENT OTITIS MEDIA WITH EFFUSION

Duration of Middle Ear Effusion
Following an Episode of Acute Bacterial Otitis Media

The duration of middle ear effusion after successful treatment for AOM has been documented by several investigators. In essentially every otitis treatment study, this outcome is determined on days 10–14 and days 28–35 after initiating therapy. A summary of the observations in three studies is provided in Table 10. These studies are limited by lack of knowledge of middle ear status before the case of AOM that led to inclusion in the study. Children who had middle ear effusion (OME) before the identifying case of AOM may have been more likely to have persisting effusion after AOM resolution. Furthermore, the data are censored by children who have recurrent AOM during the follow-up period. In many AOM treatment trials, close to 30% of children experience a recurrent AOM episode within 30 days.

The probability of persistent middle ear fluid following AOM has been substantially higher in children less than 24 months of age than in

Table 10. Persistence of middle ear effusion after successful treatment of acute suppurative OM

| Reference | Proportion effusion free by indicated no. of days | | | | | |
	14	20	30	41	62	90
Shurin et al. (1979)	n/a	12%	16%	26%	50%	58%
Schwartz et al. (1982)	50%	n/a	70%	n/a	86%	94%
Mandel et al. (1982)	49%	n/a	n/a	68%	n/a	n/a

n/a, not available.

older children. Shurin, Pelton, Donner, and Klein (1979) observed continued persistent effusion for at least 90 days in 55% of children less than 2 years old compared with 21% of older children. Mandel et al. (1982) observed persistent effusion at 14 days in 74% of children less than 2 years of age compared with 42% of older children. Persistent effusion at the end of antibiotic treatment is equally common among children who have a bacterial etiology identified, as in those with sterile middle ear fluid cultures at the time of diagnosis of AOM. The type of antibiotic treatment employed is irrelevant as long as the middle ear fluid is sterilized.

Isolation of Bacteria from Children with Persistent Nonpurulent Otitis Media with Effusion

In the late 1970s a series of articles provided data indicating that bacterial pathogens typical of AOM could be isolated from middle ear fluid samples obtained from a subset of children with persistent nonpurulent OME. The results of three of those studies are tabulated in Table 11. It is reasonable to conclude from these studies that a small percentage of ears (15%–20%) with nonpurulent OME contain viable bacteria relevant to otitis pathogenesis. With these findings established, investigators hypothesized that antibiotic treatment might promote resolution of nonpurulent middle ear effusion in a subset of children.

Resolution of Nonpurulent Middle Ear Effusion with Antibiotic Treatment

Several researchers have conducted randomized trials of short courses (2–4 weeks) of antibiotic treatment in children with persistent nonpurulent OME. Studies have usually focused on children with a minimum of 8–12 weeks of continuous effusion; a range of 65%–85% of study subjects had bilateral OME. In no study was antibiotic efficacy related to the presence of bacterial infection at entry into the trial.

In general, there has been a consistent trend for an increased likelihood of resolution of effusion among children randomized to antibiotic

Table 11. Microbiology of persistent nonpurulent OME

| Reference | N (ears) | Proportion of samples yielding pathogen | | | |
		S. pneumoniae	H. influenzae	M. catarrhalis	Any[a]
Healy & Teele (1977)	96	.10	.07	.04	.23
Riding et al. (1978)	274	.03	.07	.03	.16
Giebink et al. (1979)	140	.01	.10	.0	.13

[a]Included among "any" were S. pyogenes and S. aureus (if external canal cultures were negative for these species).

therapy, with little difference among antibiotic treatment options (amoxicillin, trimethoprim–sulfamethoxazole, cefaclor, erythromycin–sulfisoxazole). The differences in rates of resolution of effusion between placebo and antibiotic recipients have been typically modest. In general, resolution of effusion within 4 weeks is observed in 15%–25% of ears of placebo recipients compared with 25%–50% of ears of antibiotic recipients. Studies have varied in their inclusion of children of different ages. Children 2–5 years of age have constituted the largest proportion of study subjects in most trials, and some investigators have excluded children less than 2 years old. In no report has variability of antibiotic efficacy been examined by subject age or by history of child care attendance. A summary of four trials that used otoscopic criteria to define eligibility and outcome is presented in Table 12.

It is probably reasonable to conclude from available data that children 2–5 years of age with persistent OME of 8–12 weeks' duration or longer may benefit from a 10- to 14-day course of antibiotic treatment using agents with optimum potency against typical otitis pathogens. Such treatment might result in approximately a 15% increased likelihood of effusion resolution. This point of view is compatible with the Clinical Practice Guideline on OME in young children (Stool et al., 1994). The efficacy of short-course antibiotic treatment in OME has not been documented for the subgroup of children 6–24 months of age. In this age group, frequent (closely spaced) URIs are common and the likelihood of intercurrent AOM is high. The strong association of these factors with persistent and recurrent middle ear effusion suggests that a single 10- to 14-day course of antibiotics would be unlikely to have an impact on prolonged OME in most infants or young toddlers. Prior to the rapid emergence and dissemination of antibiotic-resistant pneumococci, continuous (4- to 6-month) antibiotic prophylaxis might have been a rea-

Table 12. Antibiotic treatment and resolution of prolonged nonpurulent OME

Reference	Treatment[a]	N	Outcome		
			Bilateral	Unilateral	No effusion
Mandel, Rockette,	Amoxicillin	213	.42	.28	.30
Bluestone, Paradise,	Placebo	113	.57	.29	.14
& Nozza (1987)					
Ernston & Anari (1985)	Cefaclor	46	.24	.24	.52
	Placebo	45	.60	.29	.11
Healy (1984)	TMP/SMZ	96	.32	.09	.58
	Placebo	93	.70	.24	.06
Mandel, Rockette,	Amoxicillin	79	.68 (bi + uni)	nr[b]	.32
Paradise, Bluestone,	Cefaclor	77	.78	nr	.22
& Nozza (1991)	Erythro-sulfa	80	.79	nr	.21
	Placebo	78	.86	nr	.14

[a]TMP/SMX, trimethoprim–sulfamethoxazole; Erythro-sulfa, erythromycin–sulfisoxazole.
[b]nr, not reported.

sonable option for children in this age group with persistent OME, particularly the subset prone to recurrent bouts of purulent otitis media. With the increasing prevalence of antibiotic resistance among otitis pathogens, this management option should be restricted to a highly select subgroup experiencing the highest rates of recurrent AOM (see previous discussion of antibiotic prophylaxis for prevention of recurrent suppurative otitis media).

Corticosteroid administration also has been studied as a possible adjunct to antibiotics in clearing OME (Table 13). In most studies, children had had persistent OME for a minimum of 8 weeks; the doses of prednisone ranged from 1.0 to 2.0 mg/kg/day and the drug was given for 7–14 days (with longer courses steroids were typically tapered during the second week). In three of four studies children in a comparison group received antibiotics only; Daly et al. (1991) used a comparison group that received placebos for both prednisone and antibiotics. The number of subjects included in these trials has been substantially smaller than in antibiotic treatment trials. In three of four trials listed in Table 13, the proportion of children with bilateral OME at the end of 2 weeks of treatment was lower when prednisone was administered. The relationship of age to treatment effect was not addressed in most studies; however, Daly et al. observed no effect of prednisone in children 6–24 months of age, and two trials included only children greater than 24 months of age.

With the small sample sizes, confidence intervals for the differences are obliged to be quite broad, limiting general acceptance of the positive findings. Furthermore, there is minimal evidence available regarding steroid use in children 6–24 months of age, when the prevalence of OME is highest. Available evidence suggests a lack of efficacy in this

Table 13. Effectiveness of antibiotics and prednisone compared to antibiotics alone in prolonged nonpurulent OME

Reference	Treatment[a]	N	Age (yr)	Outcome Bilateral	Outcome Unilateral	Outcome None
Berman et al. (1990)	T/S + Pred	26	3 (mean)	.11	.11	.77
	T/S	27		.48	.11	.33
Daly et al. (1991)	T/S + Pred	21	0.5–8	.38	.14	.48
	Placebo	21		.72	.14	.14
Lambert (1986)	Amox + Pred	32	2–15	.56[b]		.44
	Amox	28		.50[b]		.50
Podoshin, Fradis, Ben-David, & Faraffi (1990)	Amox + Pred	50	4–8	.20	.40	.40
	Amox	49		.59	.10	.31

[a]T/S, trimethoprim–sulfamethoxazole; Pred, prednisone; Amox, amoxicillin.
[b]Children with either bilateral or unilateral effusion reported.

age group. The Clinical Practice Guideline does not endorse prednisone as an effective medical alternative for management of persistent non-purulent middle ear effusion in children less than 3 years of age.

CONCLUSIONS

Acute otitis media is diagnosed in approximately 30% of preschool children being evaluated for acute illnesses in the outpatient setting. Skill in the physical diagnosis of purulent otitis media must be high if antibiotic treatment is to be restricted to children with the highest likelihood of having active bacterial infections. Rational decisions regarding use of antimicrobial agents in these patients can only be made with a thorough understanding of the antibacterial potency and pharmacokinetics of available antibiotics. Nonpurulent middle ear effusion frequently follows AOM, regardless of etiology or therapy; at least 50% of children less than 2 years of age can be expected to have middle ear effusion for at least 30 days following successful treatment for AOM. Overall, medical treatment of prolonged nonpurulent OME has a minimal impact on the condition; however, in a subset of children (approximately 15% and usually children over 2 years of age), OME may resolve in association with a 2-week course of antibiotic treatment. There is not a convincing body of evidence supporting the use of oral steroids in persistent OME, particularly in children less than 2 years old. It is hoped that the coming years will bring new progress in vaccine development for both the viral and bacterial pathogens of otitis media.

REFERENCES

Arola, M., Ziegler, T., & Ruuskanen, O. (1990). Respiratory virus infection as a cause of prolonged symptoms in acute otitis media. *Journal of Pediatrics, 116,* 697–701.

Barry, A.L., Pfaller, M.A., Fuchs, P.C., & Packer, R.R. (1994). In vitro activities of 12 orally administered antimicrobial agents against four species of bacterial respiratory pathogens from U.S. medical centers in 1992 and 1993. *Antimicrobial Agents and Chemotherapy, 38,* 2419–2425.

Berman, S., Grose, K., Nuss, R., Huber-Navin, C., Roark, R., Gabbard, S.A., & Bagnall, T. (1990). Management of chronic middle ear effusion with prednisone combine with trimethoprim-sulfamethoxazole. *Pediatric Infectious Disease Journal, 9,* 533–538.

Berman, S., & Lauer, B.A. (1983). A controlled trial of cefaclor versus amoxicillin for treatment of acute otitis media in early infancy. *Pediatric Infectious Disease, 2,* 30–33.

Berman, S., Nuss, R., Roark, R., Huber-Navin, C., Grose, K., & Herrera, M. (1992). Effectiveness of continuous vs. intermittent amoxicillin to prevent episodes of otitis media. *Pediatric Infectious Disease Journal, 11,* 63–67.

Bland, R.D. (1972). Otitis media in the first six weeks of life: Diagnosis, bacteriology, and management. *Pediatrics, 49,* 187–197.

Block, S.L., Harrison, C.J., Hedrick, J.A., Tyler, R.D., Smith, R.A., Keegan, E., & Chartrand, S.A. (1995). Penicillin-resistant Streptococcus pneumoniae in acute otitis media: Risk factors, susceptibility patterns, and antimicrobial management. *Pediatric Infectious Disease Journal, 14,* 751–759.

Bluestone, C.D., Stephenson, J.S., & Martin, L.M. (1992). Ten-year review of otitis media pathogens. *Pediatric Infectious Disease Journal, 11,* S7–11.

Brook, I., & Yocum, P. (1995). Bacteriology and beta-lactamase activity in ear aspirates of acute otitis media that failed amoxicillin therapy. *Pediatric Infectious Disease Journal, 14,* 805–808.

Casselbrant, M.L., Kaleida, P.H., Rockette, H.E., Paradise, J.L., Bluestone, C.D., Kurs-Lasky, M., Nozza, R.J., & Wald, E.R. (1992). Efficacy of antimicrobial prophylaxis and of tympanostomy tube insertion for prevention of recurrent acute otitis media: Results of a randomized clinical trial. *Pediatric Infectious Disease Journal, 11,* 278–286.

Chonmaitree, T., Owen, M.J., Patel, J.A., Hedgpath, D., Horlick, D., & Howie, V.M. (1992). Effect of viral respiratory tract infection on outcome of acute otitis media. *Journal of Pediatrics, 120,* 856–862.

Coffey, J.D. Jr., Booth, H.N., & Martin, A.D. (1966). Otitis media in the practice of pediatrics: Bacteriological and clinical observations. *Pediatrics, 38,* 25–32.

Daly, K., Giebink, G.S., Batalden, P.B., Anderson, R.S., Le, C.T., & Lindgren, B. (1991). Resolution of otitis media with effusion with the use of a stepped treatment regimen of trimethoprim-sulfamethoxazole and prednisone. *Pediatric Infectious Disease Journal, 10,* 500–506.

Engelhard, D., Strauss, N., Jorczak-Sarni, L., Cohen, D., Sacks, T.G., & Shapiro, M. (1989). Randomised study of myringotomy, amoxycillin/clavulanate, or both for acute otitis media in infants. *Lancet, 2,* 141–143.

Ernstson, S., & Anari, M. (1985). Cefaclor in the treatment of otitis media with effusion. *Acta Oto-Laryngologica. Supplement, 424,* 17–21.

Ford, K.L., Mason, E.O. Jr., Kaplan, S.L., Lamberth, L.B., & Tillman, J. (1991). Factors associated with middle ear isolates of *Streptococcus pneumoniae* resistant to penicillin in a children's hospital. *Journal of Pediatrics, 119,* 941–944.

Fung-Tomc, J.C., Huczko, E., Stickle, T., Minassian, B., Kolek, B., Cenbleyker, K., Bonner, D., & Kessler, R. (1995). Antibacterial activities of cefprozil compared with those of 13 oral cephems and 3 macrolides. *Antimicrobial Agents and Chemotherapy, 39,* 533–538.

Giebink, G.S., Mills, E.L., Huff, J.S., Edelman, C.K., Weber, M.L., Juhn, S.K., & Quie, P.G. (1979). The microbiology of serous and mucoid otitis media. *Pediatrics, 63,* 915–919.

Halstead, C., Lepow, M.L., Balassanian, N., Emmerich, J., & Wolinsky, E. (1968). Otitis media: Clinical observations, microbiology, and evaluation of therapy. *American Journal of Diseases of Children, 115,* 542–551.

Healy, G.B. (1984). Antimicrobial therapy of chronic otitis media with effusion. *International Journal of Pediatric Otorhinolaryngology, 8,* 13–17.

Healy, G.B., & Teele, D.W. (1977). The microbiology of chronic middle ear effusions in children. *Laryngoscope, 87,* 1472–1478.

Henderson, F.W., Collier, A.M., Sanyal, M.A., Watkins, J.M., Fairclough, D.L., Clyde, W.A., Jr., & Denny, F.W. (1982). A longitudinal study of respiratory viruses and bacteria in the etiology of acute otitis media with effusion. *New England Journal of Medicine, 306,* 1377–1381.

Henderson, F.W., Gilligan, P.H., Wait, K., & Goff, D.A. (1988). Nasopharyngeal carriage of antibiotic resistant pneumococci by children in day care. *Journal of Infectious Diseases, 157,* 256–263.

Howie, V.M., & Ploussard, J.H. (1969). The "in-vivo sensitivity test" bacteriology of middle ear exudate during antimicrobial therapy in otitis media. *Pediatrics, 44,* 940–944.

Howie, V.M., Ploussard, J.H., & Lester, R.L. (1970). Otitis media: A clinical and bacteriological correlation. *Pediatrics, 45,* 29–35.

Kaleida, P.H., Casselbrant, M.L., Rockette, H.E., Paradise, J.L., Bluestone, C.D., Blatter, M.M., Reisinger, K.S., Wald, E.R., & Supance, J.S. (1991). Amoxicillin or myringotomy or both for acute otitis media: Results of a randomized clinical trial. *Pediatrics, 87,* 466–474.

Klein, J.O. (1993). Microbiologic efficacy of antibacterial drugs for acute otitis media. *Pediatric Infectious Disease Journal, 12,* 973–975.

Klimek, J.J., Bates, T.R., Nightingale, C., Lehmann, W.B., Ziemniak, J.A., & Quintiliani, R. (1980). Penetration characteristics of trimethoprim-sulfamethoxazole in middle ear fluid of patients with chronic serous otitis media. *Journal of Pediatrics, 96,* 1087–1089.

Krause, P.J., Owens, N.J., Nightingale, C.H., Klimek, J.J., Lehmann, W.B., & Quintiliani, R. (1982). Penetration of amoxicillin, cefaclor, erythromycin-sulfisoxazole, and trimethoprim-sulfamethoxazole into the middle ear fluid of patients with chronic serous otitis media. *Journal of Infectious Diseases, 145,* 815–821.

Lahikainen, E.A. (1953). Clinico-bacteriologic studies on acute otitis media. *Acta Oto-Laryngologica, 107,* S1.

Lambert, P.R. (1986). Oral steroid therapy for chronic middle ear perfusion: A double-blind crossover study. *Otolaryngology—Head and Neck Surgery, 95,* 193–199.

Linares, J., Alonso, T., Perez, J.L., Ayats, P.J., Dominguez, M.A., Pallares, R., & Martin, R. (1992). Decreased susceptibility of penicillin-resistant pneumococci to twenty-four β-lactam antibiotics. *Journal of Antimicrobial Chemotherapy, 30,* 279–288.

Liston, T.E., Foshee, W.S., & Pierson, W.D. (1983). Sulfisoxazole chemoprophylaxis for frequent otitis media. *Pediatrics, 71,* 524–530.

Mandel, E.M., Bluestone, C.D., Rockette, H.E., Blatter, M.M., Reisinger, K.S., Wucher, F.P., & Harper, J. (1982). Duration of effusion after antibiotic treatment for acute otitis media: Comparison of cefaclor and amoxicillin. *Pediatric Infectious Disease Journal, 1,* 310–316.

Mandel, E.M., Rockette, H.E., Bluestone, C.D., Paradise, J.L., & Nozza R.J. (1987). Efficacy of amoxicillin with and without decongestant-antihistamine for otitis media with effusion in children. *New England Journal of Medicine, 316,* 432–437.

Mandel, E.M., Rockette, H.E., Paradise, J.L., Bluestone, C.D., & Nozza, R.J. (1991). Comparative efficacy of erythromycin-sulfisoxazole, cefaclor, amoxicillin or placebo for otitis media with effusion in children. *Pediatric Infectious Disease Journal, 10,* 899–906.

Marchant, C.D., Carlin, S.A., Johnson, C.E., & Shurin, P.A. (1992). Measuring the comparative efficacy of antibacterial agents for acute otitis media: The "Pollyanna phenomenon." *Journal of Pediatrics, 120,* 72–77.

Maynard, J.E., Fleshman, K., & Tschopp, C.F. (1972). Otitis media in Alaskan Eskimo children. *Journal of the American Medical Association, 219,* 597–599.

Mortimer, E.A. Jr., & Watterson, R.L. Jr. (1956). A bacteriological investigation of otitis media in infancy. *Pediatrics, 17,* 359–366.

Perrin, J.M., Charney, E., MacWhinney, J.B., McInerny, T.K., Miller, R.L., & Nazarian, L.F. (1974). Sulfisoxazole as chemoprophylaxis for recurrent otitis media. *New England Journal of Medicine, 291,* 664–667.

Pichichero, M.E., & Pichichero, C.L. (1995). Persistent otitis media: I. Causative pathogens. *Pediatric Infectious Disease Journal, 14,* 178–183.

Podoshin, L., Fradis, M., Ben-David, Y., & Faraffi, D. (1990). The efficacy of oral steroids in the treatment of persistent otitis media with effusion. *Archives of Otolaryngology—Head and Neck Surgery, 116,* 1404–1406.

Riding, K.H., Bluestone, C.D., Michaels, R.H., Cantekin, E.I., Doyle, W.J., & Poziviak, C.S. (1978). Microbiology of recurrent and chronic otitis media with effusion. *Journal of Pediatrics, 95,* 739–743.

Rosenfeld, R.M., Vertrees, J.E., Carr, J., Cipolle, R.J., Uden, D.L., Giebink, G.S., & Canafax, D.M. (1994). Clinical efficacy of antimicrobial drugs for acute otitis media: Meta-analysis of 5400 children from thirty-three randomized trials. *Journal of Pediatrics, 124,* 355–367.

Rudberg, R.D. (1954). Acute otitis media: Comparative therapeutic results of sulphonamide and penicillin administered in various forms. *Acta Oto-Laryngologica, 113,* S1–S79.

Ruuskanen, O., & Heikkinen, T. (1994). Otitis media: Etiology and diagnosis. *Pediatric Infectious Disease Journal, 13,* S23–S26.

Sanyal, M.A., Henderson, F.W., Stempel, E.C., Collier, A.M., & Denny, F.W. (1980). Effect of upper respiratory tract infection on eustachian tube ventilatory function in the preschool child. *Journal of Pediatrics, 97,* 11–15.

Schwartz, R.H., Puglise, J., & Rodriguez, W.J. (1982). Sulphamethoxazole prophylaxis in the otitis-prone child. *Archives of Disease in Childhood, 57,* 590–593.

Shurin, P.A., Howie, V.M., Pelton, S.I., Ploussard, J.H., & Klein, J.O. (1978). Bacterial etiology of otitis media during the first six weeks of life. *Journal of Pediatrics, 92,* 893–896.

Shurin, P.A., Marchant, C.D., Kim, C.H., Van Hare, G.F., Johnson, C.E., Tutihasi, M.A., & Knapp, L.J. (1983). Emergence of beta-lactamase producing strains of *Branhamella catarrhalis* as important agents of acute otitis media. *Pediatric Infectious Disease Journal, 2,* 34–38.

Shurin, P.A., Pelton, S.I., Donner, A., & Klein, J.O. (1979). Persistence of middle ear effusion after acute otitis media in children. *New England Journal of Medicine, 300,* 1121–1123.

Spangler, S.K., Jacobs, M.R., Pankuch, G.A., & Appelbaum, P.C. (1993). Susceptibility of 170 penicillin-susceptible and penicillin-resistant pneumococci to six oral cepahlosporins, four quinolones, desacetylcefotaxime, Ro 23-9424 and RP 67829. *Journal of Antimicrobial Chemotherapy, 31,* 273–280.

Stool, S.E., Berg, A.O., Berman, S., Carney, C.J., Cooley, J.R., Culpepper, L., Eavey, R.D., Feagans, L.V., Finitzo, T., Friedman, E., Goertz, J.A., Goldstein, A.J., Grundfast, K.M., Long, D.G., Macconi, L.L., Melton, L., Roberts, J.E., Sherrod, J.L., & Sisk, J.E. (1994). *Otitis media with effusion in young children: Clinical practice guideline, No. 12* (AHCPR Publication No. 94-0622). Rockville, MD: Agency for Health Care Policy and Research.

Sung, B.S., Chonmaitree, T., Broemeling, L.D., Owen, M.J., Patel, J.A., Hedgpeth, D.C., Howie, V.M. (1993). Association of rhinovirus infection with poor bacteriologic outcome of bacterial-viral otitis media. *Clinical Infectious Diseases, 17,* 38–42.

Teele, D.W., Klein, J.O., Rosner, B., & the Greater Boston Otitis Media Study Group. (1989). Epidemiology of otitis media during the first seven years of life in children in greater Boston: A prospective cohort study. *Journal of Infectious Diseases, 160,* 83–93.

Teele, D.W., Pelton, S.I., & Klein, J.O. (1981). Bacteriology of acute otitis media unresponsive to initial antimicrobial therapy. *Journal of Pediatrics, 98,* 537–539.

Tetzlaff, T.R., Ashworth, C., & Nelson, J.D. (1977). Otitis media in children less than 12 weeks of age. *Pediatrics, 59,* 827–832.

10

Surgical Management of Otitis Media with Effusion

Douglas H. Todd
and Sylvan E. Stool

The surgical treatment of middle ear effusion is the most frequent reason for administering general anesthesia to children in the United States (Stool et al., 1994). Historically, multiple surgical interventions have been utilized in the treatment of otitis media with effusion (OME) (Bluestone & Klein, 1988). The use of surgical procedures for the treatment of middle ear fluid was well documented in 1801 by Sir Ashley Cooper in the *Philosophical Transactions of the Royal Society* (Alberti, 1974) when he reported a series of patients treated with myringotomy for hearing loss. In this article, he discussed his diagnostic technique using a Hunter's watch as a measure of auditory acuity and to determine the presence of a conductive hearing loss. He observed that, if a patient heard the watch better when it was held on the mastoid process than when held over the external auditory canal, he or she would benefit from an operation. The instrument Cooper used to perform the operation was a lancet. Myringotomy was performed without the benefit of anesthesia, which was not available. This procedure did not achieve widespread popularity at the time because results were of short duration. However, there are subsequent historical reports of myringotomy followed by insertion of a foreign object to keep the incision from closing.

This chapter discusses the various procedures currently used for the surgical treatment of middle ear fluid. First, middle ear anatomy and physiology are discussed. Next, the different surgical procedures for treatment of OME are described, followed by a review of the effectiveness of these procedures.

ANATOMY AND PHYSIOLOGY OF THE MIDDLE EAR

There is great variation throughout the world in the approach to the clinical problem of OME and in the rationale for surgical therapy (Bluestone & Stool, 1995; Gates, Avery, Cooper, & Prihoda, 1989; Lous, 1995; Paparella & Froymovich, 1994; Paparella & Schachern, 1994; Thomsen et al., 1989). The reasons for this variation are many, including the classification of disease states, the facilities available, the age of the patient, and other socioeconomic factors. Middle ear effusions can be characterized in a number of ways, such as duration, bacteriology, biochemical properties, and consistency (i.e., serous, mucoid, or purulent). A combination of these factors is a common guide for surgical intervention.

A knowledge of the pneumatic system is helpful in understanding the indications used in the treatment of fluid in the middle ear. This system contains gas that is very similar in content to air but is slightly modified by its contact with mucosa. The eustachian tube may be considered as the valve that opens the middle ear cleft. Its major function is middle ear ventilation and protection of the middle ear from nasopharyngeal secretions. Fluid that accumulates within the system is usually drained by the eustachian tube (Figure 1). Conditions that alter eustachian tube function may lead to accumulation of fluid in the middle ear and mastoid cavity or to the inability of the system to remove fluid.

The middle ear cleft contains the ossicular chain (Figures 2 and 3). The volume of this cleft is approximately 1.5 ml. It is divided into compartments labeled relative to the ossicular chain. The mucosa of the middle ear is highly vascular and contains goblet cells that produce mucus. The major volume of gas within the system is contained in the mastoid cavity, a honeycomb like structure composed of multiple small bony air cells. The middle ear and the mastoid cavity are connected by a narrow passage called the aditus ad antrum.

When the gas in the pneumatic system is replaced by fluid, this affects the function of the middle ear and consequently alters the auditory acuity. The type of fluid is not as important as the quantity. A small amount of fluid may allow motion of the tympanic membrane and ossicular chain. A large amount of fluid may prevent propagation of sound to the inner ear. If the fluid contains bacteria, an infection may

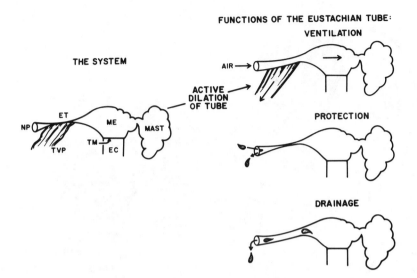

Figure 1.   Functions of the eustachian tube include ventilation, protection, and drainage of the middle ear. NP, nasopharynx; ET, eustachian tube; TVP, tensor veli palatini muscle; TM, tympanic membrane; ME, middle ear; EC, external auditory canal; MAST, mastoid cavity. (From Bluestone, C.D. & Klein, J.O. [Eds.]. [1988]. *Otitis media in children*, p. 16. Philadelphia: W.B. Saunders; reprinted by permission.)

develop that can destroy mucosa and surrounding bone. Inflamed mucosa may prevent further drainage of the system, necessitating surgical intervention. Figure 4 demonstrates the pathogenesis of otitis media with effusion and retraction of the tympanic membrane. Reflux of nasopharyngeal secretions occurs when the eustachian tube remains open, aspiration of nasopharyngeal secretions occurs when the middle ear has a relatively negative pressure, and retraction of the tympanic membrane occurs when the middle ear has a relatively negative pressure and the eustachian tube is closed. Otitis media with effusion may persist if the eustachian tube remains closed.

SURGICAL INTERVENTIONS IN THE MANAGEMENT OF OTITIS MEDIA WITH EFFUSION

Tympanocentesis

Tympanocentesis is the simplest of the surgical interventions. It is needle aspiration of the middle ear space.

Indications   Indications for this procedure include identification of organisms in middle ear effusions in children who are toxic secondarily to presumed otitis media, in children with effusion unresponsive to antibiotic therapy, in children with onset of otitis media while on antibiotics, in children with suspected suppurative complications of otitis

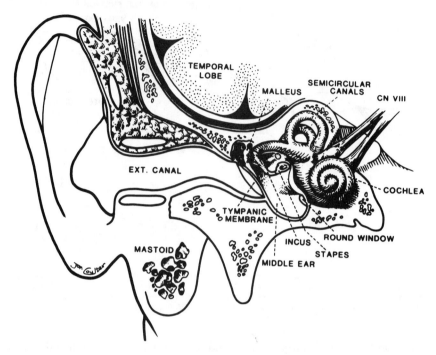

Figure 2.   Illustration of relationship of middle ear (ME) to external and inner ears. (From Bluestone, C.D. & Klein, J.O. [Eds.]. [1988]. *Otitis media in children,* p. 11. Philadelphia: W.B. Saunders; reprinted by permission.)

media, and in immunocompromised children with otitis media unresponsive to antibiotic therapy.

Procedure   Tympanocentesis is usually performed without general anesthesia. However, sedation with a short-acting barbiturate is often useful. A small amount of phenol placed on the tympanic membrane can also be used as a local anesthetic. Immobilization is essential in conscious patients. The procedure can be performed with a hand-held otoscope or an operating microscope.

To begin, culture of the external auditory canal is obtained with a Calgiswab that is moistened with trypticase soy broth. The external auditory canal is then filled with lukewarm 70% ethanol for a period of 1 minute. The alcohol is then suctioned from the ear and discarded. Tympanocentesis is then performed using an 18-gauge spinal needle attached to a 5-ml syringe or collection trap. The needle should enter the front lower quadrant of the tympanic membrane, avoiding the ossicles above and to the rear and the carotid artery above and to the front. The Alden-Senturia trap with needle attached can be utilized as illus-

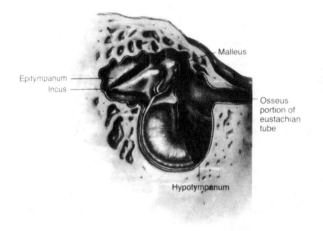

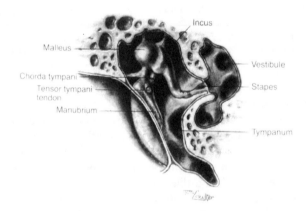

Figure 3. Anatomy of the middle ear viewed from the external auditory canal (top) and in a coronal (frontal) plane (bottom). (From Bluestone, C.D., & Klein, J.O. [1996]. Otitis media, atelectasis, and eustachian tube dysfunction. In C.D. Bluestone & S.E. Stool [Eds.], *Pediatric otolaryngology*, [3rd ed., p. 402]. Philadelphia: W.B. Saunders; reprinted by permission.)

trated in Figure 5. The middle ear aspirate is then sent to the microbiology lab for Gram Stain, culture, and sensitivity. A myringotomy can be performed after tympanocentesis to provide adequate drainage.

   Complications Complications are generally minimal when the procedure is performed correctly. Potentially, a dehiscent (malpositioned) jugular bulb could be encountered, resulting in brisk bleeding. Packing of the external auditory canal is appropriate initial treatment for uncontrolled bleeding.

Pathogenesis

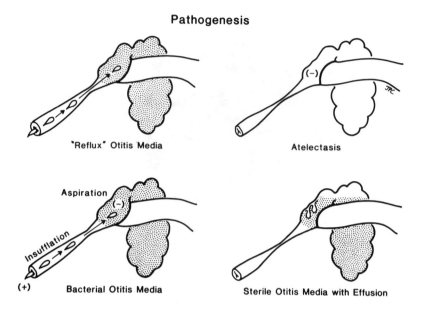

Figure 4.   Pathogenesis of OME. Shaded areas represent middle ear effusion. (From Bluestone, C.D., & Klein, J.O. [Eds.]. [1988]. *Otitis media in infants and children* [p. 23]. Philadelphia: W.B. Saunders; reprinted by permission.)

Myringotomy

Myringotomy became popular as a treatment for acute otitis media prior to the availability of antibiotics. Currently, myringotomy is used most frequently by otolaryngologists in children with acute otitis media or mastoiditis as a middle ear drainage procedure. Usually, tympanocentesis is performed as a diagnostic procedure prior to myringotomy.

Indications   Indications for myringotomy include the suspicion of complications of suppurative otitis media, such as facial paralysis, meningitis, or mastoiditis, and relief of severe otalgia (ear pain) secondary to otitis media or mastoiditis. Myringotomy is not routinely used in treatment of common otitis media unless a complication is diagnosed.

Procedure   Anesthetic considerations, visualization, and immobilization are similar to those described for tympanocentesis. We recommend the following procedure for myringotomy. Initially, the external auditory canal is cleaned with ethyl alcohol as described for tympanocentesis. Then a widefield incision is placed inferiorly in the pars tensa using the myringotomy knife. Alternatively, a radial incision can be made in the upper front quadrant (Figure 6). The middle ear effusion can then be aspirated. Fluid can be collected in a trap and sent to the microbiology laboratory if needed for diagnosis.

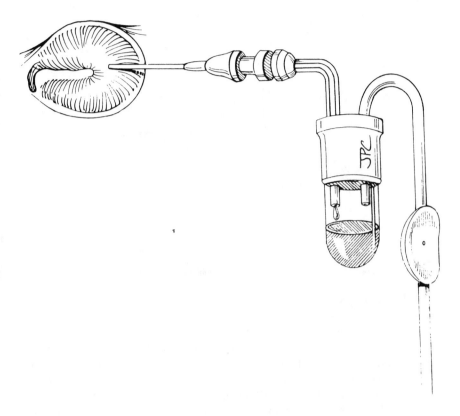

Figure 5.   Tympanocentesis is performed with an Alden-Senturia trap (Storz Instrument Co., St. Louis, MO). (From Bluestone, C.D., & Stool, S.E. [Eds.]. [1995]. *Atlas of pediatric otolaryngology* [p. 31]. Philadelphia: W.B. Saunders; reprinted by permission.)

Complications The family should be cautioned that otorrhea (discharge from the ear) may persist following the procedure. Likewise, the physician should be aware that an infectious dermatitis may develop. Ototopical antibiotic drops are usually helpful in preventing secondary external auditory canal or middle ear infections following myringotomy.

Complications of myringotomy in experienced hands are minimal. The most common sequelae are persistent perforation, possibly requiring future myringoplasty, and atorphic scar formation (myringosclerosis), which is usually aysmptomatic. Dreaded complications such as injury to the ossicles or laceration of the facial nerve or dehiscent jugular bulb are very rare among experienced surgeons.

Myringotomy with Tympanostomy Tube Insertion
Myringotomy with tympanostomy tube insertion is the most common surgical procedure performed in children that requires general anesthe-

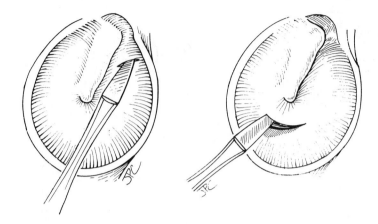

Figure 6. A widefield incision is made in the inferior portion of the pars tensa (right). A radial incision is made in the upper front quadrant of the pars tensa (left). (From Bluestone, C.D., & Stool, S.E. [Eds.]. [1995]. *Atlas of pediatric otolaryngology* [p. 33]. Philadelphia: W.B. Saunders; reprinted by permission.)

sia. The reported rate of myringotomy with or without tympanostomy tube insertion in 1986 was nearly 58,000 cases (Stool et al., 1994).

Indications   Indications for myringotomy and tympanostomy tube insertion for otitis media with effusion include recurrent acute otitis media refractory to antibiotic therapy (Bluestone & Klein, 1988) or persistent OME present for greater than 3 months with an associated hearing loss of greater than 20 dB in the better hearing ear (Stool et al., 1994). Placement of tympanostomy tubes can also be considered for treatment of problematic eustachian tube dysfunction (Roddey, Earle, & Haggerty, 1966).

Procedure   Myringotomy with placement of tympanostomy tubes is performed under general anesthesia in young children. In older cooperative patients, this procedure may be performed under topical or local anesthetic.

Utilizing the otologic operating microscope and working through the external auditory canal via an ear speculum, a myringotomy is performed as described earlier. A radial incision in the upper front quadrant or a widefield incision in the lower front quadrant can be utilized. The middle ear contents are then aspirated with a Frazier Tip suction catheter. Alligator forceps are then used to insert the tympanostomy tube into the myringotomy incision. Figure 7 demonstrates the technique of myringotomy and tympanostomy tube insertion.

Complications   Complications associated with tympanostomy tube insertion are similar to those for myringotomy. Table 1 illustrates the benefits and risks of various treatments for OME. Approximately 50 different tympanostomy tubes are available currently. Most tubes are constructed of plastic, metal, or Teflon. Variations in tube design reflect

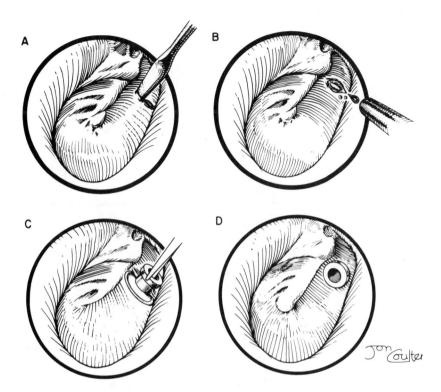

Figure 7.   A review of myringotomy with tympanostomy tube insertion. A, A widefield incision is made in the pars tensa. B, suction is used to remove middle ear fluid. C, An alligator forceps is used to insert the tympanostomy tube. D, View of completed tube insertion. (From Bluestone, C.D., & Klein, J.O. [1996]. Otitis media, atelectasis, and eustachian tube dysfunction. In C.D. Bluestone & S.E. Stool [Eds.], *Pediatric otolaryngology* [3rd ed., p. 545]. Philadelphia: W.B. Saunders; reprinted by permission.)

attempts to improve tube insertion, removal, longevity in the middle ear, and antimicrobial activity. Data comparing the effectiveness of various tubes are sparse. Persistent otorrhea is usually treated effectively with antibiotic eardrops. We recommend protecting the ear with ear plugs while swimming or bathing. Patients are seen routinely 2–3 weeks after surgery and then every 3–4 months thereafter for the duration of tympanostomy tube presence in the middle ear. Tympanostomy tubes generally remain in place for 3–12 months depending on the specific type used. Permanent tubes can also be placed if indicated for problematic eustachian dysfunction.

Exploratory Tympanotomy, Middle Ear Reconstruction, and Mastoidectomy

In some patients, inadequately treated acute otitis media or persistent OME can lead to intractable disease and its sequelae. Intratemporal

Table 1. Risks and harms of myringotomy and tympanostomy tube insertion[a]

Intervention	Benefits[b]	Harms[b]
Observation	Base case	Base case
Antibiotics	Improved clearance of effusion at 1 month or less, 14.0% (95% CI [3.6%, 24.2%]) Possible reduction in future infection	Nausea, vomiting, diarrhea (2%-32% depending on dose and antibiotic) Cutaneous reactions ($\leq$5%) Numerous rare organ system effects, including very rare fatalities Cost Possible development of resistant strains of bacteria
Antibiotics plus steroids	Possible improved clearance at 1 month, 25.1% (95% CI [−1.3%, 49.9%])[c] Possible reduction in future infections	See antibiotics and steroids separately
Steroids alone	Possible improved clearance at 1 month, 4.5% (95% CI [−11.7%, 20.6%])[c]	Possible exacerbation of varicella Long-term complications not established for low doses Cost
Antihistamine/ decongestant	Same as base case	Drowsiness and/or excitability[d] Cost
Myringotomy with tubes	Immediate clearance of effusion in all children Improved hearing	Invasive procedure Anesthesia risk Cost Tympanosclerosis Otorrhea Possible restrictions on swimming
Adenoidectomy	Benefits for young children have not been established	Invasive procedure[d] Anesthesia risk Cost
Tonsillectomy	Same as base case	Invasive procedure[d] Anesthesia risk Cost

From Stool, S.E., Berg, A.O., Berman, S., Carney, C.J., Cooley, J.R., Culpepper, L., Eavey, R.D., Feagans, L.V., Finitzo, T., Friedman, E.M., Goertz, J.A., Goldstein, A.J., Grundfast, K.M., Long, D.G., Macconi, L.L., Melton, L., Roberts, J.E., Sherrod, J.L., & Sisk, J.E. (1994). *Otitis media with effusion in young children: Clinical practice guideline, No. 12* (ACHPR Publication No. 94-0622). Rockville, MD: Agency for Health Care Policy and Research. .

[a]The target patient is an otherwise healthy child age 1 through 3 years with no craniofacial or neurologic abnormalities or sensory deficits.

[b]Outcomes are reported as differences from observation, which is treated as the base case. When possible, meta-analysis was performed to provide a mean and associated confidence interval (CI).

[c]Difference from base case not statistically significant.

[d]Risks were not examined in detail because no benefits were identified.

complications and sequelae may include hearing loss, chronic tympanic membrane perforation, cholesteatoma, retraction pocket, tympanosclerosis, ossicular discontinuity and/or fixation, acute and chronic mastoiditis, petrositis, labyrinthitis, perilymphatic fistula, facial paralysis, cholesterol granule, infectious eczematoid dermatitis, and otitis externa. Intracranial suppurative complications of otitis media and mastoiditis include meningitis, extradural abscess, subdural abscess, focal otitic encephalitis, brain abscess, lateral sinus thrombus, and otitic hydrocephalus. Exploratory tympanotomy, reconstruction of the middle ear, and mastoidectomy are commonly used to treat intratemporal and intracranial complications of otitis media. Exploratory tympanotomy is performed through a transcanal, endaural, or posterior auricular approach. The middle ear is evaluated microscopically and pathologic tissue such as granulation tissue or cholesteatoma is removed. If the ossicles are eroded or missing, the hearing apparatus may be reconstructed utilizing an ossiculoplasty procedure. If a chronic tympanic membrane perforation is present, a transcanal myringoplasty or more complex tympanoplasty is utilized to graft the perforation. Mastoidectomy is performed when conservative management of chronic otitis media fails or if cholesteatoma is suspected. A detailed discussion of these procedures is beyond the scope of this text.

Adenoidectomy and Tonsillectomy
Adenoidectomy performed either alone or in conjunction with tonsillectomy has been the most common *major* surgical procedure performed for the prevention of otitis media historically. Despite frequent use, the justification for these procedures for the treatment of OME has never been established through controlled clinical trials for children less than 4 years old (Gates et al., 1987). Indeed, the Agency for Health Care Policy and Research (AHCPR) Clinical Practice Guideline on OME in young children states that adenoidectomy and tonsillectomy are not indicated in the treatment of OME in a child age 1–3 years in the absence of specific oral or pharyngeal pathology (Stool et al., 1994).

EFFICACY OF SURGICAL MANAGEMENT OF OTITIS MEDIA

Myringotomy
The clinical efficacy of surgical management of otitis media with effusion has been addressed in multiple clinical studies. Table 2 reviews the outcomes of studies conducted in the past to determine the efficacy of myringotomy for acute otitis media (Bluestone, Stool, & Kenna, 1996). In the first study (Roddey et al., 1966), all children included in the study received antibiotics. Approximately one half of these children received

Table 2. Percentage of patients with persistent middle ear effusion after initial myringo-tomy and antimicrobial therapy, compared with those receiving antimicrobial therapy alone for acute otitis media

Reference	Procedure[a]	No. of subjects	Percentage with effusion 10–14 days	4 weeks	Statistical significance
Roddey et al. (1966)	AB	121	35	7	No
	AB&M	94	24	9	
Herberts et al. (1971)	AB	81	10	—	No
	AB&M	91	18	—	
Lorentzen & Haugsten (1977)	AB	190	16	6	No
	AB&M	164	20	6	
Puhakka et al. (1979)	AB	90	78	29	Yes
	AB&M	68	29	—	
Qvarnberg & Palva (1980)	AB	151	50	—	Yes
	AB&M	97	28	—	
Schwartz & Schwartz (1980)	AB	361	47	—	No
	AB&M	451	51	—	
Engelhard et al. (1989)	AB	55	40	—	No
Kaleida et al. (1991)	AB	167	61	—	No
	AB&M	104	56	—	

Adapted from Bluestone, Stool, and Kenna (1996).
[a] AB, antibiotic therapy; AB&M, antibiotic therapy and myringotomy.

myringotomy as well. The only significant difference between the two groups was more rapid relief of otalgia in patients who received myringotomy. Children who received both myringotomy and antibiotics also had a lesser prevalence of OME, although this difference was not statistically significant. Another study (Herberts et al., 1971) found no significant difference in the percentage of children with otitis media with persistent effusion 10 days after treatment with either antibiotics alone or antibiotics and myringotomy. Lorentzen and Haugsten (1977) had similar results comparing myringotomy, antibiotics, and myringotomy with antibiotic therapy. Puhakka and colleagues (1979) repeated the same study with 158 children. They found that, 4 weeks after the onset of acute otitis media, the children treated with antibiotics alone had a 71% cure rate, whereas the children treated with antibiotics and myringotomy had a 90% cure rate. This study achieved statistical significance. The authors concluded that myringotomy clearly accelerates the recovery rate from acute otitis media.

Qvarnberg and Palva (1980) studied 248 children comparing penicillin V and myringotomy, penicillin V alone, and amoxicillin alone. Their statistically significant study indicated that antibiotics with myringotomy result in cure as a rule. Either antibiotic alone resulted in a 10% failure rate with patients running a prolonged course. Schwartz and Schwartz (1980) treated 776 children with various antibiotics, with half of the children also receiving myringotomy without aspiration. They found no significant difference in pain relief or persistence of effusion 10 days after treatment. In reviewing these studies, however, Bluestone et al. (1996) indicated that each had a design or methodologic flaw resulting in difficulty in result interpretation.

An excellent study by Engelhard and co-workers (1989) randomly assigned 105 infants with acute otitis media into one of three treatment groups: 1) amoxicillin–clavulanate alone, 2) myringotomy plus placebo tablet, and 3) amoxicillin–clavulanate and myringotomy. The two myringotomy groups were double blinded, and otoscopy was used to determine outcome. In infants treated with antibiotics with or without myringotomy, a 60% recovery rate was noted. In infants treated with myringotomy and placebo, a 23% recovery rate was noted. The authors concluded that the addition of myringotomy to antibiotic therapy did not appear to affect the persistence of infection or effusion. A 1991 study by Kaleida and colleagues randomly assigned children with severe otitis media to receive 10 days of amoxicillin, myringotomy with placebo, or both myringotomy and amoxicillin. Infants in the study received amoxicillin with or without myringotomy. Outcome was tested by otoscopy, tympanogram, and acoustic reflex. The authors found that there were more initial treatment failures in children receiving myringotomy alone than in children receiving antibiotics with or without myringotomy. The investigators concluded that amoxicillin is indicated for the treatment of otitis media and that the data did not support the routine use of myringotomy as initial treatment of acute otitis media. The authors did, however, recommend myringotomy for selected infants for symptomatic antimicrobial treatment failures or when a complication of suppurative otitis media was present.

Myringotomy with Tympanostomy Tube Placement
A multitude of studies have addressed the efficacy of myringotomy with insertion of tympanostomy tubes for the treatment of otitis media with effusion. The most definitive review of the literature to date is the ACHPR Clinical Practice Guideline on OME in young children (Stool et al., 1994). The guideline panel employed explicit, science-based methods and expert clinical judgment to develop specific statements on management of OME in young children. Extensive literature searches were conducted and critical reviews were used to evaluate empirical and scientific evidence and significant outcomes. Peer review and field re-

view were also undertaken. When the scientific data were incomplete, the guideline recommendations reflect the professional judgment of panel members and consultants.

Regarding the surgical management of OME in young children, the guideline panel made the following recommendations:

1. Myringotomy with or without the insertion of tympanostomy tubes should not be performed for initial management of OME in an otherwise healthy child.

2. Antibiotic therapy or bilateral myringotomy with insertion of tympanostomy tubes *may* be chosen to manage bilateral otitis media with effusion that has lasted a total of 3 months in an otherwise healthy child age 1–3 years who has a bilateral hearing deficit defined as 20 dB hearing level or worse in the better hearing ear.

3. Bilateral myringotomy with insertion of tympanostomy tubes *is* recommended to manage bilateral OME that has lasted a total of 4–6 months in an otherwise healthy child age 1–3 years who has a bilateral hearing deficit as described in recommendation 2.

The interested reader is referred to the guideline (Stool et al. (1994) for a more detailed review of this topic.

Bluestone and Klein (1988) also contains an excellent review of the literature regarding surgical management of otitis media. Shah (1971) performed myringotomy and aspiration of the middle ear in one ear and tympanostomy tube insertion in the other ear in children with OME. Additionally, adenoidectomy was performed in children receiving tympanostomy tubes. Follow-up at 6 and 12 months revealed better hearing in the operated ears. Kilby, Richards, and Hart (1972) performed a similar study without performing an adenoidectomy at time of tympanostomy tube insertion. These investigators found no difference in hearing between the two ears at 2-year follow-up when all tubes had extruded. Tos and Poulsen (1976) performed myringotomy with tympanostomy tube insertion and adenoidectomy in 108 children. Follow-up at 5–8 years revealed that only 2.5% of children had a hearing loss. Tympanic membrane scarring was reported as a frequently observed finding. Gates and associates (1987) evaluated 578 children ages 4–8 years in a study that randomly assigned children who had chronic OME refractory to antimicrobial therapy into one of four surgical treatment groups: myringotomy, myringotomy with tympanostomy tube insertion, adenoidectomy and myringotomy, and adenoidectomy with myringotomy with tympanostomy tube insertion. All three options with tympanostomy tube insertion did better than myringotomy alone.

Mandel and colleagues (1989) evaluated the effectiveness of surgical treatment of OME in two studies. In the first, 109 children who had chronic OME unresponsive to antimicrobial therapy were studied. Subjects were randomly assigned to receive either 1) myringotomy, 2) myringotomy and tympanostomy tube insertion, or 3) no surgery. In this 3-year trial, subjects were evaluated monthly and whenever an ear, nose, or throat illness occurred. Patients with tympanostomy tubes had less middle ear disease and better hearing than children receiving either myringotomy or no surgery. Half of the children in the myringotomy-alone group required tympanostomy tube placement during the first year to control their disease. Likewise, half of the control group required tympanostomy tube placement during the course of the year because of development of "significant" hearing loss associated with their chronic middle ear disease. None of the involved children had that degree of hearing loss when they entered the study. Two of the children treated with tympanostomy tube insertion developed chronic otorrhea that required intravenous antibiotics to control. One patient developed chronic tympanic membrane perforations after tube extrusion that required bilateral tympanoplasties. The investigators concluded that myringotomy with tympanostomy tube insertion provided more effusion-free time and better hearing than either myringotomy alone or no surgery. The researchers considered the interpretation of their study to be difficult secondary to complexities of design. They therefore revised their protocol and a second clinical trial was conducted.

The second study (Mandel et al., 1992) included 111 children who were randomized into the same three groups as the first study: myringotomy, myringotomy and tympanostomy tube insertion, and no surgery. As in the first study, individuals were examined at least every 3 months for 1 year. Outcomes similar to the first study were observed in this trial. Patients with myringotomy and tympanostomy tube insertion had less time with middle ear effusions and better hearing than the children in the myringotomy alone or control groups. Similar to the first trial, 41% of patients randomized to the tympanostomy tube group developed some otorrhea. Three subjects developed chronic tympanic membrane perforation, two of which required tympanoplasty. On the basis of these two randomized clinical trials that evaluated a total of 220 subjects, the investigators recommended watchful waiting with periodic hearing assessment or myringotomy with tympanostomy tube insertion. Recommendations, however, should be individualized for each child. Myringotomy with tympanostomy tube insertion was recommended as the *surgical* procedure of choice, rather than myringotomy alone, for children with otitis media refractory to antibiotic therapy with effusion lasting greater than 4 months. Although Gates and co-workers (1987) recommended myringotomy with tympanostomy tube insertion and adenoidectomy as the initial surgical treatment of choice for refractory

OME, their study suggested that the addition of adenoidectomy in their population resulted in only slightly more benefit than myringotomy and tympanostomy tube insertion alone. Mandel and co-workers (1992) therefore recommended reserving adenoidectomy for children who failed their first tympanostomy tube insertion and developed recurrent OME after extrusion of the initial tympanostomy tubes. However, if a child undergoing tympanostomy tube insertion had significant nasal obstruction secondary to adenoid hypertrophy, then adenoidectomy was considered a reasonable option.

Three other randomized clinical trials that tested the efficacy of tympanostomy tube insertion for the treatment of acute otitis media are also instructive (Bluestone & Klein, 1988). Gebhart (1981) evaluated otitis media–prone infants, treating half with tympanostomy tubes and half with no surgery. Efficacy was demonstrated; however, the study was limited because follow-up was only 3 months and infants with middle ear effusions were also included.

Gonzales and co-workers (1986) performed a multicenter study involving otitis media–prone infants in a trial that randomized subjects into three groups: 1) sulfisoxazole prophylaxis, 2) tympanostomy tube insertion, and 3) placebo. Similar to Gebhart's (1981) trial, infants with middle ear effusion were included in the study and follow-up was only 6 months. Infants in the tympanostomy groups with middle ear effusion present did significantly better. However, effusion-free infants did not have a significantly reduced rate of acute otitis media.

Casselbrant and colleagues (1992) studied 264 children randomly assigned into three groups: 1) amoxicillin prophylaxis, 2) myringotomy and tympanostomy tube insertion, and 3) placebo. Unlike the two prior studies, only children free of middle ear effusions were allowed in the study. Follow-up was monthly for 2 years, and children were also seen when complaining of ear, nose, or throat problems. The average rate of new infections was significantly reduced in the amoxicillin group. There was no significant difference for this outcome measure between the tympanostomy tube and placebo group. In the tympanostomy tube group, otorrhea was considered an infection, although it was usually asymptomatic and less troublesome than in the amoxicillin or placebo group children with acute otitis media. The tympanostomy tube group did have less time with otorrhea than the other groups. The amoxicillin group had 7% adverse side effects, usually urticaria and vaginitis. The tympanostomy tube group had a 3.9% persistent tympanic membrane perforation rate, all of which subsequently healed spontaneously. Only one of the patients assigned to the tympanostomy tube group required a surgical procedure. A second set of tubes was required by 26%, and one child required three sets of tubes. The investigators therefore recommended amoxicillin prophylaxis as the first method of treatment for prevention of recurrent acute otitis media. For prophlaxis failures, tympanostomy tube insertion would be considered the next option. Followup of children on prophylaxis was recommended because middle ear effusions can be asymptomatic.

Lee, Freeman, and Fireman (1991) performed an interesting prospective controlled study of the efficacy and sequelae of tympanostomy tube insertion. They included 44 children with history of recurrent acute otitis media (>6 episodes/year) and 13 children with history of bilateral persistent middle ear effusions lasting more than 3 months. They then randomly placed a tympanostomy tube into one of the ears. The contralateral ears were randomized to receive either myringotomy alone or no surgery. Clinical, otoscopic, tympanometric, and audiologic examinations were performed before the study and at 3-month intervals for up to 2–3 years. Antibiotic therapy and prophylaxis were used when indicated. Tympanostomy tubes remained functional for a mean of 10 months. Ears with tympanostomy tubes had significantly fewer episodes of otitis media ($p < .001$; 95% confidence intervals -0.7 and -1.7) and had better hearing ($p = .005$, 95% confidence intervals -5.9 and -1.2) than the contralateral ears. After tube extrusion, there was a non–statistically significant tendency for surgically treated ears to have more otitis and worse hearing. Tympanosclerosis, retraction, and atrophy were likewise more common in operated ears.

Review of the literature demonstrates that myringotomy with tympanostomy tube insertion can be beneficial in selected infants and children because middle ear disease is reduced and hearing is improved. However, there are well-known risks, complications, and sequelae associated with tympanostomy tube insertion. Recommendations regarding watchful waiting, antibiotic therapy, or surgical intervention should be individualized by patient needs, history, physical exam, and tympanometric and audiologic findings.

FUTURE DIRECTIONS AND RESEARCH ISSUES

Although the medical literature regarding OME is voluminous, there are general areas in which research studies are needed. Well-designed randomized, controlled studies are needed in evaluating natural history, diagnosis, prevention, interventions, and long-term outcomes of otitis media with effusion.

Key issues regarding the natural history of otitis media with effusion include determining when medical and surgical intervention are indicated (considering the natural course of the disease usually follows a benign path). Information on long-term effects of chronic or fluctuating hearing loss on speech, language, learning, and behavior is needed. Diagnostic criteria and algorithms for primary care physicians regarding otoscopy, pneumatic otoscopy, and tympanometry would be useful. Detailed studies to evaluate the association of OME and environmental risk factors are needed. Most prior studies are descriptive and open to criticism. Intervention and outcome studies are needed to determine the effectiveness of various treatments—antibiotic prophylaxis, steroid therapy, surgery, allergy treatment, and others.

CONCLUSIONS

Although the efficacy of surgical management of OME has not been well documented in controlled clinical studies, clinical practice guidelines have been established to assist the practitioner in critical decision making. Generally, we believe that tympanocentesis is indicated for the identification of a resistant organism causing clinically significant acute otitis media or persistent OME. Myringotomy is not commonly needed in OME; it is useful, however, in treatment of acute otitis media with significant otalgia or as a drainage procedure if complications arise. Tympanostomy tube insertion is indicated in recurrent acute otitis media refractory to antibiotic therapy, in young children with OME present for more than 3 months and a conductive hearing loss greater that 20 dB in the better ear, and in eustachian tube dysfunction. Tympanoplasty, exploratory tympanotomy, ossiculoplasty, and mastoidectomy are reserved for treatment of significant intratemporal or intracranial complications of otitis media. Tonsillectomy and adenoidectomy are not recommended for the treatment of OME in children under the age of 3 in the absence of discrete adenotonosillar pathology. Adenoidectomy may be helpful in children over 4 years of age.

REFERENCES

Alberti, P.W. (1974). Myringotomy and ventilating tubes in the 19th century. *Laryngoscope, 84,* 805–815.

Bluestone, C.D., & Klein, J.O. (Eds.). (1988). *Otitis media in infants and children.* Philadelphia: W.B. Saunders.

Bluestone, C.D., & Stool, S.E. (Eds.). (1995). *Atlas of pediatric otolaryngology.* Philadelphia: W.B. Saunders.

Bluestone, C.D., Stool, S.E., & Kenna, M.A. (1996). Otitis media, atelectasis, and eustachian tube dysfunction. In C.D. Bluestone & S.E. Stool (Eds.), *Pediatric otolaryngology* (3rd ed., pp. 402–595). Philadelphia: W.B. Saunders.

Casselbrant, M.L., Kaleida, P.H., Rockette, H.E., Paradise, J.L., Bluestone, C.D., Kurs-Lasky, M., Nozza, R.J., & Wald, E.R. (1992). Efficacy of antimicrobial prophylaxis and of tympanostomy tube insertion for prevention of recurrent acute otitis media: results of a randomized clinical trial. *Pediatric Infectious Disease Journal, 11,* 278–286.

Engelhard, D., Cohen, D., Strauss, N., Sacks, T.G., Jorczak-Sarri, L., & Shapiro, M. (1989). Randomised study of myringotomy, amoxycillin/clavulanate, or both for acute otitis media in infants. *Lancet, 2,* 141–143.

Gates, G.A. (1994). Adenoidectomy for otitis media with effusion. *Annals of Otology, Rhinology, and Laryngology, 163,* 54.

Gates, G.A., Avery, C., Cooper, J.C. J., & Prihoda, T.J. (1989). Chronic secretory otitis media: Effects of surgical management. *Annals of Otology, Rhinology, and Laryngology. Supplement, 138,* 2–32.

Gates, G.A., Avery, C.S., Prihoda, T.J., et al. (1987). Effectiveness of adenoidectomy and tympanostomy tubes in the treatment of chronic otitis media with effusion. *New England Journal of Medicine, 317,* 1444.

Gebhart, D.E. (1981). Tympanostomy tubes in the otitis media-prone child. *Laryngscope, 91,* 849.

Gonzalez, C., Arnold, J.E., Erhardt, J.B., et al. (1986). Prevention of recurrent acute otitis media: Chemoprophylaxis versus tympanostomy tubes. *Laryngoscope, 96,* 1330.

Herberts, G., Jeppson, P.H., Nylen, O., et al. (1971). Acute otitis media. *Practical Otology, Rhinology, and Laryngology, 33,* 191.

Kaleida, P.H., Casselbrant, M.L., Rockette, H.E., Paradise, J.L., Bluestone, C.D., Blatter, M.M., Reisinger, K.S., Wald, E.R., & Suppance, J.S. (1991). Amoxicillin or myringotomy or both for acute otitis media: Results of a randomized clinical trial. *Pediatrics, 87,* 466–474.

Kilby, D., Richards, S.H., & Hart, G. (1972). Grommets and glue ears: Two year results. *Journal of Laryngology and Otology, 86,* 881.

Lee, C.T., Freeman, D.W., & Fireman, B.H. (1991). Evaluation of ventilating tubes and myringotomy in the treatment of recurrent or persistent otitis media. *Pediatric Infectious Disease Journal 10,* 2–11.

Lorentzen, P., & Haugsten, P. (1977). Treatment of acute suppurative otitis media. *Journal of Laryngology and Otology, 91,* 331.

Lous, J. (1995). Secretory otitis media in school children: Is screening for secretory otitis media advisable? *Danish Medical Bulletin, 42,* 71–99.

Mandel, E.M., Rockette, H.E., Bluestone, C.D., et al. (1989). Myringotomy with and without tympanostomy tubes for chronic otitis media with effusion. *Archives of Otolaryngology, 115,* 1217.

Mandel, E.M., Rockette, H.E., Bluestone, C.D., et al. (1992). Efficacy of myringotomy with and without tympanostomy tubes for chronic otitis media with effusion. *Pediatric Infectious Disease Journal 11,* 270.

Paparella, M.M., & Froymovich, M.D. (1994). Surgical advances in treating otitis media. *Annals of Otology, Rhinology, and Laryngology, Supplement, 163,* 48–53.

Paparella, M.M., & Schachern, P. (1994). New developments in treating otitis media. *Annals of Otology, Rhinology, and Laryngology. Supplement, 163,* 7–10.

Puhakka, H., Virolainen, E., Aantaa, E., et al. (1979). Myringotomy in the treatment of acute otitis media in children. *Acta Otol-Laryngologica, 88,* 122.

Qvarnberg, Y., & Palva, T. (1980). Active and conservative treatment of acute otitis media: Prospective studies. *Annals of Otology, Rhinology, and Laryngology, 89,* 269.

Roddey, O.F. Jr., Earle, R., Jr., & Haggerty, R. (1966). Myringotomy in acute otitis media: A controlled study. *Journal of the American Medical Association, 197,* 849.

264   TODD AND STOOL

Schwartz, R.H., & Schwartz, D.M. (1980). Acute otitis media: Diagnosis and drug therapy. *Drugs, 19,* 107.

Shah, N. (1971). Use of grommets in "glue" ears. *Journal of Laryngology and Otology, 85,* 283.

Stool, S.E., Berg, A.O., Berman, S., Carney, C.J., Cooley, J.R., Culpepper, L., Eavey, R.D., Feagans, L.V., Finitzo, T., Friedman, E.M., Goertz, J.A., Goldstein, A.J., Grundfast, K.M., Long, D.G., Macconi, L.L., Melton, L., Roberts, J.E., Sherrod, J.L., & Sisk, J.E. (1994). *Otitis media with effusion in young children: Clinical practice guideline No. 12 (AHCPR Publication No. 94-0622).* Rockville, MD: Agency for Health Care Policy and Research.

Thomsen, J., Sederberberg-Olsen, J., Balle, V., Vejlsgaard, R., Stangerup, S.E., & Bondesson, G. (1989). Antibiotic treatment of children with secretory otitis media: A randomized, double-blind, placebo-controlled study. *Archives of Otolaryngology—Head and Neck Surgery, 115,* 447–451.

Tos, M., & Poulsen, G. (1976). Secretory otitis media: Late results of treatment with grommets. *Archives of Otolaryngology 102,* 672.

IV

INTERNATIONAL PERSPECTIVES AND FUTURE DIRECTIONS

11

An International Perspective on Otitis Media with Effusion

Incidence, Prevalence, Management, and Policy Guidelines

Richard Maw
and Anthea Counsell

Health care delivery systems vary widely. There is variation within and between countries and within and between cultures. There is also variation in management strategies for similar conditions between hospitals and units within different regions of the same country. Individual specialists recommend different treatment regimens for identical conditions. Invariably these differences in management are not substantiated by evidence from carefully controlled studies. Frequently management is learned from taught courses or teacher-based instructions that are unsupported by statistically sound factual evidence.

Even for commonly occurring conditions, such as acute suppurative otitis media or otitis media with effusion (OME) in childhood, data collection and analysis are not uniform and are incomplete within most health care systems. This is often a reflection of the structure of the system. There are usually public and private sectors that are often in competition and usually without a means of communication of data between them. Within such sectors there may be general practice and hospital-based systems of care that also do not exchange data. Within hospitals or units, inpatient and outpatient management of similar conditions are separated and segregated in terms of data access. The purchaser–provider split of health care management may affect and distort the sequential collection of data over time by transferring resources and contracts. Budget limitations of purchaser contracts may shift workload from hospital-based services to the community, thus making serial analysis of trends in patient care difficult. Fundholding general practices in the United Kingdom (U.K.) may develop services previously provided in the hospital setting, distorting the statistical analysis of such activity.

All these aspects of health care delivery will affect the unit, regional, or national collection of data concerning management and case load. The differences that are created in data collection for the same condition make comparison of outcome following treatment virtually impossible. This is certainly the case with respect to otitis media and OME.

This chapter summarizes available data for incidence and prevalence of OME from a variety of countries with different health care delivery systems. We have assessed national statistical data for rates of intervention for surgical treatment of OME. The data are limited by failure of some countries to include all procedures carried out in various nationalized and private systems of care and to include operations performed both on an outpatient basis (so-called day care management in Europe and elsewhere) and as inpatient admissions.

IDENTIFICATION AND
SCREENING OF OTITIS MEDIA WITH EFFUSION
Prevalence and incidence rates for both otitis media and OME have been and are still being reported, and the wide range of rates from different countries suggests variability in the parameters used to report the data. The detection of OME by screening is not universal. In the United Kingdom, most health authorities screen at 7 months of age and at preschool entry in 4- to 5-year-olds. Only 60% of these authorities continue to fund an intermediate screen at 3½ years of age. There are differences in the performance of the screen, in terms of both the tester and the test equipment. Screening may be carried out by nonmedically trained "health visitors," school or other nurses, audiometric technicians or scientists, or medically trained staff, including senior clinical medical officers (audiology) or general practitioners. Screening may involve distraction testing, audiometry, or tympanometry. A variety of tympano-

metric equipment is available. Different and subjective thresholds may be applied to the results of screening. The "take-up" rate in screening programs varies and may omit the most needy in terms of severity of disease and potential for treatment. Parental concern may overstate the clinical situation and pressurize the threshold for intervention. Overzealous screening for OME using tympanometry with low-pass thresholds will undoubtedly present large numbers of children for consideration of treatment.

Estimation of the subjective effects of OME in childhood is difficult. This is particularly so in relation to the secondary effects of the hearing loss resulting from OME. It is especially difficult where the condition fluctuates in severity and where the clinical course relapses and remits.

The threshold of severity of hearing loss required to justify treatment of OME is not known. Similar levels of audiometric hearing loss seem to affect different children to a different extent. The effect may depend on numerous factors, including age, level of attainment of speech and language ability, laterality and symmetry of the condition, socioeconomic status, and educational ability and support. Treatment options may be described in relation to four parameters:

1. *Correction of hearing loss* may occur spontaneously as the condition resolves, and such resolution may be during what has now become known as a period of "watchful waiting." Amplification may be provided by parents and teachers or by use of a hearing aid. The effect of hearing loss on speech and language may benefit from appropriate speech therapy.

2. There may be *manipulation of environmental risk factors* known to be associated with OME, such as reduction or elimination of parental smoking and alteration of child care facilities.

3. *Treatment of the pathologic changes* within the middle ear may be achieved medically or surgically. Apart from a short-term benefit from antibiotics, there is no evidence for any sustained cure of chronic OME from any of the wide range of medications that have been investigated.

4. *Surgical treatment* with myringotomy and aspiration of middle ear fluid has a short-term benefit before the fluid reaccumulates. Insertion of a ventilation tube delays fluid reaccumulation. Tubes remain in place for a variable period depending on the structure and type of the tube. Adenoidectomy produces a long-term resolution of OME (up to 4 years), with the best overall resolution resulting from combination of adenoidectomy and insertion of ventilation tubes (Maw & Bawden, 1993). Adenoidectomy also reduces the need for

tube reinsertion (Maw & Bawden, 1994). Management of allergy may reduce the overall severity of the problem.

Relatively few of these treatment options have been properly evaluated, and only a few have been subject to cross-cultural studies between nations. There have been a number of randomized, controlled trials of surgical treatment with myringotomy, ventilation tubes, adenoidectomy, and adenotonsillectomy. The difficulty of interpreting the results of these trials is due to the use of different entry criteria, to the numerous associated variables that are frequently not controlled for, and to the variation in outcome criteria and duration of follow-up. These difficulties are compounded by the paucity of reliable national data on numbers of procedures carried out on an annual basis. The differences seen in the data that are available suggest that, first, different criteria are used within and between countries to assess prevalence of OME. Similar differences suggest that different thresholds for surgical intervention exist both within and between different countries. All of these variations indicate a need to rationalize health care delivery for the management of OME in children. Already bulletins, protocols, and guidelines have been developed by various groups.

INTERNATIONAL PERSPECTIVE ON THE PREVALENCE OF OTITIS MEDIA WITH EFFUSION

Most of the published material on the prevalence of OME is from studies in Europe, the United States, New Zealand, and Japan (Table 1). From these studies, it appears that the most important factor for prevalence is the age of the child. Studies invariably report point and not period prevalence rates. Most studies use tympanometric profiles based on Fiellau-Nikolajsen's (1983) modification of Jerger's classification. Not all results relate only to Type B tympanograms; some studies include Type C2 traces as evidence of OME. Also, some studies report prevalence data for ears, giving lower rates than those reporting rates for children.

Prevalence Data from Selected Countries

Belgium   A prospective study of 2,069 Belgian children between 2.5 and 6 years of age was carried out by van Cauwenberge and Kluyskens (1984) between 1979 and 1980. Type B tympanograms were found in 12% of left and 11.5% of right ears. The highest prevalence was at 36–48 months of age, and the number of Type B tympanograms decreased after 4 years of age.

Denmark   Three studies have been reported from Denmark. Fiellau-Nikolajsen (1983) reported data on 404 3-year-olds and found that 17%–20% of children (13%–16% of ears) had OME. Lous and

Table 1. International prevalence rates for OME

Country and reference(s)	n	Children 1.5–6		Children 7–8		Children 8–11	
		Age (yr)	Prevalence (%)	Age (yr)	Prevalence (%)	Age (yr)	Prevalence (%)
Belgium van Cauwenberge & Kluyskens (1984)	2,069	2.5–6	11.5–12 (ears)				
Denmark Fiellau-Nikolajsen (1983)	404	3	13–16 (ears)				
Lous & Fiellau-Nikolajsen (1981)	387			7	9		
Tos et al. (1988)	560	2–4	7–19 (children)	7	7	8–10	2.4
Netherlands Zielhuis et al. (1990)	1,439	2–4	25 (ears)				
Spain Suárez Nieto et al. (1983)	5,414	2	38 (children)			11	1.1
United Kingdom Williamson et al. (1994)	856	5	17 (children)	8	6		
Japan Takasaka (1990)	14,509	4	19.3 (ears)	8	3.6		
Yamaguchi et al. (1994)	443	4–5	4–9 (ears)				
Kobayashi et al. (1994)	4,339	1.5	8.7 (ears)				
		3	8.4 (ears)				
United States Casselbrant et al. (1985)	103	2–6	5–35 (children)				
Saudi Arabia El-Sayed & Zakzouk (1995)	4,214	2–3	21 (children)	7–8	6		
New Zealand Chalmers et al. (1989)	1,768	5	10.5 (ears)	7	6.5	11	2.4

Fiellau-Nikolajsen (1981) reported a point prevalence of 9% for 7-year-old Danish children. Tos, Stangerup, Hvid, and Andreassen (1988) followed three cohorts of healthy children. Point prevalence of Type B tympanograms ranged between 7% and 19% in 2- to 4-year-olds. By 7 years of age it was 7% and by 8–10 years it was 2%–4%.

Netherlands Zielhuis, Rach, and van den Broek (1990) studied 1,439 2-year-old children from Nijmegen using serial tympanometry on nine consecutive occasions up to 4 years of age. They showed an overall OME prevalence of 33% of unilateral of bilateral disease in children and a rate of 25% for ears.

Spain In Spain, Suárez Nieto, Malluguiza Calvo, and Barthe García (1983) recorded a prevalence rate of 8.7% in 5,414 Spanish children between 2 and 12 years of age. The prevalence decreased from 38% at 2 years to 1.1% at 11 years.

United Kingdom Williamson, Dunleavy, Bain, and Robinson (1994) have reported prevalence rates for 856 English schoolchildren ages 5–8 years using serial tympanometry on a seasonal basis over 3 years. Annual prevalence rates decreased from 17% for 5-year-olds to 6% for 8-year-olds. There was a significant variation in relation to seasonal change.

Japan Takasaka (1990) studied 14,509 ears in Japanese children ages 4–8 years and found a prevalence of Type B and C2 tympanograms in 8.7%. The rate was 19.3% in 4-year-olds, decreasing to 3.6% in 8-year-olds. Yamaguchi, Nakashima, and Kumagami (1994) screened almost all preschool children ages 4–5 years in the town of Izuhara Machi. More than 400 children were screened, and the prevalence of Type B tympanograms during the period 1989–1991 was 4%–9% of ears. Kobayashi, Hirata, Gyo, Yanagihara, and Saiki (1994) screened 4,339 children in Matsutama City between 1989 and 1990. A Type B tympanogram was present in 8.7% of ears from children age 1.5 years, and at age 3 there were still 8.4% of ears with Type B tympanograms.

United States Casselbrant et al. (1985) studied 103 2- to 6-year-old children at a child care center in Pittsburgh between 1981 and 1983. Using otoscopy, tympanometry, and acoustic reflex measures, the point prevalence was found to range from 5% to 35%.

New Zealand In New Zealand, Chalmers, Stewart, Silva, and Mulvena (1989) studied a large cohort of children over a 6-year period. Prevalence rates of OME for ears were 10.5% and 6.5% at 5 and 7 years of age, respectively, and 3% and 2.4% at 9 and 11 years of age, respectively.

Saudi Arabia El-Sayed and Zakzouk (1995), from Saudi Arabia, reported a random community study of 4,214 children ages 1–8 years. The point prevalence rates of unilateral and bilateral Type B tympanograms were 5.7% and 8.1%, respectively. The point prevalence rate for ears was 10.9%. This rate was approximately 21% in children 2–3 years of age and 6% in those age 7–8 years.

Summary
These international studies show various prevalence rates with a particular trend toward decreasing prevalence with increasing age. From the 13 representative studies presented here based on nearly 35,000 children, average prevalence rates can be approximated. For children between 1.5 and 6 years of age, the rate for ears is 13.5% and for children is 21.4%. For children ages 7–8 years, the average overall rate is 6.3%, and for those age 10 or 11 years it is 2% (see Table 1).

INTERNATIONAL PERSPECTIVE ON RISK FACTORS
Many epidemiologic studies have reported racial and seasonal differences in the prevalence of OME. Both have significant implications in relation to protocols and guidelines for management. Eskimos (Pedersen & Zachau-Christiansen, 1986), Native Americans (Todd & Bowman, 1985), and Australian Aborigines (McCafferty, Lewis, Coman, & Mills 1985) have a higher incidence of middle ear problems, including OME, than Caucasians. Black races have a lower incidence than Caucasians (Griffith, 1989). However, the measured racial differences in incidence of OME may not have accounted for other confounding variables, such as socioeconomic conditions, patterns of use and availability of health care, and health behaviors. Goycoolea, Goycoolea, and Farfan (1988) have shown that Easter Islanders of mixed or continental origin have a higher point prevalence of OME than genetically pure native children.

The majority of the studies listed in Table 1 show differences in prevalence as a function of the season and climatic change. Van Cauwenberge and Kluyskens (1984) screened a small group ($n = 97$) of their sample on a monthly basis to examine the effect of season on OME. The results showed the highest number of Type B tympanograms (26.7% of ears) in December, compared with 15% in May. Worldwide, there is a higher incidence of OME in winter months, probably in association with the increased incidence of infection caused by respiratory syncytial virus.

Suárez Nieto et al. (1993) demonstrated different prevalence rates in different climatic regions of Spain in children ages 6–8 years but not in younger children. Casselbrant et al. (1985), Chalmers et al. (1989), and Williamson et al. (1994) showed the prevalence of OME to be greater in the winter than the summer. Casselbrant et al. found rates of 22%–33% in winter compared with less than 10% in summer. The difference was related to the seasonality of upper respiratory tract infections. Of those children with infective episodes during their monthly evaluation, 35% had OME compared with only 11% of those without infection.

INTERNATIONAL PERSPECTIVE
ON MANAGEMENT STRATEGIES

The best indication for an international perspective on the management of OME should come from the data relating to surgical management, including myringotomy, ventilation tube insertion, and adenoidectomy procedures. Data on tonsillectomy, although not relevant to the management of OME, should provide further comparisons for validation. Unfortunately, data on surgical management of OME are often problematic. For example, certain international comparisons suggest rates for ventilation tube insertion between 0.1% and 0.3% per capita total population. However, few countries provide data of sufficient accuracy for intervention rates to be quoted with convincing reliability. There is a need for uniformity of recording such information.

Data on management of OME are collected in one form or another by most health care systems. However, the overriding impression from trying to obtain such information is that it is not readily available and, where it is obtainable, various qualifications are required to interpret the data. Usually data existed only for procedures carried out in public hospitals. Information was not usually collected on a national basis from private hospitals. However, health insurance companies may collect certain data, particularly from private institutions. Often only inpatient information is available and, given the frequency of outpatient surgical management for OME, such data represent often gross underestimates. Different classification coding systems are used in different countries, making comparisons difficult. Finally, selective sampling procedures are often used, resulting in problems estimating the true rate for the entire population.

These constraints make it difficult to establish from reported figures the reason for any trends in surgical management that may be apparent. For example, if a decline is noted, this may be due either to a reduction in the prevalence of the condition, to a change in the management, or to a change in the recording methods. Notwithstanding these limitations, some hard data are available from Europe, New Zealand, and the United States.

Netherlands

Data from the Netherlands SIG Health Care Information (1984–1993) include procedures performed in hospital otolaryngology departments. However, since the mid-1980s there has been a change toward outpatient surgical care, and not all hospital registrations include such management. The information for 1993 shows a total of 43,197 ventilation tube procedures all performed on an outpatient surgery basis. By contrast, there were 25,639 adenoidectomies, 21,645 adenotonsillectomies, and 12,437 tonsillectomies in children less than 15 years of age.

England and Wales
In the 1980s, data collection was accomplished by means of the Hospital Inpatient Enquiry (HIPE), an annual survey based on a 10% sample of inpatient discharges from National Health Service nonpsychiatric hospitals in England and Wales. HIPE data were last collected and processed in 1985, and the system was replaced by the Korner data system. In 1985, there were 59,160 ventilation tube procedures, 17,210 adenoidectomies, and 30,410 adenotonsillectomies in children under 15 years of age.

More recent data are based on Hospital Episode Statistics (Department of Health, 1995). Table 2 shows the change in numbers of surgical procedures between 1989 and 1994. There has been a decrease in the number of ventilation tube insertions, from 57,509 in 1989–1990 to 47,944 in 1993–1994. The data exclude operations carried out in private hospitals. Nicholl, Beeby, and Williams (1989) suggested that, in 1986, 16% of otolaryngology operations were performed in the private sector.

An Effective Health Care Bulletin on the treatment of persistent glue ear (OME) in children was published in the United Kingdom in November 1992. It represents a view of the effectiveness of health service interventions. It was funded by the Department of Health and was designed for decision makers with the National Health Service. A significant recommendation for management of OME was to introduce a period of "watchful waiting" together with development of protocols by purchasers in conjunction with relevant professionals. The bulletin

Table 2. Hospital episode statistics for England and Wales (1989–1994)

Code	Procedure	No. of procedures (Prevalence rate)				
		1989–90	1990–91	1991–92	1992–93	1993–94
D15.1	Insertion of ventilation tube	57,509 (40%)	52,537 (38%)	58,376 (39%)	57,925 (38%)	47,944 (34%)
E20.1	Adenoidectomy alone	18,350 (13%)	16,562 (12%)	18,344 (12%)	18,142 (12%)	16,110 (11%)
F34	Tonsillectomy alone or with adenoidectomy	65,606 (47%)	68,307 (50%)	74,421 (49%)	75,772 (50%)	77,109 (55%)
Total		141,465	137,406	151,141	151,839	141,163

Data from Department of Health (1995).

estimated that the average rate of treatment for OME in England was 4.7 per 1,000 children under the age of 15. However, this estimate was based on information supplied in 1989–1990. Following publication of the bulletin, there has been a reduction by approximately 17% in the number of ventilation tube insertions carried out between 1992–1993 and 1993–94 (see Table 2).

New Zealand

The main source of information on surgical management of OME in New Zealand is the Hospital and Selected Morbidity Data from the Ministry of Health (1989–1992). The data appear relatively complete in that they include both outpatient and inpatient data as well as figures for public and private hospitals. Table 3 shows data for myringotomy and ventilation tube procedures, tonsillectomy, adenotonsillectomy, and adenoidectomy alone. Outpatients and inpatients in public and private systems are recorded for 1989. Table 4 shows that the total number of these operations has increased from 14,005 in 1989 to 21,286 in 1992. The number of myringotomy and tube procedures has doubled from 5,349 in 1989 to 11,219 in 1992. Tonsillectomies increased from 2,805 in 1989 to 4,034 in 1992. Myringotomy and ventilation tube insertions accounted for 38% of procedures in 1989 and 53% in 1992. Overall,

Table 3. Numbers of procedures in New Zealand in each age group for public and private cases treated as inpatients (ip) and as outpatients (op) (1989)

| Code | Procedure | | Age (yr) | | | | |
			0–5	5–10	10–15	15+	Total
200	Myringotomy	Public/ip	310	716	115	165	1,306
	and ventilation	Public/op	585	882	174	85	1,726
	tubes	Private/ip	164	230	27	60	481
		Private/op	1,102	595	60	79	1,836
		Total	2,161	2,423	376	389	5,349
282	Tonsillectomy	Public/ip	37	240	373	1,224	1,874
		Public/op	0	0	4	2	6
		Private/ip	29	116	186	579	910
		Private/op	3	2	3	7	15
		Total	69	358	566	1,812	2,805
283	Tonsillectomy	Public/ip	299	1,104	301	60	1,764
	with	Public/op	7	16	1	2	26
	adenoidectomy	Private/ip	512	1,064	390	646	2,612
		Private/op	102	98	8	5	213
		Total	920	2,282	700	713	4,615
286	Adenoidectomy	Public/ip	125	336	66	11	538
		Public/op	108	259	32	1	400
		Private/ip	15	24	10	6	55
		Private/op	126	103	11	3	243
		Total	374	722	119	21	1,236

Data from Ministry of Health, New Zealand (1995).

Table 4.   Total numbers of procedures for *all* ages in New Zealand treated both as inpatients and as outpatients in public and private care, 1989–1992

Code	Procedure	No. of procedures (prevalence rate)			
		1989	1990	1991	1992
200	Myringotomy and ventilation tube insertion	5,349 (38%)	6,908 (44%)	8,776 (47%)	11,219 (53%)
286	Adenoidectomy alone	1,236 (9%)	1,335 (9%)	1,734 (9%)	1,795 (8%)
282 283	Tonsillectomy alone or with adenoidectomy	7,420 (53%)	7,208 (47%)	8,173 (44%)	8,272 (39%)
Total		14,005	15,451	18,683	21,286

Data from Ministry of Health, New Zealand (1989–1992).

60% of operations were performed in public hospitals in 1992, compared with 55% in 1989. For adenoidectomy, there was a large increase in procedures performed on an outpatient surgery basis in public hospitals, from 32% in 1989 to 67% in 1992.

Summary of Data from Netherlands, England, Wales, and New Zealand   These international statistics appear relatively complete. They are summarized in Table 5, which shows comparative data for annual numbers of myringotomy and ventilation tube procedures, adenoidectomy, tonsillectomy, and adenotonsillectomy for children less than 15 years of age for the Netherlands in 1993, for England and Wales in 1993, and for New Zealand in 1992. It shows the rate of operations versus the estimated total population for myringotomy and tube insertion and for all four procedures. The rates for New Zealand and the Neth-

Table 5.   International comparison of data from the Netherlands, England and Wales, and New Zealand for children less than 15 years old

Procedure	Netherlands 1993 (15,000,000)[a]	England and Wales 1993 (50,000,000)[a]	New Zealand 1992 (3,500,000)[a]
Myringotomy with unilateral or bilateral ventilation tube insertion	43,197 (0.29%)[b]	47,944 (0.1%)	10,784 (0.31%)
Adenoidectomy	25,639	16,110	1,764
Tonsillectomy	12,437	} 77,109	1,513
Adenotonsillectomy	27,645		4,066
Total	65,721 (0.44%)[b]	93,219 (0.19%)	7,343 (0.21%)

Data from Department of Health (1995), Ministry of Health (1989–1992, 1995), and Netherlands SIG Health Care Information (1984–1993).

[a] Total population.

[b] Rates per capita population.

erlands are very similar and are significantly greater than the rate for England and Wales. However, it is estimated that an additional 16% of procedures are carried out privately in England and Wales that are not included in these data.

Denmark

Data were obtained from the Danish National Authorities (Sundhedsstyrelsen) for children less than 14 years of age for procedures carried out in Denmark. However, they only include those patients hospitalized for at least 1 day. Because adenoidectomy and tube insertion are increasingly being performed on an outpatient surgery basis, the figures are a gross underestimation. The number of reported procedures has remained constant during the period 1989–1993.

Information was also obtained from the National Authorities for primary health care in Copenhagen County. This covers a population of 620,000, representing 12% of the national total. The data confirmed the number of operations carried out by specialists in private practice. If the rates for Copenhagen are representative of the whole country, then the total number of procedures for Denmark in 1994 would be 2,000 adenoidectomies, 200 tonsillectomies with or without adenoidectomy, and 51,400 myringotomies with tube insertion. The latter would give a rate per capita for the total population of 1.028%, which is high. Thus there is a need to reconcile information from outpatient surgery centers, inpatient units, and private practice.

Sweden

The National Board of Health and Welfare Centre for Epidemiology in Stockholm provides data for children less than 19 years of age, but only for cases managed as inpatients. Data for private cases and outpatient surgery are not available.

United States

A number of national data systems provide surgical discharge information in the United States. These include the National Hospital Discharge Survey (NHDS) of the National center for Health Statistics, The American Hospital Association's Hospital Panel, and the Professional and Hospital Discharge Data System of the Health Care Financing Administration. The NHDS is based on a 5% national sample of short-stay, general, and specialty noninstitutional hospitals, excluding military and Veterans Administration facilities. The other two main sources of information do not come from a national probability sample of surgical discharges. In comparing the number of operative procedures, these different sources estimate their reliability to be acceptable, with general agreement between the different methods (Lubitz, 1981).

Rutkow (1986) has reported rates for otolaryngology operations in the United States using the ICD-9–coded data from the National Center for Health Statistics based on the NHDS. In 1983, ear, nose, and throat operations represented 9% of all surgical operations performed. Tonsillectomy together with adenoidectomy was the most frequently performed such procedure. A total of 496,000 were carried out in 1983, with a rate of 230 operations per 100,000 population. Derkay (1993), also using NHDS data, updated Rutkow's results. Examining specifically pediatric otolaryngology procedures, he noted a substantial decline in the absolute number and in the rate per 100,000 (Table 6). During the period 1977–1987, the total number of inpatient otolaryngology procedures declined by 60% from 1,605 to 633 per 100,000. Myringotomy, with or without insertion of ventilation tubes, showed a decline of 71% in inpatient numbers and a 73% decrease from 430 to 118 procedures per 100,000 between 1977 and 1987. The rate of tonsillectomy with or without adenoidectomy declined by 61% from 787 to 303 per 100,000. Adenoidectomy declined by 84% from 164 to 24 per 100,000. Derkay noted that, in 1983, adenotonsillectomy ranked 8th in a list of surgical inpatient procedures, but by 1987 it was 24th.

Statistics from the NHDS have been published for 1992 for all listed procedures for inpatient discharges for nonfederal hospitals by ICD-9 codes. The rates are given in thousands and compare with the absolute numbers noted by Derkay in 1987. In that year there were 62,000 myringotomy and tube insertions, whereas in 1992 there were 54,000 (Vital and Health Statistics, 1994).

As part of the U.S. National Health Examination Survey in 1988, the Medical Device Implementation Supplement was used to obtain the first population estimates of the prevalence of implanted tympanostomy tubes. It was estimated that 13 per 1,000 children in the general population had received these implants (Bright et al., 1993). By contrast, a population-based study in Montreal, Canada, estimated the overall prevalence of myringotomy, tube insertion, or both as 1.7% of 3-year-olds and 1% of 7-year-olds (Croteau, Hai, Pless, & Infante-Rivard, 1990).

These figures do not represent the overall level of surgical activity in the United States. There is a growing trend toward outpatient and ambulatory surgery that affects the collection of national data on otolaryngology operations in the United States. The NHDS includes outpatient procedures requiring bed occupancy for an extended period of postoperative recuperation. However, minor procedures at the lower end of the ambulatory scale performed in outpatient clinics or physician offices would be excluded from the NHDS. Also excluded are those procedures performed in freestanding hospital- or non–hospital-owned

Table 6. Absolute numbers (Ab. no.) and rates per 1,000 pediatric population, 1977–1987, and ICD-9–coded operations for inpatient discharges from short-stay, nonfederal hospitals in the United States, 1992

	1977	1978	1979	1980	1981	1982	1983	1984	1985	1986	1987	1992
Myringotomy with or without tubes												
Rate	4.3	4.1	4.0	*	*	2.78	3.27	2.33	1.72	1.40	1.18	
Ab no.	2.16	2.08	2.02	2.02	1.7	1.44	1.69	1.21	0.89	0.73	0.62	0.54
Tonsillectomy with or without adenoidectomy												
Rate	7.87	6.92	6.08	5.74	5.64	5.23	5.41	4.34	3.48	3.39	3.03	
Ab no.	4.14	3.60	3.13	2.94	2.89	2.69	2.79	2.24	1.97	1.77	1.59	
Adenotonsillectomy												
Rate	*	*	5.42	*	*	*	4.50	3.58	*	2.75	2.48	
Ab no.	*	*	2.71	*	*	*	2.32	1.85	*	1.44	1.30	0.30
Tonsillectomy												
Rate	*	0.95	0.83	*	*	*	0.91	0.78	*	0.63	0.55	
Ab no.	*	0.48	0.42	*	*	*	0.47	0.40	*	0.33	0.29	
Adenoidectomy												
Rate	*	1.64	1.60	*	*	*	0.97	0.64	*	0.27	0.25	
Ab no.	*	0.03	0.03	*	*	0.02	0.02	0.01	*	0.01	0.02	0.08

Data from Derkay (1993).

*Data unavailable

units. The apparent decline noted in the figures for otolaryngology procedures is therefore partly illusory because it lacks information on ambulatory procedures and also on those performed in military units. A greater involvement in family medical care by military medical centers took place during the 1980s, and increasingly they have provided medical and surgical care to large numbers of pediatric patients.

POLICY GUIDELINES FOR
TREATMENT OF OTITIS MEDIA WITH EFFUSION

In the 1990s, several groups from different countries have developed policy guidelines for the treatment of OME. Several of these guidelines are reviewed in this section.

United Kingdom

In November 1992 in the United Kingdom, an Effective Health Care Bulletin reported on the treatment of persistent glue ear (OME) in children. The bulletin addressed only surgical issues and made no recommendations regarding antimicrobial treatment. This may reflect the bias of the bulletin toward hospital practice. In the United Kingdom, almost all cases of acute otitis media and of OME are initially treated by general practitioners, and most children have already had at least some antimicrobial treatment before they are referred for an otolaryngologic opinion in hospital. The Effective Health Care Bulletin (1992) recommended a period of watchful waiting of unspecified duration, with continued observation and testing. It suggested that a child be placed on a provisional waiting list throughout the period of watchful waiting before surgery was carried out. On reaching the top of the list, patients are called for surgery and are assessed immediately prior to surgery to ensure persistence of middle ear fluid. The importance of establishing those cases most likely to benefit from surgical intervention was emphasized. It was recommended that persistence and severity of the condition should be confirmed. In addition to consideration of the history and otoscopic findings, repeat audiometric and tympanometric studies should be performed at the start and finish of this period of watchful waiting. In 1995, the *Drugs and Therapeutic Bulletin* produced by the Consumers Association (1995) has recommended even longer periods of watchful waiting, with extension from 3 to 6 months.

New Zealand

The treatment policy report from New Zealand (Ministry of Health, 1994) was the result of a consensus conference that highlighted recommendations for OME management. After appropriate primary care, it was recommended that specialist assessment should take place within

4 weeks of referral, with priority to those children under 3 years of age. Appropriate medical management was considered to be prolonged antibiotics with a watchful waiting period of 12 weeks to allow resolution before surgical intervention was considered. The surgical management of choice was ventilation tube insertion as an outpatient surgical procedure. A booking system in which patients are given a precise date for surgery, rather than a waiting list system, was recommended for children under 3 years of age and for those with severe associated problems who should have tubes inserted within 1 month of specialist assessment, compared with 3 months for other children.

United States

In 1994, the Agency for Health Care Policy and Research published a guideline for OME limited to young children between 1 and 3 years of age (Stool et al., 1994). The American Academy of Pediatrics, together with the American Academy of Family Physicians and the American Academy of Otolaryngology—Head and Neck Surgery, developed the guidelines. Recommendations were made regarding diagnosis, evaluation, and management of OME and a detailed algorithm was produced. The recommendations were categorized into those that could be supported by the literature and those that were clinical options not strongly supported by the literature but that could be implemented as part of clinical practice. Management recommendations were divided into those used on initial presentation and those for OME lasting 3 months and lasting 4–6 months or more. When OME was first diagnosed, risk factor control and antimicrobial therapy were options. After 3 months of OME, antimicrobial therapy was again an option but, in addition, myringotomy and tube insertion became clinical options. By 4–6 months, tube insertion was a moderate recommendation. It was emphasized that, for OME present for more than 3 months, consideration must be given to the hearing status of the child.

Australia

The guidelines on management of pediatric middle ear disease published by the New South Wales Health Department Working Party in Australia produced vastly simplified recommendations but an algorithm similar to the American model (Chani et at., 1993). In general, a course of an appropriate antimicrobial agent was recommended to precede surgical intervention. Amoxicillin for 10–28 days was a first recommendation. Ventilation tube insertion was thought to be the appropriate surgical management for OME of more than 3 months' duration, especially if hearing loss was associated with behavioral or learning difficulties or if there were pathologic changes in the middle ear.

CONCLUSIONS

Antimicrobial treatment is effective in approximately one of four or five cases of OME and only in the short term. A meta-analysis shows a limited short-term cure for OME of 3%–30%, with a mean of 14% (Rosenfeld & Post, 1992). There are only a few studies with small numbers of cases showing the effects of steroids alone or in combination with antimicrobial therapy for OME. A meta-analysis shows that for steroids alone the short-term cure rate is 18%–21% (−2% to −43% confidence interval); for steroids and antimicrobial treatment the range is 25%–32% (−9% to −71% confidence interval). Thus the effect is not statistically significant.

The significant difference in recommendations for prescription of antimicrobial treatment between European countries and the United States and Australia requires further evaluation. Generally speaking, antimicrobial treatment for OME is withheld in Europe where it is not considered to effect a long-term cure of the condition. However, in the United Kingdom, many children will receive short courses of antimicrobial treatment in general practice. By comparison, particularly in the United States, prolonged antimicrobial treatment appears to be an almost invariable recommendation. There have recently been contentious discussions and publications in relation to this practice (Cantekin, Mcguire, & Potter, 1990).

Following watchful waiting, with or without medical treatment, if the condition persists and if there are clinically obvious effects on speech, language, learning, and behavior resulting from the hearing loss, then further treatment will be required. The options for children less than 3½ years of age without gross upper airway obstruction caused by adenoid or tonsillar enlargement are ventilation tube insertion or the use of a hearing aid. In children older than 3½ years, there is good evidence that the best overall resolution of chronic OME is achieved from a combination of ventilation tube insertion and adenoidectomy. Tonsillectomy does not appear to confer any additional benefit with respect to resolution of OME compared with adenoidectomy alone.

Consensus must be extended internationally, first for disease coding, second for data collection and analysis, and third for evaluation of comparable cases to demonstrate the effects of acceptable management regimens.

REFERENCES

Bright, R.A., Moore, R.M., Jeng, L.L., Sharkness, C.M., Hamburger, S.E., & Hamilton, P.M. (1993). The prevalence of tympanostomy tubes in children in the United States, 1988. *American Journal of Public Health, 83,* 1026–1028.

Cantekin, E.I., Mcguire, T.W., & Potter, R.L. (1990). Biomedical information, peer review and conflict of interests as they influence public health. *Journal of the American Medical Association, 263,* 1427–1430.

Casselbrant, M.L., Brostoff, L.M., Cantekin, E.I., Flaherty, M.R., Doyle, W.J., Bluestone, C.D., & Fria, T.J. (1985). Otitis media with effusion in pre-school children. *Laryngoscope, 95,* 428–436.

Chalmers, D., Stewart, I., Silva, P.L., & Mulvena, A. (1989). Otitis media with effusion in children—the Dunedin Study. *Clinics in Developmental Medicine, 108.*

Chani, K., Murphy, E., Lyle, D., Nudd, B., Isaacs, D., Starte, D., Harrison, H., Vandeleur, T., Many, M.L., & Clyne, P. (1993). Guidelines on the management of paediatric middle ear disease. *Medical Journal of Australia, (159* Suppl.), S1–S8.

Consumers Association. (1995). Management of acute otitis media and glue ear. *Drugs and Therapeutic Bulletin, 33,* 12–15.

Croteau, N., Hai, V., Pless, I.B., & Infante-Rivard, C. (1990). Trends in medical visits and surgery for otitis media among children. *American Journal of Diseases of Children, 144,* 535–538.

Department of Health. (1995). *Hospital episode statistics for England and Wales.* London: Author.

Derkay, C.S. (1993). Paediatric otolaryngology procedures in the United States: 1977–1987. *International Journal of Pediatric Otorhinolaryngology, 25,* 1–12.

Effective Health Care Bulletin. (1992). *The treatment of persistent glue ear in children.* Leeds, England: University of Leeds.

El-Sayed, Y., & Zakzouk, S. (1995). Point prevalence of type B tympanogram in Riyadh. *International Journal of Pediatric Otorhinolaryngology, 31,* 53–61.

Fiellau-Nikolajsen, M. (1983). Epidemiology of secretory otitis media: A descriptive cohort study. *Annals of Otology, Rhinology, and Laryngology, 92,* 172–177.

Goycoolea, H.G., Goycoolea, M.V., & Farfan, C.R. (1988). Racial and familial factors in otitis media: A point prevalence study on Easter Islands. *Archives of Otolaryngology—Head and Neck Surgery, 114,* 147–149.

Griffith, T.E. (1989). Epidemiology of otitis media—an interracial study. *Laryngoscope, 8,* 22–30.

Kobayashi, T., Hirata, T., Gyo, K., Yanagihara, N., & Saiki, T. (1994). Prospective tympanometry in one and a half year old children. In G. Mogi, I. Honjo, & T. Ishi (Eds.), *Recent advances in otitis media* (pp. 171–174). Amsterdam: Kugler.

Lous, J., & Fiellau-Nikolajsen, M. (1981). Epidemiology of middle ear effusion and tubal dysfunction: A one year prospective study comprising monthly tympanometry in 387 non-selected seven year old children. *International Journal of Pediatric Otorhinolaryngology, 3,* 303–317.

Lubitz, J. (1981, Spring). Different data systems, different conclusions? Comparing hospital use data for the aged from four data systems. *Health Care Finance Review,* pp. 41–56.

Maw, A.R., & Bawden, R. (1993). Spontaneous resolution of severe chronic glue ear in children and the effect of adenoidectomy, tonsillectomy and ventilation tubes (grommets). *British Medical Journal, 306,* 756–760.

Maw, A.R., & Bawden, R. (1994). Does adenoidectomy have an adjuvant effect on ventilation tube insertion and thus reduce the need for re-treatment? *Clinical Otolaryngology and Allied Sciences, 19,* 340–343.

McCafferty, G.J., Lewis, A.N., Coman, W.B., & Mills, C. (1985). A nine year study of ear disease in Australian aboriginal children. *Journal of Laryngology and Otology, 99,* 117–125.

Ministry of Health, New Zealand. (1989–1992). *Hospital and selected morbidity data.* Wellington, New Zealand: Author.

Ministry of Health, New Zealand. (1994). *Management of waiting times for specialist assessment and treatment for children with persistent OME: A consensus report to the Ministry of Health and Regional Health Authorities.* Wellington, New Zealand: Author.

Ministry of Health, New Zealand. (1995). *Hospital and selected morbidity data.* Wellington.

Netherlands SIG Health Care Information (1984–1993).

Nicholl, J.P., Beeby, N.R., & Williams, B.T. (1989). Role of the private sector in elective surgery in England and Wales 1986. *British Medical Journal, 298,* 243–247.

Pedersen, C.B., & Zachau-Christiansen, B. (1986). Otitis media in Greenland children: Acute, chronic and secretory otitis media in 3 to 8 year olds. *Journal of Otolaryngology, 15,* 332–335.

Rosenfeld, R.M., & Post, J.C. (1992). Meta-analysis of antibiotics for the treatment of otitis media with effusion. *Otolaryngology Head and Neck Surgery, 106,* 378–386.

Rutkow, I.M. (1986). Ear, nose and throat operations in the United States, 1979–1984. *Archives of Otolaryngology—Head and Neck Surgery, 112,* 873–876.

Stool, S.E., Berg, A.O., Berman, S., Carney, C.J., Cooley, J.R., Culpepper, L., Eavey, R.D., Feagans, L.V., Finitzo, T., Friedman, E.M., Goertz, J.A., Goldstein, A.J., Grundfast, K.M., Long, D.G., Macconi, L.L., Melton, L., Roberts, J.E., Sherrod, J.L., & Sisk, J.E. (1994). *Otitis media with effusion in young children: Clinical practice guideline No. 12* (AHCPR Publication No. 94-0622). Rockville, MD: Agency for Health Care Policy and Research.

Suárez Nieto, C., Malluguiza Calvo, J.R., & Barthe García, P. (1983). Aetiological factors in chronic secretory otitis media in relation to age. *Clinical Otolaryngology, 8,* 171–174.

Takasaka, T. (1990). Epidemiology of otitis media with effusion in Japan. *Annals of Otology, Rhinology, and Laryngology, Supplement, 149,* 13–16.

Todd, N.W.J., & Bowman, C.A. (1985). Otitis media at Canyon Day, Arizona: A 16 year follow-up in Apache Indians. *Archives of Otolaryngology, 111,* 606–608.

Tos, M., Stangerup, S., Hivid, G., & Andreassen, U.K. (1988). Epidemiology and natural history in secretory otitis. In D.J. Lim, C.D. Bluestone, J.O. Klein, & J.D. Nelson (Eds.), *Recent advances in otitis media with effusion* (pp. 29–34). Philadelphia: B.C. Decker.

van Cauwenberge, P.B., & Kluyskens, P.M. (1984). Some predisposing factors in otitis media with effusion. In C.D. Bluestone, J.O. Klein, & J.D. Nelson (Eds.), *Recent advances in otitis media with effusion* (pp. 28–32). Philadelphia: B.C. Decker.

Vital and Health Statistics, detailed diagnoses and procedures, National Hospital Discharge Survey 1992. (1994, August). *Series 13: Data from the National Health Survey, 118.* (DHSS Publ. No. PHS94-1779.)

Williamson, I.G., Dunleavy, J., Bain, J., & Robinson, D. (1994). The natural history of otitis media with effusion—a 3 year study of the incidence and prevalence of abnormal tympanograms in four South West Hampshire infant and first schools. *Journal of Laryngology and Otology, 108,* 930–934.

Yamaguchi, T., Nakashima, S., & Kumagami, H. (1994). Tympanometric screening for otitis media with effusion in pre-school children: Clinical study on isolated island. In G. Mogi, I. Honjo, & T. Ishi (Eds.), *Recent advances in otitis media* (pp. 157–162). Amsterdam: Kugler.

Zielhuis, G.A., Rach, G.H., & van den Broek, P. (1990). The occurrence of otitis media with effusion in Dutch pre-school children. *Clinical Otolaryngology and Allied Sciences, 15,* 147–153.

12

Developmental Outcomes in Relation to Early-Life Otitis Media

Present and Future Directions in Research

Jack L. Paradise

The question of whether persistent otitis media (OM) early in life results in lasting developmental impairments remains unresolved and a matter of controversy. This chapter discusses the background of the question, its component elements, approaches to its resolution, and the integrally related issue of tympanostomy tube placement for persistent otitis media with effusion (OME) in infants and young children.

BACKGROUND

Otitis Media and
Developmental Outcomes: Reported Relationships
Otitis media, whether acute (AOM) or secretory (OME), is accompanied by a variable degree of conductive hearing loss, ranging from negligible

This chapter was supported in part by Grant HD26026 from the National Institute of Child Health and Human Development.

The author is grateful to his colleagues, Thomas F. Campbell, Ph.D., Christine A. Dollaghan, Ph.D., Heidi M. Feldman, M.D.,Ph.D., Janine E. Janosky, Ph.D., and Diane L. Sabo, Ph.D., for their helpful suggestions.

to as much as 50 dB hearing level (HL). Most affected ears show losses in the range of 21–30 dB HL (Fria, Cantekin, & Eichler, 1985). This episodic and variable hearing impairment, occurring during supposedly "critical" or "sensitive" developmental periods limited to the first few years of life, has been held responsible by a number of authors for various types of developmental impairments found in later childhood, after both OM and hearing loss presumably have been resolved.

As discussed in earlier chapters, impairments of development have been reported in four separate domains: speech, language, cognition, and psychosocial development. These four domains encompass a variety of key developmental tasks. Most notably, the young child must be able to listen, learn, understand, think, speak, and get along with others, and the school-age child must be able to listen in noisy environments, pay attention, concentrate, integrate information, read, write, and cope with various stresses imposed by the school setting, not the least of which is the necessity to interrelate with a host of unfamiliar children and adults.

Concerning each of these developmental tasks, one or another study has found children's performance to be related inversely to their earlier OM experience—that is, the more OM they had, the less favorable their performance. Accordingly, if these study findings are valid, they would indicate that infants and young children who develop persistent OME are at risk of growing up less bright, less articulate, less accomplished, less attentive, less capable, and less well adjusted than they otherwise would have been. However, as discussed later, the studies reporting these findings have all had important limitations, and certain other studies—albeit also characterized by limitations—have failed to show such relationships.

Official Pronouncements,
Expert Recommendations, and Current Practices
Despite uncertainty about whether persistent early-life OME actually causes long-term developmental impairments, various authorities have called for mass screening for asymptomatic middle ear effusion (MEE) in young children, on the basis that "fluctuating hearing loss" may result in "linguistic, intellectual, social, and educational developmental lags" (American Speech-Language-Hearing Association, 1979, p. 283). By 1985, mass screening programs of one kind or another were in effect in at least 24 of the 50 states in the United States (Bluestone, Fria, & Arjona, 1986). In 1995, a position statement issued by representatives of the American Academy of Pediatrics, the American Academy of Audiology, the American Academy of Otolaryngology, the American Speech–Language–Hearing Association (ASHA), and the Directors of Speech and Hearing Programs in State Health and Welfare Agencies

"recognizes the adverse effects of fluctuating conductive hearing loss from persistent or recurrent otitis media with effusion (OME) and recommends monitoring infants with OME for hearing loss" (Joint Committee on Infant Hearing, 1995, p. 152). Also, the publication *Middle Ear Fluid in Young Children: Parent Guide* published by the U.S. Agency for Health Care Policy and Research (AHCPR) for general distribution, states, "Experts are not sure if hearing loss from middle ear fluid can cause delays in learning to talk, and sometimes later on, problems with school work. They do not know for sure what the long-term effects of middle ear fluid are" (AHCPR, 1994, p. 3).

More materially, concerns about presumed developmental effects of OME have been advanced (Daly et al., 1988; Gates, Avery, Prihoda, & Cooper, 1987; Teele, Klein, Rosner, & the Greater Boston Otitis Media Study Group, 1984) as providing potential or definite justification for surgical interventions, the most common of which, by far, is tympanostomy tube placement. These publications and programs, together with extensive treatment of the issue over the years in the lay press, have contributed to a now well-established practice of performing tympanostomy tube placement in infants and young children with persistent OME as a measure specifically to reduce the risk of developmental impairment. Over the years, estimates of the annual number of tympanostomy tube placement operations in the United States have ranged from 1 million (Paradise, 1977) to 400,000 (Gates, 1983). A systematic national survey in 1988 found that approximately 600,000 such operations had been performed during the preceding year in children under 18 years of age, and approximately 250,000 in children under 3 years of age (Moss, Hamburger, Moore, Jeng, & Howie, 1991).

Implications of Supposed Relationships
Definitive determination of whether these supposed relationships between early-life OME and later developmental outcome indeed exist would have not only major developmental implications but also major quality-of-life and health care implications. The developmental implications, of course, concern the nature of important psycholinguistic, cognitive, and behavioral processes and mechanisms, as discussed extensively in earlier chapters. The quality-of-life implications concern the risk for very large numbers of individuals—because of the prevalence of early-life OME—of long-term adverse effects on psychological well-being, performance, interpersonal relationships, and academic, social, and economic achievement. The health care implications stem mainly from two facts: that OME in infants and young children is usually asymptomatic and often difficult to diagnose and that the only treatment methods known to have more than short-term efficacy are surgical (i.e.,

tympanostomy tube placement, adenoidectomy, or both) (Gates et al., 1987; Paradise, 1982; Paradise et al., 1990).

Under these circumstances, if the relief of persistent OME in infants and young children by early tympanostomy tube placement were shown to be beneficial developmentally, it would follow that efforts by physicians to detect OME in infants and young children should be intensified by means of more frequent and more careful otoscopic examination, that mass screening programs for OME using tympanometry should be instituted widely, and that the numbers of children subjected to tympanostomy tube placement, adenoidectomy, or both should increase.

The health care statistics are already formidable. In the United States, about 20 million nonhospital office visits to physicians per year are made by children for OM (Stool et al., 1994), of which about 10 million are made by children less than 3 years of age. As noted previously, children in this age group receive an estimated 250,000 tympanostomy tube placement operations per year—at a cost of about $0.625 billion. Increases in these health care efforts and expenditures would further strain the health care system and the economy, but the increases would presumably be justified by the improvements in children's development that would be expected to result, with accompanying beneficial impact on their educational achievement, social and behavioral competence, quality of life, and social and economic status.

Conversely, if OME at commonly encountered levels of frequency and duration were shown *not* to be a developmental risk factor and if early tympanostomy tube placement in children with persistent OME were found *not* to be beneficial developmentally, surveillance for OME in otherwise well children would undoubtedly decrease, monitoring of children after episodes of AOM would undoubtedly be relaxed, and the numbers of children undergoing tympanostomy tube placement, adenoidectomy, or both probably would substantially decrease, because many tube operations, particularly in asymptomatic children, are being performed primarily because of concern about developmental outcomes. Under such circumstances, current health care efforts and expenditures could be reduced substantially without risk to children's development or to their later psychological, emotional, social, or economic well-being.

The Critical Period Hypothesis and Children's Development

Controversy exists concerning the relative fragility or resilience of early speech, language, and cognitive development to disruptions of various kinds (Goldin-Meadow, 1982). Language development, in particular, has been scrutinized in light of the hypothesis that there exists a "critical period" early in life during which language learning is particularly rapid and particularly vulnerable to disruption (Locke, 1994: Mayberry, 1994). Evidence supporting the critical period hypothesis remains weak, but, indisputably, many rapid and crucial linguistic developments take place during the first 3 years of life (Best, 1994; Eimas & Clarkson, 1986; Strange, 1986), and the evidently cumulative nature of such developments give credence to concerns about the potential impact of even short-term disruptions of speech and language development. Whether a critical period exists regarding cognitive and psychosocial development seems even more uncertain, because both cognitive and psychosocial development clearly evolve throughout the childhood years. Studies aimed at determining whether critical periods exist are necessarily indirect and fraught with conceptual and methodologic hazards. For example, if persistent or recurrent early-life OM is eventually shown to result in developmental impairments, an alternative mechanism by which impairments develop might involve illness chronicity and the attendant discomfort and disruption of normal activities (Jenkins, 1986).

Previous Studies of Relationships
The first study suggesting an association between early-life OM and later life developmental impairment was reported in 1969 (Holm & Kunze, 1969). A number of studies followed, varying widely in design, methods, and quality and in the specific developmental domains—speech, language, cognitive, and/or psychosocial—being tested. The findings were mixed. Some of the studies found associations between early OM and later developmental impairments of one type or another (Bennett, Ruuska, & Sherman, 1980; Brandes & Ehinger, 1981; Brookhouser & Goldgar, 1987; Feagans, Sanyal, Henderson, Collier, & Applebaum, 1987; Forgays, Hasazi, & Wasserman, 1992; Friel-Patti & Finitzo, 1990; Friel-Patti, Finitzo-Hieber, Conti, & Brown, 1982; Gottlieb, Zinkus, & Thompson, 1979; Gravel & Wallace, 1992, 1995; Hagerman & Falkenstein, 1987; Hersher, 1978; Howie, 1977; Howie, Jensen, Fleming, Peeler, & Meigs, 1979; Hubbard, Paradise, McWilliams, Elster, & Taylor, 1985; Hutton, 1983; Jerger, Jerger, Alford, & Abrams, 1983; Kessler & Randolph, 1979; Masters & Marsh, 1978; Menyuk, 1986; Needleman, 1977; Peters, Grievink, van Bon, & Schilder, 1994; Rach, Zielhuis, & van den Broek, 1988; Roberts, Burchinal, Koch, Footo, & Henderson, 1988; Roberts et al., 1989; Sak & Ruben, 1981; Silva, Chambers, & Stewart, 1986; Silva, Kirkland, Simpson, Stewart, & Williams, 1982; Teele et al., 1984, 1990; Thielke & Schriberg, 1990; van Cauwenberge, van Cauwenberge, & Kluyskens, 1985; Zinkus & Gottlieb, 1980; Zinkus, Gottlieb, & Schapiro, 1978). Other studies did not find such associations (Allen & Robinson, 1984;

Arcia & Roberts, 1993; Bishop & Edmondson, 1986; Fischler, Todd, & Feldman, 1985; Grievink, Peters, van Bon, & Schilder, 1993; Hoffman-Lawless, Keith, & Cotton, 1981; Lous, 1990, 1993; Lous & Fiellau-Nikolajsen, 1984; Lous, Fiellau-Nikolajsen, & Jeppesen, 1988; Roberts, Burchinal, Davis, Collier, & Henderson, 1991; Roberts et al., 1986; Schilder et al., 1993; Wright et al., 1988). One of the studies found an association between early OM and language delay, but not between early hearing impairment and language delay (Friel-Patti et al., 1982). Statistically significant associations in particular developmental domains were found in some studies but not in others. In short, the results of studies of relationships between early-life OM and later life developmental deficits have been confusingly contradictory.

Limitations of Studies   Many of the previously cited studies have been subjected to critical review (Feldman & Gelman, 1986; Paradise, 1980, 1981; Paradise & Rogers, 1986; Rapin, 1979; Ventry, 1980). Most of the studies employed retrospective, case–control designs and suffered from two principal limitations largely inherent in such designs: 1) inadequate ascertainment of the presence of OM early in life in cases and of its absence in controls (information having been based only on parental recall or on medical records), coupled with little or no information about the presence or absence of hearing loss; and 2) uncertainty that cases and controls were adequately matched to minimize the impact of potentially confounding variables. Other limitations common among these studies—as well as among the relatively few prospective, cohort studies—included

- Small sample size
- Nonrepresentativeness of subjects (e.g., subjects were low-birth-weight or high-risk graduates of neonatal intensive care units, or both, had learning disabilities, or were from disadvantaged backgrounds or ethnic groups or both)
- Selection bias
- Exclusive reliance on tympanometry for diagnosing OM
- Failure to differentiate unilateral from bilateral OM
- Presence of mild hearing loss or tympanometric abnormalities—or lack of information concerning these variables—at the time of developmental testing
- Questionable age appropriateness, validity, reliability, and comprehensiveness of developmental tests
- Inadequate blinding of examiners
- Selective presentation or emphasis of positive findings

These various limitations in both the case–control and cohort studies have contributed to uncertainty as to whether associations actually exist between early-life OM occurring at common levels of frequency and duration and later life development impairments.

Association versus Causality   Each of the previously cited studies was a study of *association*—that is, of whether developmental impairments were *associated with* excessive degrees of OM in earlier childhood. However, even if the positive studies had not had the limitations cited and an association between early OM and later developmental impairments had indeed been established, the question of *causality* would remain because it is possible, if not likely, that various factors—genetic, constitutional, perinatal, or environmental—may predispose children *both* to early-life OM *and* to later life developmental impairments. Under such circumstances, early OM would be *associated* with the impairments, but not *causally,* and might be considered a marker or predictor rather than a cause. If early OM is found actually to be associated with developmental impairments, demonstration of causality is crucial for justifying any type of treatment of OM (e.g., tympanostomy tube placement) as an appropriate means of preventing or lessening future impairments. For this purpose, multivariate adjustment procedures are not sufficient (Feinstein, 1977; Fletcher, Fletcher, & Wagner, 1988). Only if groups with, respectively, more and less early-life OM had had equivalent development potential from the outset could differences between them in later developmental outcomes be reasonably ascribed to the difference between them in the amounts of OM they had experienced (Feinstein, 1977, pp. 71–88). Yet, inherently, all of the previously cited associational studies lacked evidence of equivalence at baseline regarding developmental potential between the "more otitis" and "less otitis" groups.

Conditionality, Reversibility, and Preventability   If a causal association between early OM and later developmental impairment were to be established, it would be important to determine whether adverse effects of OM were 1) linear or threshold, 2) permanent or reversible, and 3) preventable or not preventable by early intervention that relieved MEE and restored hearing to normal. A few studies of children with developmental impairments and also histories of long-standing OM suggest that, once OM has subsided and normal or near-normal hearing has been recovered, the originally noted impairments may become less severe or no longer evident (Brookhouser & Goldgar, 1987; Dalzell & Owrid, 1976; Needleman, 1977; Schilder et al., 1993).

Recognized Importance of the Question
National symposia and panels convened in the United States since the 1970s and prompted wholly or in part by concern about the question of the relation of early-life OM to later life developmental impairment have

included a symposium on screening for OM held in 1977 with Public Health Service support (Harford, Bess, Bluestone, & Klein, 1978); a workshop convened by the Communicative Disorders Program of the National Institute of Neurological Diseases, Communicative Disorders and Stroke in 1978 (Hanson & Ulvestad, 1979); subsequent workshops on effects of OM in 1982 (Bluestone, Klein, & Paradise, 1983) and on screening for OM in 1985 (Bluestone et al., 1986); a conference convened by the National Institute of Child Health and Human Development (NICHD) in 1985 (Kavanagh, 1986); and a panel assembled by the AHCPR that in 1993–1994 developed a guideline for the management of OME in young children (Stool et al., 1994).

NECESSARY ELEMENTS FOR A DEFINITIVE STUDY

Specific Questions to Be Answered

To meet the needs of professionals in the various concerned disciplines who are involved, in one way or another, in child health care management or programmatic decisions, or both, a definitive study should answer four main questions:

1. Are there, in fact, associations between OME occurring at common levels of frequency and duration during the first few years of life and lasting impairments of speech, language, cognitive, or psychosocial development?
2. If such associations exist, are they causal in nature, or are they attributable instead to common underlying factors?
3. If persistent OME *causes* developmental impairments of one kind or another, what is the subsequent course of the impairments? Are they transient or fixed, reversible or irreversible?
4. In infants and young children with persistent OME, does prompt tube placement result in improved developmental outcomes?

Appropriate Research Design

To satisfactorily address all of these questions while avoiding the design problems discussed previously, a study incorporating the following elements would appear appropriate:

- A large and, if possible, sociodemographically diverse population of typical children is enrolled in early infancy and monitored prospectively with frequent, valid observations of middle ear status in order to document the presence or absence, extent (unilateral or bilateral), and duration of episodes of MEE, comprising both AOM and OME.
- In subjects developing persistent OME, hearing acuity is monitored at reasonably frequent intervals.

- Subjects who sooner or later during the first 3 years of life develop MEE that persists for extended periods of specified duration are designated "experimental."
- Experimental subjects are assigned randomly to one of two groups: those who receive tympanostomy tube placement promptly (the "early" group), and those who receive tube placement only after a specified period (e.g., 6–9 months—provided that MEE is still present at the termination of that period (the "late" group). Because the early and late groups are formed as a consequence of random assignment from the pool of experimental subjects, they may be assumed to be, at baseline, at equally high overall risk for OM and also prognostically equivalent to each other in regard to subsequent speech, language, cognitive, and psychosocial development. Subjects in the early group will, following tube placement, have immediate restoration of hearing to normal and predictably less OM so long as tubes remain functional, whereas some proportion, at least, of subjects in the late group will have continuing MEE and varying degrees of conductive hearing loss.
- Except for the timing of tube placement for persistent MEE, all aspects of the overall management of OM are standardized for all subjects according to a uniform protocol.
- A third, comparison group is selected, consisting of a sample of subjects who have failed, by age 3 years, to develop enough MEE to meet criteria as experimental subjects. This sample is selected so as to constitute a spectrum ranging from those who had developed little or no MEE to those who fell just short of meeting experimental criteria.
- At age 3 years, all subjects not in an experimental group or the comparison group are discharged, whereas experimental and comparison group subjects continue to receive close monitoring of middle ear status and hearing acuity.
- From age 3 years onward, all experimental and comparison group subjects who develop persistent MEE receive tube placement according to a uniform protocol.
- Beginning at age 3 years, and at intervals until at least age 6 years, all experimental and comparison group subjects receive a battery of standardized, age-appropriate, comprehensive tests of speech, language, cognitive, and psychosocial status, administered by qualified examiners blinded to the subjects' OM histories.
- Sample sizes are large enough to permit determination of the presence or absence of small differences in outcome between the two experimental groups, and within the comparison group, with reasonable statistical power.

Inferences and Conclusions in Relation to Findings

In the proposed study as outlined previously, depending on the developmental outcomes in the various groups of children, any of four alternative sets of inferences and conclusions might be justified:

1. If, in experimental subjects, those who received early tube placement *do* have better developmental outcomes than those who received late or no tube placement and if, within the comparison group, persistent early-life OME *is* found to be associated with poorer developmental outcomes later, one would infer that early prolonged OME, within the limits specified, *does* lead to later developmental impairment and that timely tube placement *is* efficacious in preventing or lessening the impairment.

2. If, in experimental subjects, those who received early tube placement *do* have better developmental outcomes than those who received late or no tube placement, but if, within the comparison group, persistent early-life OME is found *not* to be associated with poorer developmental outcomes later, one would infer that modest degrees of OME in most children are *not* discernible risk factors for development, but that extreme degress of OME *do* have adverse developmental effects that can be mitigated by early tube placement.

3. If, in experimental subjects, those who received early tube placement *do not* have better developmental outcomes than those who received late or no tube placement and if, within the comparison group, early-life OME is found *not* to be associated with poorer developmental outcomes later, one would infer that early, prolonged OME, within the limits specified, *neither causes nor is associated with* later developmental impairment. One would conclude that early tube placement for the purpose of preventing or lessening later developmental impairment would *not* be warranted.

4. If, in experimental subjects, those who received early tube placement *do not* have better developmental outcomes than those who received late or no tube placement, but if, within the comparison group, persistent early-life OME *is* found to be associated with poorer developmental outcomes later, one would infer *either* that common underlying factors had predisposed both to early OME and to later developmental impairment *or* that the benefits of early tube placement were offset by the operation's side effects, complications, or sequelae. In either case, one would again conclude that early tube placement in order to lessen later developmental impairment would *not* be warranted.

Pittsburgh-Area Child
Development/Otitis Media Study

In June 1991, with support mainly from the NICHD and also from the AHCPR, we began a study at Children's Hospital of Pittsburgh that incorporates each of the elements just outlined. Over a period of 4½ years, some 6,300 healthy infants less than 2 months of age and representing a broad sociodemographic spectrum have been enrolled at two hospitals and six private pediatric group practices in the greater Pittsburgh area.

Middle ear status in enrolled subjects is monitored monthly by study clinicians, whose otoscopic diagnostic reliability also is monitored regularly. Subjects who develop AOM or persistent OME receive antimicrobial treatment. Audiometry is scheduled monthly in subjects who have had MEE for as long as 8 weeks. Stringent criteria regarding persistence and apparent quantity of MEE are used in determining eligibility for randomization to early or late tube placement.

In all subjects, language and behavioral development are assessed subjectively at ages 1 and 2 years via parent questionnaires. At ages 3, 4, and 6 years, randomized subjects, subjects whose parents declined randomization, and subjects selected for the comparison group receive formal developmental tests, administered by qualified examiners blinded to the subjects' OM histories. To the extent practicable, all children are tested at times when their hearing is normal. Outcomes are measured in five developmental domains: lexicon, speech production, language processing, cognition, and psychosocial function. The study's sample size estimate of 396 randomized subjects—198 in each treatment group—was based on an assumption that a between-group difference as large as 0.33 standard deviation on any developmental outcome measure may be clinically important. To allow for estimated attrition, the goal of the study is to randomize a total of 513 subjects. At present writing (August 1996), 490 children have met randomization criteria and 378 of these (77.1%) have been assigned randomly to the early or late treatment group. Follow-up in the study is projected to end in late 2001, when the last enrolled subject will reach 6 years of age.

RELATED RESEARCH NEEDS

Irrespective of whether persistent OME early in life has long-term developmental effects, better understanding is needed of possible immediate or short-term developmental effects.

Fluctuating Hearing Loss and Impact on Speech and Language

Hearing loss associated with OME is known to be variable (Fria et al., 1985), and it also has often been described as "fluctuating" (ASHA,

1979; Joint Committee on Infant Hearing, 1995). However, the extent to which hearing loss actually fluctuates in the course of individual episodes of OME in individual children remains unclear. To resolve the issue would require serial—perhaps even daily or more often—audiometric testing of children of varying ages with documented OME, a task undoubtedly most feasible in group child care or residential settings. If substantial fluctuation were found, a related question requiring more intensive investigation would concern the impact, if any, of the fluctuation itself on speech and language comprehension and production.

Effects of OME and of Related Hearing Loss on Speech Sound Perception, Learning Tasks, and Attention

Information is needed in infants and young children, when they have OME and when they do not, on 1) relationships between hearing sensitivity, perception of individual speech sounds or groups of sounds, and production of those sounds; 2) relationships between hearing sensitivity and performance on language-learning tasks, including those that require the child to discern subtle differences between similar-sounding words; and 3) relationships between hearing sensitivity and measures of attention. Satisfactory investigation of these relationships would require intensive study longitudinally of individual children who, at varying ages, begin to develop recurrent episodes of OME; for such investigations, relatively small numbers of children would likely suffice.

Early Effects of Tympanostomy Tube Placement on Language and Behavior

After tube placement in young children with persistent OME, parents commonly report prompt surges in language development, sharp improvements in functional status (e.g., lessened irritability, improved behavior, and improved sleep patterns), or both. To the extent possible, it is important to determine whether these outcomes result from relief of OME itself, from resolution of previously unrecognized middle ear infection (as distinct from presumably sterile middle ear effusion), from improvement in auditory function, from the powerful placebo effect of surgery (Brody, 1982), or from combinations of these factors. To accomplish this in a study of any design will require, in addition to careful parental observation and documentation, intensive professional evaluation over periods of weeks or, at most, months, of young children who receive tube placement.

Either of two design strategies might be appropriate. In one, in a relatively small-scale randomized clinical trial, children would be assigned to receive one of three treatment plans: 1) tube placement; 2) a remedial program—because sham surgery (i.e., taking the child to the operating room and going through the appropriate motions but not actually performing surgery) is not ethically acceptable—aimed at improving both language and behavior, and including, where appropriate, amplification to improve hearing levels; or 3) tube placement in addition to the remedial program. Such a trial would necessarily incorporate 1) stringent eligibility criteria regarding persistent MEE; 2) appropriate stratification by, or adjustment for, age gruop, MEE duration, and hearing sensitivity; and 3) careful clinical and microbiological observations at surgery.

An alternative strategy would look to a single-subject study design (Janosky, Al-Shboul, & Pellitieri, 1995; Weiner & Eisen, 1985) in which each child serves as his or her own control. In studies with this design, a small number of children who receive tube placement under somewhat variable circumstances and after variable MEE durations would be studied intensively for short periods both before and after the operation.

Prevention of Recurrent Acute Otitis Media and Management of Otitis Media with Effusion

Concern about possible developmental consequences of persistent OME would abate dramatically if consistently effective, safe, and relatively inexpensive means were at hand to 1) prevent recurrent AOM, episodes of which are commonly followed by persistent OME; and 2) shorten the course of OME once it develops, whether as the aftermath of AOM or de novo (Paradise el al., 1993). The management approaches currently available have been discussed in detail in Chapter 9 and are summarized here only briefly, as background for the need for further research.

Prevention of Recurrent Acute Otitis Media Antimicrobial *prophylaxis* has long been used with some success to protect against AOM recurrences (Paradise, 1989). Currently, however, because of the probable contribution of antimicrobial usage to the development of antibiotic resistance by strains of *Streptococcus pneumoniae* (Reichler et al., 1992), subjecting children routinely to sustained antimicrobial prophylaxis seems dubious, its risks potentially outweighing its benefits (Paradise, 1995). This seems particularly so for children in group child care, who in any case are at increased risk of colonization with multiply resistant *S. pneumoniae* (Breiman, Butler, Tenover, Elliott, & Facklam, 1994; Reichler et al., 1992). *Tympanostomy tube placement* also is reasonably effective in preventing AOM recurrences in the short term (Casselbrant et al., 1992), but also is associated with both short- and long-term risks (Lildholdt, 1983; Paradise, 1977; Tos & Stangerup, 1989). For children who have undergone tube placement and who, after extrusion of the tubes, continue to develop OM, *adenoidectomy* is efficacious to a limited extent in reducing the risk of subsequent recurrences

(Paradise et al., 1990). Finally, *influenza vaccine* may provide limited protection against AOM recurrences (Heikkinen et al., 1991), and *polyvalent pneumococcal vaccine,* in children over age 2 years, may protect against pneumococcal episodes specifically, but without reducing recurrences overall (Bluestone & Klein, 1990).

In summary, current methods of preventing recurrent AOM fall far short of being entirely satisfactory. Our current best hope appears to lie in the development of conjugate pneumococcal vaccines, which may protect infants and children less than 2 years of age, as well as older children, against pneumococcal AOM—generally the most severe form of the disease. However, the effectiveness of such vaccines remains to be established, and they cannot, of course, be expected to protect against otitis caused by bacteria other than the pneumococcus or by viruses. Broader range protection, through vaccines, against the manifold viral respiratory infections that often serve as initiating factors in AOM is not on the near horizon. Thus, although we may be able to limit to some extent the development of recurrent AOM by encouraging breast feeding, by restricting group child care to the extent feasible, and by judicious use of the measures described here, it seems inevitable that, for at least the foreseeable future, recurrent AOM will continue to affect large numbers of infants and young children.

Management of Otitis Media with Effusion In children with OME, antimicrobial treatment has afforded improved rates of near-term resolution of effusion (Mandel, Rockette, Bluestone, Paradise, & Nozza, 1987; Rosenfeld & Post, 1992), but again, routinely invoking such treatment is currently questionable because of its potential contribution to increases in the prevalence of infection caused by multiply resistant strains of *S. pneumoniae.* Nonetheless, antimicrobial treatment should virtually always be undertaken before deciding to resort to tympanostomy tube placement. Tube placement affords substantial sustained efficacy (Mandel, Rockette, Bluestone, Paradise, & Nozza, 1992), but the operation poses the risks cited in the previous section. Studies to date of the efficacy of corticosteroid treatment have given mixed results (Rosenfeld, Mandel, & Bluestone, 1991), and definitive study is urgently needed, particularly because receipt of a recently available, effective varicella vaccine by many children who have not had natural varicella has substantially allayed fears about the use of systemic corticosteroids in such children. No other promising modalities appear currently to be available for treating OME in infants and young children, but some comfort may be taken from the fact that the prevalence of OME falls off progressively as children grow older. Explaining why and how that happens will add to the challenges of future researchers.

REFERENCES

Agency for Health Care Policy and Research, U.S. Department of Health and Human Services. (1994). *Middle ear fluid in children: Parent guide* (AHCPR Publication No. 94-0624). Rockville, MD: Author.

Allen, D.V., & Robinson, D.O. (1984). Middle ear status and language development in preschool children. *Asha, 26,* 33–37.

American Speech-Language-Hearing Association. (1979). Guidelines for acoustic immitance screening of middle-ear function. *Asha, 21,* 283–288.

Arcia, E., & Roberts, J.E. (1993). Otitis media in early childhood and its association with sustained attention in structured situations. *Developmental and Behavioral Pediatrics, 14,* 181–183.

Bennett, F.C., Ruuska, S.H., & Sherman, R. (1980). Middle ear function in learning-disabled children. *Pediatrics, 66,* 254–260.

Best, C.T. (1994). The emergence of native-language phonological influences in infants: A perceptual assimilation model. In J.C. Goodman & H.C. Nusbaum, (Eds.), *The development of speech perception: The transition from speech sounds to spoken words* (pp. 167–224). Cambridge, MA: MIT Press.

Bishop, D.V.M., & Edmondson, A. (1986). Is otitis media a major cause of specific developmental language disorders? *British Journal of Disorders of Communication, 21,* 321–338.

Bluestone, C.D., Fria, T.J., Arjona, S.K. (Eds.). (1986). Controversies in screening for middle ear disease and hearing loss in children. *Pediatrics, 77,* 57–70.

Bluestone, C.D., & Klein, J.O. (1990). Otitis media, atelectasis, and eustachian tube dysfunction. In C.D. Bluestone & S.E. Stool (Eds.), *Pediatric otolaryngology* (2nd ed., pp. 320–486). Philadelphia: W.B. Saunders.

Bluestone, C.D., Klein, J.O., & Paradise, J.L. (Eds.). (1983). Workshop on effects of otitis media on the child. *Pediatrics, 71,* 639–652.

Brandes, P.J., & Ehinger, D.M. (1981). The effect of early middle ear pathology on auditory perception and academic achievement. *Journal of Speech and Hearing Disorders, 46,* 250–257.

Breiman, R.F., Butler, J.C., Tenover, F.C., Elliott, J.A., & Facklam, R.R. (1994). Emergence of drug-resistant pneumococcal infections in the United States. *Journal of the American Medical Association, 271,* 1831–1835.

Brody, H. (1982). The lie that heals: The ethics of giving placebos. *Annals of Internal Medicine, 97,* 112–118.

Brookhouser, P.E., & Goldgar, D.E. (1987). Medical profile of the language-delayed child: Otitis-prone versus otitis-free. *International Journal of Pediatric Otorhinolaryngology, 12,* 237–271.

Casselbrant, M.L., Kaleida, P.H., Rockette, H.E., Paradise, J.L., Bluestone, C.D., Kurs-Lasky, M., Nozza, R.J., & Wald, E.R. (1992). Efficacy of antimicrobial prophylaxis and of tympanostomy tube insertion for prevention of recurrent acute otitis media: Results of a randomized clinical trial. *Pediatric Infectious Disease Journal, 11,* 278–286.

Daly, K., Giebink, G.S., Le, C.T., Lindgren, B., Batalden, P.B., Anderson, R.S., & Russ, J.N. (1988). Determining risk for chronic otitis media with effusion. *Pediatric Infectious Disease Journal, 7,* 471–475.

Dalzell, J., & Owrid, H.L. (1976). Children with conductive deafness: A follow-up study. *British Journal of Audiology, 10,* 87–90.

Eimas, P.D., & Clarkson, R.L. (1986). Speech perception in children: Are there effects of otitis media? In J.F. Kavanagh (Ed.), *Otitis media and child development* (pp. 139–159). Parkton, MD: York Press.

Feagans, L., Sanyal, M., Henderson, F., Collier, A., & Applebaum, M. (1987). Relationship of middle ear disease in early childhood to later narrative and attention skills. *Journal of Pediatric Psychology, 12,* 581–594.

Feinstein, A.R. (1977). *Clinical biostatistics.* St Louis: C.V. Mosby.

Feldman, H., & Gelman, R. (1986). Otitis media and cognitive development: Theoretical perspectives. In J.F. Kavanagh (Ed.), *Otitis media and child development* (pp. 27–41). Parkton, MD: York Press.

Fischler, R.S., Todd, N.W., & Feldman, C.M. (1985). Otitis media and language performance in a cohort of Apache Indian children. *American Journal of Diseases of Children, 139,* 355–360.

Fletcher, R.H., Fletcher, S.W., & Wagner, E.H. (1988). *Clinical epidemiology: The essentials* (2nd ed., pp. 125–126). Baltimore: Williams & Wilkins.

Forgays, D.K., Hasazi, J.E., & Wasserman, R.C. (1992). Recurrent otitis media and parenting stress in mothers of two-year-old children. *Journal of Developmental and Behavioral Pediatrics, 13,* 321–325.

Fria, T.J., Cantekin, E.I., & Eichler, J.A. (1985). Hearing acuity of children with otitis media with effusion. *Archives of Otolaryngology—Head and Neck Surgery, 111,* 10–16.

Friel-Patti, S., & Finitzo, T. (1990). Language learning in a prospective study of otitis media with effusion in the first two years of life. *Journal of Speech and Hearing Research, 33,* 188–194.

Friel-Patti, S., Finitzo-Hieber, T., Conti, G., & Brown, K.C. (1982). Language delay in infants associated with middle ear disease and mild, fluctuating hearing impairment. *Pediatric Infectious Disease Journal, 1,* 104–109.

Gates, G.A. (1983). Socioeconomic impact of otitis media. *Pediatrics, 71,* 648–649.

Gates, G.A., Avery, C.A., Prihoda, T.J., & Cooper, J.C. Jr. (1987). Effectiveness of adenoidectomy and tympanostomy tubes in the treatment of chronic otitis media with effusion. *New England Journal of Medicine, 317,* 1444–1451.

Goldin-Meadow, S. (1982). The resilience of recursion: A study of a communication system developed without a conventional model. In E. Wanner & L. Gleitman (Eds.), *Language acquisition: The state of the art* (pp. 51–77). Cambridge, England: Cambridge University Press.

Gottlieb, M.I., Zinkus, P.W., & Thompson, A. (1979). Chronic middle-ear disease and auditory perceptual deficits: Is there a link? *Clinical Pediatrics, 18,* 725–732.

Gravel, J.S., & Wallace, I.F. (1992). Listening and language at 4 years of age: Effects of early otitis media. *Journal of Speech and Hearing Research, 35,* 588–595.

Gravel, J.S., & Wallace, I.F. (1995). Early otitis media, auditory abilities, and educational risk. *American Journal of Speech-Language Pathology, 4,* 89–94.

Grievink, E.H., Peters, S.A.F., van Bon, W.H.J., & Schilder, A.G.M. (1993). The effects of early bilateral otitis media with effusion on language ability: A prospective cohort study. *Journal of Speech and Hearing Research, 36,* 1004–1012.

Hagerman, R.J., & Falkenstein, A.R. (1987). An association between recurrent otitis media in infancy and later hyperactivity. *Clinical Pediatrics, 26,* 253–257.

Hanson, D.G., & Ulvestad, R.F. (1979). Otitis media and child development: Speech, language and education. *Annals of Otology, Rhinology, and Laryngology, 88(Supplement 60),* 1–111.

Harford, E.R., Bess, F.H., Bluestone, C.D., & Klein, J.O. (Eds.). (1978). *Impedance screening for middle ear disease in children*. New York: Grune & Stratton.

Heikkinen, T., Ruuskanen, O., Waris, M., Ziegler, T., Arola, M., & Halonen, P. (1991). Influenza vaccination in the prevention of acute otitis media in children. *American Journal of Diseases of Children, 145*, 445–448.

Hersher, L. (1978). Minimal brain dysfunction and otitis media. *Perceptual and Motor Skills, 47*, 723–726.

Hoffman-Lawless, K., Keith, R.W., & Cotton, R.T. (1981). Auditory processing abilities in children with previous middle ear effusion. *Annals of Otology, Rhinology, and Laryngology, 90*, 543–545.

Holm, V.A., & Kunze, L.H. (1969). Effect of chronic otitis media on language and speech development. *Pediatrics, 43*, 833–839.

Howie, V.M. (1977). Acute and recurrent otitis media. In B. Jaffe (Ed.), *Hearing loss in children* (pp. 421–429). Baltimore: University Park Press.

Howie, V.M., Jensen, N.H., Fleming, J.W., Peeler, M.B., & Meigs, S. (1979). The effect of early onset of otitis media on educational achievement. *International Journal of Pediatric Otorhinolaryngology, 1*, 151–155.

Hubbard, T.W., Paradise, J.L., McWilliams, B.J., Elster, B.A., & Taylor, F.H. (1985). Consequences of unremitting middle-ear disease in early life: Otologic, audiologic, and developmental findings in children with cleft palate. *New England Journal of Medicine, 312*, 1529–1534.

Hutton, J.B. (1983). Effect of middle ear pathology on selected psychoeducational measures following surgical treatment. *Perceptual and Motor Skills, 57*, 1095–1100.

Janosky, J.E., Al-Shboul, Q.M., & Pellitieri, T.R. (1995). Validation of the use of a nonparametric smoother for the examination of data from a single-subject design. *Behavior Modification, 19*, 307–324.

Jenkins, J.J. (1986). Cognitive development in children with recurrent otitis media: Where do we stand? In J.F. Kavanagh (Ed.), *Otitis media and child development* (pp. 211–221). Parkton, MD: York Press.

Jerger, S., Jerger, J., Alford, B.R., & Abrams, S. (1983). Development of speech intelligibility in children with recurrent otitis media. *Ear and Hearing, 4*, 138–145.

Joint Committee on Infant Hearing. (1995). Joint Committee on Infant Hearing 1994 position statement. *Pediatrics, 95*, 152–156.

Kavanagh, J.F. (Ed.). (1986). *Otitis media and child development*. Parkton, MD: York Press.

Kessler, M.E., & Randolph, K. (1979). The effect of early middle ear disease on the auditory abilities of third grade children. *Journal of the Academy of Rehabilitative Audiology, 12*, 6–20.

Lildholdt, T. (1983). Ventilation tubes in secretory otitis media: A randomized, controlled study of the course, the complications, and the sequelae of ventilation tubes. *Acta Oto-Laryngologica. Supplement, 398*, 5–28.

Locke, J.L., (1994). Gradual emergence of developmental language disorders. *Journal of Speech and Hearing Research, 37*, 608–616.

Lous, J. (1990). Secretory otitis media and phonology when starting school. *Scandinavian Audiology, 19*, 215–222.

Lous, J. (1993). Silent reading and secretory otitis media in school children. *International Journal of Pediatric Otorhinolaryngology, 25*, 25–38.

Lous, J., & Fiellau-Nikolajsen, M. (1984). A 5-year prospective case-control study of the influence of early otitis media with effusion on reading achievement. *International Journal of Pediatric Otorhinolaryngology, 8,* 19–30.

Lous, J., Fiellau-Nikolajsen, M., & Jeppesen, A.L. (1988). Secretory otitis media and language development: A six-year follow-up study with case-control. *International Journal of Pediatric Otorhinolaryngology, 15,* 185–203.

Mandel, E.M., Rockette, H.E., Bluestone, C.D., Paradise, J.L., & Nozza, R.J. (1987). Efficacy of amoxicillin with and without decongestant-antihistamine for otitis media with effusion in children: Results of a double blind, randomized trial. *New England Journal of Medicine, 316,* 432–437.

Mandel, E.M., Rockette, H.E., Bluestone, C.D., Paradise, J.L., & Nozza, R.J. (1992). Efficacy of myringotomy with and without tympanostomy tubes for chronic otitis media with effusion. *Pediatric Infectious Disease Journal, 11,* 270–277.

Masters, L., & Marsh, G.E. II. (1978). Middle ear pathology as a factor in learning disabilities. *Journal of Learning Disabilities, 11,* 54–57.

Mayberry, R.I. (1994). The importance of childhood to language acquisition: Evidence from American Sign Language. In J.C. Goodman & H.C. Nusbaum (Eds.), *The development of speech perception: The transition from speech sounds to spoken words* (pp. 57–90). Cambridge, MA: MIT Press.

Menyuk, P. (1986). Predicting speech and language problems with persistent otitis media. In J.F. Kavanagh (Ed.), *Otitis media and child development* (pp. 83–96). Parkton, MD: York Press.

Moss, A.J., Hamburger, S., Moore, R.M. Jr., Jeng, L.L., & Howie, L.J. (1991). *Use of selected medical device implants in the United States, 1988* (Advance Data No. 91) Rockville, MD: National Center for Health Statistics.

Needleman, H. (1977). Effects of hearing loss from early recurrent otitis media on speech and language development. In B. Jaffe (Ed.), *Hearing loss in children* (pp. 640–649). Baltimore: University Park Press.

Paradise, J.L. (1977). On tympanostomy tubes: Rationale, results, reservations, and recommendations. *Pediatrics, 60,* 86–90.

Paradise, J.L. (1980). Otitis media in infants and children. *Pediatrics, 65,* 917–943.

Paradise, J.L. (1981). Otitis media during early life: How hazardous to development? A critical review of the evidence. *Pediatrics, 68,* 869–873.

Paradise, J.L. (1982). Editorial retrospective: Tympanometry. *New England Journal of Medicine, 307,* 1074–1076.

Paradise, J.L. (1989). Antimicrobial drugs and surgical procedures in the prevention of otitis media. *Pediatric Infectious Disease Journal, 8* (Suppl.): S35–S37.

Paradise, J.L. (1995). Managing otitis media: A time for change. *Pediatrics, 96,* 712–715.

Paradise, J.L., Bernard, B.S., Colborn, D.K., Smith, C.G., Rockette, H.E., & the Pittsburgh-Area Child Development/Otitis Media Study Group. (1993). Otitis media with effusion (OME): Highly prevalent and often the forerunner of acute otitis media (AOM) during the first year of life [Abstract]. *Pediatric Research, 33,* 121A.

Paradise, J.L., Bluestone, C.D., Rogers, K.D., Tayor, F.H., Colborn, D.K., Bachman, R.Z., Bernard, B.S., & Schwarzbach, R.H. (1990). Efficacy of adenoidectomy for recurrent otitis media in children previously treated with tympanostomy-tube placement: Results of parallel randomized and nonrandomized trials. *Journal of the American Medical Association, 263,* 2066–2073.

Paradise, J.L., & Rogers, K.D. (1986). On otitis media, child development, and tympanostomy tubes: New answers or old questions? *Pediatrics, 77,* 88–92.

Peters, S.A.F., Grievink, E.H., van Bon, W.H.J., & Schilder, A.G.M. (1994). The effects of early bilateral otitis media with effusion on educational attainment: A prospective cohort study. *Journal of Learning Disabilities, 27,* 111–121.

Rach, G.H., Zielhuis, G.A., & van den Broek, P. (1988). The influence of chronic persistent otitis media with effusion on language development of 2- to 4-year-olds. *International Journal of Pediatric Otorhinolaryngology, 15,* 253–261.

Rapin, J. (1979). Conductive hearing loss effects on children's language and scholastic skills: A review of the literature. *Annals of Otology, Rhinology, and Laryngology. Supplement, 60,* 3–12.

Reichler, M.R., Allphin, A.A., Breiman, R.F., Schreiber, J.R., Arnold, J.E., McDougal, L.K., Facklam, R.R., Boxerbaum, B., May, D., Walton, R.O., & Jacobs, M.R. (1992). The spread of multiply resistant *Streptococcus pneumoniae* at a day care center in Ohio. *Journal of Infectious Diseases, 166,* 1346–1353.

Roberts, J.E., Burchinal, M.R., Collier, A.M., Ramey, C.T., Koch, M.A., & Henderson, F.W. (1989). Otitis media in early childhood and cognitive, academic, and classroom performance of the school-aged child. *Pediatrics, 83,* 477–485.

Roberts, J.E., Burchinal, M.R., Davis, B.P., Collier, A.M., & Henderson, F.W. (1991). Otitis media in early childhood and later language. *Journal of Speech and Hearing Research, 34,* 1158–1168.

Roberts, J.E., Burchinal, M.R., Koch, M.A., Footo, M.M., & Henderson, F.W. (1988). Otitis media in early childhood and its relationship to later phonological development. *Journal of Speech and Hearing Disorders, 53,* 424–432.

Roberts, J.E., Sanyal, M.A., Burchinal, M.R., Collier, A.M., Ramey, C.T., & Henderson, F.W. (1986). Otitis media in early childhood and its relationship to later verbal and academic performance. *Pediatrics, 78,* 423–430.

Rosenfeld, R.M., Mandel, E.M., & Bluestone, C.D. (1991). Systemic steroids for otitis media with effusion in children. *Archives of Otolaryngology—Head and Neck Surgery, 117,* 984–989.

Rosenfeld, R.M., & Post, J.C. (1992). Meta-analysis of antibiotics for the treatment of otitis media with effusion. *Otolaryngology—Head and Neck Surgery, 106,* 378–386.

Sak, R.J., & Ruben, R.J. (1981). Recurrent middle ear effusion in childhood: Implication of temporary auditory deprivation for language and learning. *Annals of Otology, Rhinology, and Laryngology, 90,* 546–551.

Schilder, A.G.M., van Manen, J.G., Zielhuis, G.A., Grievink, E.H., Peters, S.A.F., & van den Broek, P. (1993). Long-term effects of otitis media with effusion on language, reading and spelling. *Clinical Otolaryngology, 18,* 234–241.

Silva, P.A., Chambers, D., & Stewart, I. (1986). Some audiological, psychological, educational and behavioral characteristics of children with bilateral otitis media with effusion: A longitudinal study. *Journal of Learning Disabilities, 19,* 165–169.

Silva, P.A., Kirkland, C., Simpson, A., Stewart, I.A., & Williams, S.M. (1982). Some developmental and behavioral problems associated with bilateral otitis media with effusion. *Journal of Learning Disabilities, 15,* 417–421.

Stool, S.E., Berg, A.O., Berman, S., Carney, C.J., Cooley, J.R., Culpepper, L., Eavey, R.D., Feagans, L.V., Finitzo, T., Friedman, E.M., Goertz, J.A., Goldstein, A.J., Grundfast, K.M., Long, D.G., Macconi, L.L., Melton, L., Roberts, J.E., Sherrod, J.L., & Sisk, J.E. (1994). *Otitis media with effusion in young children. Clinical practice guideline No. 12* (AHCPR Publication No. 94-0622). Rockville, MD: Agency for Health Care Policy and Research.

Strange, W. (1986). Speech input and the development of speech perception. In J.F. Kavanagh (Ed.), *Otitis media and child development* (pp. 12–26). Parkton, MD: York Press.

Teele, D.W., Klein, J.O., Chase, C., Menyuk, P., Rosner, B.A., & the Greater Boston Otitis Media Study Group. (1990). Otitis media in infancy and intellectual ability, school achievement, speech, and language at age 7 years. *Journal of Infectious Diseases, 162,* 685–694.

Teele, D.W., Klein, J.O., Rosner, B.A., & the Greater Boston Otitis Media Study Group. (1984). Otitis media with effusion during the first three years of life and development of speech and language. *Pediatrics, 74,* 282–287.

Thielke, H.M., & Shriberg, L.D. (1990, January). Effects of recurrent otitis media on language, speech, and educational achievement in Menominee Indian children. *Journal of American Indian Education,* pp. 25–35.

Tos, M., & Stangerup, S.E. (1989). Hearing loss in tympanosclerosis caused by grommets. *Archives of Otolaryngology—Head and Neck Surgery, 115,* 931–935.

van Cauwenberge, P., van Cauwenberge, K., & Kluyskens, P. (1985). The influence of otitis media with effusion on speech and language development and psycho-intellectual behavior of the preschool child—results of a cross-sectional study in 1,512 children. *Auris-Nasus-Larynx, 12*(Suppl. I): S228–S230.

Ventry, I.M. (1980). Effects of conductive hearing loss: Fact or fiction. *Journal of Speech and Hearing Disorders, 45,* 143–156.

Weiner, I.S., & Eisen, R.G. (1985). Clinical research: The case study and single-subject designs. *Journal of Allied Health, 14,* 191–201.

Wright, P.F., Sell, S.H., McConnell, K.B., Sitton, A.B., Thompson, J., Vaughn, W.K., & Bess, F.H. (1988). Impact of recurrent otitis media on middle ear function, hearing, and language. *Journal of Pediatrics, 113,* 581–587.

Zinkus, P.W., & Gottlieb, M.I. (1980). Patterns of perceptual and academic deficits related to early chronic otitis media. *Pediatrics, 66,* 246–253.

Zinkus, P.W., Gottlieb, M.I., & Schapiro, M. (1978). Developmental and psychoeducational sequelae of chronic otitis media. *American Journal of Diseases of Children, 132,* 1100–1104.

Appendix

Managing Otitis Media
with Effusion in Young Children:
Clinical Practice Guideline

PURPOSE AND SCOPE

Otitis media (inflammation of the middle ear) is the most frequent primary diagnosis at visits to U.S. physician offices by children younger than 15 years. Otitis media particularly affects infants and preschoolers: Almost all children experience one or more episodes of otitis media before age 6.

The American Academy of Pediatrics, the American Academy of Family Physicians, and the American Academy of Otolaryngology—Head and Neck Surgery, with the review and approval of the Agency for Health Care Policy and Research of the U.S. Department of Health and Human Services, convened a panel of experts to develop a guideline on otitis media for providers and consumers of health care for young children. Providers include primary care and specialist physicians, professional nurses and nurse practitioners, physician assistants, audiologists, speech-language pathologists, and child development specialists. Because the term *otitis media* encompasses a range of diseases, from acute to chronic and with or without symptoms, the Otitis Media

From Stool, S.E., Berg, A.O., Berman, S., Carney, C.J., Cooley, J.R., Culpepper, L., Eavey, R.D., Feagans, L.V., Finitzo, T., Friedman, E.M., Goertz, J.A., Goldstein, A.J., Grundfast, K.M., Long, D.G., Macconi, L.L., Melton, L., Roberts, J.E., Sherrod, J.L., & Sisk, J.E. (1994). *Managing otitis media with effusion in young children: Quick reference guide for clinicians, No. 12* (AHCPR Publication No. 94-0623). Rockville, MD: Agency for Health Care Policy and Research.

Guideline Panel narrowed the topic. Two types of otitis media often encountered by clinicians were considered:

- **Acute otitis media**—fluid in the middle ear accompanied by signs or symptoms of ear infection (bulging eardrum usually accompanied by pain; or perforated eardrum, often with drainage of purulent material)
- **Otitis media with effusion**—fluid in the middle ear without signs or symptoms of ear infection

The *Clinical Practice Guideline, Otitis Media with Effusion in Young Children*, and this *Quick Reference Guide for Clinicians, Managing Otitis Media with Effusion in Young Children*, based on the *Guideline*, discuss only otitis media with effusion. Further, the *Guideline* and this *Quick Reference Guide* narrow their discussion of the identification and management of otitis media with effusion to a very specific "target patient":

- A child age 1 through 3 years
- With no craniofacial or neurologic abnormalities or sensory deficits
- Who is healthy except for otitis media with effusion

When the scientific evidence for management permitted, Guideline recommendations were broadened to include older children.

HIGHLIGHTS OF PATIENT MANAGEMENT

Congenital or early-onset hearing impairment is widely accepted as a risk factor for impaired speech and language development. In general, the earlier the hearing problem begins and the more severe it is, the worse its effects on speech and language development. Because otitis media with effusion is often associated with a mild to moderate hearing loss, most clinicians have been eager to treat the condition to restore hearing to normal and thus prevent any long-term problems.

Studies of the effects of otitis media with effusion on hearing have varied in design and have examined several aspects of hearing and communication skills. Because of these differences, the results cannot be combined to provide a clear picture of the relationship between otitis media with effusion and hearing. Also, it is uncertain whether changes in hearing due to middle ear fluid have any long-term effects on development. Evidence of dysfunctions mediated by otitis media with effusion that have persisted into later childhood, despite resolution of the middle ear fluid and a return to normal hearing, would provide a compelling argument for early, decisive intervention. There is, however, no consistent, reliable evidence that otitis media with effusion has such long-term effects on language or learning.

The following recommendations for managing otitis media with effusion are tempered by the failure to find rigorous, methodologically sound research to support the theory that untreated otitis media with effusion results in speech-language delays or deficits.

Recommendations and options were developed for the diagnosis and management of otitis media with effusion in otherwise healthy young children. The following steps parallel the management algorithm provided later (see Figure 1).

Diagnosis and Hearing Evaluation

1. Suspect otitis media with effusion in young children.

Most children have at least one episode of otitis media with effusion before entering school. Otitis media with effusion may be identified following an acute episode of otitis media, or it may be an incidental finding. Symptoms may include discomfort or behavior changes.

2. Use pneumatic otoscopy to assess middle ear status.

Pneumatic otoscopy is recommended for assessment of the middle ear because it combines visualization of the tympanic membrane (otoscopy) with a test of membrane mobility (pneumatic otoscopy). When pneumatic otoscopy is performed by an experienced examiner, the accuracy for diagnosis of otitis media with effusion may be between 70% and 79%.

3. Tympanometry may be performed to confirm suspected otitis media with effusion.

Tympanometry provides an indirect measure of tympanic membrane compliance and an estimate of middle ear air pressure. The positive predictive value of an abnormal (Type B, flat) tympanogram is between 49% and 99%; that is, as few as half of ears with abnormal tympanograms may have otitis media with effusion. The negative predictive value of this test is better—the majority of middle ears with normal tympanograms will in fact be normal. Because the strengths of tympanometry (it provides a quantitative measure of tympanic membrane mobility) and pneumatic otoscopy (many abnormalities of the eardrum and ear canal that can skew the results of tympanometry are visualized) offset the weaknesses of each, using the two tests together improves the accuracy of diagnosis.

- **Acoustic reflectometry** has not been studied well enough for a recommendation to be made for or against its use to diagnose otitis media with effusion.

- **Tuning fork tests:** No recommendation is made regarding the use of tuning fork tests to screen for or diagnose otitis media with effusion, except to note that they are inappropriate in the youngest children.

4. **A child who has had fluid in both middle ears for a total of 3 months should undergo hearing evaluation. Before 3 months of effusion, hearing evaluation is an option.**

A change in hearing threshold is both a clinical outcome and a possible indicator of the presence of otitis media with effusion. Methods used to determine a child's hearing acuity will vary depending on the resources available and the child's willingness and ability to participate in testing. Optimally, air and bone conduction thresholds can be established for 500, 1,000, 2,000, and 4,000 Hz, and an air conduction pure-tone average can be calculated. This result should be verified by obtaining a measure of speech sensitivity. Determinations of speech reception threshold or speech awareness threshold alone may be used if the child cannot cooperate for pure-tone testing. If none of the test techniques is available or tolerated by the child, the examiner should use his or her best judgment as to adequacy of hearing. In these cases, the health care provider should be aware of whether the child is achieving the appropriate developmental milestones for verbal communication.

Although hearing evaluation may be difficult to perform in young children, evaluation is recommended after otitis media with effusion has been present bilaterally for 3 months, because of the strong belief that surgery is not indicated unless otitis media with effusion is causing hearing impairment (defined as equal to or worse than 20 decibels hearing threshold level in the better hearing ear).

Natural History

Longitudinal studies of otitis media with effusion show spontaneous resolution of the condition in more than half of children within 3 months from development of the effusion. After 3 months the rate of spontaneous resolution remains constant, so that only a small percentage of children experience otitis media with effusion lasting a year or longer. In most children, episodes of otitis media with effusion do not persist beyond early childhood. The likelihood that middle ear fluid will resolve by itself underlies the recommendations made for management of otitis media with effusion.

Environmental Risk Factors

Scientific evidence showed that the following environmental factors may increase potential risks of getting acute otitis media or otitis media with effusion:

- Bottle feeding rather than breast feeding infants
- Passive smoking
- Group child care facility attendance

Because the target child for Guideline recommendations is beyond the age when the choice of breast feeding versus bottle feeding is an issue, this risk factor was not considered at length.

Passive smoking (exposure to another's cigarette smoke) is associated with higher risk of otitis media with effusion. Although there is no proof that stopping passive smoking will help prevent middle ear fluid, there are many health reasons for not exposing persons of any age to tobacco smoke. Therefore, clinicians should advise parents of the benefits of decreasing children's exposure to tobacco smoke.

Studies of otitis media with effusion in children cared for at home compared to those in group child care facilities found that children in group child care facilities have a slightly higher relative risk (less than 2.0) of getting otitis media with effusion. Research did not show whether removing the child from the group child care facility helped prevent otitis media with effusion.

Therapeutic Interventions

5. **Observation OR antibiotic therapy are treatment options for children with effusion that has been present less than 4–6 months and at any time in children without a 20-decibel hearing threshold level or worse in the better hearing ear.**

Most cases of otitis media with effusion resolve spontaneously. Meta-analysis of controlled studies showed a 14 percent increase in the resolution rate when antibiotics were given. Length of treatment in these studies was typically 10 days.

The most common adverse effects of antibiotic therapy are gastrointestinal. Dermatologic reactions may occur in 3 to 5 percent of cases; severe anaphylactic reactions are much rarer; severe hematologic, cardiovascular, central nervous system, endocrine, renal, hepatic, and respiratory adverse effects are rarer still. The potential for the development of microbial resistance is always present with antibiotics.

6. **For the child who has had bilateral effusion for a total of 3 months and who has a bilateral hearing deficiency (defined as a 20-dB hearing threshold level or worse in the better hearing ear), bilateral myringotomy with tube insertion becomes an additional treatment option. Placement of tympanostomy tubes is recommended after a total of 4–6 months of bilateral effusion with a bilateral hearing deficit.**

The principal benefits of myringotomy with insertion of tympanostomy tubes are the restoration of hearing to the preeffusion threshold and clearance of the fluid and possible feeling of pressure. While patent and in place, tubes may prevent further accumulation of fluid in the middle ear. Although there is insufficient evidence to prove that there are long-term deleterious effects of otitis media with effusion, concern about the possibility of such effects led the panel to recommend surgery, based on their expert opinion. Tubes are available in a myriad of designs, most constructed from plastic and/or metal. Data comparing outcomes with tubes of various designs are sparse, and so there were assumed to be no notable differences between available tympanostomy tubes.

Insertion of tympanostomy tubes is performed under general anesthesia in young children. Calculation of the risks for two specific complications of myringotomy with tympanostomy tube insertion showed that tympanosclerosis might occur after this procedure in 51 percent, and postoperative otorrhea in 13%, of children.

A number of treatments are not recommended for treatment of otitis media with effusion in the otherwise healthy child age 1–3 years.

- **Steroid medications** are not recommended to treat otitis media with effusion in a child of any age because of limited scientific evidence that this treatment is effective and the opinion of many experts that the possible adverse effects (agitation, behavior change, and more serious problems such as disseminated varicella in children exposed to this virus within the month before therapy) outweighed possible benefits.
- **Antihistamine/decongestant therapy** is not recommended for treatment of otitis media with effusion in a child of any age, because review of the literature showed that these agents are not effective for this condition, either separately or together.
- **Adenoidectomy** is not an appropriate treatment for uncomplicated middle ear effusion in the child younger than age 4 years when adenoid pathology is not present (based on the lack of scientific evidence). Potential harms for children of all ages include the risks of general anesthesia and the possibility of excessive postoperative bleeding.
- **Tonsillectomy, either alone or with adenoidectomy,** has not been found effective for treatment of otitis media with effusion.
- **The association between allergy and otitis media with effusion** was not clear from available evidence. Thus, although close anatomic relationships between the nasopharynx, eustachian tube, and middle ear have led many experts to suggest a role for allergy management

in treating otitis media with effusion, no recommendation was made for or against such treatment.

- **Evidence regarding other therapies for the treatment of otitis media with effusion** was sought, but no reports of chiropractic, holistic, naturopathic, traditional/indigenous, homeopathic, or other treatments contained information obtained in randomized controlled studies. Therefore, no recommendation was made regarding such other therapies for the treatment of otitis media with effusion in children.

TREATMENT OUTCOMES

Table 1 summarizes the benefits and harms identified for management interventions in the target child with otitis media with effusion.

ALGORITHM (FIGURE 1)

Notes to Algorithm
The following notes are an integral part of the algorithm in Figure 1.

(A) Otitis media with effusion (OME) is defined as fluid in the middle ear without signs or symptoms of infection; OME is not to be confused with acute otitis media (inflammation of the middle ear with signs of infection). The Guideline and this algorithm apply only to the child with otitis media with effusion. This algorithm assumes follow-up intervals of 6 weeks.

(B) The algorithm applies only to a child age 1–3 years with no craniofacial or neurologic abnormalities or sensory deficits (except as noted) who is healthy except for otitis media with effusion. The Guideline recommendations and algorithm do not apply if the child has any craniofacial or neurologic abnormality (for example, cleft palate or mental retardation) or sensory deficit (for example, decreased visual acuity or preexisting hearing deficit).

(C) The Panel found some evidence that pneumatic otoscopy is more accurate than otoscopy performed without the pneumatic test of eardrum mobility.

(D) Tympanometry may be used as confirmation of pneumatic otoscopy in the diagnosis of OME. Hearing evaluation is recommended for the otherwise healthy child who has had bilateral OME for 3 months; before 3 months, hearing evaluation is a clinical option.

(E) In most cases, OME resolves spontaneously within 3 months.

(F) The antibiotic drugs studied for treatment of OME were amoxicillin, amoxicillin–clavulanate potassium, cefaclor, erythromycin,

Table 1. Outcomes of treating otitis media with effusion[a]

Intervention	Benefits[b]	Harms[b]
Observation	Base case	Base case
Antibiotics	Improved clearance of effusion at 1 month or less, 14.0% (95% CI [3.6%, 24.2%]) Possible reduction in future infection	Nausea, vomiting, diarrhea (2%-32% depending on dose and antibiotic) Cutaneous reactions (≤5%) Numerous rare organ system effects, including very rare fatalities Cost Possible development of resistant strains of bacteria
Antibiotics plus steroids	Possible improved clearance at 1 month, 25.1% (95% CI [−1.3%, 49.9%])[c] Possible reduction in future infections	See antibiotics and steroids separately
Steroids alone	Possible improved clearance at 1 month, 4.5% (95% CI [−11.7%, 20.6%])[c]	Possible exacerbation of varicella Long-term complications not established for low doses Cost
Antihistamine/ decongestant	Same as base case	Drowsiness and/or excitability[d] Cost
Myringotomy with tubes	Immediate clearance of effusion in all children Improved hearing	Invasive procedure Anesthesia risk Cost Tympanosclerosis Otorrhea Possible restrictions on swimming
Adenoidectomy	Benefits for young children have not been established	Invasive procedure[d] Anesthesia risk Cost
Tonsillectomy	Same as base case	Invasive procedure[d] Anesthesia risk Cost

[a] The target patient is an otherwise healthy child age 1 through 3 years with no craniofacial or neurologic abnormalities or sensory deficits.

[b] Outcomes are reported as differences from observation, which is treated as the base case. When possible, meta-analysis was performed to provide a mean and associated confidence interval (CI).

[c] Difference from base case not statistically significant.

[d] Risks were not examined in detail because no benefits were identified.

erythromycin–sulfisoxazole, sulfisoxazole, and trimethoprim–sulfamethoxazole.

(G) Exposure to cigarette smoke (passive smoking) has been shown to increase the risk of OME. For bottlefeeding versus breast feed-

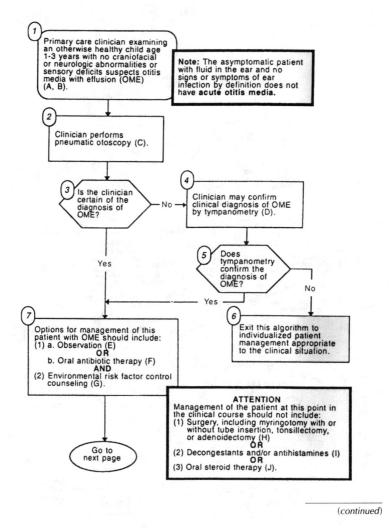

Figure 1.   Algorithm for managing otitis media with effusion in an otherwise healthy child age 1–3 years.

ing and for child care facility placement, associations were found with OME, but evidence available to the Panel did not show decreased incidence of OME with breast feeding or with removal from child care facilities.

(H)   The recommendation against tonsillectomy is based on the lack of added benefit from tonsillectomy when combined with adeno-

Figure 1. *(continued)*

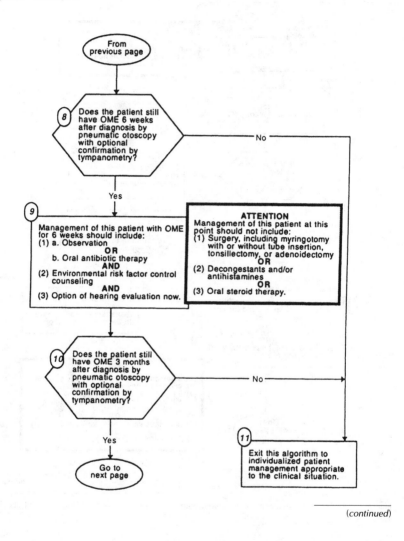

(continued)

idectomy to treat OME in older children. Tonsillectomy and adenoidectomy may be appropriate for reasons other than OME.

(I)   The Panel found evidence that decongestants and/or antihistamines are ineffective treatments for OME.

(J)   Meta-analysis failed to show a significant benefit for steroid medications without antibiotic medications in treating OME in children.

Figure 1. (*continued*)

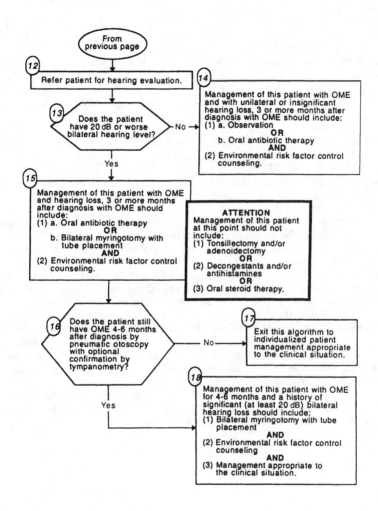

From previous page

⑫ Refer patient for hearing evaluation.

⑬ Does the patient have 20 dB or worse bilateral hearing level?

No →

⑭ Management of this patient with OME and with unilateral or insignificant hearing loss, 3 or more months after diagnosis with OME should include:
(1) a. Observation
    OR
   b. Oral antibiotic therapy
    AND
(2) Environmental risk factor control counseling.

Yes

⑮ Management of this patient with OME and hearing loss, 3 or more months after diagnosis with OME should include:
(1) a. Oral antibiotic therapy
    OR
   b. Bilateral myringotomy with tube placement
    AND
(2) Environmental risk factor control counseling.

ATTENTION
Management of this patient at this point should not include:
(1) Tonsillectomy and/or adenoidectomy
    OR
(2) Decongestants and/or antihistamines
    OR
(3) Oral steroid therapy.

⑯ Does the patient still have OME 4-6 months after diagnosis by pneumatic otoscopy with optional confirmation by tympanometry?

No →

⑰ Exit this algorithm to individualized patient management appropriate to the clinical situation.

Yes

⑱ Management of this patient with OME for 4-6 months and a history of significant (at least 20 dB) bilateral hearing loss should include:
(1) Bilateral myringotomy with tube placement
    AND
(2) Environmental risk factor control counseling
    AND
(3) Management appropriate to the clinical situation.

SELECTED BIBLIOGRAPHY

Black, N. (1985). The aetiology of glue ear—a case-control study. *International Journal of Pediatric Otorhinolaryngology, 9*(2), 121–133.

Cantenkin, E.I., Mandel, E.M., Bluestone, C.D., Rockette, H.E., Paradise, J.L., Stool, S.E., Fria, T.J., & Rogers, K.D. (1983). Lack of efficacy of a decongestant-antihistamine combination for otitis media with effusion ("secretory" otitis media) in children: Results of a double-blind, randomized trial. *New England Journal of Medicine, 308*(6), 297–301.

Casselbrant, M.L., Brostoff, L.M., Cantekin, E.I., Flaherty, M.R., Doyle, W.J., Bluestone, C.D., & Fria, T.J. (1985). Otitis media with effusion in preschool children. *Laryngoscope, 95,* 428–436.

Etzel, R.A., Pattishall, E.N., Haley, N.J., Fletcher, R.H., & Henderson, F.W. (1992). Passive smoking and middle ear effusion among children in day care. *Pediatrics, 90*(2), 228–232.

Friel-Patti, S., & Finitzo, T. (1990). Language learning in a prospective study of otitis media with effusion in the first two years of life. *Journal of Speech and Hearing Research, 33,* 188–194.

Maw, A.R. (1991). Development of tympanosclerosis in children with otitis media with effusion and ventilation tubes. *Journal of Laryngology and Otology, 105*(8), 614–617.

Rosenfeld, R.M., Mandel, E.M., & Bluestone, C.D. (1991). Systemic steroids for otitis media with effusion in children. *Archives of Otolaryngology—Head and Neck Surgery, 117,* 984–989.

Rosenfeld, R.M., & Post, J.C. (1992). Meta-analysis of antibiotics for the treatment of otitis media with effusion. *Otolaryngology—Head and Neck Surgery, 106,* 378–386.

Teele, D.W., Klein, J.O., Rosner, B., & the Greater Boston Otitis Media Study Group. (1983). Middle ear disease and the practice of pediatrics: Burden during the first five years of life. *Journal of the American Medical Association, 249*(8), 1026–1029.

Teele, D.W., Klein, J.O., Rosner, B., & the Greater Boston Otitis Media Study Group. (1984). Otitis media with effusion during the first three years of life and development of speech and language. *Pediatrics, 74*(2), 282–287.

Toner, J.G., & Mains, B. (1990). Pneumatic otoscopy and tympanometry in the detection of middle ear effusion. *Clinical Otolaryngology, 15*(2), 121–123.

Williams, R.L., Chalmers, T.C., Stange, K.C., Chalmers, F.T., & Bowlin, S.J. (1993). Use of antibiotics in preventing recurrent acute otitis media and in treating otitis media with effusion: A meta-analytic attempt to resolve the brouhaha. *Journal of the American Medical Association, 270*(11), 1344–1351.

Zielhuis, G.A., Straatman, H., Rach, G.H., & van den Broek, P. (1990). Analysis and presentation of data on the natural course of otitis media with effusion in children. *International Journal of Epidemiology, 19*(4), 1037–1044.

INDEX

Page numbers followed by *f* denote figures; those followed
by *t* denote tables.

319